Miracles in Concrete

Structural Engineer August Komendant

Edited by: Carl-Dag Lige, Estonian Museum of Architecture

Translation from Estonian into English: Refiner Translations (Aksel Haagensen, Margus Elings)

Translation from Spanish into English: David Gouverneur, Oscar Tenreiro

Consulting engineer: Tiit Masso

Copy-Editing: Juta Ristsoo, Refiner Translations (Michael Haagensen, Wendy Smith)

Project management: Freya Mohr

Layout, cover design, typesetting and colour correction: Marje and Martin Eelma, Tuumik Stuudio

Paper: Pergraphica Rough Natural, Galerie Art Gloss, Keaykolour Indian Yellow (cover) and Keaykolour Lichen (cover)

Printing: Printon AS, Tallinn, Estonia

Cover illustration: Kimbell Art Museum, architect Louis I. Kahn, structural engineer August Komendant, 1966–1972. Original Merike Komendant Phillips, August E. Komendant Collection, The Architectural Archives, University of Pennsylvania by the gift of Merike Komendant Phillips and G. Jüri Komendant; stylized by Marje and Martin Eelma

Publication of this book was supported by:

Heldur Meerits

Merike Komendant Phillips

George Jüri Komendant

Estonian Concrete Association

Estonian Ministry of Education and Research

Tallinn University of Technology Library

Tuumik Stuudio

Peeter Kangur, Heiko Raschinski, Cultural Endowment of Estonia, Estonian Association of Civil Engineers, Estonian National Culture Foundation, Estonian Society of Art Historians and Curators, the Government of the Republic of Estonia, Graham Foundation fo Advanced Studies in the Fine Arts, National Archives of Estonia, Astlanda Ehitus, Betoneks, Betoonimeister, E-Betoonelement, Ehitustrust, Estconde Invest, EstKonsult, Fund Ehitus, HC Betoon, IB PIKE, IB Telora, Ikodor, In Nomine, Ithal-Kraanad, KontekInt, Kunda Nordic Tsement, Kuubik Projekt, Mainor Ülemiste, Mapri Ehitus, Maru Betoonitööd, Merko Ehitus Eesti, Mira Ehitusmaterjalid, Nordecon Betoon, Novarc, Peri, PR Betoo Ramm Ehitus, Rudus, Saint-Gobain Ehitustooted, Savekate, Tajumaailm, Tartu Mill, TMB Element, VMT Betoon, YIT Eesti

MIX
Paper from responsible sources
FSC® C068125
FSC www.fsc.org

Library of Congress Control Number: 2022930908

Bibliographic information published by the German National Library

The German National Library lists this publication in the Deutsche Nationalbibliografie; detailed bibliographic data are available on the Internet at http://dnb.dnb.de.

ISBN 978-3-0356-2512-7

e-ISBN (PDF) 978-3-0356-2513-4

Estonian Print-ISBN 978-9916-9638-3-8

P.O. Box 44, 4009 Basel, Switzerland

Part of Walter de Gruyter GmbH, Berlin/Boston

9 8 7 6 5 4 3 2 1 www.birkhauser.com

Miracles in Concrete

Structural Engineer August Komendant

Edited by Carl-Dag Lige

Birkhäuser Verlag, Basel; Estonian Museum of Architecture, Tallinn

2022

Table of Contents

Foreword

Triin Ojari
Director, Estonian Museum of Architecture

Modern architecture, as it developed during the twentieth century and the forms that it took, would be unthinkable without a close relationship with engineering. Without talented structural engineers, without innovation in building and material technology. Also, architecture always mirrors the technology of its era, and excellent and high-quality spatial solutions are born when all the participants in a project value creative thought and strive toward a common goal. The story of twentieth-century Western architecture includes only a few famous projects, like the Sydney Opera House or the Centre Pompidou in Paris, in which the importance of the engineer is emphasized. In Estonia, the Tallinn Song Festival venue, as a technological achievement from the Soviet era when it was almost impossible to create anything innovative in construction, is probably the best-known example. And yet modern architecture has increasingly developed in the direction of greater complexity and interdisciplinarity. It's no longer true that "architecture begins where engineering ends" (as architect Walter Gropius once said). Instead, every good building is based primarily on teamwork and, to some extent, this provides an opportunity for architectural history to view the building arts from a broader and less person-centered perspective.

The concept of innovative technology is global in nature, and we are more aware of this today than ever before. However, it requires a good and inspiring environment in order to germinate. After World War II, the structural engineer August Komendant had the opportunity to build a career in the economically successful United States. He worked with the top architects of his era, most closely with Louis I. Kahn. Komendant's presence is also apparent in many of Kahn's perfected spaces. He thinks creatively, honors the architect's ideas and strives to realize the vision without any compromises so as not to ruin a whole that is refined to the nth degree. There are few such dedicated relationships in the history of architecture, and even fewer books that describe the collisions and collaborations of those two worlds better than Komendant's *18 Years with Architect Louis I. Kahn* (1975), which was recently also published in Estonian (2019).

The exhibition *Miracles in Concrete. Structural Engineer August Komendant*—first exhibited at the Estonian Museum of Architecture in 2020—, with the accompanying book, provides the first survey of the life and work of August Komendant as Estonia's most international structural engineer, and manifests his astuteness as a designer in very different projects and more broadly in his role as an engineer in the creation of buildings of architectural integrity. In reality, great things are often comprised of small decisions, and every role is important when giving birth to a good living environment.

For the Estonian Museum of Architecture, this has been a large-scale international research project in which the challenge was to deal, on the one hand, with the periphery of architecture as a profession, and on the other, with classic examples of modern architecture. I would like to thank curator Carl-Dag Lige for his very dedicated and thorough work in researching Komendant's legacy and for his level-headed elucidation of the intrigue that exists between architecture and engineering. The support of August Komendant's children—architect Merike Komendant Phillips and structural engineer George Jüri Komendant—was very helpful. And the excellent collaboration with the Architectural Archives of the University of Pennsylvania and William Whitaker, the Curator made this entire project possible.

Foreword

William Whitaker
Curator, The Architectural Archives, University of Pennsylvania

The fact that August Komendant made important contributions to twentieth-century architecture is not lost to history. He wrote a gripping account of his experiences in *18 Years with Architect Louis I. Kahn*, and Komendant's seminal collaborations with Kahn form the foundation of a series of enlightening academic and scholarly studies.

The Kahn-Komendant collaboration has dominated interest in the engineer's work, with much of that interest directed at examining the development of Kahn's Richards Medical Research Laboratories, the Salk Institute for Biological Studies, and the Kimbell Art Museum. This is not a surprise. There is much to learn from these examples of the successful collaborations between architects and engineers, and their example has done much to dispel the myth of the lone genius in architecture. Kahn, of course, worked with and benefited from the insights of others; in fact, he thrived on these inputs to stimulate his remarkable powers of synthesis. However, Komendant—as an observer, critic, and collaborator—remains, an equal of Kahn, singularly impactful in his dealings with the architect, not only as a professional, but also as a friend and fellow countryman.

Komendant's respect for and friendship with the architect put him at the forefront of the supporters of Kahn's legacy at the University of Pennsylvania, and his generosity helped to establish the Architectural Archives within the Graduate School of Fine Arts (now the Weitzman School of Design). Two distinct archival collections related to August Komendant are now housed there.

The first of these collections, comprising exactly 150 drawings and 1,264 pages of computations, is stored in the Archives' Louis I. Kahn Collection. Komendant collaborated with Kahn on over a dozen projects, from the competition for an Enrico Fermi Memorial to an unrealized high-rise for Kansas City. These drawings and computations, while a relatively small number when compared the 36,000 drawings and 150 boxes of papers in the Kahn Collection, are an integral part of the collection, and the related projects would not be complete or understandable without the inclusion of Komendant's originals.

The reason for keeping these materials alongside Kahn's was, initially, driven by practical considerations: to expedite copying as needed during construction. When the architect died in March 1974, his archives were quickly put into storage and Komendant informed that it would not be possible to return his originals before Kahn's estate was settled. This was not an easy task. Kahn was $469,350 in debt ($39,695 owed to Komendant), and it took an extraordinary effort by his closest supporters to achieve a solution that paid off the debt in full and kept his archives intact. Kahn's collection, acquired by the Commonwealth of Pennsylvania, was formally entrusted to the University of Pennsylvania in 1976 and subsequently opened to the public in 1979. Komendant made a gift of this first collection to the newly established Architectural Archives the following year. To date, this material has remained integrated with Kahn's.

The second collection is more extensive. Komendant worked out of his home in Upper Montclair, New Jersey. Built into a steep slope, the living areas on the upper floor had magnificent views of the New York City skyline; his lower level workroom housed Komendant's remaining professional records—his preliminary study drawings and computations, the related project files and correspondence, photo albums, and his extensive writings. These records illuminate Komendant's thinking process and his own critical reflections on his practice. This collection, donated in 1993 (a year after his death), came to the Archives through the generosity of Komendant's daughter, Merike, and son, Jüri. Helmi Aren facilitated the transfer with her gracious hospitality, support, and encouragement.

Importantly, the opening up of the Komendant Collections established new lines of inquiry into the engineer's origins and development, raising questions about his early work in his native Estonia (of which almost no record survives among Penn's holdings), and laying out his work independent of Kahn, including his intensive collaborations with architects Moshe Safdie and David Rinehart in realizing Habitat '67 in Montreal, among others. Obviously, there was more to the story, and it became clear that a broader study was necessary to assess Komendant's full body of work and impact.

Thankfully, with this book and the eponymous exhibition *Miracles in Concrete. Structural Engineer August Komendant*, the Estonian Museum of Architecture significantly enhances our understanding of Komendant's life and work. On behalf of The Architectural Archives, I extend my gratitude to Carl-Dag Lige, the lead curator of the project, for the tireless efforts, and his colleagues at the Museum for taking on this important and long-overdue project.

For me, simply returning to Komendant's drawings and looking intensively at his carefully composed sheets, one comes to appreciate the unique way he draws; his use of soft lead pencils; the density and feeling for every element therein. You won't find scale figures in his drawings, but you feel the human presence in the knowing placement of elements; as if in his own mind's eye he sees and feels concrete at the molecular level and visualizes all the forces within in active flex. It is remarkable that Komendant did this work without the benefit of computer analysis; it was all done on paper based on his brilliant, insightful mastery of mathematics.

When you work closely with an archive you learn the value of such material observations and how a telling object can reveal individual talent and perspective. Such objects become a sort of instigation, demanding a return and thoughtful consideration. I vividly recall sorting through the many photographs Komendant took while working for the U.S. Army in the years immediately following World War II. He spent weeks on the road examining the engineering of Germany's Autobahn and innovative road and river bridges in concrete. He used some of these photographs to illustrate his detailed reports assessing the future potential of concrete and to highlight new technologies worthy of investment. In one report, he described—with astonishing ease—how bridges constructed using the posttensioning methods, which he later built his reputation on, could be restored: a seemingly simple operation of repositioning the fallen pieces, recasting the broken elements, and retensioning of the cable elements, thereby restoring the bridge to full use. After many years of fear and the horrors of war, Komendant possessed within himself the sublime confidence that it can all be put back together again.

Is it not, perhaps, the greater gift of engaging with these collections, having the opportunity to creatively restore these linkages with the past; to "re-stress," as Komendant might describe it, the energized creative environment that leads to impactful work? Together, these collections provide an essential ingredient for scholars, architectural conservators, curators, and most significantly, young architects to engage with the remarkable work of August Komendant. The Architectural Archives is dedicated to supporting and encouraging their efforts.

Introduction

Miracles in Concrete is the first comprehensive assessment of the legacy of structural engineer August Komendant (1906–1992). The book, in conjunction with an exhibition of the same name—first exhibited at the Estonian Museum of Architecture from January 10 through July 26, 2020—provides an overview of Komendant's long career spanning from the 1930s to the 1980s. Komendant's portfolio contains more than 200 projects—some of which he designed independently, others in collaboration with architects and fellow engineers. The most significant of these projects can be found on the more than 400 pages that follow. The book also features the voices of some of Komendant's contemporaries and loved ones. The interviews conducted during the research help to understand the background of the projects and paint a portrait of August Komendant as a person. This book should be seen primarily as an introduction—research into Komendant's legacy should certainly continue.

Structure of the book

This book is divided into two major parts, the first being text-based and the second image-based. The first part contains essays by renowned architectural historian Professor Kenneth Frampton and the editor of this book Carl-Dag Lige, as well as selected articles by August Komendant and several interviews. Komendant's own writings included in this volume are "Design and Its Critical Evaluation" (1972), which may be read as the author's personal architectural or design theory, and "Architect–Engineer Relationship" (1986), in which Komendant discusses the greatest challenges in the collaboration between an architect and engineer based on his work with Louis Kahn.

The only known in-depth interview with August Komendant—a conversation with architect Oscar Tenreiro in 1985—is published here for the first time in English. Interviews with architects Moshe Safdie, Robert Geddes and Oscar Tenreiro, who reflect on their experience of working with Komendant, were conducted especially for this book. Among the interviews you will also find conversations with the children of August Komendant: architect Merike Komendant Phillips and structural engineer George Jüri Komendant. All these conversations highlight August Komendant's personality as well as his professional values as a structural engineer.

The second, larger part of the book provides a visually rich overview of August Komendant's most important works during his career as a structural engineer—from the early concrete structures in his native Estonia in the 1930s to the masterpieces of world architecture in North America in the 1960s and 1970s. A majority of these drawings and photographs are published for the first time. A separate section offers a brief biographical glimpse of August Komendant's family, education, and working life.

In the final section of the book, you will find a comprehensive list of August Komendant's work, including the key details of each project, and a selected bibliography, which includes both Komendant's own publications and writings by others on his work.

Acknowledgments

The Estonian Museum of Architecture has researched the legacy of August Komendant for more than five years. Throughout this time, the family of August Komendant has been an irreplaceable support to the museum. Our special thanks go to his children, Merike Komendant Phillips and George Jüri Komendant. Martin Komendant has assisted with valuable materials.

The whole project would not have been possible without the professional and friendly staff at the Architectural Archives of the University of Pennsylvania—William Whitaker, Allison Olsen and Heather Isbell Schumacher. Jennifer Garland (McGill University Library), Tess Beckingham (Safdie Architects) and Elena M. García Orozco (The Architectural and Construction Archives, University of Puerto Rico) have also been instrumental in working with the archival material.

Among the architects, our greatest thanks go to Oscar Tenreiro, who donated valuable drawings and photographs from his collection and shared his personal memories of working with August Komendant. Architects Moshe Safdie, Robert Geddes, Jaan Holt, Ilmar Reinvald, Frank Sherwood, and Nader Ardalan also contributed to creating the content of the book. We would especially like to thank Professor Kenneth Frampton, who wrote the introductory essay.

The wonderfully thorough and sensitive design of the graphic part of the book and the exhibition are by Marje Eelma. We thank Tomomi Hayashi and Andrea Ainjärv for the warm and evocative design of the exhibition space, and Ago Märjama with his colleagues for the construction and installation. The production team at the Estonian Museum of Architecture—Triin Ojari, Maili Rajamägi, Epp Alatalu, Anna-Liisa Simm, Laos Koort, Anne Lass, Jarmo Kauge, Koit Randmäe, Sandra Mälk, Kadi Kriit, Kerly Ritval, Inna Lauk, and Ksenia Vaher—made great contributions.

Epp Aareleid, Kai Aareleid, Mari Klein, Kerli Linnat, Tiit Masso, Juta Ristsoo, Jelena Rõbakova, David Gouverneur, Refiner Translations, and Birkhäuser Verlag have been a great help with translating and editing the texts.

The publication of this book was only possible thanks to our friendly supporters. Our greatest personal thanks go to Heldur Meerits, Merike Komendant Phillips, George Jüri Komendant, Tiit Roots, Imre Leetma, Toomas Vainola, Toomas Kään, Tõnis Liibek, Feliks Mägus, Margus Nõlvak, Emil Urbel, and Indrek Allmann.

For their help with putting the book and exhibition together, we also wish to thank Ahti Vuks, Allan E. Laupa, Allan Laupa Jr., Andreas Ignacio Hinojosa, Andres Ojari, Andrew Benner, Andrus Komendant, Anna Zsoldos, Are and Epp Tsirk, Ariel Vazquez, Astrid Aavola, Augusto Teran, Bill Gregg, Birgit Pikk, Brita Arnover, Carl-David Randviir, Cathryn Copper, Constance Clement, Daryn Jankovic, David Geddes, Eero Pank, Egle Tamm, Enrique Vivoni Farage, Eva-Liisa Lepik, Eva-Riin Joosti, Gabriele Neri, Heie Treier, Heige Peets, Heino Ainso, Helen Kask, Helin Vahter, Henry Kuningas, Heryk Tomassini, Ingrid Ruudi, Ivo Pilve, Jana Antonova, Jari Jetsonen, Jarmo Kauge, Josue Hurtado, Jutta Wiese, Kaarel Mikkal, Kaarel Siim, Kalev Ramjalg, Karen Jagodin, Karin Sõmer, Karl Erik Miller, Karl Õiger, Kaspar Marli, Katariina Grib, Katarina Klaamas, Kristi Kalev, Käti Erit, Kätlin Piht, Larry Eubank, Laura Susi, Lauri Lenk, Linda Calvin, Ljudmilla Georgijeva, Loora Orav, Mait Väljas, Mari Luukas, Marika Luite, Maris Mändel, Mark Fischer, Mark Gunderson, Markus Pihla, Mart Kalm, Martin Eelma, Martin Kukk, Martin Sermat, Martin Siplane, Mathieu Pomerleau, Mati Pihlak, Matthias Beckh, Mikk Meelak, Mikk Roben, Milvi Vahtra, Nancy Sparrow, Nele-Kateriin Määrits, Nubia Rodríguez de Tenreiro, Olavi Sikka, Oliver Orro, Peep Roosmann, Rain Robert Randväli, Ralf Tamm, Ramon Jose Fermin, Raul Kalvo, Reio Avaste, Relika Kala, Richard H. Klumb, Riho Oras, Robert Treufeldt, Roland May, Ronald Kiipus, Signe Jantson, Siim Sokk, Siim Välkmann, Steven Lawrey, Tarmo and Merle Toom, Tõnis Arjus, Tõnu Peipman, Villu Urban, Estonian Academy of Arts, Koko architects, Motor, Nordic Hotels, and Tallinn University of Applied Sciences,.

The editor would like to thank the team at Birkhäuser Verlag, led by Alexander Felix, who helped prepare the publication of the English version of the book.

Personally, I am grateful to my loved ones and friends who have provided support during this long journey.

I dedicate this book to the memory of my grandfather, structural engineer Uno Lige (1931–2018).

I hope you enjoy exploring the book.
Carl-Dag Lige, editor

Essays and interviews

August Komendant: A Preface

Kenneth Frampton

August Komendant was one of those rare structural engineers whose own cultivation plus an innate sense of structural elegance make them particularly susceptible to working with talented architects, particularly when the latter's sensibility gravitates toward the expressivity of structural form. Louis Kahn was just such an architect, and it was this, above all other factors, which rendered their fertile collaboration possible. However, apart from the odd fact that they had both been born in Estonia, it is difficult to imagine two figures who were more opposed not only in terms of their formation but also with regard to temperament and experience, for where the one was a hypersensitive architect, trained according to the ethos of the École des Beaux-Arts, who went on, during World War II, to design low-cost social housing under the auspices of the New Deal, the other was trained at the Technical University of Dresden (1929–1934) before the war and somehow, subsequently ending up in the States, served under the demanding General Patton during the post D-Day invasion of Europe.

Kahn was initially attracted to Komendant by the latter's reputation as a pioneer of prefabricated, prestressed reinforced concrete, for which he was already renowned by the mid-1950s—not only as a designer thereof but also as someone who was producing precast concrete elements wholesale in a prestressing plant in Lakewood, New Jersey, for which he was a consulting engineer. At Komendant's invitation, Kahn first visited the Lakewood plant in 1956, spending virtually a whole day there, touring the on-line production with a group of his students from the University of Pennsylvania. Kahn was particularly intrigued by the exquisite precision and elegance of the prefabricated pieces, which, in many respects, promised to be the final answer to his intuitive search for a mode of concrete construction which would have the lightness and precision of steel space-frame construction. This had long been his aspiration, as is evident from the pseudo space-frame concrete floors of his Yale Art Gallery in New Haven completed in 1953. Of even greater import at the time was what the group learned from Komendant about quality concrete production. As Komendant put it in 1975:

A Vierendeel truss being shipped to the construction site of the Richards Medical Research Laboratories, 1959

> *I gave them all kinds of explanations starting with concrete mix, aggregate, and type of cement. In a small plant testing laboratory they were amazed how different were the qualities of cement. Only two cement types of the thirty-one tested were suitable for architectural concrete. In their minds all cements were the same, but now they found out that this was not the case and that thorough testing is required to determine cement suitability and to avoid corrosion of surfaces exposed to severe climatic conditions. Also the vibration for placing concrete and after-treatment aroused many questions. Kahn [...] could at first not understand that concrete quality is improved considerably after vibration with high-frequency surface vibrators, about two or three hours after it was placed. [...] After he saw how much water came to the surface during after-treatment and [...] in addition, seeing compressive tests carried out with nontreated and after-treated samples which had about 20 to 30 percent higher strength, Kahn fully understood its meaning.*

I have cited from Komendant's memoir at length because for Kahn this visit was a revelation not only because of what he learned about the manufacture of high-quality concrete but also because the technique of prestressed, prefabricated concrete promised to be the one material he had been searching for since the mid-40s, namely a lightweight, fireproof, hollow construction in concrete, which is exactly what Komendant provided for him in his Richards Medical Laboratories, completed as a research complex for the University of Pennsylvania in 1961.

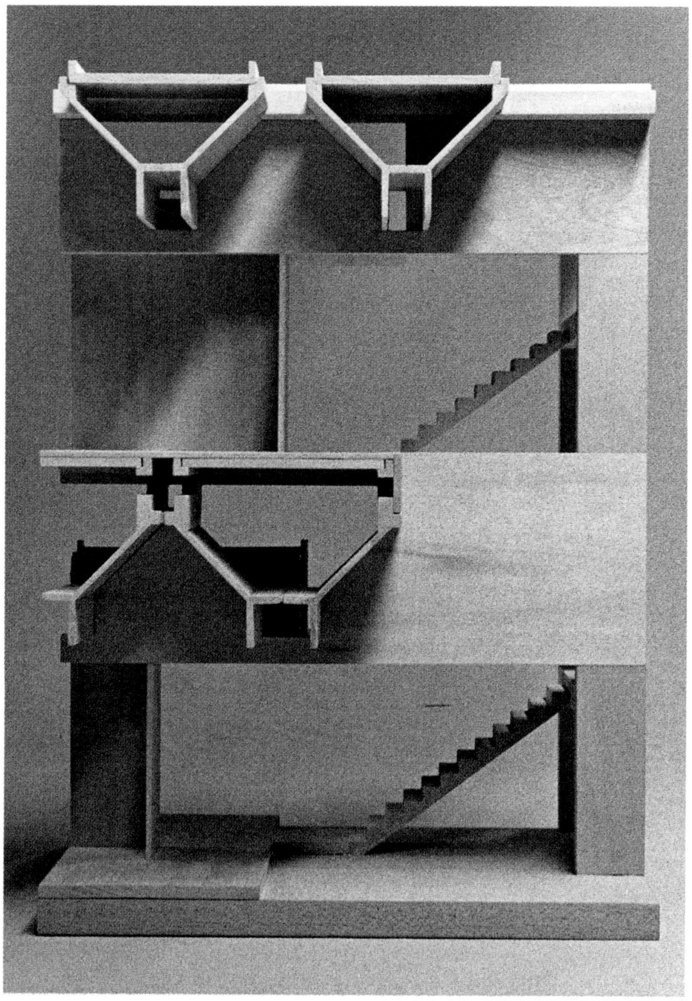

Model of the preliminary structural system of the Salk Institute

Komendant's audacious introduction of this highly sophisticated European technique brought him into conflict with the retardataire American building industry, which resisted departing from its established ways and, in any case, favored steel rather than concrete. Despite this, Komendant often prevailed by virtue of being able to demonstrate the economic advantage of the new technique. Even so, contractors did in fact outwit him from time to time, as in the case of his first scheme of 1959 for the interstitial floors of Kahn's Salk Institute in La Jolla, California, which was eventually realized in 1965. The prestressed, prefabricated box-truss girders spanning 100 feet of Komendant's original scheme with prestressed folded plates spanning 50 feet in between eventually had to give way, under contractor and client pressure, to posttensioned in situ reinforced concrete Vierendeel trusses, 9 feet in depth, spanning 62 feet at 20-feet centers, supported on a separate columnar system. In the end, the flat soffits to these interstitial floors deprived the laboratory space of what would have been an undeniably strong tectonic character.

Perhaps the most interesting aspect of their eighteen year long collaboration was the fact that Komendant was the only critical voice that Kahn would accept, with the result that without Komendant's backing, many of Kahn's projects failed to see the light of day, either because the format was inappropriate or because Kahn on his own was incapable of coming up with a conceiving concept. In many works it seems that Komendant himself took the lead, as was the case with the *Tribune Review* newspaper building realized in Greensburg, Pennsylvania in 1962. Much the same could be said of the large single-story factory built for Olivetti in Harrisburg, Pennsylvania, in 1970. In the first instance, Komendant's presence is suggested by the expressive detailing, most particularly for the way in which narrow prestressed reinforced concrete beams were brought down onto load-bearing concrete block walls. In the second instance, with the Olivetti factory, Komendant came up with the overall structural concept, since Kahn seemed unable to arrive at a solution. Both of these works demonstrate Komendant's capacity as a master builder. In the first instance by precisely calculating the load-bearing capacity of the concrete block, and in the second, by coming up with the idea of a 56 by 56 foot reiterated prismatic shell structure, that is, to say a structural module, octagonal in plan, which was carried, in each instance, on a single in situ concrete column 30 inches square with a cast-in-place downpipe, draining the roof of each bay. Typical of Komendant's ingenuity was the way in which these concrete shells were posttensioned across their rims and fill the rotated square openings between the octagonal shells either with roof lights or air-conditioning units. The lucidity and simplicity of this invention, capable of infinite reiteration, says everything about Komendant as a comprehensive problem-solver.

Despite the profound differences of their approach, which often led to acrimonious arguments, the two men had an intensely symbiotic relationship with one another and it is a question whether either of them could have achieved what they did without the other. The only major departure from this symbiosis was by far the largest and most monumental structure that Komendant would ever design or have the chance to realize, namely, the large megastructure that he designed for the young architect Moshe Safdie, who commissioned him with the challenge of building his brilliant Habitat '67, a totally radical residential format underwritten by the Canadian government and erected on the occasion of the Montreal Expo of 1967. As intimated at the beginning, Komendant, like the illustrious Ove Arup or Pier Luigi Nervi, was one of those exceptionally gifted engineers whose innate feeling for structure put them into a class of their own. That he should finally be recognized, albeit posthumously, as being of this calibre is surely one of the main goals of the exhibition and book *Miracles in Concrete. Structural Engineer August Komendant*.

Habitat '67 after completion

August Komendant, ca. 1928

Miracles in Concrete. Structural Engineer August Komendant

Carl-Dag Lige

August Eduard Komendant (1906–1992) was an Estonian-American structural engineer, whose collaboration with famous architects and engineers resulted in several masterpieces of twentieth-century architecture. His professional career spanned more than half a century from the 1930s to 1980s and coincided with an era characterized by modernization, urbanization and the rapid development of technology.

By the middle of the twentieth century, reinforced concrete had become one of the most popular structural materials for building new living environments. A strong and durable composite emerges when liquid concrete, a mixture of water, cement, and aggregate (sand, gravel, crushed stone, etc.), solidifies around reinforcing steel bars. Concrete was increasingly used for both residential buildings and public structures. A material which many people consider to be bleak, cold, and dull was August Komendant's passion for decades. He brought concrete to life in a way that left its mark on the history of both twentieth-century construction and architecture. He consistently demanded quality starting from the recipe for the concrete mix to the finishing of the completed structures, and would not tolerate any concessions. He was interested in the technology of prestressed concrete and using precast elements in building because he valued the effective and economical use of the material. His beliefs were based on knowledge complemented by a refined sense of aesthetics, which helped him understand even the most lyrical architect-artists, such as Louis I. Kahn (1901–1974), who spent his early childhood in Saaremaa, Estonia.

Through time, architecture and building have been collective disciplines in which the best results are born of creative disputes and well-reasoned positions. The idea and spatial character of a building is usually designed by the architect. This is done by considering the choice of materials, arrangement of the volumes, organization of movement within the space, its suitability to the surrounding environment, etc. The role of the engineer is to help the architect realize this vision, to "interpret" it from the realm of the imagination into actual space. Creative engineers with their knowledge can transform the architect's vision into something that is feasible, tangible, and can be directly experienced.

During his career, August Komendant had several architects as dialogue partners, but the one who was closest to him was Louis I. Kahn. Many researchers believe that both of their most important projects resulted from their collaboration. Their mutual trust enabled them to communicate in a way that interwove both the spiritual and prosaic dimensions of the building arts. In addition to Louis Kahn, Komendant also worked closely with other famous architects, including Moshe Safdie, Henry Klumb, Robert Geddes, Romaldo Giurgola, Oscar Tenreiro, and, at the beginning of his career, Estonian architects Eugen Sacharias and Elmar Lohk.

If one has to select three emblematic buildings from Komendant's long career, let them be the Kadriorg Stadium grandstand in Tallinn (architect Elmar Lohk, 1936–1938), the Habitat '67 experimental housing complex in Montreal, Canada (architect Moshe Safdie, 1963–1967) and the Kimbell Art Museum in Fort Worth, Texas, USA (architect Louis I. Kahn, 1966–1972). If the grandstand, with its 12.8-meter cantilevered roof, expresses a young engineer's desire to prove himself, and Habitat '67 indicates the comprehensive competence of a consulting engineer, then the Kimbell structure is a refined synthesis of the knowledge, experience, and exacting choices made by a mature, but still ambitious, structural engineer. All these buildings are examples of the creative cooperation between an engineer, architect, and builder focused on quality.

Early Career: Estonia, 1934–1944

August Komendant graduated from the Paide Co-educational Secondary School in 1927. After military service, he was sent to the school for noncommissioned officers, and from there to a military school for his postgraduate studies. He left the military as a junior officer (1929) and went to study in Germany. In 1934 he graduated from the Sächsische Hochschule zu Dresden (from 1961, the Technische Universität Dresden, better known as TU Dresden) as a certified structural engineer specializing in the statics of reinforced concrete. The previous year he had

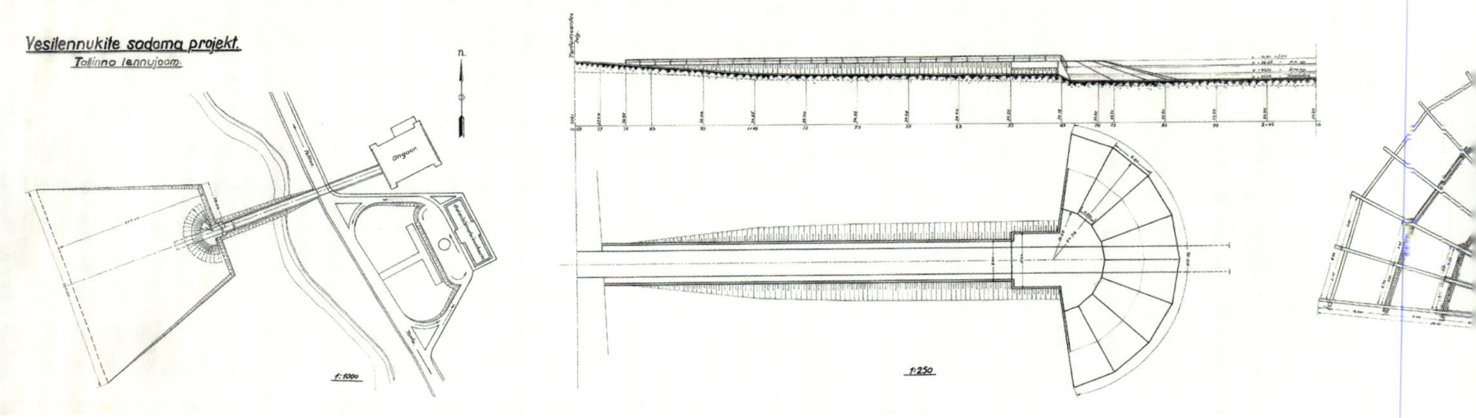

August Komendant. Seaplane Harbor of the Ülemiste Airport, 1934

been appointed as an assistant researcher to his professor Kurt Beyer. However, as the National Socialist Party and Adolf Hitler came to power and encouraged foreigners to leave the country, Komendant decided to return to his native Estonia.[1]

During the interwar period, from the 1920s to the 1930s, both the construction and architectural fields developed rapidly. Urban populations increased, and the shortage of housing caused by war damage advanced the development of new technologies, which enabled faster construction, the economical use of materials, and the creation of architecture that suited modern lifestyles. Likewise, in Estonia, people tried to keep up with contemporary technologies and architectural concepts.

August Komendant started working as a civil engineer at a time (1934) when modernist architecture had matured and the use of reinforced concrete as an innovative building material became increasingly widespread. In the second half of the 1930s, Komendant became one of the most highly regarded designers of reinforced concrete structures in Estonia. In collaboration with local architects and engineers, he contributed to the development of the local building culture and modernization of the living environment.

During the first decade of his professional career as a structural engineer, Komendant designed approximately 50 buildings or structures, around half of which were built. Most of those structures were either industrial or infrastructure-related projects in Estonia, with a few small-scale exceptions in Helsinki, Finland (concrete floors for a university building extension; petroleum tanks for an oil-shale company).[2]

The scarcity of Estonian structural engineers with good knowledge of concrete structures meant that Komendant was instantly hired upon his return to Estonia in 1934. One of his first projects was the new sausage factory for the Võhma Eksporttapamaja (Võhma Export Slaughterhouse) in Võhma, Viljandi County.[3] Architect Hendrik Otloot designed a modern extension to an existing building. Komendant obtained the commission through the contractor Estoruss, led by Komendant's family friend and influential Estonian engineer, Konstantin Zeren (1883–1944).

Soon after the Võhma project was completed, Komendant was hired by the Ministry of Roads—the main institution responsible for designing and constructing public buildings in Estonia at the time. He worked as a staff engineer in the Construction Department at the Ministry; it is likely that it was Zeren's idea to hire Komendant, as Zeren was then head of the department.

Structural design as well as supervisory responsibilities poured in quickly for Komendant. He helped design and supervise the construction of the first international airport in Estonia (see pp. 106–109). The Ülemiste complex in Tallinn included a harbor and landing bridge for seaplanes on Lake Ülemiste, and concrete runways, hangars and a nearby customs building for the main airfield. Yet, the first major design by Komendant was not for the Tallinn airfield, but for the Raadi military airfield near Tartu, in South Estonia.

The Military Aircraft Hangar in Tartu was designed by Komendant in May 1935 and completed a year later (see pp. 110–115). Its design was based on German examples, which Komendant learned about either during his studies in Dresden or from the professional books and magazines he had acquired. There are no indications that Komendant had any help from an architect with this project. Before World War II, it was quite common for engineers to design industrial and military structures independently of architects.

The hangar in Tartu is strikingly modern, not only in its structural design (prestressed concrete), but also in its architectural features (Modernism). Komendant became interested in prestressed concrete early on, as he actively followed what Franz Dischinger, Eugène Freyssinet, and other innovative structural engineers were doing in the field of concrete structures, both in theory and in practice.[4] The Aircraft Hangar in Tartu is probably the first structure in Estonia where the prestressing of concrete was implemented. The main part of the hangar's structure consists of six concrete frames. The horizontal tie rods on the floor level, which help brace the frames together, were manually pretensioned with wrenches, and then cast into the concrete floor.

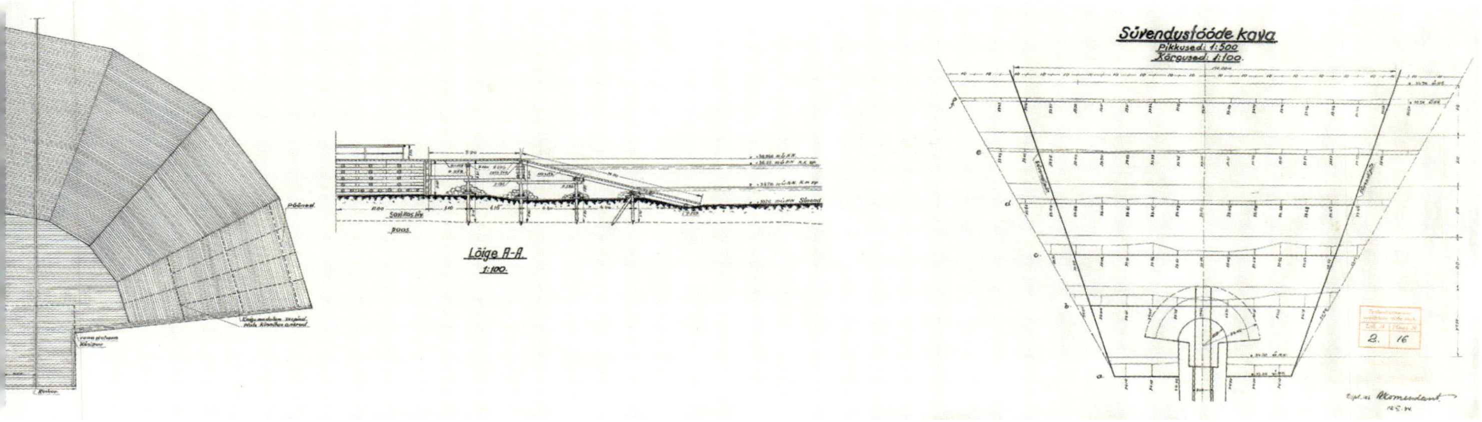

Kadriorg Stadium Grandstand, 2016

In 1936 Komendant left the public position at the ministry and soon established his own design and consulting office. That same year architect Elmar Lohk won the architectural competition for the new Kadriorg Stadium grandstand in Tallinn (see pp. 118–127). Lohk, who was influenced—if not inspired—by the new Olympic Stadium grandstand in Helsinki (architects Yrjö Lindgren, Toivo Jäntti, 1934–1938), proposed a long, reinforced concrete grandstand with a large cantilevered roof above its central section. Komendant, assisted by Tarmo Randvee and Heinrich Laul, both engineering students at the time, provided the structural design and working drawings, and also provided construction supervision services for the architect Lohk.

The grandstand in Kadriorg, still standing proudly, is among the prime examples of Modernist architecture in Estonia; it is

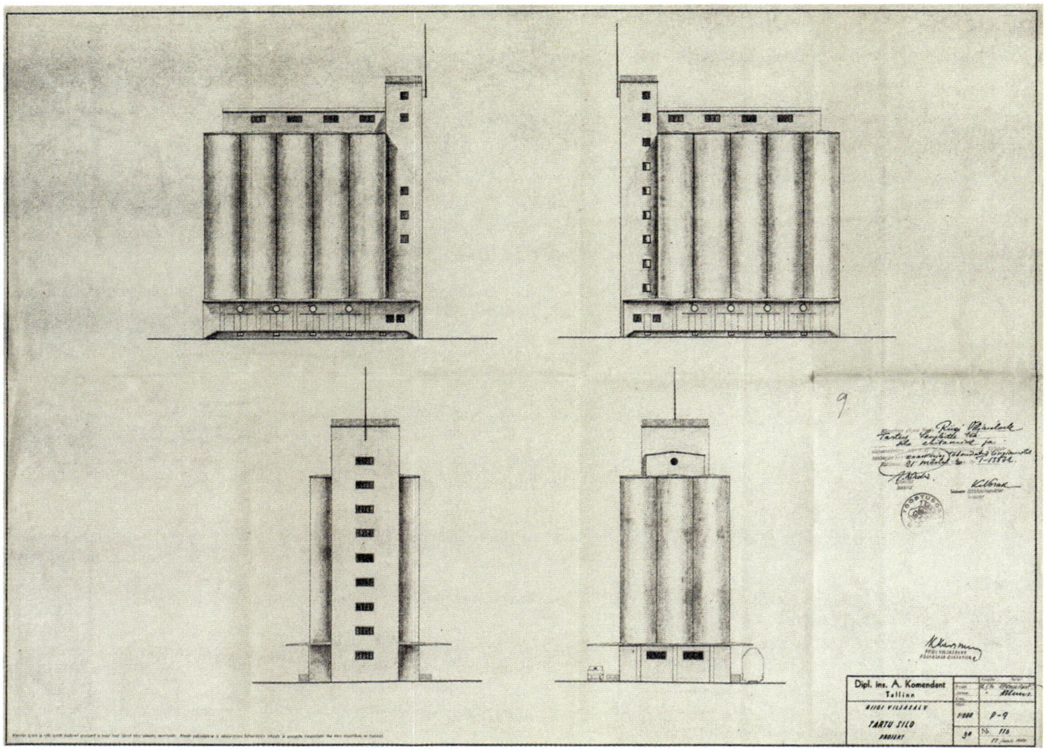

August Komendant. Tartu grain silo, elevations, 1940

Construction of the Tartu grain silo using sliding formwork, 1940

a feat of structural engineering. The grandstand is comprised of 26 parallel reinforced concrete frames, of which the 12 middle ones support the 12.8-meter cantilevered roof plate, which is 12 centimeters thick. The grandstand is 112.3 meters long and initially had 3,500 seats, of which 2,000 were under the roof.

Komendant was among the first structural engineers to introduce so-called mushroom slab to Estonian architecture and structural engineering. In 1939, together with architect Ernst Kesa, he designed the National Grain Silo in Tartu, completed in 1941 (see pp. 132–139), where he used mushroom slabs (column/capital/flat slab) on its ground floor. The grain storage facility is also remarkable because of its innovative construction method—sliding formwork, still new in Estonia at the time, was used to cast the concrete silos. Attempts were made to destroy the structure during World War II. The stair tower collapsed, but the monolithic block of 15 silos only tilted to one side. It was straightened after the war, and is still being used to store grain.

Another remarkable structure designed by Komendant, this time in collaboration with architect Roman Koolmar, was a large cold storage for food exports in Tallinn harbor (designed in 1937, unfinished, destroyed in World War II, see pp. 130–131). All five floors of the cold storage had mushroom slabs (column/capital/drop-plate/flat slab).

The last large-scale commission Komendant received before leaving Estonia was a group of industrial buildings for Estonian Phosphorite Ltd., in Maardu, Harju County (architect Eugen Saarelinn (Sacharias), 1939–1941, completed after World War II, see pp. 140–145). The largest part of the complex was the enrichment factory, a limestone-clad building with reinforced concrete structure. The building has been out of use for several decades and has lost many of its interior details, but the massive concrete bunkers and high ceilings are still impressive.

Via Germany to the United States

In autumn 1944 August Komendant—like thousands of other people from the Baltic States—fled the front lines of the war with his family. The family ended up in Dresden where Komendant was hoping to finish his doctoral thesis under the supervision of Professor Kurt Beyer. As the war was approaching its dreadful end game, work and study at TU Dresden became exceedingly difficult. The building of the Engineering Faculty of TU Dresden was miraculously saved in the infamous bombing of the city in February 1945, but it was clear that Komendant's preparations for defending his thesis could not continue under such circumstances. Once again, the family escaped the war front, this time reaching the Western Allies' side. Leaving TU Dresden meant that Komendant's PhD thesis remained indefinitely undefended, although his professors supposedly told him that in principle he was entitled to have the degree.[5] Therefore, in the whirlwind of World War II, Komendant was not able to defend his PhD, but his fellow faculty members and later colleagues always called him Dr. Komendant. His friends simply called him Doc.

Due to favorable circumstances and possibly a stroke of luck, Komendant was soon (that is, in the spring or early summer of 1945) hired by the US European Command in Germany. During the next five years, Komendant conducted various engineering studies, the majority of them concerning war-damaged reinforced concrete structures. It was clear that there were not enough resources to rebuild all the German cities and infrastructure from scratch. Many of the damaged edifices had to be reconstructed using parts that remained intact. Komendant worked extensively on the damaged highway bridges of the Rhine Valley. Most of those bridges were relatively new—built during the 1930s. They provided Komendant ample practical knowledge about the latest innovations in German engineering, particularly prestressed concrete. He also studied how the structures had behaved under and reacted to extreme circumstances (explosions and intentional damage during the war).[6]

As stated above, Komendant was interested in innovation related to reinforced concrete structures from the beginning of his engineering career. Under the guidance of the forward looking faculty members at TU Dresden, he received the best possible education, which covered the theoretical aspects of concrete as well as its application. The development of prestressed concrete technology became one of the central themes of his work, but Komendant was also fascinated by the promotion of precast concrete construction in order to speed up the building process and make it more efficient. Komendant was also keen to find uses for concrete in high-quality architecture.

When the United States opened its borders to World War II refugees from Europe, Komendant decided to move to the New World. His knowledge of English had improved considerably during the years he served the US Armed Forces in Germany. These language skills helped him establish a position as a respected engineer soon after his arrival in the United States. In 1952 Komendant published a book on prestressed concrete structures, which gained attention among structural engineers and eventually architects.[7] Prestressing technology was not common in the US at the time. Komendant used both his practical and theoretical knowledge to introduce the potential this technology could hold for the American construction industry and contemporary architectural design.

Reinforced concrete as a material and its rapid development could be considered one of the symbols of the modernization process throughout the Western world from the late nineteenth century to the present day. During the last century, many of the world's cities were built of concrete. At the same time, it is a controversial material; building concrete structures is an energy-intensive activity, and the nature of concrete—gray, hard and cold—is unappealing to many people. However, no material is bad in and of itself. Everything depends on how it is used. Komendant was passionate about concrete and tried to get the best out of it.

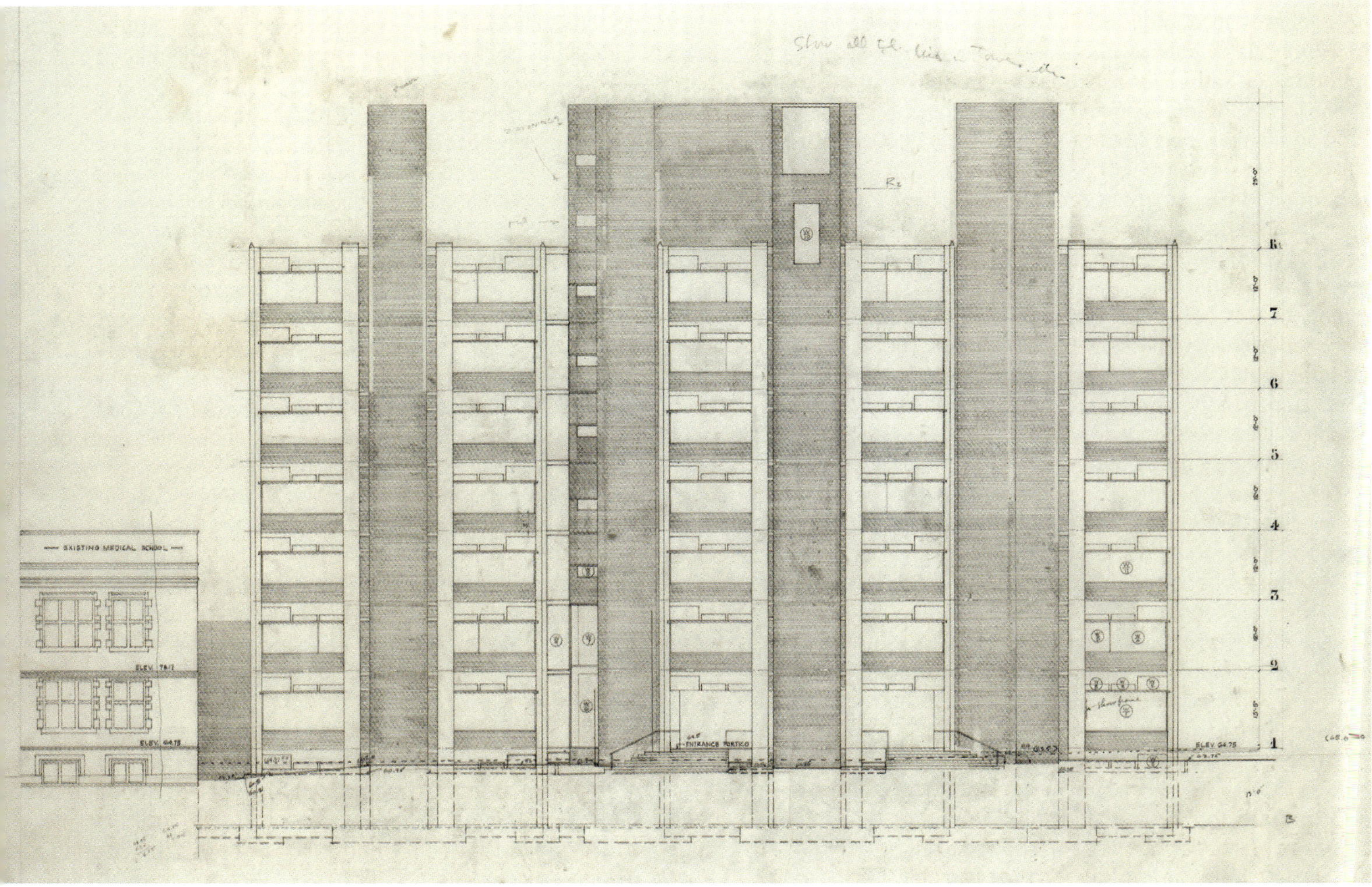

Office of Louis Kahn. Richards Medical Research Laboratories, north elevation, 1958

Throughout the 1950s, Komendant helped establish several concrete factories and promote precasting; that is, using factory-made concrete elements in the construction process. He was closely involved with the Lakewood Prestressing Company, Inc. (see pp. 146–147) and Atlantic Prestressed Concrete Co., the latter ended up producing precast elements for Louis Kahn's world-famous Richards Medical Laboratories building in Philadelphia, Pennsylvania (1957–1965, see pp. 150–165).

Construction of the Richards Medical Research Laboratories

Breakthrough and career highlights

Raymond Hood of the Keast & Hood engineering company first introduced Komendant to the architect Louis Kahn. Hood was aware of Komendant's recently published book on prestressed concrete structures and suggested that Kahn consult Komendant for the design of the Enrico Fermi Memorial competition in Chicago.[8] This was in 1956. Kahn and Komendant, both originally from Estonia, found many things in common and remained in close contact for the next eighteen years, until Kahn's unexpected death in 1974.

Although Louis Kahn was just one of many architects Komendant collaborated with, his designs have had the greatest

Kimbell Art Museum, back entrance after completion

international impact in architectural as well as engineering history. Komendant and Kahn worked together on at least fifteen designs, seven of which were eventually built. The three most important projects from their collaborative years are, arguably, the Richards Medical Research Laboratories (1957–1965), the Salk Institute for Biological Studies (La Jolla, California, 1959–1965, see pp. 194–211) and the Kimbell Art Museum (Fort Worth, Texas, 1966–1972, see pp. 268–285). Among their unrealized projects, the Palazzo dei Congressi (Venice, Italy, 1968–1974, see pp. 290–297) has had the greatest international impact.

The Richards laboratory complex is one of the symbols of twentieth-century architecture. It was the first large project that Kahn and Komendant collaborated on and provided the impetus for the further careers of both men. The structural solution of the building supports the architectural idea that envisions laboratories as studios for researchers. The floor-slab system is striking and economical. It is comprised of precast Vierendeel trusses and edge members, which, after being lifted into place by crane, were connected and posttensioned into unity with steel cables.[9]

Dr. Jonas Salk, founder of the Salk Institute for Biological Studies, wanted to create a research center for the world's top scientists. The beautiful location, on a hillside near the Pacific

Interior of the Kimbell Art Museum

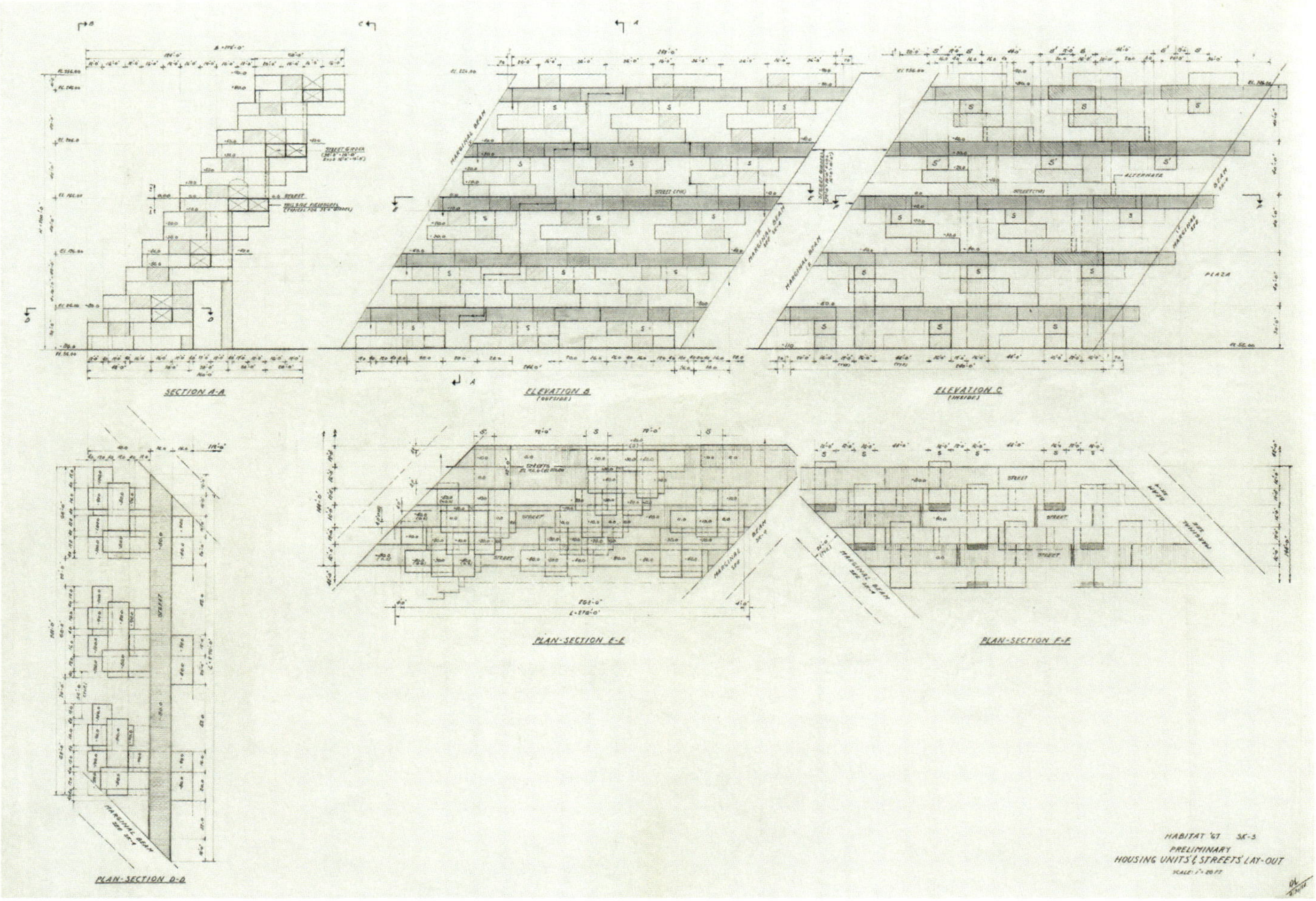

August Komendant. Habitat '67, early structural study, 1964

August Komendant visiting the Habitat '67 housing complex after completion

Ocean in La Jolla, California, inspired Kahn's sensitive design for the ensemble, in which aesthetics and technology are blended. Along with ensuring that the complex could withstand an earthquake, another important structural challenge was posed by the long span of the spacious laboratories. The initial structural proposal was comprised of box girders and folded plates. However, in the completed building, the main components are large Vierendeel trusses, which form separate mechanical floors.[10]

The Kimbell Art Museum is a temple of art built for an extraordinary private collection, and a museum building that is unique in the world. Louis Kahn paid special attention to the use of natural light and dignified materials—concrete, travertine, wood, glass, and polished metal. Kimbell could be considered a culmination of a collaboration between a mature architect (Kahn) and his consulting engineer of many years (Komendant). The central part of the structure is comprised of cycloid shells, which delicately disperse light. The cycloid shape was proposed by Marshall Meyers, the project architect from Louis Kahn's office. The shells are built of monolithic reinforced concrete, are posttensioned with steel cables, and carry the marginal beams with spans of more than 30 meters.[11]

The rapid technological development, urbanization and population increase of the 20th century caused fundamental changes in the field of construction and architecture. The idea of the modular organisation of space became popular among architects (for instance, Le Corbusier's Dom-Ino House, 1914–1915) and this concept was extensively implemented in the design of modern residential, commercial, and industrial environments. The mechanized production of building materials and details, and their on-site assembly, accelerated the building process.

August Komendant was an ardent supporter of modular construction. It was not only faster and more efficient to build using factory-made concrete products, but it also enabled the design of a new and different kind of architecture. The systems that made designing and building faster, more economical, and flexible did not necessary lead to a loss of creativity or architectural quality. Habitat '67, an experimental apartment building in Montreal, Quebec, Canada (1963–1967, see pp. 220–243), comprised of 354 concrete modules, is still one of the most ambitious examples of modular construction. Here Komendant collaborated with the Israeli-Canadian architect Moshe Safdie, whom he had met in 1962, when Safdie was briefly working in Louis Kahn's office in Philadelphia.

The Habitat '67 residential complex was built for the Expo 67 world's fair and symbolises the social optimism and technological advances of the 1960s. Architect Safdie wanted to create a modular urban ensemble that provides the comforts of private houses—spacious balconies, plenty of light and sufficient privacy. Komendant helped not only with providing the structural solution, but also with organising the production and construction process. All the housing units and smaller details of Habitat '67 were produced in a temporary concrete factory installed next to the building site. The concrete modules were put in place by crane and then connected and posttensioned into unity with steel cables. The static calculations were challenging for Komendant and his assistants due to the large number of cantilevered surfaces and the need to make the building earthquake-resistant.[12]

After the passing of Louis Kahn, it was the Venezuelan architect Oscar Tenreiro Degwitz who became Komendant's closest ally among architects, and remained as such until the end of Komendant's professional career. Between 1976 and 1987 they collaborated on eleven projects, ranging from conceptual architecture competitions to large-scale urban ensembles. Unfortunately, only two projects reached the construction phase, and only the Plaza Bicentenario ensemble was more or less completed.[13]

Built next to the Presidential Palace of Venezuela—Palacio de Miraflores—the Plaza Bicentenario and the Presidential Palace Extension (1982–1987, unfinished, see pp. 334–341) were part of Oscar Tenreiro's proposed master plan to construct a number of cultural venues and open public areas in central Caracas. Tenreiro designed not only the Plaza Bicentenario but also the National Gallery GAN (see pp. 312–323), and the Teatro del Oeste dance theater (see pp. 328–333).

The Plaza Bicentenario has parking spaces underneath the plaza as well as galleries and office spaces on the edges of the site. Most of the load-bearing structures are of posttensioned reinforced concrete, designed in close collaboration between Tenreiro and Komendant. The dance theater construction was also well under way, but was halted due to financial difficulties. It has been standing as a concrete ruin in central Caracas for more than three decades.

The National Gallery GAN (1980–1986, unbuilt) complex was, arguably, the most important project on which Tenreiro and Komendant collaborated. It was planned for the vicinity of the presidential palace and the dance theater. The galleries of the monumental museum were organised around four spacious courtyards. Natural light, directed by screen walls and skylights, was designed to dominate the interior. The structure of the building was developed in close dialogue between Tenreiro and Komendant. They intended to use long-span posttensioned folded plates separated by skylight ribbons. Elastically controlled joints with sponge rubber would have been used to provide earthquake resistance.

August Komendant's legacy

Throughout his career August Komendant played a variety of roles in the construction industry. In the 1930s, he was a construction supervisor and entrepreneur, and in the second half of the same decade, he was a faculty member and structural designer. After World War II, he was primarily a consulting engineer. He felt just as comfortable on building sites as he did at the drawing table, and rumbling concrete mixers were just as familiar to him as graphite pencils and slide rules. Before the computer age, all drawings and calculations were done by

Plaza Bicentenario after the completion of the first construction phase

hand. This required great concentration and precision. During his career, Komendant prepared thousands of drawings and hundreds of calculations. He had many assistants, including his life partner Helmi Aren, who was talented in music and mathematics as well as technical drawing.

Komendant was also a successful educator. As a young engineer, he gave lectures on concrete structures at Tallinn University of Technology (1937–1939). After emigrating to the US, he became a visiting professor at the University of Pennsylvania, where, together with Louis Kahn, he primarily taught architectural students. In the 1970s, Komendant taught a course in the philosophy of technology at the renowned Pratt Institute in New York. The students appreciated "Dr. Komendant" for his knowledge, experience, and directness. He was convinced that a good education did not mean acquiring lots of facts but learning how to think.

During his lifetime, Komendant wrote four books, of which the most famous is his retrospective *18 Years with Architect Louis I. Kahn* (1975). The other three are technical works. *Prestressed Concrete Structures* (1952), as mentioned previously, was his first book published in the US and introduced Komendant to local architects and engineers. A curious fact: unbeknownst to its author, the book was translated into Russian in the USSR (1959). Komendant also authored *Contemporary Concrete Structures* (1972; second printing 1977) and *Practical Structural Analysis for Architectural Engineering* (1987). In addition to books, Komendant wrote scientific articles for technical publications as well as popularizing texts for the general public.

The construction and design of buildings is always associated with numbers and calculations—whether related to money, materials, or structures. However, calculations alone cannot create architecture and a living environment that touches the soul. Starting with his engineering studies in the 1930s, it was clear to August Komendant that, in addition to the wise use of technology and skillful arrangement of spaces, every structure also requires a component of artistic creativity.

Classical ideas, along with those relevant to modern building culture, were intertwined in Komendant's aesthetic perceptions. Just like Vitruvius, Leon Battista Alberti, Ove Arup, and other major figures in the history of construction, Komendant was convinced that every building—be it a residence, industrial building, or museum—has its own aesthetic character and distinctive atmosphere. Komendant considered it important for buildings to indicate their intended purpose and constructional nature. He believed that every building must be able to "explain" how it is able to stand up and why its appearance is appropriate.

Every building is constructed for a definite purpose—churches for religious services, schoolhouses for learning, factories for manufacturing, and residential buildings as homes. When the spaces are arranged compactly, with structural elements designed to last, building materials used economically, and the appearance integral, it is most likely a good building. In a situation where the aesthetic, functional, and technological components form an integral whole, a kind of qualitative surplus develops, which simultaneously belongs to everyone and no one. It remains elusive but is felt and perceived by almost everyone using the space.

Such spatial quality is usually aspired to in houses of worship and symbolic public buildings—churches, museums, and concert halls. And yet it can also appear in many ordinary environments, even in industrial and utilitarian buildings. August Komendant helped to create several amazingly complete buildings. Many believe the most impactful of them is the Kimbell Art Museum, designed in collaboration with architect Louis Kahn and located in Fort Worth, Texas.

The buildings and projects that were completed with August Komendant's participation demonstrate how to see and sense the whole, and to parse out what is most important from a large body of information. He was a well-educated and highly experienced specialist who worked across national borders but remained faithful to his heritage and native language. If today creativity often has to retreat in the face of efficiency, higher productivity, and limited time then, as an engineer, Komendant valued Architecture with a capital *A*—its timeless dimension and lasting quality. He knew that miracles need more than spreadsheets and a budget—a creative impulse is vital. Creating a high-quality, excellent and inspiring space motivated him, and should also inspire all those who plan and build our living environment today.

1 August Komendant, "Konstantin Zeren ehitajana" [Konstantin Zeren as a Builder], in *Liivika võõrsil: Üliõpilasselts Liivika 75. aasta koguteos*, ed. Elmar Järvesoo and Leo Koobas (Toronto: Üliõpilasselts Liivika Kirjastus, 1984), 96–99.

2 See the List of Works, pp. 410–412.

3 Komendant, "Konstantin Zeren ehitajana," 97.

4 See architect Oscar Tenreiro's interview with August Komendant (1985) in this volume, pp. 41–59.

5 Author's conversation with George Jüri Komendant, son of August Komendant, September 27, 2018.

6 A substantial amount of material related to Komendant's work for the US European Command can be found in the August E. Komendant Collection at the Architectural Archives of the University of Pennsylvania (AAUP).

7 August Komendant, *Prestressed Concrete Structures* (New York: McGraw-Hill, 1952).

8 August Komendant, *18 Years with Architect Louis I. Kahn* (Englewood, NJ: Alloray, 1975), 1–3. Alternatively, it might have been Nicholas Gianopulos, structural engineer and principal of Keast & Hood, who introduced Komendant to Kahn. William Whitaker's e-mail to the author, February 4, 2022.

9 A detailed account from the perspective of construction history of the Richards Medical Research Laboratories can be found in Roberto Gargiani, *Louis. I. Kahn: Exposed Concrete and Hollow Stones* (Lausanne: EPFL Press; Oxford: Routledge, 2014), 130–181.

10 On the design and construction history of the Salk Institute, see Anna Rosellini, *Louis. I. Kahn: Towards the Zero Degree of Concrete* (Lausanne: EPFL Press; 2014), 9–129.

11 The Kimbell Art Museum has been analyzed from the perspective of construction history in Thomas Leslie, *Louis. I. Kahn: Building Art, Building Science* (New York: George Braziller Inc., 2005), 177–225. See also Rosellini, *Louis. I. Kahn: Towards the Zero Degree of Concrete*, 281–345.

12 A detailed account of Habitat '67's design and construction history is provided in Réjean Legault, "The Making of Habitat 67: A Tense *Pas de Deux* between Moshe Safdie and August Komendant," *Journal of the Society for the Study of Architecture in Canada / Le Journal de la Société pour l'étude de l'architecture au Canada* 46, no. 1 (2021): 30–50.

13 A comprehensive overview of architect Oscar Tenreiro's oeuvre can be found in *Todo Llega Al Mar: Pensamiento y obra del arquitecto Oscar Tenreiro* [Everything Flows into the Sea. The Thought and Works of Architect Oscar Tenreiro] (Valencia: Ediciones ETSAV, 2019).

Design and Its Critical Evaluation (1972)

August Komendant

Approach to a design

Any creative activity within man's experience involves four basic phases:

1. *Image*—the processing of ideas, concepts, and meanings, the weighing of possibilities, and the analysis of meanings. The process is purely abstract, free from limitations. It is an entirely immeasurable phase of a design.

2. *Design*—the realization of the image. This phase is not abstract. It involves practical consideration and is largely controlled by limitations.

3. *Construction*—the building of reality.

4. *Critical evaluation* of the finished product. This, too, is an immeasurable phase.

The last phase—critical evaluation—must also be an integral part of the first three phases, as guidance to the creator himself. Without it, the finished product—building, bridge, etc.—is not even worth evaluating.

There are two basic approaches to developing the first two phases of a design: artistic and philosophic. The artistic approach makes use of forms and patterns as the universal elements in the creation of architecture as well as art. In this approach, architecture is regarded as research for the right forms for making useful spaces. Thus, the creative architectural impulse is primarily an impulse to form.

Using form and pattern as the operational bases for architecture and assuming that the design phase (from abstraction to reality) is correct, the following questions immediately arise: Is form really immeasurable and impersonal? What produces an emotional response—forms and their relations? If so, what are the right forms and relations?

An objective, direct answer to these questions, so fundamental in architecture, is not possible. Supporters of the artistic approach, not being able to answer these vital questions, claim that such questions are irrelevant and meaningless in architecture. They use intuition for guidance in their aims and decisions and, very often, undefined architectural or structural reasons as justification of their choices and actions. Therefore, the artistic approach in architecture leads to confusion, aimlessness, and experimentation. It is highly subjective, being based primarily upon feeling and thus lacking the objective principles required for any applied art, such as architecture, and as such, it is disputable.

The philosophic approach considers form not as a primary element in architecture, but rather as a result of abstract and physical relations the treatment of which is no longer elementary. The form does not necessarily determine the end in view because the form is only part of the meaning. The order and position of elements define the form; that is, how the materials or elements are ordered determines what the form means. The vital union of form and matter does not necessarily produce a complete integration or a desired harmony. Also, it may not realize the intended meaning.

Thus a combination of forms and elements can become mere artifice, an added attraction or concealment, empty of content.

The only basis which allows us to answer all vital questions objectively and which provides guidance through all the creative phases of a design is the function. The function is dynamic, it represents and cannot be represented, and as such, it is immeasurable. The upper boundary of a function is a mathematical idea—a pure concept, very abstract and rationally manipulatable, whose meaning does not flow from the accident of its existence. The lower boundary of the function is represented by certified facts and thus independent of our control; it is the last instance against which our competence and validity of abstract concepts can be checked.

Since a function is dictated by an "inner reasoned certainty," it is not disputable, and this makes all the difference. Thus the philosophic approach, using function as the basis for all phases of design, is conclusive and convincing. It is the only acceptable approach for the contemporary mind because it creates an emotional response—"a mysterious present-field of functions"—and guides the creator from the beginning to the end of his work. The ever-present field of functions is the only medium by which the creator and the observers of his work are related.

The Means of Realization

As the image, the design, and their realization are closely related, the quality of the finished product—the structure or building—is determined already in the design phase by the choice of structural and mechanical systems, materials, and methods of construction. If these choices are not correctly made, intentions and accomplishments will commonly be out of scale and the work will not carry out the intention.

Since the structure basically serves some purpose, the purpose will most likely limit the choice of structural and mechanical systems, and these, in turn, will control the materials and methods of construction to be used.

There are four basic carrying actions—suspension, arch, beam, and shell—and a variety of combinations of these basic actions, such as beam-arch action and beam-suspension action. Also, there are four basic materials: wood, masonry, steel, and reinforced concrete. The physical characteristics of the materials and the structural peculiarities of the carrying actions determine their relationship. For example, the suspension action involves only tensile stresses and can currently be accomplished with steel cables and strands. True arch action involves only compressive stresses and can be accomplished most efficiently with masonry, concrete, or steel. Beam action involves three types of stresses—compressive, tensile, and shear—and can be accomplished with wood, prestressed concrete, and steel. Beam action accomplished with reinforced concrete involves an additional stress, namely, bond stress. Shell action involves mainly two types of stresses—shear and compressive—and can be accomplished with reinforced and prestressed concrete.

The number of stresses involved indicates the span limits and the economy of the carrying action. Thus the most uneconomical carrying action with limited spans is beam action. The longest spans that are economically possible can be obtained by suspension and arch actions or by a combination of both, that is, by a trussed system.

Rarely can an efficient and acceptable structural system be accomplished by one carrying action. Beam action is generally required to obtain the stability and flexibility needed to meet local conditions and satisfy architectural requirements.

The shape of the structural member or members making up the system is controlled mainly by the physical characteristics of the material, the type of stresses involved, and their distribution over the cross-sectional area and along its length. The color and texture of surfaces and the pattern of members, as well as the shapes and connections, are atmosphere-creating qualities and are controlled by the image.

Selection of the method of construction is controlled mainly by considerations of economy, but whatever method is used, the finished product must clearly indicate what that method was, that is, how the structure was built and the required quality obtained.

Engineering science at present is at such a level that the strength of materials produced, the deformations of a structural element or system under any known loading it may be subject to, and its stability and carrying capacity can be computed with sufficient accuracy that any conceivable project can be carried out with reasonable safety and quality. As a result, methods and systems are changing more rapidly than ever before. This progress demonstrates the ability and face of contemporary architecture and engineering.

Critical Evaluation

Before the critical evaluation of any design can be started, the basis of such an evaluation must be established. The more conscious the designer is about what constitutes good design, the more successful he can be in pursuing his aim, the sounder his concept will be of the correct way of deciding what is right or wrong, and the more rational his decisions are likely to be. It is quite possible to be a good designer without ever philosophizing about the basic principles of engineering, but the advancement of engineering depends upon someone's deep and persistent thinking about methods and meanings, about why and how to apply certain theories, using assumptions and weighing validities, justifications, etc. Thus to be a good and progressive engineer, it is not enough to accumulate a vast amount of facts, data, and experience in one's specialized field. Facts and data that are not ordered by reason and understanding into constructive relations may be called "knowledge," but they are not significant in themselves unless they suggest ideas combined into theories. Engineering as an applied science is simply not a two-dimensional affair, composed of factual knowledge lacking depth and stability. The third dimension, which is required for stability, is provided by theories, which are the only means of advancing engineering and of discovering what the advancement signifies.

Generally the evaluation of any design makes use of the following three criteria:

1. Rational solution

2. Aesthetic quality

3. Economy

One is immediately confronted with the following question: What are the relative degrees of importance of these criteria? For example, is a sound structural solution more important than aesthetic quality or economy? Probably no one could lay down beforehand a complete set of such rated criteria to take care of all eventualities. Even if that were possible, what about the value judgment of the end in view itself—the finished product whose quality is based upon a single order that will somehow take account of all three criteria? It is this that usually creates the conflict among the engineer, architect, public, and owner. In most cases, the owner's part in this dispute is assumed to be cancelled out by fixing limits for expenditures and establishing the program to be completed within the financial limits. However, confining the program and funds available does not satisfy the third criterion—economy—it merely establishes the size of the project.

Before the problem can be investigated further, the value-judgment criteria must be clarified, defined, and analyzed explicitly in detail.

Rational Solution

What is understood by a "rational" structural solution? The term "rational" has many meanings and therefore must be fixed in the context of this particular usage. Let us assume, for example, that a preliminary image and schedule are created for a particular design, to be executed in a definite location under local conditions, and that data such as materials, equipment, and labor available and soil, seismic, and climatic conditions are known. There is, in this case, only one rational structural solution: The solution which carries out the purpose of the project and satisfies all conditions with maximum efficiency. Furthermore, a rational structural system (or systems) is one that does not interfere with the functions the structure is designed for. It must correspond to the image or architectural solution, and thus it should be aesthetically acceptable. All these factors considered, any other structural solution will have a lower degree of rationality. A further question that arises in connection with these statements is: What sort of evidence is required to prove that the structural solution is rational under given conditions? This question cannot be answered directly; it requires a broad and thorough study based upon the following fundamental concepts:

1. The structural system and shapes must correspond with the special physical characteristics of the material to be used.

2. Each structural member as a component of the structural system must be designed so that its relative function, type of carrying action, and degree of importance in the structural system are clearly pronounced.

3. The number of members or elements to accomplish the overall carrying action of a structural system should be the minimum possible.

4. A structural member serving functions additional to its structural one has a higher degree of importance, which must be indicated.

5. The use of materials should be efficient and balanced within the structural system.

6. The materials of the members used should be stable and durable under normally existing and possible expected conditions.

7. The design must be simple, honest, and easy to construct under given conditions, and the method of construction should be visible.

The simultaneous satisfaction of all these fundamental concepts is a rather complex problem. It requires both a profound structural and mathematical knowledge and the understanding and experience that result in a trained intuition. By "trained intuition" we mean a faculty for contemplating a set of possibilities and then arriving almost at once at a valid rational solution, which is suggested by the given architectural image and set of local conditions. Without such intuition, the resulting design seldom approaches the set standards or required results.

Aesthetic Quality

The second criterion, aesthetic quality, is more difficult to define than the first because the term is subjective and therefore one cannot be fully guided by reason. But even when one cannot formulate the concept exactly, it is possible to distinguish between external and internal evidence of the aesthetic quality of a structure.

External evidence of aesthetic quality can be derived from direct inspection of the structure, whereas the internal evidence of quality requires a knowledge of background, function, and relations and of the architectural image and design itself. The external qualities can be seen by anyone who has had some previous acquaintance with the general idea of the structure or the method of construction. It would not be difficult to select a set of characteristic qualities in a finished structure which the majority of observers would feel similarly satisfied about. However, such qualities must be real, that is, must embody the structure's own characteristics, and not simply the illusory qualities which, by ordinary standards, one may expect or hope to see because the structure has been designed by a well-known architect or engineer having a high degree of prestige or for some other, similar reason. Also, the decorative effect of a structure, which very often is confused with its external quality, must be taken into consideration. A decorative effect usually does not have duration; it is like fashion without depth, creating only temporary response. Real aesthetic quality is self-contained, independent, free of artificial effects, and capable of maintaining its own value; as such, it is timeless and universal.

For the characteristics of a finished structure that may serve as evidence for aesthetic quality, the following postulates are suggested:

a) Expressiveness

b) Atmosphere

c) End-means relation

Before one can make fair sense of these qualitative characteristics, they must be explained, if possible, in terms of their meaning, their interrelationship, and the means by which a designer can control them.

Expressiveness in this context means the relationship between a design and its objective or the relationship between a structural member or members and their real function. If a building or structure is designed for a particular purpose, the design must exhibit the characteristics that indicate its purpose, function, and performance capacity. The appearance of a structure should express all its embodied qualities and, without any mystery, should make the observer directly aware of what the structure is or is expected to be. The shapes and forms should grow freely out of the nature of the purpose itself instead of being forced or borrowed from elsewhere.

Atmosphere is a quality which cannot be analyzed into simpler qualities or defined precisely because the term is not only subjective but also psychological, closely related to the perceptual conditions on which it largely depends. Therefore, it can be made meaningful more by explanations and proper illustrations than by definitions. For example, atmosphere makes the difference between a house and a home, between a warehouse and a library, or between a theater and a nightclub, which have similar functions for different people at different times, namely, relaxation, enjoyment, etc. Thus the real difference is in the atmosphere. Churches, museums, schoolhouses, factories, laboratories, etc., differ by their atmosphere, as do apartment houses and office buildings. Of two structural systems designed for the same purpose and having the same numerical factor of safety, one may create a safe atmosphere and the other may lack it or have it to a lesser degree, even though the second structure may appear more massive than the first (a quality which is often assumed to be synonymous with strength). Nobody can dispute the simple truth that the proper atmosphere of a building is an indispensable quality which makes a design significant. When a building, whatever its purpose may be, lacks the expected atmosphere and rationality, it reveals only its struggle between hope and despair in every aspect.

The *end-means relation* is, in the true sense, an alternative means to the same end: to obtain the highest degree of expressiveness and desired atmosphere by natural, nonintellectual, and material means. The first two postulates—expressiveness and atmosphere—are both more or less relative and subjective in nature, involving the observer's response to the structure. This type of evidence for the aesthetic quality of a structure is as often asserted as denied by different people. Therefore, subjective external evidence does not carry positive conviction unless it is supported by more objective internal qualities—qualities which are supported by reason and which are expressed by the third postulate, the end-means relation.

Now, what are these internal qualities? Before this question can be answered, a more profound problem must be clarified. Expressiveness and atmosphere are, in a sense, effects, that is, results of a certain cause or a complex of causes. Very often, the significance in a design of the cause-effect or, more explicitly, end-means relation is overlooked or not understood. Thus, confusingly, the structural design is regarded only as satisfying all the structural fundamentals (concepts 1 to 7), and the engineer's task as a whole is considered to be like that of a mathematician—solving a problem described by a set of impersonal equations with given boundary conditions. However, it is true that a proper structural solution is, almost by its very nature, aesthetically satisfying; even when a structural solution is based only on the principle of efficiency and on the satisfaction of functional purpose, the results, while they may be aesthetically insignificant, are never irritating. But also nobody can argue the simple truth that however well a structure performs its function, some alternative structural solution, almost equally efficient, can often add to the structure as a whole something that raises its quality. This "something" is the difference between static computations—dimensioning the carrying elements and analyzing the stresses—and making a structural design. To make this more explicit, the structural design requires, besides the technical data and factual knowledge, a deep understanding of structural systems, related materials, their behavior under conditions the structure will be subjected to, mechanical installation, construction methods, etc., which are inseparable parts of any design. The problems involved in a contemporary design are extremely complicated. It is not a process in which an idea simply forms in the designer's mind and is mechanically worked out in accordance with some accepted method and in available materials.

As in any other creative work, the concept of a design most suitable to accomplish an architectural image develops and ripens gradually in the mind before the actual mechanical designing process starts. The process involves recognizing and weighing the possibilities inherent in the particular structural system, materials, and method of construction to be used. The designer must be aware of what causes a certain effect and what effects a structural system, members, arrangement of members, and shape and form of members are capable of yielding. Also, distinction between the quality of effects is most significant.

The effects caused by the design itself—such as the choice of structural system and materials and the form and shape of the members, which result in effects of completeness, power, order, degree of heterogeneity, etc.—or effects caused by the surface characteristics and color of the material without any addition to the design besides those elements that contribute to its capacity to serve its purpose, have aesthetic value of a higher degree because the external qualities are supported by internal evidence or rational reasoning.

All other effects, produced by addition to the structural design for concealment, etc., have a lesser degree of aesthetic value or no value at all. It is perhaps not feasible to try to account for all the casual features which might influence the aesthetic quality of a design, but at least these factors are objectively true, that is, connected to knowledge and understanding and not based only on purely subjective judgments, such as liking. The perception of the aesthetic quality of a design, especially of a structural design, must be based upon conceptual content and must be free from irrelevant subjective distortions. Therefore, a progressive and good engineer must always be conscious of what he is doing and must control his actions by asking the philosophical questions *why* and *if*: What are the results and what are the rational means to obtain the desired results—safety, efficiency, expressiveness, and atmosphere—without losing sight of the end-means relation?

Expressiveness

The essentials of expressiveness are simplicity, clarity, and above all, modesty. These qualities can be achieved by means of the following principles: The function and degree of importance of each element in the structural system must be meaningful and unmistakably pronounced by mass-space relations or even more explicitly by scale, form, and shape of the elements. The arrangement of the elements in the overall system must show the flow of forces and how they are led into the supporting elements. The type of loads the system is subjected to must appear from the shape as well as from the arrangement of elements in the carrying system. The overall carrying system must be homogeneous, have novelty, etc., and individual secondary elements should not dominate but should fuse freely and naturally into the system so that not a single element could be removed without the carrying system losing its wholeness.

The degree of expressiveness can be controlled by the choice of carrying system, by variation of mass-space relation, by the number and combination of elements constituting a carrying system, by the shape of elements, by the choice of materials the elements are made of, and by the surface qualities (color, texture, etc.).

Atmosphere

The atmospheric qualities are obtained by the choice of qualities of expressiveness and as such can also be controlled by the proper choice of the structural system, materials, surface texture, color, and arrangement of lighting.

For example, a quiet, neutral atmosphere is promoted by the completeness of the structural system, by simplicity and simple order—all that is needed must be there modestly. The elements should be balanced and in equilibrium. The system should not be analyzable into more simple secondary systems. The number of elements in the system should be minimized. The materials should be concrete, masonry, or wood.

A vivid atmosphere can be most successfully produced by complexity: two-directional space systems, trusses, systems composed with harmonically ordered elements. Also, heterogenic systems with periodically ordered members are suitable.

In general, a similarity of members or elements creates harmony, clarity, and completeness—in other words, safety.

Expressiveness and atmosphere are closely associated, and their relationship can be explained most simply by using an example. Let us analyze the structural system for a church. The desired atmosphere requires that the system should have a relatively low degree of expressiveness, that it should not dominate the visual field and should not attract any direct attention. However, it must create an effect of power—even, in an indirect way, of mystery and greatness. The proper structural solution by which such qualities can be obtained is the use of arches and shells, relatively flat folded plates, or a highly unified structural system composed of similar, simple, harmoniously ordered elements fusing naturally into unity.

Whatever the purpose of a building, the relationship between expressiveness and atmosphere is established by the architectural image. The structural system must correspond directly to that image without affecting its carrying action and structural clarity. To the degree of conformity of the perceptual and conceptual images the design owes its power and aesthetic value.

End-Means Relation

The end-means relation postulate is truly a critical accomplishment, connecting quality judgment directly with knowledge and understanding. To satisfy the end-means postulate requires a high degree of imagination and thoroughly up-to-date knowledge, both theoretical and practical, of parts-whole relationships, space-mass relationships, etc., because this type of knowledge is indispensable to the achievement of desired qualities and also to the balancing and ordering of complex qualities into the single quality of the finished product. The basis for the evaluation of the end-means relation involves, besides originality and novelty, the principle of intellectual economy: the most by the least.

Many critics deny that knowledge is essential for evaluating the aesthetic qualities of a structure. They insist that such judgments should be based only upon the appearance or perceptual image, and thus only upon external evidence. If this were true, how could one judge a dishonest structure? For example, in terms of appearance, a structure may seem to be a reinforced concrete shell when structurally it is not a shell at all but only a shell-shaped plastic ceiling hung from a truss. Before one is able to pass any judgment of aesthetic quality, one must distinguish aesthetic quality itself from its effects. As another example, the color of a surface may be the natural color of the material or it may be a painted imitation. The paint may actually be more attractive to some observers, but for one having knowledge of how the texture and color are obtained, it will have no quality at all.

On the other hand, a building with a high degree of aesthetic quality may not serve the purpose it was designed for or may be too rich for this particular purpose—for example, a factory designed as a library or a laboratory that looks like a monument. When the observer is aware of such a discrepancy, even the most beautiful building will lose all its aesthetic qualities and only look funny.

Economy

The third criterion, economy, depends mainly on the efficient use of materials, on the simplicity and efficiency of the structural system, and on the individual members of the system—factors already included in the first criterion. However, in some cases the efficiency of the structure has to be sacrificed to realize the image, and here lies the difference between a proper structural system and a structural system which satisfies only the structural needs. Besides these main factors in achieving economy, there are secondary factors, such as assigning other services to a structural member, for example, embedment of ducts, utilities, etc. The installation and maintenance of such services should be easy. Furthermore, extensive economy is achieved by using efficient construction methods and materials which correspond to the structural solution and time schedule.

In many designs the aesthetic criterion, based only on the perceptual image, is overemphasized at the expense of the conceptual image and other criteria, or vice versa. In the first case, the resulting design tends to be decorative, and in the second case, "functional." Commonly both such designs lack significance because the intention and accomplishment contradict each other. Such conflicts seem to be almost common among advanced and complex contemporary designs.

To conclude, the value judgment of a design is based upon the evaluation of all the criteria and their relations in terms of rationality—maximum results at minimum cost within the limits of the funds available. This principle is the only sound basis for a value judgment of any design because it combines all the essential and rational factors: knowledge, understanding, imagination, local conditions, and the technical and cultural standards of the country in which the structure under evaluation is located.

This article was first published in August Komendant's book *Contemporary Concrete Structures* (New York, NY: McGraw-Hill, 1972; 2nd. ed., Huntington, NY: Krieger, 1977), 3–15.

Architect–Engineer Relationship (1986)

August Komendant

For the contemporary design and construction of concrete structures, the importance of close-absolute rapport between architect and engineer is a must. Very often this "must" is ignored and due to this there are so many fiascos and so few successes.

Architects usually consider engineers as unavoidable nuisances, who spoil architectural qualities for so-called structural reasons. In [the] architect's mind [the] engineer is an outsider, as far as design is concerned, and his task is only like that of a mathematician solving structural problems by a set of impersonal equations with given load factors and boundary conditions. This prevailing attitude of architects is completely wrong. The engineer's contribution to a contemporary unified design is not only to satisfy the structural needs, but his skills, knowledge, understanding of structural systems and materials are valuable to the architecture as a whole. Nobody can argue the simple truth that however well a certain structural system performs its carrying functions, the facts are overwhelming that some other, alternate structural solution adds to the design something that raises its quality. This "something" is the difference between a unified architectural-structural design and a structural design consisting only of stress analysis and dimensioning the carrying elements. In a unified design the structure is an integral part of architecture—it is the architecture.

Basically architecture is part art and part engineering. The basis of art is form and architecture as art consists of looking for proper forms and their relations in order to obtain the architectural aims. In engineering the basic element is function and the proper forms are those which carry out their functions most efficiently and effectively. Most architects like to be artists and forget the engineering part in architecture.

In art only one person—the artist—carries out all three phases of his creation: the image phase, design and its realization. In contemporary architectural and engineering designs a team of specialists are involved: architects, engineers—structural and mechanical, and construction engineers. Without such teamwork the finished product seldom approaches the set standards, it lacks the expected quality and reveals its struggle and desperation in every aspect. It must be kept in mind that in a unified design the variety of functions the building reveals relates the perceptual and conceptual image and creates an emotional response. This mysterious "field of functions" is the only medium which relates the creators with the observers of their work.

Kahn was in true sense an artist. His philosophy was more poetic than a search for truth. He considered architecture as pure art—"silent music." He never accepted that architecture is only a functional or applied art. Up to his fifties he was known and admired mainly by architectural students but not really understood, mainly because Kahn always knew the question *what* but was not able to answer the following logical questions *how* and *why*. When these questions arose he smiled disarmingly and said, *It is still a secret*. Because of arbitrary choice of forms and their relations, without proper critical evaluation requiring knowledge, his intended "silent music" became just "silent noise". Among practicing architects he was almost unknown. He had only a few accomplishments as an architect, none of them significant.

As far as engineering was concerned, he did not consider it to be a creative profession—Kahn believed only artists and scientists are creative—and engineers as "sausage makers—just cranking the stuff out". This statement of Kahn's is a clear indicator that he was completely ignorant of engineering. He lacked the basic knowledge of structures and structural materials, and their special physical characteristics. He hid his lack of structural knowledge behind arrogance and his position.

Kahn's attitude about engineering changed drastically after his close association with Robert Le Ricolais and myself, as professors in the University of Pennsylvania. He learned very fast about true engineering and recognized that by using advanced structures in architecture he was able to realize his ideas beyond his earlier approach. In his lectures and speeches he still stuck to his artistic approach, but as a practicing architect he became a fundamentalist. This is proven by his well-known questions and thoughts: Is this window only an opening in the wall? What the material like brick or concrete likes to be? The structure has to tell its own story from gravel yard to the finished building. These questions and thoughts are irrelevant to an artist but vital and basic for a functional architect. Form is static, it does not talk. Function is dynamic and reveals the purpose of structural elements in [the] overall structural system. How the elements are arranged and their relationship are the basic means to create atmosphere, never the form empty of contents, because only the function gives content to the form.

Kahn's changed attitude toward engineering is most evident in his essay on "Monumentality," where he states:

> *Standardization, prefabrication, controlled experiments and tests, and specialization are not monsters to be avoided by the delicate sensibility of the artist. They are merely the modern means of controlling vast potentialities of materials for living, by chemistry, physics, engineering, production and assembly, which lead to the necessary knowledge the artist must have to expel fear in their use, broaden his creative instinct, give him new courage and thereby lead him to the adventure of unexplored places. His work will then be part of his age and will afford delight and service for his contemporaries. I do not wish to imply that monumentality can be attained scientifically or that the work of the architect reaches its greatest service to humanity by his peculiar genius to guide a concept towards a monumentality. I merely defend, because I admire, the architect who possesses the will to grow with the many angles of our development. For such a man finds himself far ahead of his fellow workers.*[1]

Kahn had a profound and deep intuition about what true architecture should be. His first architectural images for a project were almost always brilliant. Kahn never lacked ideas or dreams. In most cases his trouble was—too many ideas for a design, which made the choice rather difficult, if not agonizing. Working with Kahn one of my main duties in the image phase was to try to intensify the image so that it gained gravity and came down to reality, instead of being blown into thin air. Any creative process is considerably helped when one can discuss the problems and possibilities with a partner who has the theoretical-structural knowledge and practical experience. Kahn almost always had severe doubts about his choice of design for a particular project. He needed continuous encouragement, especially in case a solution was never used before, was a novelty and brilliant. He got irritated when he was criticized and told that his solution was nonsense and could not be done. In such cases, we had complete agreement—why not, let us do it!

Kahn's positive change toward engineering made him famous, but did not change his negative attitude about engineers, they remained still the "sausage makers" for him. Many engineers were irritated by it. Abba Tor discussing a technical problem with Kahn did not feel comfortable with the image of a sausage maker and instead substituted it with that of a "male dancer in a classical ballet who, feet firmly planted on the ground, catches the daring ballerina in midair and helps her complete her movements gracefully rather than fall on her face."[2]

Contemplating Kahn's and Tor's stand on the engineer's role in architecture, it is quite obvious that Kahn overlooks the importance of the quality of the "stuff" prepared only by the architect without any help from the engineers. Contrary to Kahn, Tor considers creation of excellent architecture as a team effort by two equal partners.

Very often an engineer finds himself in situation where a design starts with high hopes but during the design process the stuff gets thinner and thinner, and lacks substance. If there is a confirmed commitment, the engineer gets disgusted and takes the position to crank it out as quick as possible and get it over with. If some engineers' and also architects' aim is just to make money, they would not mind being ordinary "sausage makers." Such an attitude is the main reason that engineers generally have a rather low status in society. It is also responsible for [a] relatively large number of mishaps and failures in the construction industry.

The Dacca project may serve as an example. The image phase was worked out perfectly, and the approach was functional and promising. But when the design started Kahn changed the image using his earliest artistic approach. The choice of forms was confusing, arbitrary and unbalanced—empty of content. The proper relationship of materials and structural systems was entirely overlooked. Brick and concrete were put into [a] position they did not want to be in. We had a profound disagreement. Kahn became arrogant and acted like [an] immature prima donna. He tried to give me orders to carry out his designs, which I considered wrong and below my standards. I told Kahn—I am not working for you but only with you, I don't take orders. The situation grew unacceptable for both of us. It was clear to me that even my best efforts and desires could not crank his stuff into a successful conclusion. I stopped cranking, and this was the end of our association.

Our association was interrupted for about three years. In this period Kahn was not creative and was depressed. There were rumors and even an article in a professional magazine stating that Kahn has run dry of new ideas and is dead as an architect. All this was far from the truth, Kahn still had plenty of ideas but could not perform because no acceptable "sausage maker" was available.

When [the] Olivetti and Kimbell projects came along, our association was reestablished. In this period we were really perfect "dance partners." Both projects are novelties—advanced designs—and the "male dancer" had to take care of the balancing and performance. Everyone visiting these buildings can see the results obtained by [a] proper relationship between architect and engineer. All the designs and buildings we worked on together have become architectural landmarks, received numerous gold medals and national as well as international attention.

In hindsight, it was exciting to work with an architect with such [a] phenomenal mind. Sometimes he just drove me nuts, changing a design already under construction, or leaving for lectures and unimportant meetings at a time when architectural drawings and his decisions were badly needed. But even in some serious situations, he laughed disarmingly and said, *We are not in court where there has to be a decision—guilty or not guilty.*

As a true artist, Kahn had no sense of economy or time, but there was plenty of excitement—arguments, disagreements, fights and enjoyment. Never a dull moment during the eighteen years of my association with architect Louis I. Kahn.

1 Editor's note: Quoted from Louis Kahn, "Monumentality," in *New Architecture and City Planning: A Symposium*, ed. Paul Zucker (Freeport, NY: Philosophical Library, 1944), 77–88. The essay has been republished on multiple occasions, for example, in *Louis I. Kahn: Writings, Lectures, Interviews*, ed. Alessandra Latour (New York: Rizzoli, 1986), 18–27.

2 Editor's note: See consulting engineer Abba Tor's review of August Komendant's book *18 Years with Architect Louis I. Kahn*, *Architectural Record* 162, no. 3 (1977): 107.

This article is most likely a transcript or a developed version of August Komendant's lecture in the "Louis Kahn" course at the Institute for Architecture and Urban Studies (IAUS) in New York, NY, in 1980 or 1981. Originally published in English and Italian in *Louis I. Kahn: l'uomo, il maestro*, ed. Alessandra Latour (Rome: Edizioni Kappa, 1986), 315–19.

August Komendant at home, 1985

Interview. August Komendant (1985)

August Komendant and Oscar Tenreiro Degwitz
Upper Montclair, New Jersey, January 27, 1985

Oscar Tenreiro: I would like to talk about some of your personal experiences, Doctor Komendant,[1] for instance, your relation with so many different architects, and also about your views on architecture. We were talking before that most engineers are not concerned about the general results of their work, the overall result, the final building. But in your case you are very much concerned with that, and in many ways, I would say, that you are an architect in its historic meaning, in the ancient way of defining it. That is to say, a person who builds, knows how to build, and who cares about the results. What would you think of your experience with architects in general, and if we consider all the different personalities of the architects who you have worked with, which one of them do you feel closer to your own feelings?
August Komendant: I believe Lou Kahn. We had the same philosophy. Practically we had no disagreement about the philosophy. We dreamed together, we built together. You see, he was full of ideas. And whatever was an advanced design, he was interested, very much interested. Many people would say no, it cannot be done, for example, the Kimbell Museum—nobody has used cycloids before because it's very difficult to handle mathematically. They all said no, and advised Kahn to use another approach. We came together, and it was interesting. We said, let's do it. [Chuckles] And we did it! This was also true with the Olivetti building. Practically, also with the Salk Laboratories. You see, it always worked out because we both had the same attitude.[2]

The structure is an integral part of architecture, because that is the architecture. Let's say, all the buildings we designed with Lou—it's structure! What else?! It is structure arranged in a way that it became architecture. Balancing masses, areas, and always keeping in mind that the building itself talks to you. Very clear, simple. Nothing artificial.

I would say, second, was [Moshe] Safdie. In the very beginning and in the meanwhile, before he became a prima donna, after Habitat, or even during Habitat.[3] But now he has learned that without proper engineering he could never carry out what he had in mind. You see, our relationship is now also philosophically very close. No monkey business. Everything has to be there, and it has to be arranged in a way that the result is beautiful, and has aesthetic appeal. I don't like to use the word beauty. Ladies have beautiful dresses, but a building has *aesthetic appeal*.

Then, you see, let's say Alvar Aalto, we also had practically the same philosophy. We talked very much, discussed it—what can be done, what is wrong, and so on.[4] So also with Henry Klumb, also [Romaldo] Giurgola. We had a very good contact. We talked the same language. It was interesting when there was a jury meeting in Philadephia, and the Pope came to Philadelphia,[5] they wanted to have all the structures and all these ones.[6] And Giurgola was the chairman of this jury. But he got a very urgent telephone call; he had to go back right away. And he turned the chairmanship over to me. The rest were architects, and they were astonished. Giurgola said, *He knows more about architecture than you, we all together*! And then he left. Nobody argued anymore. [Laughs]

You see, I have always paid very much attention to the aesthetic appeal of the structure. If you take [Paul] Rudolph, it's the opposite. ... He hides the structural systems behind dropped ceilings. Something is wrong when you hide something, use trees to hide your building behind them, as Rudolph does, and as many others do.[7] My point of view is, in jury meetings in the university, you see, you have to use the building—not renderings. You can paint wonderful renderings, and the building disappears. For example, Kimbell, we had several discussions on how to do it, from the very beginning.

I never take a project when the image has been created. I have to be a part of it, otherwise I won't do it. I never took the work when the design was ready—*now you do the dimensions and stresses, and all the junk and whatever that is required from engineers*. I said *No, I am also a designer*. This is how I worked with Safdie, Kahn, and even Klumb, from the very beginning.

Nowadays it has become fashionable to hide things, to hide the structure—
Oo yaa.

Cycloid shell covering the entrance portico of the Kimbell Art Museum

—and to express meaning in buildings. But that is taken as something you have to add to buildings, like cosmetics.
That's right.

What you're saying is something very important to be said today because the tendency is to forget the integral part of the structure in architecture, as you said.
That is very true in many, many designs, usually because you cannot ask an architect to know everything what is available. You have to point out, according to your own view, what would be suitable, what creates an effect. Because everybody is after effect, some like to have effect by decorations. But it's never considered what is actually the value of the effect, how it has been obtained. It can be simple, rational means, or decorations. If it's obtained by decoration, it has no value whatsoever. It may have appeal, yes, but that's temporary.

It will depend on taste, fashion ...
Yes, of course, fashion! Now, let's take this postmodern architecture ... there are no principles! Borrowing from the past not knowing how to use it. And they believe that it's ... They call it a new style, postmodern. But for some architects it's only a trademark. They don't even know what this style means, you see. And it is dead before it's born. That's the case. This young Philip Johnson's group, they're all promoters, and when you see their designs, they're different from what they talk about.[8] As I've said before, we all borrow from where our roots are. Greece, Italy, even Egyptians, Babylonians. All these ... But we like to modernise it up to the technical standard. Not just because it was once used, and carried out in some way. Viaducts in Italy, for example. You see, even all these arches and domes in cathedrals, they are very beautiful. We don't use them, and there are reasons for that. There's no skilled labor for this, because there's no demand. Yet, there is something very similar in which we can use the same idea. And that is actually flat slabs arranged in different ways. In hotel lobbies, for example, [the slabs] are very suitable for this purpose. It can be arranged. All the capitals in a modern way, no Corinthian capitals and all that. ... We cannot do it anymore, we don't have the skilled labor, we don't have the sculptors, and we cannot afford it.

Habitat '67 housing complex after completion

Don't you think, Doctor, that maybe this attitude today towards decoration, imitations of Corinthian or Doric columns, maybe it's something that appears in the industrial world because a sort of lack of inspiration has affected the architecture being done?
Yes, that's one point of view, that is the postmodern way to do it. But you see, they don't have the knowledge, the vision, actually, to do it properly, you see. Being up-to-date, to the present state of technology, that's the trouble. That goes back to the education in the schools of architecture, schools of engineering—they are strangers to each other today. Instead, because we are in the same industry, we have to work together, to consider, make proposals, to study them, so that the final product would be appealing and up-to-date.

That is true because you have near you an engineer who is in some ways compensating the natural tendency of architects to fly above reality, to fly without support. If you don't have that at your side then you lose your balance. Maybe the problem is that it is so difficult to find this compensation from the technical point of view, to have at your side someone who is trying to talk to you in a creative way, to compensate your deformations, maybe that's the origin of this problem.
I always tell my students that when one likes to create something, there should be no strings attached, it has to be free as a bird. One dreams something, and wants to have something. Now, if an architect does it alone because he or she doesn't have the knowledge and means to do it, this beautiful image will go up in smoke.

As an engineer I consider it my duty to densify this image, and put it back into reality, more or less. It gains gravity, and it becomes reality. It is also the duty of the engineer to support. Habitat, for example, a wonderful idea! They said we had gone nuts, Safdie and Komendant have dreamt up something that cannot be done. It will collapse, and kill hundreds of people! There was the [municipal] advisory committee and that's exactly what they said. [Edward] Churchill[9] trusted us, and he wanted to have something appealing that would gain attention throughout the world and show how people will live in the twenty-first century. He took a great risk, he called Dr. Salk[10] in California and asked, *We have a crazy design here, and Komendant believes he can do it, and it will be safe.*

Doctor Salk answered, *Whatever he says, believe he can do it*. After that the advisory committee was sent home, and I had free hands. The building is still there, and there are so many unhappy professors because it has not collapsed. [Laughs]

The Habitat case is so interesting also because at that time architecture was dreamed very much about this supposedly new way of building housing vertically, this imitation of slopes, this addition of small cells in clusters, systems like that. So all the architectural schools and architects were dreaming about things like that, maybe some of them very much in the air. But when Habitat was actually built you had a reference, so that is the importance of building in architecture. To build you need this technological and real approach. That is maybe what is lacking today.
Yes, for example, the system of precast factory-made housing has developed a lot. Usually the tools are very expensive, for example, in Iran, we asked eight firms to use their own system to build 25,000 units in a new city close to Isfahan, 400 kilometers from Tehran.[11] Sand and limestone mountains, nothing more. Desert. Dust was flying around. And when the bids came in, I almost went into a coma—the prices were so high. And I went to the Shah and told him, because it was an Atomic City, it was the Shah's baby.[12] I went to the Shah and said, *No in good conscience all these designs are not acceptable price-wise, and also safety-wise. Because Iran is in a very unstable area: high altitude, there are earthquakes, and of all these designs, I wouldn't recommend any of them.*

What do we do? I told him, Okay, I'll think about it, and I proposed something. I developed this system which is safe and 25 percent more economical because all the eight bidders bid on my design. And that was the result. As I told you, I used cyclopean concrete.[13] They had oil, but they like to sell oil, don't they? They used solar heat. Now, how you can do it if you use, let's say, 4-inch [approx. 10 cm] walls. There is no thermal mass, you see! And the temperature difference between day and night is so extreme that you can't live in these houses. Now, what I did, I used cyclopean concrete, about 30 cm thick walls to provide thermal mass, and it was economical. I didn't use any big cranes. I went to Copenhagen to seek help in the construction of the moulds which were needed. They are actually four walls, no bottom, no top. It was easy to pour them. And the Smidth Company in Copenhagen proposed the moulds.[14] I made a proposal, they said it was perfect. And we used hot concrete for this purpose. Instead of using water for mixing, we used saturated steam. In 4 hours we had 28-day strength. We could use these expensive moulds four times in 24 hours, and when the boxes were set we put prefabricated blankets over them and also used the building for casting. We set the moulds, poured, and there was so much flexibility that we could do whatever the architects dreamed about. There was no limit. And when it was ready, we posttensioned the structure into unity to provide safety for the dynamic forces. You can have any combination, and I believe that is the future.

Each prefabricated system that had been proposed, from Denmark, Germany, France, required one $5,000,000 factory to produce around 1000 units per year. But the time schedule was five years to build 25,000 units. We had to have five factories, that is $25,000,000 for the factories; heavy cranes were required, which were not available. Then the contractors told us, *We only need forms to set them up and pour ... and if you like we can build you 10,000 units annually*. Because it is the number of forms—one set of these hydraulically opened and set forms was $75,000, and originally, using the same box girder design like we used in Habitat, it was $250,000. That was the choice. We could offer more. We needed half the number of inside moulds because we used hot concrete, and we could release the moulds in one hour and use them again and again. Outside, not to damage the surface, we had to keep them on for a little bit longer because they had to cool down to the atmospheric temperature.

A technical question, how do you mix the steam in the cement and sand?
We used a special mixer, and when the aggregates [sand, stone] were shoveled into the mixer, there was a hose where the steam came in. A very simple operation. But it was a different type of mixer which can usually stain concrete, if you don't know, it can be a problem. But we could do it.

And then to obtain this cyclopean appearance you intended to sandblast.
Yes, to expose the limestone. We had to use our own materials. Now, there was sand, plenty of it, like in any desert. But this sand had organic matter in it. It was easy, because we had to clean the sand anyway. We neutralized it by putting some lime in the washing water. This way we could use local sand. And limestone was there, no problem, we only needed a little bit of steel, only for posttensioning. Because when you have walls of 30 cm on the boxes you need some steel at the margins of the boxes. And they were all separated from each other with neoprene pads to provide flexibility.

You have to use some steel.
Yes, but I would say, in comparison with other systems, maybe only 5 percent. Not too much.

It's the same idea we used at the Danzas Venezuela building.[15] Doctor, these projects couldn't be built, but did you have any intentions of trying to develop this system?
Yes, I was asked to design a very crazy building in Australia.[16] The development of around 400 acres, [approx. 162 hectares]. There is a gulf that comes into this 400 acres and the whole building had to be in the water. The depth is 25 meters. And I used exactly the same system. Because the floors there are frames, you see, and the floors between the frames acted in [a] horizontal direction. I used the boxes as inclined columns. Easy to construct, and the only trouble was with the foundation. I made the estimate, and I believe they never believed me

Robina Casino-Hotel ensemble, presentation model

when I told them it would be cheaper than any other construction for this type of work. [Moshe] Safdie was the architect. Two pyramids facing each other, 22 floors high, and between the towers there is a gambling casino, convention hall, and on the sides, night clubs, dining halls, etc. All in the water, accessible only by boats and bridges.

When you were working with Kahn, did you have any opportunities to design or develop some housing ideas? Was he interested in housing?
Not very much, I have to say. Yes, he had some interest, but because he was considered an architect who, let's say, designed laboratories, schools, institutional buildings, nobody approached him for housing. But when Habitat was built, he became interested. There was one development in Boston. We discussed this, and he said no.

One day we will build a community of this housing. And I believe we can build it in [the] South Bronx waste area [in New York City], and we will build it so economically that everybody can use it. Half the price. And it's possible. No decorations. Pour boxes, concrete walls. The only trouble is you can't hang pictures on the walls, you have to drill.

You mean he was interested in trying to do this?
Yes.

What was his opinion of Habitat?
First of all, he didn't understand it. That was the first thing. And he didn't like it. There was a big fight in Israel between Kahn and Safdie, they hated each other. Regardless that Safdie was his and my student.[17] I told Lou, *Don't say you don't like it, because it's a fact you don't understand it. But because that's our future, you better understand it!* Explain it to me, he said, and I did. And then, like always, he said, *Yeeess that's a very nice idea, but I would not do a building like Habitat*. I said, I wouldn't either. Because I didn't have the experience, nobody had, we made many mistakes, we didn't even realise the full potentiality of this system. Now I have the experience, and the result in Iran is the proof. Now they want to use it in North Africa.[18] Two architects were sent over from Paris, two professors who had to design there, they came to my office and—

Was this recently?
I'd say last summer.

How did they learn about the system?
Oh, there are newspapers. ... They learned [about] it, and they were sent over.

That seems like something that can be interesting for countries which need to build housing ...
Economical housing! I would never say it's cheap housing! Because that's offensive. These are homes that can be built that way, in clusters. Like in Venezuela. Oh boy, you see, people don't like to live in file cabinets—that's what a high-rise building is. They like to have something where outside and inside are combined into unity.

That is very important in tropical countries.
In the tropics you need balconies, and such. ... You see, if you can sell air, you will be rich.

I think, Doctor, that architecture is still looking for an answer to massive housing in tropical countries. It's very curious that nowadays nobody seems to be interested in proposing anything.
They need to! Because the population will be two billion people more by the year 2000, maybe earlier. It's insane that in New York [City] you can't get an apartment; you have to pay $1,000 for a two-room apartment. People are on the streets, you see. Every year we lose 3,000–4,000 houses in coastal areas due to hurricanes and tornados. Why? Because we're stupid. We have all the means to do something. All the professional organizations: AIA, civil engineers, consulting engineers, and most of all, technical publications. It's their responsibility to look around and see what is possible. You go and tell them something, that you have it. [They asked me] why haven't you built it? I say I'm not in the twenty-first century yet. That's where it'll be used, somebody has to do it. Because if it is theoretically viable and sound, why not?

Don't you think it's ironic that in a country like the US you haven't been able to convince anyone to do these things because here, as you said, everything exists to do it.
Of course, you can do that in any country.

Especially here in the US.
You can do it in any country, because it's actually the responsibility of every country and professional organizations to study and propose how to solve housing problems. If I were a young fellow, I'd build up the South Bronx in two years a half the market price. In two years! All the housing required

Doctor, what do you think about the present discussion on the massive construction plans, the issue discussed is that these massive plans tend to promote a sort of nonplace city, as some people call it. That means a city in which you don't have quality urban places to enjoy. How do these things affect you?
Very much, because when you see all those satellite and new cities, how they have been designed and built. Originally we designed buildings to last. Durability is a quality. Now we don't do that anymore. The lifetime of a building is 20–25 years. They deteriorate more rapidly than we can build them. And the result is a shortage of housing.

And more so, in developing countries.
Sure. Of course they may not have the knowledge, and they come for advice, to ask from American firms, and all this

Ciba-Geigy Pharmaceutical Company buildings

But I'm sorry to say, we don't give them proper advice. Arab countries are proof of this, for example. And America has a disease of bigness. Everything has to be big. Architects have firms, 200 architects and draftsmen, engineering firms with 300 people, four computer centers, and what comes out is junk. Real junk. When individuals, you see, do something—and most improvements in any related field are achieved by individuals—the government would never approach them because you don't have 300–400 men in your office.

Why? What's your way of explaining this attitude?
Disease of bigness!

Maybe it comes from the development of capitalist society?
No, this has nothing to do with it. The capitalist method or system has nothing to do with it.

Is it more a cultural thing?
Not even cultural. I believe I would go back to education in the universities.

One of the things that has impressed me for years about what you do, is that you're a person that has the possibility of doing your work on a small scale, and I have always spoken about this to my students and my relations, as something not only to be admired, but as something very important, because you don't have to be as Americans like to be—so oversized in everything, like you said—to do proper things, but it is very curious, commercially speaking. This approach is not accepted. So when you say that you work on a small scale, everybody tends to be a little skeptic about your capacities.
Yes. Eero Saarinen once said to Louis Kahn that he badly needs an engineer, because at that time he had some projects. And he asked Lou, *Could you lend Komendant to me. But I know he's so busy, you see, all these big jobs, the biology building and all that stuff. And he has just a small firm.* Lou said, *No you're wrong, Komendant has a very big firm—he does the work of 10!* Saarinen approached me about the Yale University building. And I did it, and he was amazed that I managed to do this complicated design with crossing Vierendeel trusses arranged in the shape of a sunrise in two weeks. It was very interesting.[19]

I [also] worked with Kellermann Dragnett.[20] They had about twenty men at their office. But I made all the drawings by myself. For the Ciba-Geigy project we discussed the preliminaries.[21] We approached many firms in New York City, we had discussions. We already had the architectural sketches. I made the preliminary structural system for these buildings and described what it's all about. I didn't like to make the drawings. And I asked how long it would take you to make all the drawings, I believe about 60 to 70, and all the computations. It will be an advanced prestressed concrete design—two-way prestressed concrete. They calculated and said six engineers, six to eight months. I told Ciba-Geigy's project engineer [Augustine] Pushparaj that's no good. I will start on January 1 and the drawings will be ready by May 1.

You, alone?
Me, alone. Of course my wife, Helmi, is a mathematician, she checks my computations, and she does the lettering and layouts.[22] I usually work behind three tables.

This serves you as a reference—when you worked on the National Gallery project,[23] you did your part in a very short period, I don't remember whether it was something like two months or less.
At that time Kahn said to Saarinen, *You see, it doesn't take time when one knows how to do it.* I learned discipline during my university days. I never use drafting paper. All these computations, they're original. I never draw a line which I have to erase. I never start designing when I haven't got everything I have to use ready in my mind. Also I have the ability to estimate what's right or wrong. When I see the image, I always see the finished structure in my mind. How many times did I walk through Habitat even before the drawings were ready. When we were there with Safdie—because it was reduced from the original proposal to a much smaller version—he said, *No, it's a very small thing, I'm not interested!* And when it was ready we were walking there. ... But I had told him at the very beginning, *You see, it's a very big thing!* And when it was ready he said, *I never imagined it would be so big.* That comes back to training. In German universities that was the main thing, the imagination.

How did they develop the students' imagination?
They called it *Darstellende Geometrie* [that is, descriptive geometry]. They had some items that they turned around. Now you sketch it. They used all these types of tricks. I happened to have excellent professors in this field: Professor Benno Löser in reinforced concrete, Professor [Kurt] Beyer, the father of modern statics, and Professor [Otto] Kirschmer. [Professor Franz] Dischinger from Berlin University and Professor [Ulrich] Finsterwalder, with whom I worked, and many others. Beyer once told me, *Now, I see your drawings—but how would it look when it is ready? Close your eyes, think about it. Can you see what's wrong? And what's right?* Yes, I learned it. Now, whatever I design, when the image is ready, I see it in reality.

Maybe your training as a builder helped you.
That was a European method—you were a designer and also a builder, in contact.

That has been forgotten now.
Yes. When a modern-day architect or engineer comes to a construction site, watch out! They don't even know how to walk there. They don't climb the scaffolding. They call me a monkey! [Laughs]

Because you keep climbing on the scaffolding?
Yeah! In the very beginning, even the young engineers [were afraid]. And I climbed, they were looking at me—what?! Then they all started climbing, even faster than I would with my seventy-eight years. [Laughs] They never believe I'm seventy-eight. ...[24]

How old were you when you graduated from university?
I graduated in the second half of 1933 when Hitler came to power.[25] I was twenty-seven. Then I stayed with Professor Beyer as his private assistant for one year, until Hitler said, *All foreigners, get lost!* Beyer was like a father for me. I had to leave. I went to Tallinn, Estonia. And I opened my own engineering office, because reinforced concrete and all modern designs, they were not there yet. ... Now, of course, this was a good opportunity. Then I was asked to be professor in the Tallinn University of Technology.[26] The current [1985] president of the Academy of Science [of the Estonian SSR, Nikolai Alumäe], he is my pupil! He wrote to me and asked for information about me, he's writing an article. He wrote that he is thankful to me that I put him on the right track.[27]

At that time it was possible for you to work alone. Were you successful?
I worked from Estonia, a small country and we had an oil industry, Swedish, Germans, and Estonians. There was a factory [in Tallinn, AS Franz Krull], they were specialists in refrigeration equipment and steam turbines. At that time I worked on the biggest steel steam turbine in India—I designed the foundation for vibrations etc.[28]

Your education on prestressed concrete—was that during university?
No, in 1935 I was already a professor in Tallinn.[29] Hitler asked scientists and university professors to come to Germany, he wanted to show what he had done in three years. That he was peaceful, and the Autobahn was under construction, and all this. And community housing. He wanted to have the world's opinion changed. There were about 600 people, and I was among them. He invited people from all over the world, the US, Europe.[30]

Where did you meet?
It was in Berlin, in Charlottenburg [at the Technical University of Berlin]. We had, let's say, lectures.[31] They showed us what they wanted to do and how, and so on. There was [Eugène] Freyssinet from Paris. I was sitting with my professors [Friedrich Wilhelm] Neuffer and Beyer. There was also [Karl] Kammüller from Karlsruhe, and Freyssinet came ... there was a discussion at the table. Then, I was interested, because

Military aircraft hangar in Tartu during construction, 1935

Freyssinet was very enthusiastic about prestressing and all this. But it failed there. ... He went bankrupt because the system was excellent but not practical.

Too complicated?
Yes, because you used molds that were very strong, because it would take about 10 atmospheres pressure during hydration. The forms had to take prestressing. They were small units, for bridges etc. ... So-called bonded prestressing. And it didn't work. It was not flexible enough, it was expensive, the forms were like boilers, high-pressure boilers, 10 atmospheres!

Why?
To get very rapid hydration under steam and high pressure—he got 16,000 psi [approx. 1,125 kg/cm^2] in concrete in four hours. The forms were very expensive, he had to use them many, many times to make them economical. But it was not enough. Mainly because it was not flexible enough. He talked, and I listened as a young fellow. Never open your mouth, listen to smart people talk, and they argued. And Dischinger said, *No, Freyssinet, you are wrong. It* [that is, prestressed concrete] *is a wonderful idea, it was developed by the Dresden professor Koenen*[32]*, and it didn't work because at that time plastic flow was not known. Shrinkage—we only knew that there was something that the volume of the concrete changed. What you are trying to do ... yes, you developed the theory of shrinkage, and we learned by practice that there is such a thing as plastic flow, and this all has to be considered.* At that time Dischinger was building the Aue prestressed concrete bridge [completed in 1937].[33] When I was studying in Dresden he completed his doctorate.[34] I met him there. So we already knew each other. This idea was very appealing. There was no literature available, just using your own brain, and I designed an airplane hangar for the Estonian military, and for the first time I used prestressing.[35]

You took the essentials from Freyssinet's talk in Berlin?
Yes, the essentials were very clear on what it would be. Dischinger was more practical. Later they had a fight because Freyssinet patented his design and Dischinger tried to make it work and also patented it—so there was a clash. It was solved after the war because the Germans and all Europeans lost their patent rights.[36]

When was the hangar built, do you remember?
1936.

Is it still there?
Yes, in Dorpat [Tartu], where the university is. It is still there. Of course I was interested [in prestressed concrete], I tried [to put it in use]. When I was in the European Command,[37] steel was not available. But there were cables, high-carbon grade—plenty. Now, we had to build bridges. And of course I told them we can do prestressed concrete because there's no steel. Because steel was a dollar item, and we liked dollars very much.

If you had these essentials, and you started working on your own, did you have any communication with Dischinger or Freyssinet in terms of interchanging theories?
No, not during the war because there was no communication. Only after the war. I worked with Finsterwalder and Dischinger

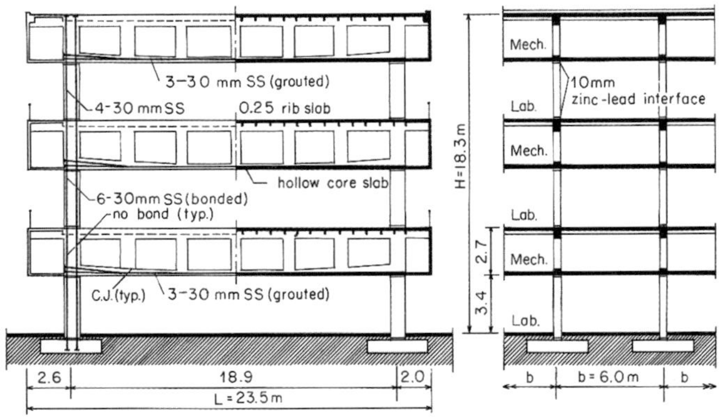

Structural system of the Salk Institute laboratories

when I was in the European Command as a top adviser for the office of the chief engineer. I called them in as my consultants, and we worked together. Then the Truman Doctrine started in Greece and Turkey. They had the same trouble at that time—steel was very expensive and not available.

You built some bridges?
Because I was in charge of communications, and all the reconstructions, and the temporary bridges, all this, I was in charge of … the river Rhine with its many, many big bridges.

When was the first time you used prestressed concrete for architectural purposes?
We built some warehouses in the European Command for our armed forces. There I used it. But it was always pretensioned, not posttensioned. In the US, the first posttensioned building was, I believe, the Richards Medical Building. No, actually, there were these car inspection buildings,[38] but Richards was the first major building. And with Saarinen I used the Vierendeels for the Yale University dining halls.

These Vierendeels for Richards, are there any structures as precedents before that?
They weren't used then in America. Mostly they were used in steel in Belgium, because Belgium was a steel country. Also in Germany, but not very much. Germany used plate girders and trusses.

In some ways was Richards with Louis Kahn an experiment for you?
No, I wouldn't call them experimentations. When I have a system that I've studied theoretically, and it is sound, I use it right away. When it's sound theoretically, it must be sound in practice. The first posttensioned building was the Merchants Refrigerating Co. building in Secaucus, I was also the contractor there.[39]

Does the Richards building have elastically controlled joints?
Yes and no, not completely. I developed the elastically controlled joints for the Salk Laboratories [completed in 1965] because it's a highly seismic area. I developed them there, and since then I've used them very successfully everywhere. In the Richards, yes, I used them too, but at that time [the first phase of the building was completed in 1961] neoprene was not available, nor was teflon. Instead of using something like I used in the Salk Labs, I used steel plates. True, we could have used lead. But there was a danger with lead. When a fire starts, it's going to melt. In Salk we already used lead, and to raise the melting point, I mixed it with zinc. Common fires go to 1000°F [approx. 538°C]. The melting point has to be higher. Lead's melting point is 400°F [approx. 204°C] or something. When mixed with zinc you can raise it. But the trouble is, you cannot mix zinc and lead. It floats out. What I did, I covered the lead with zinc, and I forced the zinc into the crystal structure of the lead.

How?
It was a long process, we did a lot of tests. There was a very interesting firm in San Diego, they were very much interested in this. We tested it and finally we succeeded.

And that's what you used in bridges?
Yes. In Richards I actually used only steel plates. And I provided elongation lengths and all these ones. … It was successful, but it's only an eight-story building.

When did neoprene become available?
I have used sponge rubber and neoprene since I built the Cincinnati Chemical buildings in Toms River in New Jersey, and we had trouble there.[40] There was a chemist, and I asked, *Do you have a material which is stable and works under pressure with constant volume*. And he said, *Yes we do, we use it for equipment to put between the supports and machinery. It dampens the vibrations*. I said, *I'd like to see it, let's go*. Sponge rubber was the same. I used no dry-packing. I always used sponge rubber for sealing because actually that's also neoprene. It's very durable, it's not affected by temperature. And the chemist said, *You see, when we ship some machinery, we use this stuff to put between the crates and essential parts of the machinery, and DuPont makes it*. Since that time, also in the Philadelphia Police Administration Building,[41] I've used plenty of neoprene, I've used plenty of sponge rubber.

How would you define, in simple words, this elastically controlled deformation principle?
Very simple. When we use steel in concrete, the ratio of the steel modulus of elasticity to concrete's modulus, called *n*, is about 6 if we have 5,000 psi concrete [approx. 350 kg/cm²]. Only six times the steel is used structurally in concrete, not more. First, if I put something elastic in between the members, it shrinks away; the modulus of elasticity relationship n for the members goes from 6 to about 15 to 20. We actually use steel three to four times more efficiently in concrete. In columns, for example at Salk. You can't use it in beams where elasticity controls. Second, if there is a dynamic force, the pressure in columns goes to one side—one side is

Richards Medical Research Laboratories, steel plates in the structural joints help regulate the elasticity of the building

compression, and the other side is tension. If I provide some elongation lengths for the reinforcing bars, using neoprene between surfaces, let's say 15 cm, steel can elongate. On the compression side, neoprene yields away usually, and compression becomes almost uniform. Some eccentricity usually disappears. That's the reason I eliminate the moments there. Not entirely, but just enough to make it economical. And also, let's say, in areas where you have dynamic forces. We call it ductility. When concrete is very rigid, the dynamic force is very high. It's the so-called D'Alembert principle, mass multiplied by acceleration.

Would you call this principle an advanced technological principle?
Oh yes, highly.

And how do you think it was understood by engineers in countries like Venezuela?
In the very beginning, they didn't understand it at all. In Habitat, for example, I used sponge rubber between the boxes, and also neoprene. And they all, the professors from the McGill University and Toronto, came and said Komendant is crazy, he puts his buildings on rubber, it won't work! They were very skeptical. If you give some flexibility, sometimes a member or element knows better how to carry out the function I designed this element to do. We call it, let's say, transfer of stresses. If it's very high here, it yields away, and helps the weakest point. That's a good quality, actually a safety valve when we make mistakes in our designs. It balances it up. The stronger part takes over the weaker part. It helps.

And that helps a lot in seismic areas.
Yes, absolutely! For example, Habitat. Montreal is a highly seismic area, like California. When I designed it I assumed that the top of the building moves, I guess, 3 inches [approx. 7.6 cm], in severe cases, and I could control how much elongation lengths I give the part. If I give only 5 cm, it elongates less, and the movement is less at the top. If it's a small building, like three stories, I have to give more because. ... When you hit rubber, there's no result. But hit glass, it breaks! So it is with a building. If we build every high-rise out of rubber, or neoprene, you see, there will be no damage no matter how severe the earthquakes. Now, you hit a building, it starts oscillating and quiets down.

Instead of following the theory that some people formulate, that specifies that a building has to be very, very light to avoid the problems of mass, what you do is you don't worry about weight, but you try to make the building flexible.
Exactly. We call it ductility. When Salk was built, they said, *No concrete buildings. We are in a severe earthquake region, and concrete will not do. We can only have steel buildings because of ductility problems.* Now I asked, *Is ductility the only problem? Oh, yes.* I asked them, *What will you do if I will give you a concrete building with more ductility than even in a steel building? Then there would be no problem,* they said, *you will get your building permit.* I said, *That's a deal.* When the drawings went in, no question was asked. And they changed the [building] code. Now we can have concrete buildings in California. Before that, no.

What is interesting is that it's a way of transferring high-level technology in a way which is nothing similar to the commercial way of doing it. It's a principle that comes from theories, from the mind, from—
From sound education.

That is true. The usual way of understanding what they call transfer of technology is through patents, through commercial agreements ...
I don't give a dime about patents! I have many of them, and I have never made money with patents.[42] I do my own design, let's say, in Venezuela. There I simply used the principle of elastically controlled joints because it is the most appropriate. I am not interested in having a patent. I have developed many things in this way. One of them was, for example, the posttension cable system fabricated integrally with its plastic casing, providing a film of a special grease for corrosion protection between the cable and the casing. I developed these conduits jointly with DuPont. They have enormous advantages because they reduce the section traditionally required by the metal casing. The cable can be directly put into position before pouring the concrete, not paying attention to separately positioning the metal casing, thereby reducing the time required. We also developed a plastic casing accommodating three cables at a time, something more or less complex because of the tendency of the cables to flatten between them when being tensioned.

Are there any other significant posttensioned projects you can refer to?
The construction of the refrigeration warehouses for a company [Merchants Refrigerating Co.] in New Jersey in the early 1960s.[43] This project was very interesting since I developed posttensioned Vierendeel trusses. Shortly after, I presented it together with the Richards towers and a posttensioned bridge which I had previously built, in a symposium of posttensioning in Italy. This was the only North American entry in the event.

The project was a consequence of a strike in the steel industry in the USA. I recall that this coincided with the beginning of the construction of the World Trade Center[44] which further reduced the supply of steel, and forced one to seek solutions using concrete as an alternative construction material. At the time, I was a partner at the Atlantic Prestressed Concrete Co., and we were contacted by a firm that originally had planned using steel for a refrigeration warehouse, and they were opting for concrete.

Time was a crucial factor since we only had twenty weeks to do the job. If we did not deliver on time, we would be fined $1,000 per day, including weekends. I agreed with this, but

Interior of the Merchants Refrigerating Co. cold storage and the load-bearing structure of precast concrete elements, 1961

Merchants Refrigerating Co. cold storage after completion

I requested equal treatment asking them: How much would they pay us by the day if we finished ahead of schedule? And they [contractors Turner and Co.] answered: *Double*. We signed the agreement. I then sought the collaboration of an aeronautical company that was being shut down, asking them to produce the metal scaffolding and the work began immediately.

I started my calculations, and I realized that the stresses were so high that they doubled the resistance capacity of the concrete solution. I did not know what to do. The contract had been signed, everybody was preparing to work and I was in a desperate situation. I walked around thinking for two weeks, not knowing what to do. I came to this piece of land, where this house [Komendant's home in Upper Montclair, New Jersey] is now, that I already had bought, a bit desperate. Should I hang myself or flee? What else could I do? One evening, in bed, I had an idea. I woke up, gave it a try and it seemed to work. It was about using the suspension principle, that is, employing posttensioned Vierendeel trusses in which the trajectory of the cables would follow the suspension principle. This would also allow reducing somewhat the sectional dimensions. As a result, we were able to finish the work in sixteen weeks instead of twenty and pocketed a nice sum.

But there was an additional economic benefit to this solution. The company used to move the products in the warehouse with a conveyor system on the ground, which reduced the storage capacity. I suggested suspending it from the ceiling. They asked me can this be done, and how much would it cost? I gave them a good price and they accepted the deal, and so we did. With these earnings, I built this [that is, Komendant's own] house.

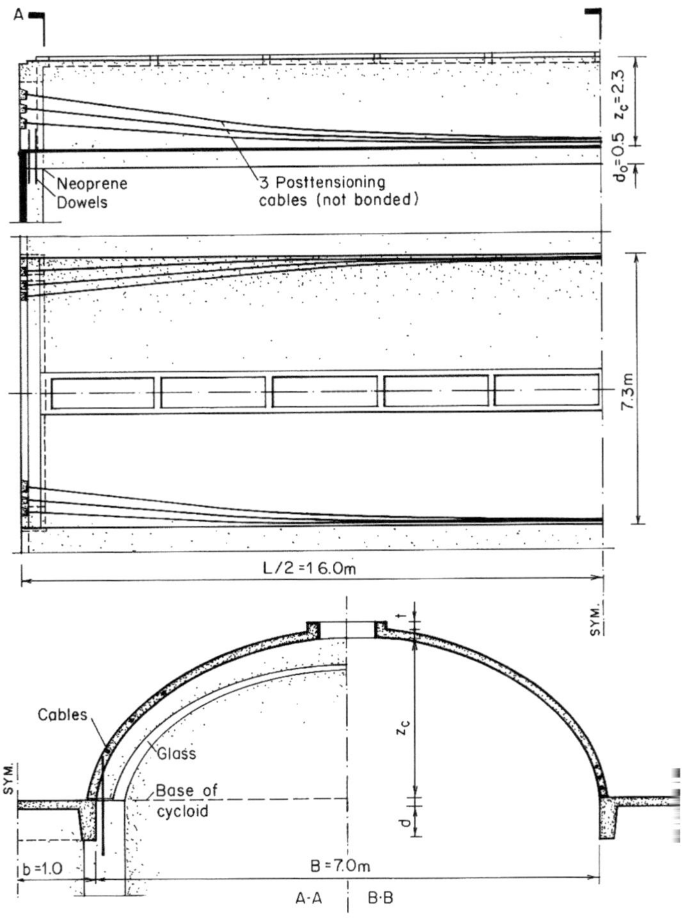

Kimbell Art Museum, structural system of the cycloid shells

So, the solution is based on the principle of suspended structures ...

Suspension is the most cost-effective load-carrying system that can be imagined. Previously, the Vierendeels were not tensioned horizontally with the suspension criteria, which made them much heavier and less efficient. This was a new approach, not tested before. I used this system in the Salk Laboratories and many times thereafter. In Vierendeels and in normal beams, I always use the suspension system. The advantage is that the suspension manages the dead weight. And usually the dead weight is twice that of the live loads. I always say that *diamonds are created under pressure*.

I would like to ask you, which do you consider the most successful and well-executed project of those you worked on with Lou Kahn?

The Kimbell Museum. I was in charge of its construction. Kahn would usually say, *Doctor, you [always] know.* ... I know the time the projects take, and what they cost. At this time, Kahn collaborated with a local [architecture] firm, Preston M. Geren, but shortly after they became very distant to the point of not talking to each other. Preston Geren would tell Kahn, *You are in Philadelphia, while I am here, I have to face the consequences; you are not a practical man, but I am; your design is not good* ... and comments of this nature. Preston Geren decided to go ahead with his design, thus there were two different projects for the museum. ... His was a very simple design with a flat roof, that was about all. And Kahn obviously said, *I am not responsible for that design, and I am not willing to accept interference*. The situation remained like that for three months. Whenever they would meet, the scene was very difficult. Preston Geren accused Kahn of using very small sections for the structure. According to their agreement Preston Geren was responsible for the engineering. I was Kahn's structural consultant and in charge of predimensioning of the structure. After analyzing the project, Geren's staff concluded that the cycloids could not be built, adding that they had never been constructed, that they had no experience with them, *And on top of it ... we don't like the SOB of ... Kahn ... he is a very difficult architect. So why deal with all these problems?*

Was their main objection, the scaffolding and things like that?

No, their concern was the static condition of the structure. They didn't take the cycloid theory seriously. They also objected to the two-directional pretensioned system I had proposed for

Library of the Kimbell Art Museum during construction

Construction site billboard of the Kimbell Art Museum

Construction site of the National Assembly in Dhaka

the lower level. Usually, when flat slabs are reinforced in both directions, full load is considered separately for each direction. Consequently, these slabs are calculated to resist twice the expected loads. In this project I designed the two-directional pretensioned system for zero deflection at the nodes. That was the reason why my dimensions where smaller.

Finally, due to all these problems, the Executive Committee decided to sue the architects, since their fees were rising and no drawings had been delivered. Dr. Brown,[45] who was the Chair of the Committee, was in a desperate position because he had been responsible for bringing Kahn and very much liked the project. He approached me and said, *Doctor, please help me. I cannot handle these two stubborn architects. They don't even talk to each other. Why don't you take over and construct the building?* I told him that this was not possible because I had a contract with Kahn and not Preston Geren. I would only accept if Preston Geren personally asked me to do it.

Geren thought that I was a "little Kahn" because we worked together. For that reason he didn't like me too much. However, sometime later he contacted me asking me to participate in the project; and I wrote a very strong draft refusing to do so. However, Kahn who was in the hospital in Philadelphia after a recent operation, when he heard about the whole thing, asked me to accept. *Take it, don't worry,* he said, *accept, I will do anything to get this project built.*

I then sent Geren another letter in which I requested to be the only one responsible for the project; that I would produce the structural drawings personally, and I would provide him with a set. If within a week's time, I had not received any observations, I would be free to make my own decisions to keep the construction on track. My fees should be guaranteed by the owner—because they were in trouble, threatened to be sued due to the considerable delay of more than a year and a half. If I was not paid, I would stop working. I would provide another set of plans to the local contractor, who went over the material I provided him without objections.

I am not an arrogant man, but this time I was, how furious I felt. I also wrote that I guaranteed that there wouldn't be delays, that I would have the drawings ready so the rhythm of construction would be kept. When my wife, Helmi, read the letter, she told me, *You can just sit down and wait, since this arrogant letter will never be answered!* I put it in the mail one Tuesday, while Helmi insisted that there would be no response. I decided to distract myself by attending our garden ... letting time pass. I then sent Geren a telegram which simply read: yes or no? The answer arrived, accepting all my conditions and asking me to go see them as soon as possible. Kahn couldn't be happier, *August, anything you do, I can make it beautiful. ...*

I began working on July 28 and submitted the drawings which allowed work on the scaffolding to start on August 15. The drawings were completed in the beginning of October. The building is beautiful and economic. This was the story, diamonds are created under pressure. Sometime later, Geren told me that whenever he speaks with other engineers about this building they say the only person that can deal with Kahn and design this type of structure is Komendant.

You once mentioned that Kahn got depressed when criticized.
Correct, he didn't like it. When we were working in Dhaka we had a disagreement because I didn't share the principles he had established.[46] In a place in the world where there is eighteen inches of rain in a month every building has to take that into account. That was not the case. I told him no, it is not going to work. But he was already famous at this point. The Salk Institute was under construction, and there were comments about his work everywhere. There was an exhibit at the Museum of Modern Art.[47] The church at Rochester had been completed, and the Richards towers were also built.[48] Of course he wanted to be a prima donna with me, *I can say anything, I am the architect.*

We went to Dhaka, and our opinions clashed. I had a good relationship with the local Finance Minister, who had participated in setting the fees of the project and establishing construction criteria.[49] One day he invited me to dinner and did not ask Kahn or Carles Vallhonrat who also had traveled with us.[50] Kahn was very offended. He asked me, *Why you?* The Finance Minister simply wanted to go over issues related to the project, paperwork, construction methods ... aspects in which Kahn was not involved. Anyway, he was upset.

What did he tell you?
Well, he reacted as a prima donna. Then I told him, *What you need is another consulting engineer. I do not work for you, I work with you. I am not your employee, and I don't receive orders from you. I follow my criteria when dealing with structures ... So, fine, good-bye*. For three years and a half, we did not speak to each other. I came back alone from Dhaka, they stayed there. We only saw each other at the university, where if he asked my opinion I answered: *No comments*. If you go over this period, you will notice that Kahn did not deliver any projects. *Progressive Architecture* published an article that stated: Kahn is dead. ... Since he had not designed any new [successful] structures. As a consequence, Lou was terribly depressed.

Did he tell you that?
No, his wife [Esther Kahn] told me. But just then, in came Olivetti. He had the commission for their factory in Pennsylvania.[51] He didn't know how to do it. Esther, his wife called me, she said, *Doctor I don't know, Kahn is depressed. You have your differences, it might be time to solve them. Three and a half years is enough time.* I answered, okay. The next day, Kahn called me, *May I come to see you?* We met and we had our "first drink" ten times, always the first, never the last. And we started again our collaboration. This was the best period of Kahn: Olivetti, Kimbell, Palazzo dei Congressi in Venice.

Then, with the Pakistan-India war, the Dhaka building, the Assembly Hall, a concrete building that was under construction, was used as a fortification and was damaged. They contacted Kahn to work on repairing it and to continue the project. The layout of the plan was such that the roof could not be done! There were even suggestions to install a metal roof. But it was a concrete building, a metal roof was not logical. Kahn came to consult me, *Help me!* I made two proposals, one was built. That was our last work at Dhaka together. I helped him to complete the building.[52]

During that time he was very depressed. Esther told me, *I don't know what is wrong with Kahn, he is not capable of anything, he is very depressed!* He was very sensitive to critics. I was the only one that could criticize him because between us there was a total agreement about that: to be honest with each other. And he was honest with me.

Did you ask him to agree on this?
Yes, from the beginning of our relationship.

When you were working on the Richards towers?
It was some time before. On the occasion of a competition for a monument in Chicago, and he needed my help. During the Richards project I gave him some suggestions. In some cases I suggested three or four possibilities. He selected and I worked accordingly. 180 articles were written on the Richards project. It was the first high-rise building to be partially factory-built here [in the US]. It made Kahn famous. We had journalists constantly around us. We went to nightclubs and bars together because I needed publicity as much as Kahn did. I wrote several articles on the construction system, including drawings. Kahn edited them. You know, prestressing was practically unknown [in the US]. Concrete was used here only in foundations. Prestressed concrete was not used in architecture.

What was your impression when he approached you the first time?
I did not know who Kahn was. His secretary called me asking me to visit him. *Who the hell is Kahn?*, I asked. *He is a very well-known architect and professor at the University of Pennsylvania*. I took the train to Philadelphia and we met. We discovered that we were both from Estonia. Our philosophies coincided very, very well, and from that moment we

began working together. I put all that into my book *18 Years with Architect Louis I. Kahn*.

So, you had a good first impression of him?
Yes, he was a dreamer, and so was I. And if he followed his dreams I would also have the opportunity to realize mine. I was known in Europe but not in the United States. I had just arrived from the European Command when I met him.[53]

It is beautiful what you say about dreams.
Without dreams, there wouldn't be development. Dreams are the beginning of development. To make dreams real, that is the base. Dreams give you the image of what could be done. They give you the possibility of making. Why not dream? To make dreams real we need basic theoretical knowledge, but because in some cases there are no theories, we have to create them.

Kahn wrote, with different words, when I received the Medal from the American Institute of Architects, ... *having Komendant's mathematical knowledge, when there was not a theory, he would develop one that he tested in his built structures, making theory and practice fully coincide*.[54]

1 August Komendant never formally defended his PhD dissertation, though was very close to doing so while working and doing research at TU Dresden under professor Kurt Beyer between the autumn of 1944 and spring of 1945. After World War II Komendant often used the title of Dr. in front of his name and was therefore also addressed as such. [All comments here and in the following by the editor of the book.]

2 For the Kimbell Art Museum, see pp. 268–285; for the Olivetti-Underwood Factory, pp. 258–267; for the Salk Institute for Biological Studies, pp. 194–211.

3 See pp. 220–243 for Habitat '67.

4 Komendant's contacts with Alvar Aalto need further research. There is no evidence that they worked on projects together, but they might have met on some formal or informal occasions.

5 Komendant is probably referring to the 1975 architectural competition for adjusting the Veterans and the John F. Kennedy Stadiums for liturgical worship during the 41st International Eucharistic Congress held August 1–8, 1976 in Philadelphia, Pennsylvania. See "Competition for Stadia Adaptation," *AIA Journal* (July 1975): 15, 56.

6 "All these ones," is an idiosyncratic expression Komendant often used in conversation.

7 "Hide behind the trees," is most likely a metaphoric expression not to be taken literally.

8 It is not clear which group of architects in relation to Philip Johnson (1906–2005) Komendant is referring to here.

9 Colonel Edward Churchill, Director of Installations for the 1967 World Exhibition in Montreal.

10 Jonas Edward Salk (1914–1995), physician, medical researcher and virologist, founder of the Salk Institute for Biological Studies in La Jolla, California.

11 Komendant was invited to consult on the Atomic City of Nuran project by architect Nader Ardalan (b. 1939) of the Mandala Collaborative in 1978. See Nader Ardalan's text, pp. 102–103, for projects they collaborated on between 1978 and 1979, all of which remained on paper due to the Iranian Revolution..

12 Mohammad Reza Pahlavi (1919–1980), the Shah (emperor) of Iran until his overthrow in the Iranian Revolution on February 11, 1979. Due to his status as the last Shah of Iran, he is often referred to as simply the Shah. It is not apparent that Komendant ever met the Shah in person.

13 "Cyclopean" refers to Cyclopean masonry, an ancient type of masonry used in the defense structures of Mycenaean Greece (1600–1100 BC). Large limestone boulders were the primary construction material to build the walls. Similarly, cyclopean concrete, proposed by Komendant, would have used large pieces of local limestone within the concrete walls. See also Nader Ardalan's text, pp. 102–103; and Pamela Karimi, *Domesticity and Consumer Culture in Iran: Interior Revolutions of the Modern Era* (New York: Routledge, 2013), 214.

14 Komendant is probably referring to the FLSmidth & Co., A/S, established in 1882, a consulting company and cement manufacturer..

15 Teatro del Oeste Dance Theater, Caracas, Venezuela, architect Oscar Tenreiro, structural consultant August Komendant, 1982–1983, unfinished; see pp. 328–333.

16 Master plan for the Robina New Town and Hotel-Casino Complex in Gold Coast, Queensland, Australia, architect Moshe Safdie, 1981–1982, unbuilt. Online database for The Moshe Safdie Archive, McGill University Library, http://cac.mcgill.ca/moshesafdie/fullrecord.php?ID=10865&d=, accessed May 3, 2020.

17 Moshe Safdie did not study under Louis Kahn nor August Komendant, but worked at Louis Kahn's office in 1962 for a period. See pp. 61–65 for Moshe Safdie's interview.

18 There is no indication that this project was ever realized, or if it was, it happened without Komendant's involvement.

19 Dining Halls of the Ezra Stiles and Samuel Morse Colleges, Yale University, New Haven, Connecticut, architect Eero Saarinen, structural consultant August Komendant, 1959–1961; see pp. 174–177.

20 Kellermann & Dragnett Inc., Consulting Engineers, a firm with which Komendant collaborated on several occasions in the late 1960s and during the 1970s.

21 New facilities for the Ciba-Geigy pharmaceutical company, Summit, New Jersey, architect Henry Klumb, structural engineer August Komendant, 1981–1986; see pp. 324–327.

22 Helmi Aren (1935–2006) and August Komendant never officially married but lived together in Upper Montclair, New Jersey, from the early 1960s until Komendant's death in 1992.

23 National Gallery GAN (Galeria de Arte Nacional), Caracas, Venezuela, architect Oscar Tenreiro, structural consultant August Komendant, 1980–1986, unbuilt; see pp. 312–323.

24 Komendant reflects on his recent visit (1983) to the construction site of the Oscar Tenreiro-designed Plaza Bicentenario in Caracas, Venezuela.

25 Komendant's diploma from the Sächsische Technische Hochschule zu Dresden (Saxon Technical University in Dresden, or TH Dresden, now TU Dresden) is dated May 18, 1934. August E. Komendant Collection, AAUP, 027.II.A2.

26 From 1934 to 1936 Komendant worked as a structural engineer and construction manager at the Department of Public Works, Ministry of Roads of the Estonian Republic. He was not a professor but served as a lecturer of reinforced concrete courses at Tallinn University of Technology between 1937 and 1939. He opened his private engineering consultancy in Tallinn in 1937. See Komendant's early curriculum vitae in *Arvustajate arvamused kandideerijate kohta puu-, massiiv- ja raudbetoonkonstruktsioonide professuurile* (Tallinn: Tallinna Tehnikaülikool, 1939), 1–2.

27 Nikolai Alumäe (1915–1992), a scholar of shell theory and one of the pioneers of cybernetics in Estonia, had a brief correspondence with Komendant in 1984. August E. Komendant Collection, AAUP, 027.II.B10. See also Alumäe's brief memoirs, "Kuidas keegi" in *Ehitusinsenerid TPI-st* [Structural Engineers from the Tallinn Polytechnic Institute] (Tallinn: Valgus, 1986), 116–17; and August Komendant's biographical entry, most likely written by Alumäe, in the same publication, p. 196.

28 As of 2020, documented information on this project has not been found. In collaboration with AS Franz Krull, Komendant also designed the cold storage at the Tallinn Old City Harbor, architect Roman Koolmar, design 1937, construction nearly completed in 1941, when it was blown up by the withdrawing Soviet Army; see pp. 130–131.

29 See note 25.

30 Construction historian Roland May: "I only see one congress as the possible venue. The IABSE, International Association for Bridge and Structural Engineering, at that time by far the most important international organization for structural engineers, held its second congress in October 1936 in Berlin and Munich. There were around 1,000 participants (some 600 foreigners) from nearly 40 countries. Even though the Nazis misused the congress for propaganda purposes, it cannot be said (as Komendant does) that Hitler asked scientists and university professors to come to Germany—it was a meeting of an international organization." Roland May's e-mail to the editor, April 28, 2020.

31 For the program and presentations of the congress see *International Association for Bridge and Structural Engineering: Second Congress. Berlin-München. 1.–11. October 1936. Preliminary Publication* (Berlin: Wilhelm Ernst & Sohn, 1936), digitized version available on ETH Zürich's e-periodica collection, https://www.e-periodica.ch/digbib/volumes?UID=bse-cr-001, accessed May 2, 2020.

32 Mathias Koenen (1849–1924), structural engineer and educator, experimented with prestressed concrete at TH Dresden in 1907, but failed due to a lack of knowledge about the shrinking and creeping of concrete. Koenen became Dr.h.c. of TH Dresden in 1908. Roland May's e-mail to the editor, April 28, 2020.

33 For an early introduction of the Aue bridge in Saxony, Germany—one of the first prestressed concrete bridges in the world—see Franz Dischinger, "Entwicklung und Fortschritte im Eisenbetonbau" in *Neues Bauen in Eisenbeton* (Berlin: Zementverlag G.M.B.H., 1937), 7–37.

34 Dischinger defended his dissertation at TH Dresden in 1929, his supervisor being professor Kurt Beyer. See his dissertation *Die Theorie der Vieleckkuppeln und die Zusammenhänge mit den einbeschriebenen Rotationsschalen* (Berlin: Ernst und Sohn, 1929).

35 Military Aircraft Hangar, Tartu, Estonia, design August Komendant 1935, completed 1936. As part of the hangar's structural system, Komendant designed pretensioned tie rods, placed beneath the floor slab, see pp. 110–115.

36 Roland May: "The patent conflict between Freyssinet and Dischinger was already resolved at that time Komendant met Freyssinet and Dischinger, as Freyssinet had been granted the German patent at the end of 1935. Also, I have never heard that after WWII all Europeans lost their patent rights." Roland May's e-mail to the editor, April 28, 2020.

37 From 1945 to 1950 August Komendant served as a consulting engineer for the United States European Command (EUCOM), one of the unified combatant commands of the United States military. For EUCOM Komendant conducted research on various types of structures and consulted on the reconstruction of war-damaged bridges.

38 Car inspection facilities for New Jersey Department of Motor Vehicles, design Frank Grad & Sons. Architects & Engineers, structural design The Glenwal Co., Inc. Engineers & Contractors, structural consultant August Komendant, 1957. Komendant's drawings in the August E. Komendant Collection, AAUP, 027.I.A32.

39 Cold storage and distribution center, Merchants Refrigerating Co., Secaucus, New Jersey, architects Abbott Merkt & Co., structural engineer August Komendant, 1960–1961; see pp. 180–183.

40 Facilities for the Cincinnati Chemical Works, Toms River, New Jersey, design A. M. Kinney Inc., structural consultant August Komendant, 1956–1957. Komendant's drawings in the August E. Komendant Collection, AAUP, 027.I.A32..

41 Philadelphia Police Administration Building, Philadelphia, Pennsylvania, architects Geddes Brecher Qualls Cunningham, structural engineer August Komendant, 1959–1963, see pp. 184–193.

42 Most important of August Komendant's patents, US4195453A, was a construction and structural system for modular, multifloor buildings of precast reinforced concrete boxes. The K-System, as Komendant himself referred to it, was largly based on experience gained at Habitat '67; see pp. 308–311.

43 See note 39.

44 Komendant might be mistaken here, as construction of the World Trade Center in New York City by architect Minoru Yamasaki did not begin until 1968.

45 Richard Fargo Brown (1916–1979), director of the Kimbell Art Museum, 1966–1979.

46 Komendant was involved with the Dhaka project from 1962 to 1964. See August Komendant, *18 Years With Architect Louis I. Kahn* (Englewood, NJ: Aloray, 1975), 75–90.

47 Exhibition, *Richards Medical Research Building, Louis I. Kahn, Architect*, June 6–July 16, 1961, Museum of Modern Art, New York. See also the *Bulletin of the Museum of Modern Art* 28, no. 1 (1961).

48 See pp. 212–219 for the First Unitarian Church in Rochester, and pp. 150–165 for the Richards Medical Research Laboratories.

49 Komendant probably refers to Muhammad Shoaib (1907–1976), Finance Minister of Pakistan. See also Komendant, *18 Years With Architect Louis I. Kahn*, 80–83.

50 Carles Enric Vallhonrat (1928–2017), architect and educator, worked at the office of Louis Kahn from 1960 to 1971, and for more than forty years at the Princeton University architecture school.

51 See pp. 258–267 for the Olivetti-Underwood Factory.

52 The authorship of the Assembly Hall's final roof structure needs further research. It is not clear whether Kahn was assisted by Komendant, Harry Palmbaum or some other structural designer.

53 Komendant exaggerates; he arrived in the US in the summer of 1950 but met Louis Kahn no earlier than autumn 1956.

54 Komendant received the medal of the American Institute of Architects in 1978. The Philadelphia Chapter of the AIA had submitted an application, including a letter of recommendation by Louis Kahn, as early as in 1973. The medal was presented to Komendant at the AIA National Convention in Dallas, Texas on May 21, 1978. Documentation related to Komendant's AIA medal can be found in the August E. Komendant Collection, AAUP, 027.II.A4.

This interview, originally conducted in English, was first published in Spanish as "Entrevista con August Komendant," in August Komendant, *18 años con el arquitecto Louis I. Kahn* (Santiago de Compostela: Colexio Oficial de Arquitectos de Galicia, 2000), 59–77. One of the original audio tapes has survived, and was the primary source for the former part of the text in the present volume. The latter part of the text was retranslated from Spanish to English, and was further edited by Oscar Tenreiro.

Architect Moshe Safdie on the construction site of Habitat '67

Interview. Moshe Safdie

Moshe Safdie and Carl-Dag Lige
Somerville, Massachusetts, October 22, 2018

Carl-Dag Lige: Would you briefly describe the circumstances under which you met August Komendant?
Moshe Safdie: In 1962 [Louis] Kahn gave me a job in his office. I had graduated in 1961 [from McGill University], come to see him and showed him my thesis. These were the days before we had portfolios ... we just showed our drawings. It was the end of the summer, he'd just had his cataract operation, and we timed it so that I would arrive when he was back in the office. Komendant was working with him and would come and go in the office, I met him there just working.

During the time at Kahn's office were you in a close relationship with Komendant, related to work? Did you discuss some issues there?
With Komendant I was more an observer than in a close relationship with him. During my time with Kahn I worked on the Mikveh Israel synagogue, and then the Indian Institute of Management, and dabbled with some drawings on the Salk [Institute].

What kind of an impression did he leave? What kind of a person, character was he?
He seemed determined, self-assured ... he had his manners, his pipe. He gave the impression of somebody who knows what he's doing. But I didn't have any interaction with the architect-engineer working together even in the discussions he had on the Salk; I was not at the table as a participant. Just before I was planning to go to India to supervise the Management Institute, my thesis advisor and professor [Sandy van Ginkel] showed up and said, *We're going to have a World's Fair* [in Montreal in 1967], *I'd like you to come and work on the master plan.* I was young and very, very cheeky and I gave him a condition—that I would go but I wanted to apply my thesis to a pavilion in the World's Fair. He said, *Wow, provided the budget, you'll have to do it on your own time.* So I went back [to Montreal] and left Kahn. Kahn didn't like people leaving him, but that's life. And soon after, as I started working on the master plan, there was an opportunity to get $50,000 from the cement companies who were giving a grant for promoting concrete at Expo. So I brought some friends from Philadelphia and we started working. [Architect] David Rinehart was the most important figure amongst them to join me.[1]

At that point David Rinehart had left Kahn's office?
Correct, he was not there anymore. At this point the question of engineering came up; whatever you do, you can't move forward without it. I remembered August in this moment, so I called him and said we have this feasibility study, and we have a bit of money, do you want to join us? He was delighted and accepted, and of course this is when we really got to know each other. The first early meetings were key—at this time we only worked with models—models, then studies, and then more models. I was still struggling with the idea of the frame and putting boxes into the frame. August suggested that because of the weight of the boxes and the need to fireproof the boxes, we should make them load-bearing. We also discussed standardization, which took some convincing on his part, and we eventually developed two systems. One was more ambitious, but never got built—the original twenty-two-story leaning membranes supported by an A-frame. The second was similar to what we actually built. We had two to three months to use the grant from the concrete industry. In the beginning there was no commitment that it had to be concrete, but finally we came to the realization it had to be concrete as there were not many other choices for fireproof materials. That still shocks me; to this day there are no more fireproof materials available, nothing has advanced.

Just to take a step back, it was your idea to invite Komendant as the structural consultant?
Yes, at that time nobody in Canada knew who he was. It took some doing.

Was it related to the fact that you got the funds from the cement companies to test the concrete possibility?
No, not at all, at this time I could basically do as I wanted. Later on it became more complicated, because when it came

Study model of Habitat '67

time for the project to be built, there were many questions about who would be the engineer of records, who would sign the drawings, what is the relationship with Komendant? And then there was the municipal Structural Committee who said his design wouldn't stand up. Luckily, I had a courageous client. But in the beginning it was just, *Come help us out!* I don't even remember if we paid him, if we paid for his travel, if he got a portion of the $50,000 ... I don't remember any of that.

Merike [Komendant Phillips, August Komendant's daughter, who worked as an architect at Safdie's office at the time] mentioned that when she joined the team, it was quite early on, that you had a very small team working on the project. David Rinehart, Merike, a couple of more architects, Merike's father and you, but later on the team grew.

The team grew as soon as it became a real project. It grew in two phases—in the beginning there was the feasibility study, I'm not sure Merike was there during that phase. We used to call her Komendant's spy. [Laughs] The first phase was in the Expo office, which lasted until we took the project to Ottawa in October 1964 to present it to the Prime Minister and the Cabinet. They approved it and gave us a budget. Then Edward Churchill, the head of Expo construction, called and said, *You're fired. Go set up your own office, you shouldn't be doing this as a government employee.*

So I chose an associate architect, I had a budget, a fee, and started hiring people. I first talked to Parkin Architects Ltd., but eventually ended up with David, Barott, Boulva, who brought about four people with them. I hired two or three people from Philadelphia, and many from Montreal—all young people. We rented a space in the low-rise building at Place Ville Marie; Expo was in the main tower. That's when we jumped from four to fifteen, and then finally to about forty employees, which is when I believe Merike joined us, in phase two. All of the people who worked with me in phase one, including Adèle Santos [on the master plan][2] who you may know about, were Expo employees, except for David Rinehart.

It must be the case, yes, that Merike joined after it became a project. But coming back to August Komendant in a more general way, in your opinion, what are his main achievements as a structural engineer? What makes his work still relevant today?

Through experience and intuition, Komendant was able to design a building spatially with all of the pieces of the building working together, well before computer programming made this commonplace. He told me that some of his theories were developed when he was doing forensic work on buildings damaged during the war in Europe—that a lot of his experience came from the forensic research he did. He was thinking about building spatially. That is how we came to a concept where the boxes [of Habitat '67] are load-bearing, that streets are taking lateral and some vertical forces, and everything is posttensioned and with neoprene pads so that things can move. The big contention with the Structural Committee was that there were no expansion joints in the building; rather it was all just working together incrementally. With concrete this is especially impressive. Concrete is more difficult in terms of analysis and in understanding how the forces work than in steel. I still go to Habitat and I am in awe that he could have figured all of that out! And it's still standing in reasonable condition fifty years later. It has even withstood one serious earthquake. It was just an amazing kind of intuitive power that Komendant had. I have worked with great engineers since, all with their own unique styles, including Peter Rice at Arup, and several other gifted engineers at Arup, and at Buro Happold.

If you compare them as characters or their approach—

As characters, nobody comes close to Komendant's eccentric character.

What do you mean by eccentric?

He was a very unpredictable guy. He was a continental gentleman, charming, but with a very dictatorial Germanic manner; he had no patience for fools. He spoke forcefully in a kind of staccato: Yup! Yah! Yes! No! Not!, etc., so he came through as a very opinionated, dominant person; he was Estonian but again, very Germanic in his manner of speaking, though I never learned his whole history before he came to the United States.

People have told me that Lou Kahn was very upset that I engaged him with Habitat. Do you have evidence of that? Have you heard that?

What Komendant says in his book[3] is that Kahn didn't like Komendant working for other architects. He probably wanted to keep good people to his own office, and was a little envious, yes.

He [Kahn] was possessive. He wasn't nice to me after I left.

Really?
Yes, on several occasions. I guess it was hard for him. It's understandable, Kahn was fifty or sixty years old when he became successful, whereas here I am a twenty-five-year-old kid and Boom! Success. It must have been difficult for him.

Psychologically—
Yes, I think so. I always had a soft spot for him despite his response.

With Komendant we had a real camaraderie. We battled together to build Habitat. It would not have happened of course without me, but it also would not have happened without him. It was both his skills as an engineer and his persona. There was a pivotal moment when the engineers of the [University of Toronto and McGill] University appointed by the municipality said that Habitat would not stand up. I saw Churchill after, and he said, *What are we going to do now?* I said, *Well, you've got these two guys and you've got Komendant, whose word do you believe?* So he said, *Who can I talk to about Komendant*? I gave him some a list, the contractors at the time who were building his other buildings, clients. He just picked up the phone and spent an hour interrogating people about him. Then he said, *We will go ahead.* He placed the report in his drawer, *I am the federal government—I am the sovereign. I do not need a building permit.* It was an amazing moment! To this day I cannot fathom that a civil servant had that kind of courage.

In terms of the local engineers—
I remember the names, [professor J. O.] McCutcheon and ... one of them was a French-Canadian [professor G. A. Kani].

Did you ever find out whether it was politics or just incompetence?
It wasn't politics, politically there was a will. They really had their doubts, and they were lacking the tools to evaluate the structure. As for the associate local engineers, the two I ended up with, Monti[4] and Adjeleian,[5] were more open-minded, because they had to put their names on the drawings. Komendant couldn't sign the drawings.

This was about the local license?
Yes.

There had to be a local office, partner.
There were two structural offices. One in Ottawa, Adjeleian, who had been my professor at McGill. The McGill architecture program was part of the School of Engineering. Unlike at most American universities, I received a lot of structural education at McGill. I even learned soil mechanics. We really had to cover a lot. I've always felt comfortable with engineering material because of that education. I joke now with my engineers, that after fifty years, I can size structural weakness quite precisely. I can figure out what's working and what's not. I've just developed an intuition over time.

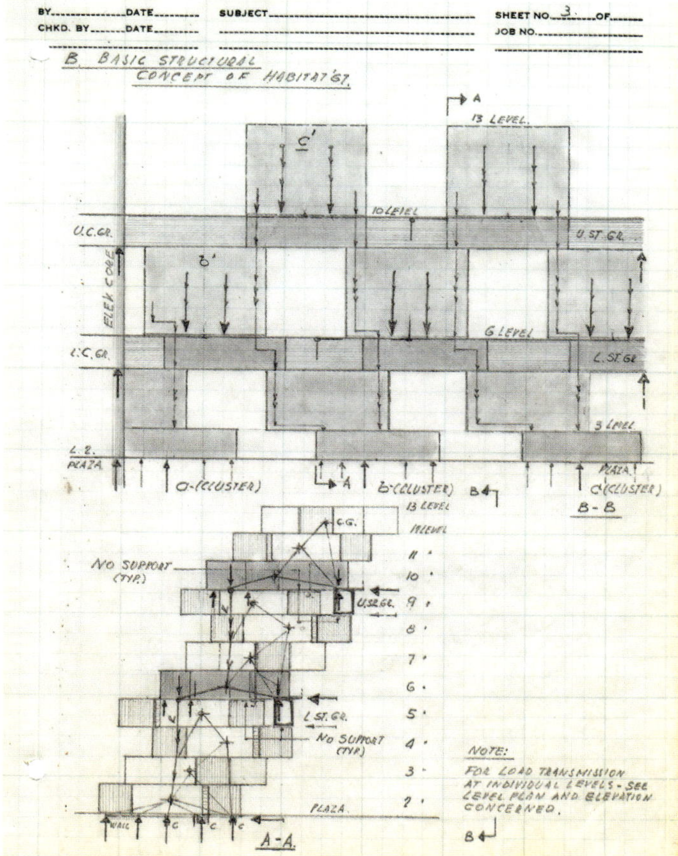

August Komendant. Static calculations of Habitat '67, force distribution, 1966

I was just going through your thesis work last week in Montreal and I was thinking, here's a young architect thinking about structure and modular space and all these things together in such a clear and ambitious way.
Lots of daring and god knows what! [Laughs]

As a historian I am interested in what the ambitious and talented engineers have said or thought about the artistic, aesthetic, creative—however you called it—side of the built environment. With Ove Arup, with Komendant, with Pier Luigi Nervi, with Peter Rice, and some others, I feel that they are engineers who are very well aware of architecture as a discipline, and about the importance of collaborating with talented architects in a teamwork manner to get a good result.
I think it is absolutely true.

What is your impression, what kind of value did Komendant attribute to this side?
It's an interesting question. I think the concept of Habitat could have gone in two different directions. One way is more reflective of the work of Archigram or Yona Friedman, or other groups like that. Space frame, plug-in elements, more mechanical in nature. It would have been different, but we would have figured it out. The other approach was more archaic. Do you know the book and exhibition *Architecture Without Architects*

Habitat '67 during construction

by Bernard Rudofsky [of 1964]? It presents the power of vernacular architecture—say an Italian hill tower. The aesthetic is really of volumes, of solids, the juxtaposition of units of space, all reading as three-dimensional units. Apart from the reality of concrete being load-bearing and heavy, and therefore let's make it all load-bearing, I think Komendant was preconditioned to strive for this kind of architecture. I think his direction and push structurally was also informed by his aesthetic preference. I think that is what differentiated Habitat immediately from the many other projects of that period that were interested in similar ideas. ... Although when somebody says, *There were so many things in the air at that time, you just happened to get yours built!* I say, *Show me*. Because I don't think there was anything on paper or in theory that combined the elements that we eventually managed to create with Habitat. I think Komendant was moved by that aspect no less than his structural rationality. I experienced this again with Peter Rice when I did the library in Vancouver [completed in 1995] and with Buro Happold for the Jewel project in Changi Airport in Singapore [completed in 2019], which is just a great big toroid[6] of steel, spanning 300 meters. These sensibilities come through in the creative process of great engineers for sure. There are others that I didn't work with, but you can see that in their work too. Great engineers like Frei Otto, Pier Luigi Nervi ... who I would have loved to collaborate with, but it didn't happen.

We briefly spoke about Komendant's character and the jobs you did together. Do you have any personal memories you consider important to share with a larger audience?
You know, Komendant always had his favorite people. He was very nourishing to them, but to others he could be indifferent. One of the people who was very important to the realization of Habitat was Cipriano Da Re.[7] He was a chief engineer, for Francon Limited, the precaster, a self-educated Italian. He worked very closely with Komendant on the detailing and a lot of the posttensioning issues that arose. Komendant loved Cipriano, along with a few others, such as a local engineer's project manager by the name of Komocki, who was Polish.[8] At that point the whole European thing took over. [Laughs] There were all of these relationships for the duration of the project, and I found myself at a very young age having to orchestrate a lot of psychological issues. The one thing I learned very quickly is the need to manage. I had to manage Komendant. He could rub people the wrong way, and I had to learn to navigate in that complicated world of the World's Fair. But people had a great deal of respect for him; there was a mystique about him.

What do you mean by mystique?
Well I think there's a mystique about Germans. Like the rocket men.[9]

He was considered a German?
I think that if you'd asked the average person on the Expo site what Komendant's nationality was they wouldn't say Estonian. I knew he was Estonian.

But again, the mystique?
A mystique in that, he commands respect; he knows what he's talking about. He acted a role, very effectively. His manner of communication and gravitas helped in a process, because when he said something, people took it seriously.

Was it even possible to argue with him if he was such a strong character with his views?
I did, but he could be tough, particularly for people on the engineering side. As an example, Komendant would come every week or two with a big roll of drawings, and a slide rule—imagine a slide rule! He would roll the drawings out and say, *See Moshe!* and he would point to a big blister he had on his finger, *That's from making all the drawings!* He was so proud that he made the drawings himself, and he must have done most of them, although he had assistance.

He had a very small office but in the case of larger projects Helmi Aren [Komendant's partner] and some other engineers and draftsmen helped him. In comparison with Ove Arup ... Arup felt like a team player, he built a large firm, was very good with people, but Komendant liked to work on his own.
I met Ove Arup personally only once, at the office of Sandy van Ginkel. And at that point it was Arup the engineer, and not Arup the big organization. Arup now is an octopus-like, far-reaching organization, but it amazes me how they maintained excellence in spite of their size and geography.

Komendant was absolutely a loner. He got help as he needed to. In a way, Kahn was also, although he had a team. He saw jobs through from A to Z, step by step. That's perhaps his biggest influence on me, I am obsessed with the same thing. Safdie Architects has maybe 60–70 employees, sometimes up to 120, but I am involved with every project from start to finish.

And you walk around the office and see the details ... what your colleagues are doing.
Every detail! I'll sit for hours on a project, drawing details of fenestration. That's what Kahn did, with every building.

1 David Rinehart (1928–2016), architect and educator, worked at the office of Louis Kahn from the end of the 1950s until 1964.

2 Adèle Naudé Santos, architect, urban designer and educator, Dean of the School of Architecture and Planning at Massachusetts Institute of Technology, 2003–2014.

3 August Komendant, *18 Years With Architect Louis I. Kahn* (Englewood, NJ: Aloray, 1975).

4 Monti, Lefebvre, Lavoie, Nadon & Associates, structural and mechanical consulting engineers.

5 John Adjeleian (1923–2004), structural engineer and educator.

6 In geometry, a toroid is a surface of revolution with a hole in the middle, like a doughnut, forming a solid body.

7 Cipriano Da Re (1924–2012), consulting engineer and specialist on prestressed concrete.

8 Jan Komocki, consulting engineer from Monti, Lefebvre, Lavoie, Nadon & Associates.

9 Moshe Safdie: "*Rocket men* here refers to the Germans who were brought to the United States to develop primarily the NASA rocket program because of their expertise in rocketry. More specifically, before and after World War II many scientists, physicists, and chemists came from Germany and greatly enriched the United States. There was the assumption that they were capable, and Komendant enjoyed the standing of the German Dr. or Professor from Germany." Moshe Safdie via Tess Besckingham's e-mail to the editor, May 8, 2020.

August Komendant and architect Robert Geddes (*right*) on the construction site of the Philadelphia Police Administration Building, 1961

Interview. Robert Geddes

Robert Geddes and Carl-Dag Lige
Skillman, New Jersey, October 26, 2018

Carl-Dag Lige: Would you briefly explain the circumstances surrounding how you first met August Komendant?
Robert Geddes: I don't know. [Laughs] We met, obviously, at the University [of Pennsylvania], at the faculty meetings, but I don't recall a specific time when we would have met first. It must have been in 1958 or 1959, because he was the structural engineer for the [Philadelphia] Police Headquarters.[1] The key people in my office who really worked with Komendant were George Qualls, but most of all Barney Cunningham.[2] We liked him [Komendant] enormously. We called him "Gus." He was a wonderful team player. He enjoyed us, and we enjoyed him.

What kind of an impression did you have of him as a person?
Well, in addition to sharing the brilliance and competence he had as a builder-engineer, he was open in the best sense of the word. He liked conversation, and we all enjoyed it together. It was jovial. If I had known then that you were going to ask me these questions, I'd be better prepared. [Laughs] I'll give you an example. When the Police building was under construction, one Friday afternoon there appeared to be a crack in the structure. The city building department called a halt to the construction. Those people—it was not an easy building to get approved, accepted, and understood. If you had any reason to be against the building in any way—architecturally, socially, politically—the cracks there really, really hurt.

What we discovered that weekend was that Komendant was not only an engineer, he was, essentially, a builder. I think there are several kinds of structural engineers. There are planners. I would probably suspect Ove Arup was an excellent planner, but I'm not sure. Anyway, I think there are planner engineers. And builder engineers. And then there are artists. Those three types. And that is what Komendant was—he was a builder. What he did that Saturday morning ... Barney Cunningham and I met him there on the site. He took these pieces [of concrete], broke them apart, and discovered what he had guessed was the problem. The US testing lab had given us a certification that all the reinforcing and stirrups were in place. In fact, for reasons that I still can't understand, the construction company [without consulting Komendant or GBQC] decided that it was too difficult to put concrete around the stirrups and [in the areas where the cracks occurred] they didn't put them in at all! Therefore, the pieces, they cracked. Komendant knew that was going to happen! As soon as he saw it, he was there and said, I'll show you. So, we had to replace it all. That is probably the liveliest example of him actually being able to build, to fabricate, to produce. He had our respect and our loyalty.

What was different about Komendant compared to other engineers?
First of all, Komendant's work did not directly follow the development of the modern architecture of Le Corbusier and others developing frame systems. I don't know for a fact, but Komendant never in my work nor in Kahn's work made a frame. The form itself became the structure. In the obvious examples of form becoming the structure, in the case of Richards [Medical Building], I mean, the structure was the whole thing. In our case he also carried it to, I think, a high level.

[For the Police building] we had a block in Philadelphia, a city block, with a street coming in diagonally at this point in what would have otherwise been part of a city grid. Ironically or strangely, the site did not include the corner; the underground subway went through there. We really had to fight to have this corner knocked off. What I argue in *FIT*[3] is that you are either going to fit in or you are going to stand out. There's a reason why you do this [that is, fit in], and a reason why you do that [that is, stand out]. Given this situation in the city and its civic purpose, it was correct to stand out *and* fit in. What we did, really—well, I'll show you on the plan. We built three subcenters. There are two cores for the police [on the sides] and one core for the public [in the middle]. Do you know Piranesi's drawing of Rome's Campo Marzio? If you look at it, you will see many times that he was playing around with the notion of there being a building with more than one center.

I have to say that Komendant and Cunningham made a great team, because the Police building has very complicated geometry. When we built, even the last piece fit! Almost didn't, but it fit.

Philadelphia Police Administration Building on the day the construction was temporarily halted, August 18, 1961

Did you consider using precast elements for the structural system from the beginning of the project?
It is hard for me to remember. This was our [GBQC's] second building. Our first building was the Pender Labs for the Moore School [of Electrical Engineering] at Penn, where we used a precast edge piece, which acted as a restraining section for the structure. It always seemed reasonable to us to do the two things together—the structure and the exterior surface combined. I think we are putting too much emphasis on exterior at the moment.

There are two ways in which, I think, modern architecture had real problems. One was on the exterior wall and the other was on the interior ceiling—and we gave up [control of] both of them to simple, dumb modular hung ceilings, and simple dumb exterior walls. There's not much left to architecture when you give up ceilings and walls! So, we [GBQC] strove to have an integral system for exterior wall and interior pieces.

You gave up the idea of the curtain wall and integrated the facade and ceilings as one structural system.
Yes, exactly. [In the Police building] that was the real achievement. I have to credit Barney Cunningham. Barney was as much an engineer-builder as Komendant was a builder-engineer. The tragedy of life is that the Schokbeton[4] system didn't exist very long.

Was the concrete wall surrounding the site there from the beginning?
No. It was all open. [The wall] was put up a couple of weeks after the building opened, [and is antithetical to our concept]. As you probably noticed, it's not precast concrete, it's ordinary gray concrete. [The wall] was added. In fact, if the building stays, the first thing to do is to take the wall down. Put in a double row of trees. That would be beautiful. An administration building is an office building. A *headquarters* is also more symbolic. I'm sorry they ever changed the name.

Why didn't GBQC continue working with Komendant after the Police building?
I don't know. I'm guessing. The structural failure was a big shock to us, and we never again tried to build at the cutting edge of technology. I think we retreated. Whether we should have or not, I don't know. But we did. From that point on we

built concrete buildings, reinforced concrete buildings, but they were no more advanced than Auguste Perret's buildings.

At Penn I used to have a favorite question for students at the jury when they presented their work, I would say: what is the building made of? One day a student said it's made of *precast ideas*. [Laughs] I didn't mind that. Well, I knew what he meant.

I should show you how far away from the avant-garde structural question we [GBQC] went—when we did the new college for New Jersey, the Stockton College, we set up several sub-systems: structure, interior partitions, mechanical, etc. And we set up performance specs. We didn't ask that there be concrete or brick or steel or whatever. But the winning systems were steel structure, aluminum exterior; concrete didn't come into it at all. The subsystems that won on the basis of performance were what mattered. I think it's really a terrible shame. If Schokbeton had continued in business, it would have become a dominant element in American architecture. But it didn't.

Facade panels of the Philadelphia Police Administration Building, 2019

What kind of importance did Komendant give to the artistic, creative, aesthetic side of the built environment? Do you feel he considered it important?

No, I think he was a builder engineer. He produced. He worked with Lou, he worked with me and others, but I don't think he was himself the generator of form. It's terribly sad that Carles Vallhonrat[5] died recently. He could have answered that. Carles came and taught with me at Princeton. He would've known exactly, precisely how Komendant fit into this conversation.

Frank Lloyd Wright supposedly said that every engineer is a frustrated architect.

Frank Lloyd Wright was very fortunate to have Wes Peters as an engineer! No, I don't think that Komendant was frustrated. He completely enjoyed sitting around the table and thinking this is how it could be done. If Schokbeton had continued, the development of modern architecture in this country [USA] would have been very different. It wouldn't have gone to the thin glass wall. It would have been a much more ... *Expressionism* is the term they use. I think the Police building would not have been such an unusual building. It was unusual then, and still is, I suppose. But I think there would've been many rectilinear *and* curvilinear ones. Don't assume that the curvilinear aspect [of the Police building] is the key. Somebody once asked James Stirling, what are the building types he was working on. He said there are two: linear and centroidal. [Laughs] I think it's true. The fact that Komendant did a centroidal, a curvilinear building with us, doesn't mean he couldn't have contributed greatly to a gridded, multigridded building.

1 Robert Geddes taught architecture and civic design at the Graduate School of Fine Arts (later School of Design), University of Pennsylvania from 1951 to 1965. Komendant joined the faculty in 1959. For more on the work and career of Robert Geddes see www.robertgeddesarchitect.com, accessed September 9, 2021. For the Philadelphia Police Administration Building, see pp. 184–193.

2 George Wyckoff Qualls (1923–2001) and Warren W. "Barney" Cunningham (1922–2013), architects and educators, from 1960 partners in Geddes Brecher Qualls Cunningham. For more on the firm GBQC and each architect individually, see www.philadelphiabuildings.org, accessed September 9, 2021.

3 Robert Geddes, *FIT: An Architect's Manifesto* (Princeton, NJ: Princeton University Press, 2013).

4 For the history of Schokbeton's patented concrete technology, see Lucas van Zuijlen and Jack Pyburn speaking at the *Docomomo* National Symposium, Minneapolis, Minnesota, June 4–7, 2015, www.docomomo-us-mn.org/concrete-and-schokbeton.html, accessed September 9, 2021.

5 Carles Enric Vallhonrat (1928–2017), architect and educator, worked for several years in the office of Louis Kahn and at the Princeton University School of Architecture.

Merike has stolen her father's pipe and glasses, 1976

Interview. Merike Komendant Phillips

Merike Komendant Phillips and Carl-Dag Lige
Kenosha, Wisconsin, April 25, 2018

Carl-Dag Lige: What was your father like as a person? How would you describe his personality?
Merike Komendant Phillips: He was a very nice person, a very interesting person. When he talked, he always looked at the "big picture," he didn't get bogged down in the small details. Always very sociable, they had lots and lots of friends. And I don't remember him ever being angry with us. I guess we were very well behaved children. Well, maybe my brother Jüri not so much. [Laughs] But yes, he was a very, very interesting person. I was aware of this from a very early age.

He studied in Germany and seemed to be quite cosmopolitan by nature. Was he interested in world affairs?
It's hard for me to say, I was still a kid at the time. Work was the most important thing for him. He was also interested in politics and culture. We always had newspapers delivered and he read those. When he was older he read every evening, various subjects. About mathematics, history, different theories.

Which newspapers did he read?
In America he read the *Vaba Eesti Sõna* (Free Estonian Word), the *New York Times*, the *New Republican*. He was an ardent Republican. I must say that there were very few Democrats among Estonians [the Estonian immigrants living in the United States] because they felt that the Russians [the Soviet regime] were allowed to annex Estonia because our president [Democrat Franklin D. Roosevelt] gave Estonia away at the Yalta Conference [1945]. They were very critical of this. All the stories I remember reviled the Russians. But I don't think that they [with his wife, Erna; his later partner, Helmi; or his acquaintances] would always talk about politics.

What topics did he like to talk about with friends?
Philosophy, culture, architecture, also art and music. Maybe less about music with [Louis] Kahn. And I don't remember them discussing politics with Kahn at all.

How would you describe his approach to life?
He got up early in the morning and always worked hard. Then there was lunch; Helmi made something beautiful and delicious. In the afternoon they said they would have "friends" over. *What friends?*, I asked. It turned out they would be watching TV! [Laughs]

Yes, my father worked all the time. Even when I was there [as an adult, visiting], my father was always in his office. For the whole day. In the evening we ate together, had a drink and a nice chat. Sometimes friends came to visit. They [with Helmi] were very, very sociable. Made a lot of jokes. They were also visited by important guests, [conductor] Neeme Järvi, for example. I didn't know them all, but there were writers and artists, mainly from the Estonian community in New York. I know that they were not active participants in the work of the Estonian community, but they made donations. When we were in a refugee camp in Germany and he worked for the American army, I know he made a lot of donations, he made all sorts of small gifts for the children of the [Estonian] school. Because he could buy stuff from the PX [Post Exchange, military stores]. In this way he was able to help many people.

What do you consider to be his greatest professional achievements?
That he introduced prestressed concrete to the United States. Certainly also that he proposed very interesting [structural] solutions to very complicated problems. He would have a goal. Everything would be clear to him right away! And then he just wrote or drew it on a piece of paper. For him, the structure was very important—it had to be "clean" and to fit the architecture. Structure was as important to him as architecture. But this was not at all typical [among engineers at the time]. Usually the architect drew up the project and then the engineer had to look at how it could be built and how it would stand up. But he wanted to be involved from the very beginning of the creative process. This was an exception.

And he was a good teacher. His students respected him. He was able to talk in an interesting manner. When I first saw my father make a presentation, it was in Montreal [1963 or 1964] before I went to work for [Moshe] Safdie. I must have just been accompanying my father. He had to give a presentation to the heads of the Expo. Safdie himself was only twenty-five years old at the time! He was young and had no experience at all. They wanted to know what this project [Habitat '67] was, and it didn't seem to be going well at all. But then my father started talking and I was startled. My mother always said that he could convince anyone! He began talking about how it could be built, that it was possible and would bring a lot of positive attention to Canada. How these [concrete] housing units could be made was something rare, and what could be built from them, and that nothing like this had been done anywhere before. And Safdie got the project! Not just because of my father, but he was the one who brought it all together. Of course, he hadn't done any calculations yet. [Laughs]

So, a good persuader?
Oh yes! He was very impressive and determined. Not in the manner of "I'm the expert and do it like this and that's it." No. Sometimes he had some tricks up his sleeves. In that book [*18 Years with Architect Louis I. Kahn*], he talks about them. There were many occasions where he knew [more than others]. And he knew how to build it! He climbed onto the roofs as the concrete was being poured and showed the workers how to install tensioning cables, etc. He was so knowledgeable that he could not be compared to anyone else. And yes, sometimes he liked to be cunning. He had very good relationships with the contractors and construction companies. He wasn't a crook, but he was cunning, with a good head for business.

He liked good liquor. If you didn't drink, you weren't a proper Estonian, something like that. [Laughs] He liked vodka, vodka cocktails. And Cuba Libres, it's rum with coke. [Juhan] Liiband was a very, very good [friend and drinking buddy]. In [the 1930s] Estonia, Liiband had been a major contractor, but in America he had a hard time finding work, even though he was a very good civil engineer. He worked for my father on the Habitat project. My father had a large number of Estonians working for him who helped and made calculations and drawings. However, Helmi was his greatest help. She was not an engineer, but she checked my father's calculations and wrote, did secretarial work. She was very precise.

One important detail. Today's engineers use computer programs that tell you that you require this and that, so much of this and so much of that and that this or that has to be this large. Otherwise, they don't know [unless the software tells them the results]. But my father was the opposite—he already knew. He used calculations as a way of checking, to confirm his knowledge.

Could one say that he had a good engineering intuition?
It wasn't intuition. It was pure knowledge based on experience. He knew how it should be, what dimensions of elements were needed, how it would work. And he knew how to construct it. In the case of Habitat, for example, the earthquake-resistant joints. The same were applied to the Salk Institute.

How would you describe the relationship between your father and Louis Kahn?
They were very good friends. I always saw Kahn in very personal settings, because we went out to eat together all the time, I was an attentive little "youngster." And it was very interesting. They didn't just discuss work things like "what is the dimension of this or that?" They knew those were subjects for the office. They talked about philosophy and the like. Kahn in his books, however, has, as they say, his head more in the clouds.

Kahn is often surrounded by a mystical aura, precisely because of his somewhat cryptic way of speaking in public. But you imply that he was a completely ordinary person?
Yes, absolutely. When I met him—he was very nice. His company did not cease all work and gather round while he gave some great lecture. He walked around the tables, observing. He was always discussing things with Anne Tyng, when I was working there. ... There were arguments, quite a lot. Nor did I always know what project he was working on. And I also didn't know that Marie Kuo was his lover. She was very beautiful, a young Chinese woman, and very talented. It was a nice little group, the four of us always went out to dinner.

You, August Komendant, Louis Kahn and Marie Kuo?
Yes, the four of us. I guess I was a chaperone. [Laughs] It was a gentlemen's club, there weren't many people there. It was very beautiful.

How did August Komendant and Louis Kahn address each other?
Kahn was always "Lou" and my father ... I think he was always "Doc."

Kahn lived in Philadelphia, your father in Upper Montclair ...
Yes, when my father went to Philadelphia, he always stayed in a beautiful hotel, two or three nights.

What do you think was the key to their successful collaboration?
They complemented each other. Lou's designs were very beautiful. ... My father provided the structure, made his designs strong. Without this, especially in the case of the Richards Laboratory, Lou would hardly have achieved such a result. He became well known for this. When I look at my father's other work, I think what he did with Lou was the best.

In the book, your father writes that they also had disagreements ...
Oh yes, it was a very difficult time. There were disagreements at the end, too, but these were never about the architecture or the engineering solution along the lines of "Oh, what you're doing isn't good enough." Maybe there were some small things when my father said he liked this or that [solution]. But this was never a criticism of the central idea. Rather, it concerned drawings not arriving at the right time and Kahn making changes [to his designs] again. ... This was especially difficult. Like, *Yes, he's changed things again!* And the boys [the architects and draftsmen at Louis Kahn's office] don't draw the plans properly, their designs were just sketches. And then about money, too. Lou was unable to manage his finances. He spent so much time on projects, so even though

the work was well paid, all the money disappeared. They agreed that my father would be paid separately, but then it turned out that Lou had used the money for something else. Such situations caused trouble. But my father never thought Lou wasn't a good architect. Eventually there was certainly a bit of bitterness as well, as Lou began to take more and more of the credit in public, without acknowledging [the contributions of others].

Did this apply only to your father or also his other partners?
It was certainly broader. We talked about [architect] David Rinehart before. ... But I don't know about the others, I was there only for two summers. In general, I did not see Kahn share credit and public attention with anyone in particular. He was the leader. However, it was not the case that he had a large group of people to do all the dirty work.

In which years did you have summer internships at Louis Kahn's office? What were your responsibilities?
I started my studies [at Syracuse School of Architecture] in 1957. I didn't work as an intern during the first summer, so in the summers of 1959 and 1960. I was a draftsman, I made working drawings—elevations, plans, etc. Of course, these were not my designs, but I drafted what was needed. I also made illustrations of projects for magazines, ink drawings. There was a house for a female artist. ... It had similar windows to the Tribune Review building. I remember this woman had a large bathroom. And a library right behind it! I also worked on the Tribune Review project. Also, if someone wanted a clean elevation or plan to be drafted.

I graduated from Syracuse University in 1962. Then we spent more than half a year traveling in America and Mexico and elsewhere. My brother, Jüri, me, our mother, and a friend. When I returned, I worked for Alfred Easton Poor in New York. It was a big company. And I had a very hard time getting a job. Although I took my dissertation and work samples and I had very good grades—I was the most successful in my class up until the final semester. But I still couldn't find work, because I was a woman!

You think it was because of your gender?
Oh yes! Absolutely. Some of my male schoolmates had been C-students, but got jobs right away. I worked on bank projects at Alfred Easton Poor, making drawings again. After I left they hired another girl, who was very good. I was like a guinea pig! [Laughs] I lived in New York, I was very self-conscious and smart and proud. [Laughs] I worked at that office for almost two years. Then I traveled around Europe, Israel, Egypt, and elsewhere with two of my girlfriends for almost six months. It was great to traipse around.

And after you returned, did you go to work for Moshe Safdie?
Yes. Safdie had a very small office back then. Maybe five architects. All of them were young. All of them had been connected to Lou Kahn's office in some way. Safdie wanted those who had worked for Kahn. I showed him my work, and Safdie accepted me.

And you started working on the Habitat '67 project?
Yes, absolutely, right from the start. All those concrete boxes. ... We had to work them out. I worked for Safdie for almost two years, I left in 1965 when I got married. So not until the end of the Habitat project.

Did your father help you get these jobs?
Yes, I believe so. But I also had to prove that I knew what I was doing. They would not have accepted me, if I hadn't been up to par.

In 1965, you married architect Bill Phillips and moved to Kenosha?
Yes, then I worked in Chicago, commuting by train. I worked for Harry Weese. He was a famous architect here. Worked on many projects in the Chicago area.

To come back to your father, in your opinion, what kind of importance did August Komendant attribute to the artistic or aesthetic component in architecture and the built environment?
I thought he thought that was of utmost importance. Very, very important. That was what you start with. No question about that. He had an intrinsic ability to evaluate it, of knowing what is true but, again, always seeing it through an engineer's [perspective]. There might have been some structures that were valid and interesting that, I think, he would not have got involved with at all. He was involved always when a structure was part of architecture. With Lou you could see that dialogue [between architect and engineer]. But you're never 100 percent on the same plane, because you *do* have different backgrounds.

Several engineers who collaborated with modernist architects considered honesty of utmost importance. The architecture is there, but its structural solution should be expressed, should be logical—
And apparent, not hidden! My father repeatedly emphasized he doesn't want the structure to be overwhelming or threatening. It has to look logical also to a person who's not familiar with the mathematics of structure. It has to be intrinsically logical. Structural honesty was paramount, always. Nowadays you don't see it that much. With computers, everything is possible. But like they used to make a joke that just because you *can* do it, doesn't mean you *should* do it. So you don't have that [structural honesty in architecture] anymore. It has kind of gotten lost in the era now, very much so.

Is there anything else you'd like to address about your father?
I thought my father was brilliant. He was unique. And not because he was my father, but because I saw his work. If he'd been a stranger, I'd have been equally impressed. He was very, very lively and interesting. He had the ability to get people enthused about a project, and to take them with him, make them feel the enthusiasm of creating these things and what it meant, not just designing a building. He was an inspiring engineer.

Little "King George" with his father in Germany in the late 1940s

Interview. George Jüri Komendant

George Jüri Komendant and Carl-Dag Lige
Kenosha, Wisconsin, April 25, 2018
Berkeley, California, September 26, 2018

Carl-Dag Lige: You are a structural engineer, like your father. Early on in your career, you also worked briefly for him. Did you go to work in his home office in Upper Montclair?
George Jüri Komendant: Yes, I lived about half an hour away. I was married to my first wife then and we lived nearby. I went to work, every day; it was very nice. It was very interesting for me to work with my father, because he was a great engineer and he was good to me—he showed me what to do and how to do it. And he gave me enough to do. I did both drawings and simple static calculations with him. I was with him for about a year and a half, from June 1967 to the end of 1968. Most of the work was to do with the Miami Airport designs, parking garages etc. I did drawings for Dad.

Did he work on Sundays?
He worked when he wanted to. When he had a job to do, he just went down to his office and worked. Of course, he also took some free time. I remember the first week of working for him. At about two o'clock he said he was leaving, as he had friends coming. I didn't think I'd heard anyone coming. The next day again he said, *I have friends coming over.* On the third or fourth day, I thought, what's going on? And I went upstairs. What I saw was Helmi [Helmi Aren, August Komendant's partner] and him watching *The Days of Our Lives* on TV! [Laughs] He watched it every day. In the evenings, he usually didn't work, and would watch TV or read something instead. When we visited, we used to drink gin and tonic and sit on the balcony—it was very enjoyable. On weekends, he only worked when he had deadlines. It wasn't like he had to work; he had an interest in it.

My sister, Merike [who is an architect by education, see pp. 71–73] also worked for Dad for some time. But she also worked for architects—Dad used to set her up to work for them. Dad also got me a job with the Atlantic Prestressed Concrete Co. I worked at their plant in Trenton but started in Delaware, where they also had a precasting plant. They made double tees there. I worked in quality control and made cylindrical test specimens. I learned a lot about prestressing there. How to use molds and so on. This was my first job in the construction industry. Then they shut down the Delaware plant and I went to Trenton. I was eighteen or nineteen, a student, and I enjoyed working there. I mainly did reinforcement work. I installed the steel rebars for concrete elements before pouring. The other workers didn't know whose son I was, but they liked my dad a lot. They usually shouted, *Hi Doc!* or *Hi Gus!* to him. Dad was very good and respectful to the workers when they did their job well.

For example, he taught the workers to vibrate concrete—he once told a foreman to put a good guy on it, not someone who doesn't know what he's doing. There are many dangers when pouring concrete. Usually, the mixture is not liquid enough to flow into every corner. That's what a concrete vibrator is for, to remove air bubbles and excess voids. If you vibrate it too much, you will extract too much water. If you don't vibrate it enough, you will leave honeycombing. You need to know what you're doing. Dad taught the workers how to vibrate properly. He took part in the construction process himself, he taught by example. That's why the concrete in Salk and elsewhere is so beautiful!

Dad was a good boss. Juhan Liiband, with whom we lived during our first month in America [in the summer of 1950], was a good Estonian friend and a good engineer. Juhan helped him get a job at DuPont at the time. Later [in the 1960s], when Dad found out that Juhan had been fired at one point, he hired Juhan to work for him.

Your father worked for the Devenco Inc. engineering firm in the early 1950s and was involved in designing several DuPont plants.
I don't know the details about these, but Dad told me why he left DuPont. They had this project—I think it was in Louisiana—and the design had rather short spans and therefore many columns and a large number of concrete piles to support the foundation. Dad suggested making longer spans and using fewer columns and piles. He showed them how to get a more efficient design. DuPont had a practice of giving 10 percent of

August Komendant's residence in Upper Montclair, New Jersey, architect Osvald Mitt, completed in 1961. Living spaces were located on the higher floor, office and drafting room on the lower floor of the building

the [savings] in profits to anyone who recommended something useful. So, Dad asked for 10 percent because they saved a lot of money thanks to his suggestions. They told him he was an in-house engineer and only doing his job, and they didn't give him his bonus. Dad had had it and said, *Okay, I quit!* I don't know if he left the same day, but he left. That was Dad. If something happened that he didn't think was right, he was happy to say, no, thank you!

It went against his professional self-esteem and sense of justice.
Yes. He gave the information to them voluntarily. It was not part of his design nor his task. But he made a suggestion about how to do it better. And they saved a lot of money as a result.

Please describe your father as a person. What was he like?
He didn't really live with us that much. In that sense, it was a little difficult. Looking back, he no longer lived with us after we arrived in the US. We didn't talk about it much; neither did Mom [August Komendant's wife, Erna], but in the end we understood. Mom said that Dad was still Dad and would visit us—every two weeks—and he always did. He spent Christmas with us and all the holidays and birthdays, too. He came, put his heart into it, was very conscientious. Even if it was hard for him. He gave Mom $250 a month, which was a very big sum of money at first. Sometimes he didn't have that much himself. But he always paid, and somehow we managed. When Merike went to college, he paid for it. And then for my college. He also helped Merike with her house. Merike told him that she would gladly accept help, but only if he also did something for Jüri. Then he helped my children around the same time.

He was a very good father. When I was little, I didn't always understand how he took care of us. He worked a lot. When he came to visit, he was with Uncle Liiband; they would have a few drinks and hang out. Of course, being able to spend some time with Liiband was part of the reason why he came. I played with the Liibands' son, and everyone was happy, and you know—but he always came.

He did some surprising things. For example, there was this game we played with little rings that you had to throw on a stick. I was always amazed that he, an esteemed professor and engineer, would come and play with us. Mom had a lot of respect for him. She always talked very highly of Dad—and so did everyone else. Dad was very smart and hard-working and took care of us, Mom always said.

In 1962 or 1963 I visited their house for the first time [the home of August Komendant and his partner, Helmi Aren in Upper Montclair, New Jersey]. I believe I went with Merike, and I met Helmi for the first time. Helmi was very nice to us, and Dad was always very, very nice. He received us warmly. He had a little dog, and we went out in the backyard, and Dad threw a ball for the dog.

What I noticed was that he loved reading philosophy. He didn't repeat what he had learned, but he did like to talk about what he had read. He read quite a lot; I saw the books he had on the shelves. Naturally, he also had a lot of engineering literature and magazines.

He read professional and philosophical literature, but was he also interested in fiction or any other field? Politics for example?
Not as much as philosophy, I guess. Although, politics too. He was a Republican. [Laughs] Everyone was back then because [Dwight D.] Eisenhower was a Republican and he helped win World War II. He was a pretty good president, especially compared to the current Republican president [Donald Trump].

Dad loved going to the opera with Helmi, in New York. He and his friends would put on tuxedos and celebrate New Year's Eve. It was interesting for me to watch, because it was like my father's other life, about which I knew nothing.

As a young engineer, what kind of responsibility did you have at your father's office?
Working with my dad was my first true engineering design job. I already had my master's [in Structural Engineering from the Georgia Institute of Technology, Atlanta, Georgia, 1967]. In 1968 I came to California to do my PhD at the University of California, Berkeley. Dad always wanted me to come back to New Jersey, but I stayed here [in California], and that was a disappointment for him.

When I was working with him, he consulted [for the engineering firm Kellerman & Dragnett Inc.] on the National Airlines terminal [in Miami, Florida]. That was interesting. He worked on the concrete parking structures, did the concrete portion of the drawings. They also had a big hangar with huge doors. It was a large span, to fit the planes in. They didn't know how to solve it, because the deflections were too big with the way that the doors were designed—hung from the top and extremely heavy. They used steel trusses, and for that depth they couldn't get the cantilever working. My dad suggested that they put a posttensioning cable in the trusses and tension it up. At that time already, they were running computer programs; so they ran the program and said the cable had no effect. My dad looked at the drawings and what they had done is put the cable ending at midspan [of the trusses]. He said, *No, no, no, you've got to put it all the way out* [at the end of the cantilever]. Once they did that, the problem was solved, and everybody was happy.

He was very protective of his own work. In a lot of ways. He did everything himself. He did hand drawings and he had his way of doing sections, etc. So he gave the original Miami drawings to Kellerman & Dragnet. When the drawings came back, he found they had taken out all his symbols and a draftsman had modified them to put in architectural type symbols just to make it consistent with their architectural drawings. He said, *No, you cannot change my drawings. I quit!* They were so apologetic, and I spent the next week [with them] changing everything back to the way it was. *They are my drawings. You cannot change them!* He stood by his drawings, and he didn't want anybody else to modify them. Which is the right thing to do, as it was his work. You can't have somebody else changing your drawings. They were trying to pretty them up, architectural drafting etc.

Some have suggested that August Komendant was not a team player and that's why he couldn't build a larger team around him, a large engineering office. He wanted to control everything. Do you agree with that?
I would phrase it a little bit differently. He worked as an individual. And he worked in an area that he knew really well at a time when very few people were familiar with it. He had a specialty. A lot of people who made suggestions to him did not understand the specifics. In that sense he controlled it, because he was the expert in the field doing the work.

You are speaking about the prestressing technology?
That's basically what he did. Most of his buildings had prestressed concrete in one form or another. He did not do typical engineers' work like stairways, etc. He had other engineers or architects doing that work. He was primarily interested in posttensioning, pretensioning, prefabrication. That's what he worked on, that was his specialty, and he did not go out and seek advice on those matters. He didn't feel he had to. So being a team player—

Is a matter of what kind of a team we are talking about. It can relate to organization or business management, but it can also relate to the content of the work.
Yes. Organization-wise, he was a consultant for organizations and for other people. But he didn't need any organization for himself. He wasn't building up a company, he was consulting on something very specific that he did not need assistance with.

Computers were coming in and people would say, *We'll give you a computer, use our computer.* And he'd say, *For what? What program do you have that does what I do?* There were no programs out there. ... Now there are programs for finite element analysis, etc. You can do a lot of things. But they weren't there initially. You may have a computer, but if you don't have a program, what do you do with it?

They would have needed him to develop the programs.
Exactly. And that was not his interest. If he had been interested, he probably could have programmed and come up with a design. But he had his own method of doing things, and he was very comfortable in that and very good at that. He did not feel he had to change, necessarily.

I've got the impression he really loved his work.
I remember one of the big contractors in New York, George Fuller, came in and wanted to do a concrete building in New York. They were in competition with a steel building and wanted to do a bid to see if concrete would even be economical. I think it was a 72-storey structure or something like that. My father sat down on Friday evening and had the whole thing sketched out by Monday. It was an apartment building that they wanted to just bid on. It did not get built. The point of that story is that he would actually sit down and engineer it. He did all the design, showed how to build it. And you probably could have built it from those drawings. I mean, he had nice, nice drawings and a layout for the contractor. The contractor just couldn't believe it. They asked him for a consultation to see if it could be done. And he gave them a whole set of drawings done over the weekend! He worked on it the whole time. He enjoyed it so much. When he found a project he enjoyed, he would just work on it. And often he didn't ask for any money. It was a boost of energy for him. If he liked the project, he would work on it. It was a challenge for him. And he wanted to come up with a solution that wasn't necessarily an ordinary solution. He wanted to come up with a solution that was unique [and appropriate for the building].

One of the parking facilities of the National Airlines at the Miami International Airport

Kimbell Art Museum during construction

He was interested in finding innovative solutions to take structural engineering further in its development.
The Merchants Refrigerating Co. had buildings that were basically not performing. The buildings were going through such big temperature changes. So [for their new cold storage design] he used posttensioning [see pp. 50–53; 180–183]. With the tie rods and other elements, the building would expand and come back together [as temperature changed] like the little man doll that you would play with when we were young. You push a button on the bottom and the little doll collapses, then you let go and it springs back. With that project he made enough money—because he solved a difficult problem for them—to build his house in Upper Montclair. By the way, the local planning department didn't want him to build that house because the site is on a heavy slope. They said that's not a buildable site. But he showed them the plans and they approved it. His was the first house on that street section.

I was in the office when the Kimbell came in [in 1968, see pp. 268–285]. He came back from Philadelphia, very excited, saying, *They're going to do a museum, the Kimbell, and Lou Kahn would like to have a cycloidal roof shell.* He explained to me what a cycloid was, that by rolling a ball you can trace the line a point made [as the ball made a full rotation]. He said, *Okay, calculate the section properties for me, for the cycloidal arch.* That was my first assignment for the Kimbell. I came up with some numbers for him, just so that he could actually put them in his own calculations. Then we talked about the cycloid. It was obvious that you can't have a thin section [at the base of the cycloid], it's just not going to work. So he modified it but tried to keep the overall feeling of a cycloid. When he did it, it was very clear how to deal with the posttensioning cables—he just looked at the shells as big beams. He figured out how to hold it all up.

Dad also said that many thought that, because the skylight was at the top of the vault, it could not be done. They thought that the shells acted on the cross section like a classic barrel vault. In that case, yes, the skylights would not have been possible. But they didn't realize that the shells could be analyzed longitudinally. An engineer is always looking at the shorter span as the more efficient. Most things are figured out based on the shorter span. But with the Kimbell, you had to look at the longer span. In fact, it was the shape of the cycloid shells that made the design efficient. For this building, the long span worked really, really well. In addition to the posttensioning, of course. All this, combined, was not the result of ordinary engineering thinking. Dad also wanted to be economical with material in order to manage with as little concrete as possible. This can be seen in the mechanical ducts between the shells. And he didn't want to hide them—he was interested in showing how the structure works. He was very interested in being able to see what the structure looks like so the viewer could understand how it carries loads. I know that when he designed Vierendeel trusses, for example, he determined the dimensions of the elements and said, that's it. Just this much and no more!

The usual story with the Kimbell is that architect Marshall Meyers proposed, and together with Louis Kahn, designed the cycloids, and then Komendant helped to figure out how they would actually stand.
Well, sure. They wanted the cycloid, that's where the architecture comes in. They come up with the initial concept. It was kind of like, is this possible? This is what we'd like to do. Can we do it? And then my dad would figure it out and say, yes, you can do this or that. So, in that sense, yes, the architects, came up with the primary design, no question about that. But without my dad figuring out how to build it, they wouldn't have this building. That's the thing.

Construction site of the Kimbell Art Museum. August Komendant and the museum director Richard F. Brown *(left)* with a foam board for the floor slab structure, 1970

What would you say was the most important part August Komendant contributed to the Kimbell project?
The long spans, the cycloid shells, and the skylights up at the top. He really liked the skylight a lot. He worked on that to make it work and enjoyed doing it. He also modified the end condition slightly. It's not a true cycloid, it sort of stops being a cycloid at its support conditions. And it's a really long span—100 feet [30.5 m]. What he liked about it is the slenderness of it. It's not massive, and he used the shape to make the structure work. Often times it's easier to design a beam, because you've got certain properties for it. But to put the posttensioning cables into that beam and have it work as a beam when it's actually a curved structure? Not everybody would be able to do that, to visualize how those cables go in. And that's what he was very good at, he could visualize the forces in a structure. He could visualize what was required, and he put the posttensioning cables where they were needed. To actually analyze this is a really difficult problem. Nowadays, you do a finite element analysis. So yes, that's a typical posttensioning shape, but to fit it into the structure and have it all working correctly and work with the architecture is [a challenge]. These cables have to curve on that curved surface and produce the result you want.

It's a double-curve structure, a three-dimensional structure.
Exactly. It's a three-dimensional design, because the cables are curving in one direction and the "arches" are curving in the other. He understood that really well.

What's interesting to me is that Dad thought of these shells, supported only on four corner columns, as longitudinally acting structures all along, unlike the architects [for whom the cross section seemed important]. It was immediately clear to him what to do. There is a lot of talk that it's a nice building and all. But it was Dad who figured out how it was possible. Kahn didn't know how to do that. Architects initially had many types of columns [along the edges of the cycloids], for example.

He also made several other corrections. He pointed out that light should enter between the sections [cycloid shells and walls] of the building. And as far as I know, this is the first time he used the polystyrene foam-filled floor slab. I remember that when the builder started to pour the concrete, the foam blocks lifted up. [Laughs] Then they called Dad in panic, what do we do? This can't be done! So, Dad told them that they first needed to press the foam down [with some concrete on top] so that it doesn't lift.

Did the use of foam blocks help save material or was there another reason to use them?
The main reason was the weight of the structure. The spans were long. Waffle slabs are often used, which have an open underside, with concrete ribs visible. The perpendicular ribs under the concrete slab make the structure stronger, providing a better moment of inertia. But if you have a concrete slab both above and below the ribs, they form a kind of system similar to wide-flange beams together with the ribs, which is much stronger and more efficient. He filled the gaps between the ribs with foam blocks and placed posttensioning cables inside the ribs. That's what made the large spans possible. It was no longer necessary to support such a great [self-weight] load. The resulting design had a very efficient section. Ultimately, such a ceiling was also cheaper because the total floor slab didn't require as much concrete. Dad probably didn't develop this type of structural approach himself, but he used it because it was innovative.

Another thing he was really good at when designing structures was that he visualized how they would move or how they would absorb energy. A lot of his designs were based on the understanding of how a building moves. Engineers come up with formulas and make things simple for themselves. And they come up with simple formulas for simple problems. But to understand how a building works, he always thought about how it moved, and what was required to handle it. That's

Precast concrete elements on the construction site of the Richards Medical Research Laboratories

where the posttensioning came in. When you have something that's very rigid, it absorbs force. When you have the cables and tie rods in there, they can extend, but not if they're locked in, so he always had [non-bonded] extensions in there so that the building could actually move in case of an earthquake or wind forces and temperature changes. He had a good knowledge of the energy. That's an important element that a lot of people probably don't realize.

To put it simply, he considered structures as dynamic entities.
Correct. Nowadays, you can do all sorts of analysis through the finite element analysis [using simulation software]. But when he was doing these buildings, before computers, engineering was about trying many solutions, and when you finally got one that worked, that was the design! But he also looked at the energy. He may have tried different things, but he was always realizing that the building has to resist dynamic forces and absorb the energy when forces are placed upon it. That energy has to be absorbed. So, how do you absorb it and how do you transmit it, and how does the building come back to its original position? He had an intuitive sense, and if you look at his calculations, he actually does some energy calculations.

In the case of his most important collaborations with Louis Kahn, people sometimes point out a development curve from Richards to Salk to Kimbell to characterize how the relationship between architecture and engineering becomes more and more organic and symbiotic from one project to the next. Do you agree that the Kimbell is the most refined collaboration between your father and Louis Kahn?
Yes, I agree. The Kimbell is more complete than Salk in the sense that you can see how the building is constructed. Salk is technically at least as sophisticated, but you don't see the structure, the Vierendeel trusses, of the mechanical floors. What is visible in Salk in structural terms is relatively ordinary. There is nothing visible to the eye to say that it is structurally unusual. Just the shape and execution of the building are very beautiful. In other words, Salk as a building does not talk about how it stands up, but the Kimbell does and therefore also stands out more.

Why do you think the Richards Medical Research Laboratories building [see pp. 50–52; 150–165] is important?
I was a student at the University of Pennsylvania at the time and saw it being built out of my dorm room window. What made it interesting was building it from precast concrete elements. They put them all together nicely, repeatedly used similar elements, and tied them together by posttensioning. In the American context, precast concrete construction was not yet widespread at that time. And of course, Kahn's design—it looked very elegant, not just a box! [Laughs] I knew right away it would be a famous building. It was in the air; people were talking about it.

I remember he was already giving lectures at Penn with Lou Kahn at the time. Every other Friday afternoon. During the first year, we didn't socialize much, but in the second and third years, I spent more time with my father and sometimes went to dinner with him and Kahn. I happened to be in downtown Philadelphia with Dad when we heard that President Kennedy had been murdered [Friday, November 22, 1963]. As a student, I could have been up to something other than hanging out with my father on Friday nights, but I liked being with him. He usually stayed at the Benjamin Franklin Hotel, and sometimes we dropped by Kahn's office and went out to dinner. Thinking back, I could have spent a lot more time with him. And I could have taken a picture with Kahn! [Laughs] One day they started talking about a project over dinner and drawing plans for it on a paper tablecloth at the restaurant. They drank vodka and made drawings. I should have kept that piece of paper! [Laughs]

Concrete service towers of the Salk Institute

He was also initially involved in Kahn's Dhaka project, wasn't he?
He was there, he worked on it, early on. What happened in Dhaka was that Juhan Liiband went there as Dad's representative on-site for about six months. But that project was more about brickwork, and Dad said there wasn't enough engineering of the kind that interested him. It is the largest, most beautiful building they have in Bangladesh.

What makes the Salk Institute [see pp. 194–211] special to your mind?
Two things. The quality of the concrete, especially how it looks—Dad played a big role here. And then the long-span Vierendeel trusses. What first strikes the eye is the beautiful design by Kahn, but for me, the beauty is mainly in the quality of the concrete. If the concrete wasn't up to scratch, the building wouldn't be particularly special. It would be interesting, but not very good. Dad explained how they did it [the long spans and open floor space laboratories] using posttensioned trusses. All of the building elements are so clean that it's just great to look at. And then he also considered that the building had to move, and used elastic joints. If there's an earthquake, the building can move. The posttensioning cables will pull the structure back into shape.

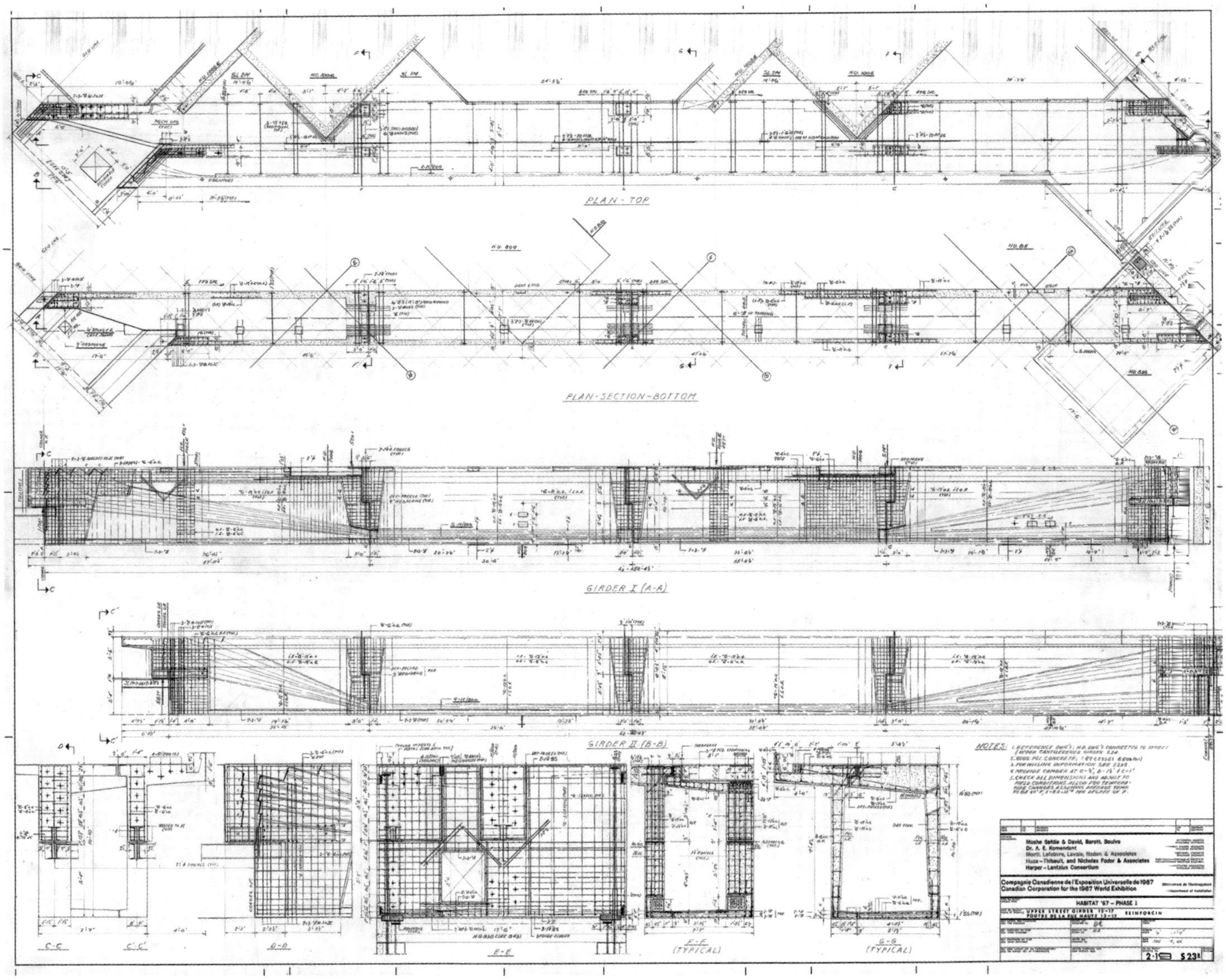

August Komendant. Upper street girder of Habitat '67, drafted by Helmi Aren, 1966

Vierendeel trusses are not widely used in the US. He studied these and other types of trusses back in Europe—he was well acquainted with this technology. I saw him design Vierendeel trusses for other projects; I saw how he calculated and put them together. The only thing he had to study when designing a truss was the diagonal ties—whether one diagonal tie should be used or if more were needed. He wasn't sure [of the number] at first because shear transfer had to be considered. Static calculations show how large the diagonals need to be and whether two or three are needed.

Olivetti [see pp. 258–267].
The Olivetti factory was under construction when I was working for my father. I didn't get very involved in the project, but we went to the construction site several times—at the beginning, when the formwork was being built, and when the reinforcement and posttensioning cables were installed. Dad told the contractor that the concrete would have to be poured from the bottom [of the shells] up, but for some reason they wanted to pour it from the top [of the shells] down. What happened was that when they started posttensioning, the concrete broke behind the anchoring because there was honeycombing in the concrete behind the plates [resulting from the contractor's choice of casting the concrete from the top downward]. Then Dad went down there and had to show them how to fix it. Dad didn't say, I told you so. But the contractor now saw that pouring from above could cause honeycombing.

Dad usually specified all the concrete mixes himself. He was no ordinary engineer—he was interested in how the concrete would look, how it would feel. It wasn't just about saying this is a "five-[cement]-bag mix" or a "six-bag mix." He put a lot of thought into the quality of the concrete. However, there was a problem with the concrete mix [used for the columns]; the concrete contractor got something wrong there.

Horizontal girders of Habitat '67 contain the mechanicals, and serve as "streets in the air"

The compressive strength of the columns ended up being very low, about 1000 psi [approx. 70,3 kg/cm^2]. They held a big meeting on whether to make concrete collars for the already finished columns or to demolish them altogether. In the end, some were salvaged but some had to be demolished.

The concept for Olivetti was elegant, but unfortunately this elegance was somewhat lost in the construction process. When we were standing on these mushroom-shaped shells during construction—the shells were not yet interconnected at the time—it was a powerful feeling. The structure itself was impressive—large shells on top of single columns. But the effect disappeared when the modules were interconnected and skylights were built in the corners [connecting the shells]. And the elegance of the columns disappeared when they had to be repaired. Naturally, Dad wasn't happy about that! When concrete was added, the columns became visually too thick.

What makes the Philadelphia Police Administration Building, designed with Geddes Brecher Qualls Cunningham [see pp. 67–69; 184–193], special?

I saw the Police building being built because I was at the University of Pennsylvania at the time. Dad came to Philadelphia, and we went to that construction site, too. I saw the building being assembled from precast elements. Dad talked a lot about it. There are curved facades, curved concrete panels. How to put it all together—plus the pretensioning and post-tensioning—is not that easy to figure out! You need to have a good imagination! When you see the result, it seems logical. But initially you have to figure out how it would be possible to build it at all. In that sense, the question *how* is even more important for the structural engineer than the end result.

There were no computers at the time. Everything was done manually; all calculations were done manually. And Dad worked with Helmi to lay out the full-scale curvature—with Helmi leaning out of the window to measure it! [Laughs] You can do some things on paper, but when you try it out one to one in space, you can see for yourself if it really works. Of course, not everything can always be tested at scale. Anyway, Dad was interested in visualizing and exploring how it would really look. In the case of the Police building, it is remarkable how the whole is formed with so few different elements. It was a huge job to come up with it.

It's like a three-dimensional puzzle.

Yes! If you are a good engineer, you must have a good sense of space. This is something that is difficult for many, because all the drawings are two-dimensional. But the buildings are spatial. It is as if you have to be able to look between the drawings—when you look at a two-dimensional drawing, you really need to think three-dimensionally. If you can't do that, it's very difficult. Now modeling is done on computers, of course. You can look at how the different parts of a building fit together. But that was not possible back then.

Do you have any stories to tell about Habitat '67 [see pp. 61–65; 220–243], which was designed in collaboration with Moshe Safdie?
I went there with my father when it was under construction. After that, we went again during the Expo in 1967. During construction, it was very interesting to see the so-called bridges, or horizontal girders that act as "streets in the air," connecting different parts of the building. During construction, the post-tensioning cables for these girders were visible, running along a special [open-sided] duct. As construction was going on, the loads were changing, the duct was open, and you could see what was happening. The builders had to tighten these prestressing cables on an ongoing basis as construction progressed and loads changed. In the end, of course, the duct was closed up. These girders had pretty long spans. They intrigued my father too, as did the way the housing modules fit together. It was interesting for my father to figure this out, to do the static calculations. These things were very difficult to calculate and difficult to execute in terms of construction.

As I mentioned, Dad knew concrete and made his own mixes. He knew how much cement, and what kind, to put in the mix, so that it changes the color and other properties of the concrete. He said that at Habitat, a month or two before the grand opening, one of the precast stairs fell down and broke during installation. They had to fix it, pour new concrete in the gaps. It was important for Dad that it shouldn't be possible to tell it had been fixed, not only in terms of strength, but also in terms of appearance. Dad did different experiments with concrete, heating it to get the same color as the concrete that was already there. It worked. I don't know if this is true, but Dad said no one could tell the difference afterwards! [Laughs] He never panicked about such things. It just had to be done.

Toward the end of his career, your father also worked closely with the Venezuelan architect Oscar Tenreiro, who has admitted that August Komendant played a very important role in his development as a young architect, being like a mentor to him. Their first project, the Caracas bus terminal, was in 1976–1977 [see pp. 298–303].
I believe that Dad gave him confidence and also reassurance that the buildings he designed could be built. That's the impression I have from my father's stories. As a young architect, I would also be happy if an experienced engineer said something like that! He spoke very positively about their projects together.

Dad usually listened to what someone had to offer. He didn't accept every job; it had to be interesting. Ordinary work, just some posttensioned floor slab somewhere—that didn't interest him. If there were long spans, a structure without columns, then he might have been intrigued. [Laughs] It also depended a lot on what he was currently working on. He loved challenges and also people who wanted to take them on. He helped them, often without asking for any money! For example, the design for George Fuller—he made all the drawings without being paid. He just loved to do it. They were astonished when Dad took the drawings to them—they weren't expecting anything, they just wanted to know if the building could be built. And Dad showed them: yes, it can. Here are the drawings! [Laughs]

Oscar Tenreiro said they once talked about the Sydney Opera House (architect Jørn Utzon, structural engineer Ove Arup, 1957–1973). They both respected Arup as an engineer but said that the Opera House is not the best building in terms of its structural integrity and in terms of its relationship to architecture. The building should express its tectonic character and primary function, but the Opera House doesn't do that necessarily—this building is more about effect than tectonics.
I happen to like it myself. It's interesting, totally different. I thought the detailing on it that I saw was pretty good. I like the way it looks. What I understand about it is that the acoustics may not be the best, which is a different issue.

Lou Kahn and my father were on the same page on that, that, when you go into a building, it has to talk to you. You have to feel, you have to know its purpose. When you mentioned that he was not a fan of the Sydney Opera House, I think it was in that vein that I heard him talk about it a little bit. He only mentioned it once or twice. It wasn't a big area of conversation, but he was somewhat critical of it when he talked about it

Do you recall any modern or contemporary buildings that he liked? Were there any favorite buildings he used as examples?
I'm sure there were. I know the Mackinac Bridge in Michigan was something he really wanted to go visit and see what it was like. But as far as other favorite buildings … that was not the type of conversation I typically had with him.

What were the typical conversations you had? You're a professional structural engineer yourself.
When we talked about structures, he talked more about the projects that he was working on. I'll give you an example. Oscar Tenreiro, a relatively young architect at the time [at the end of the 1970s] came over and showed Dad his preliminary drawings. My father would be so fascinated by them! These are the kind of things he talked about. We talked about Lou Kahn's Kansas City building [see pp. 286–289], he talked about how he wanted it built and what his philosophy on that was, and what his thinking on it was, from a structural point of view. But then he was also my father, so we didn't always talk about buildings.

There seems to be a difference between architects and engineers with regard to paper architecture or experimental architecture—spatial ideas not necessarily meant for building,

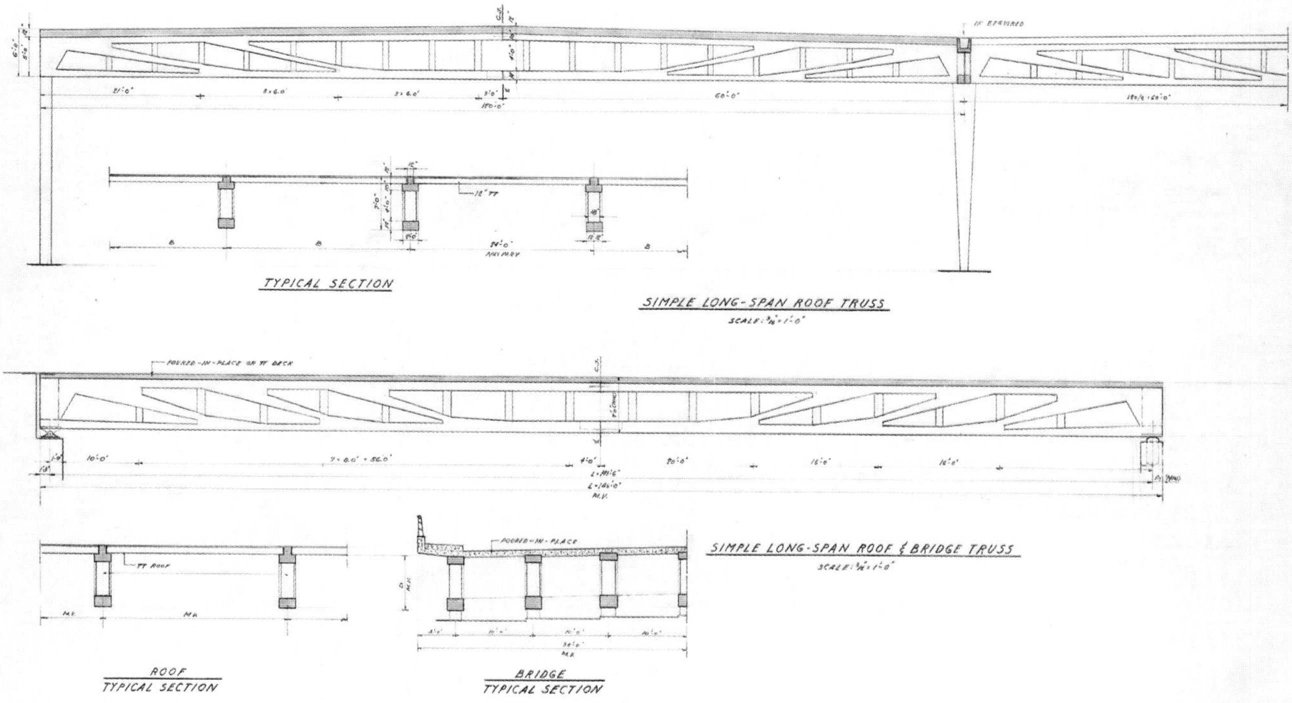

August Komendant. Long-span roof and bridge trusses, with spans of 120′ [36,6 m] and 143′ 6″ [43,7 m], respectively, conceptual design, 1959

but often considered important for testing new approaches. August Komendant, Ove Arup and some other engineers have expressed their doubts with regard to paper architecture or theoretical spatial experiments in general. Their primary interest seems to have been translating architectural ideas into built form almost as if stating that a structural idea is truly valuable only when it has been materialized. Would you agree that your father didn't care about paper architecture and spatial experiments?
No, I would not agree with that. From the late 1950s he had many projects, he was pretty busy, and didn't really have the time. But when he first came to the States he designed bridges, highway bridges, and other structures that were not necessarily meant to be built. If he had a concept of doing something, he would work on it, like he did with the cylindrical dams.

The Sylvenstein Dam with Franz Dischinger in Germany.
Yes. In the US he wrote a couple of papers on dams, and it was more about the possibility of building them than actually doing it. So he did have those interests. He sketched structures that didn't need much architecture. He had unique designs for bridges. … But he would not sketch buildings per se. Once he had a job, he would sketch the different parts of the building, and put his engineering and architectural values into that part. But he wouldn't design the whole structure. When he was working on a project, he did not try to be an architect, but he had an aesthetic value for the structure, and he wanted the structure expressed in the building—and he wanted that structure to be nice! [Laughs]

There's this common stereotype that engineers don't care about how a structure looks. What kind of importance did August Komendant attribute to artistic, aesthetic, architectural values?
I think he cared about space. He cared about the effect that a building has, and he didn't want the structure to interfere, he wanted the structure to contribute. He was very, very conscious about that. When I worked with him, he was always thinking of how it would look. Sure, you need columns, etc. But where you needed structure, he would make it blend in and be part of the whole.

Structural engineers of the modern period often emphasized structural honesty as a principle. Do you agree that August Komendant was one of them?
Yes, 100 percent.

How would you explain structural honesty to a person who doesn't know much about architecture nor about structural engineering?
He wanted a person to feel that the structure was sound by seeing it, giving him a sense of security, not by making it massive but, blending it in and making it beautiful. Not an in-your-face kind of structure. But if you looked at it, you would realize that it is there, it is visible, but it also blends in. He did not try to hide the structure, he was very opposed to putting a facade on a structure and hiding it. That was a great sin for him. He wanted the structure to be there, and he wanted it to be part of it all. He'd be very offended if you hid the load-bearing structure, that would be very offensive to him.

You mentioned that the *how*, rather than the *what*, is often more exciting for a creative engineer.
The architect offers the spatial idea. The engineer offers the structural idea—how it would be possible to build, to put the different components together. Before making the drawings and calculations, Dad had already thought about how the concrete elements would fit together, how the whole system would work. That is the original idea of the engineer. It is only on this basis that the individual components can be developed.

The architect answers the question *what*, while the engineer answers the question *how*.
I would say the architect makes the outward appearance of a person for others to see, while the engineer puts a skeleton inside so that the person can stand up and walk around. [Laughs] An architect can make a gorgeous person, but you need a skeleton inside! The three-dimensional skeleton is vital. This is also evident in the Philadelphia Police building, where he dealt with curved facades and floor panels. When he started designing the individual elements, he already had a clear general solution and therefore knew exactly where to place the posttensioning cables, for example.

The construction sequence must also be taken into account—how and when everything will be done. This directly affects the building's structural design. Even if the contractor is the one who builds it in the end, the engineer has to figure out how to do things and in what order. That was a particular strength of my father's. That's why people came to consult him. He would come up with a general solution very quickly. Static calculations came later.

Interview. Oscar Tenreiro

Oscar Tenreiro Degwitz and Carl-Dag Lige
Alto Hatillo, Caracas, Venezuela
April 17–20, 2018; edited January 6, 2022

Architect Oscar Tenreiro (*right*) visiting August Komendant at his office, ca. 1980

Carl-Dag Lige: How did you discover August Komendant as a potential structural consultant for your projects?
Oscar Tenreiro: How did Dr. Komendant appear on the scene? I had seen and partially read his book, *18 Years with Architect Louis I. Kahn* [1975]. The reason? Lou Kahn was a very admired architect at the time, universally. I also ran into a review of this book in *Progressive Architecture*, which started with a quote, *No architect is a hero for his engineer.* Then I read the book and said to myself, well, this is the kind of person I need for my project. That was the Caracas bus terminal [see pp. 289–303].

Dr. Komendant's relationship with Kahn seemed very important to me because it placed Kahn not as an idol but as a partner. I felt there was something important going on between them. So I called him. He asked me to send a letter, and that is how it started. Then I sent him the bus terminal model and visited him in New Jersey to talk about the project. That was my first encounter with him, in the fall of 1976.

For the terminal, I had the idea of using a steel structure. But he didn't like to work with steel, he wanted to do it in concrete. That was his material. We did the proposal, but it didn't become a project. The government changed, and the proposal didn't progress.

A little later you developed the K-System Apartment Building [see pp. 304–309].
I thought [Louis Kahn's] Kansas City Office Building [see pp. 286–289] was such an interesting concept in terms of form, in terms of the liberation of the ground floor and in terms of construction technology. I said to Dr. Komendant, *Why don't we apply similar principles to an apartment building?* He said, *Okay, let's do it.* He came here [to Caracas] and we went to meet a local German engineer, Johannes Johanson, the best structural engineer we had in Venezuela. Dr. Komendant explained the project to him. Johanson had many doubts about it—corrosion for example. When we left, Dr. Komendant said, *Well, he's a conservative guy.* [Laughs] But together with him we continued to develop the project. I didn't pay him a dollar for it. He did it for fun. The project was meant to be built here [in Venezuela] on Margarita Island. Dr. Komendant joined this project without knowing if it was possible to build it or not. He even went to Miami once to introduce the project, and paid for his own trip. I paid for his trips to Caracas, though. He liked it here.

When did August Komendant visit Caracas?
He came to visit in 1976, 1981 and 1983. His last trip was for the Plaza Bicentenario when it was being built, in August 1983. Before that, in 1976, he came for the Pandock project to talk to its manager and engineers. But that project didn't go any further either. He also came for the National Gallery [GAN] project in 1981, to meet my structural engineers Martin Meiser, a German, and Andres Prypchan, a Ukrainian.

In hindsight, and despite the fact that it remained on paper, the National Gallery or GAN [see pp. 312–323] project in Caracas stands out as, arguably, your most important collaboration with August Komendant. What made this project significant?
The GAN was conceived as part of the master plan for the Parque Cultural [Park of Culture]—an initiative to revitalize public areas and build new cultural institutions in the proximity of the Presidential Palace, Palacio de Miraflores. I received the commission. It was supposed to be a sequence of public spaces, something for the people. It is an interesting part of the city, with a great potential as a link between the low

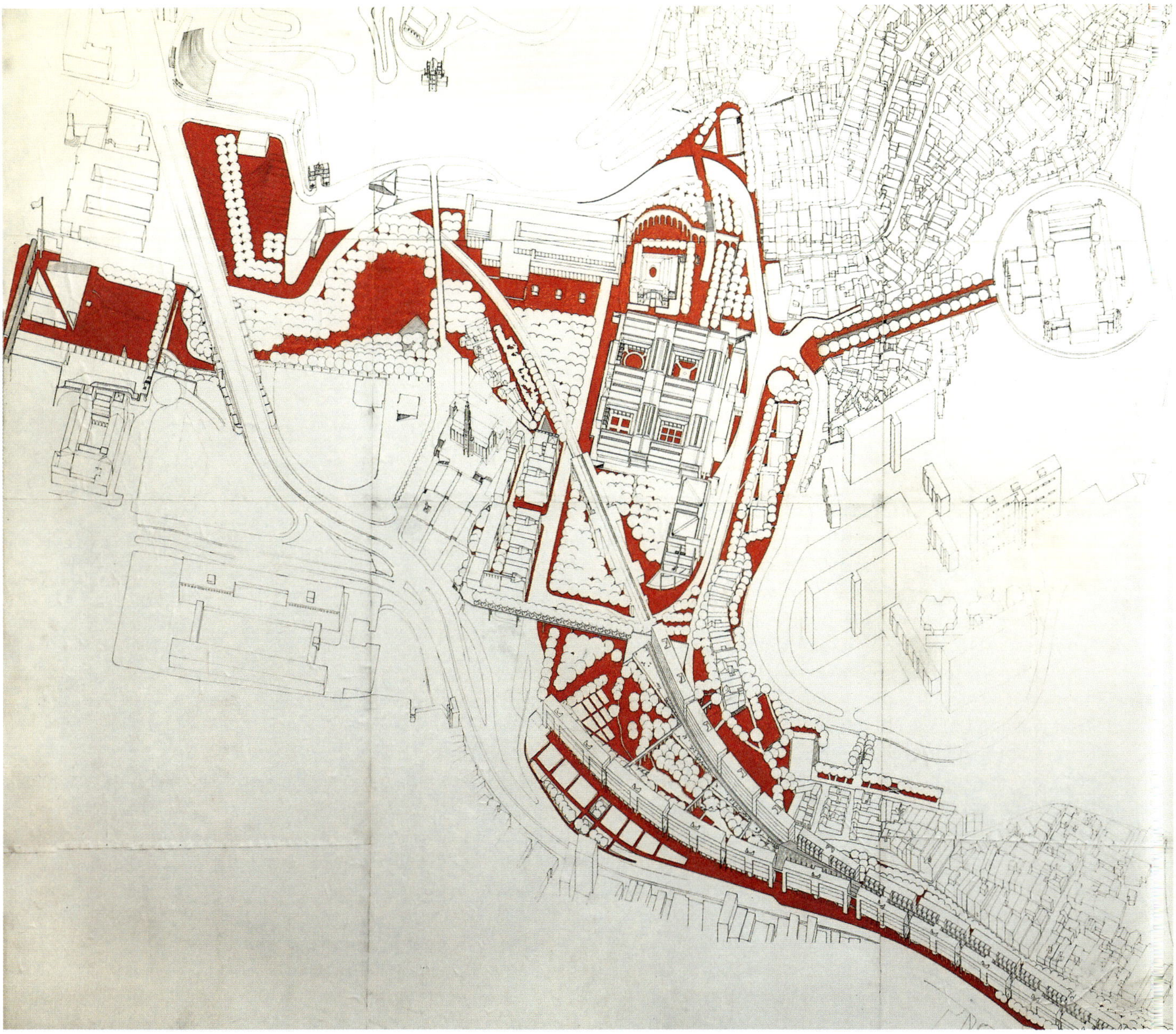

Office of Oscar Tenreiro. The Park of Culture master plan, Caracas, with the Plaza Bicentenario on the left edge, and the National Gallery (GAN) with its four patios in the middle

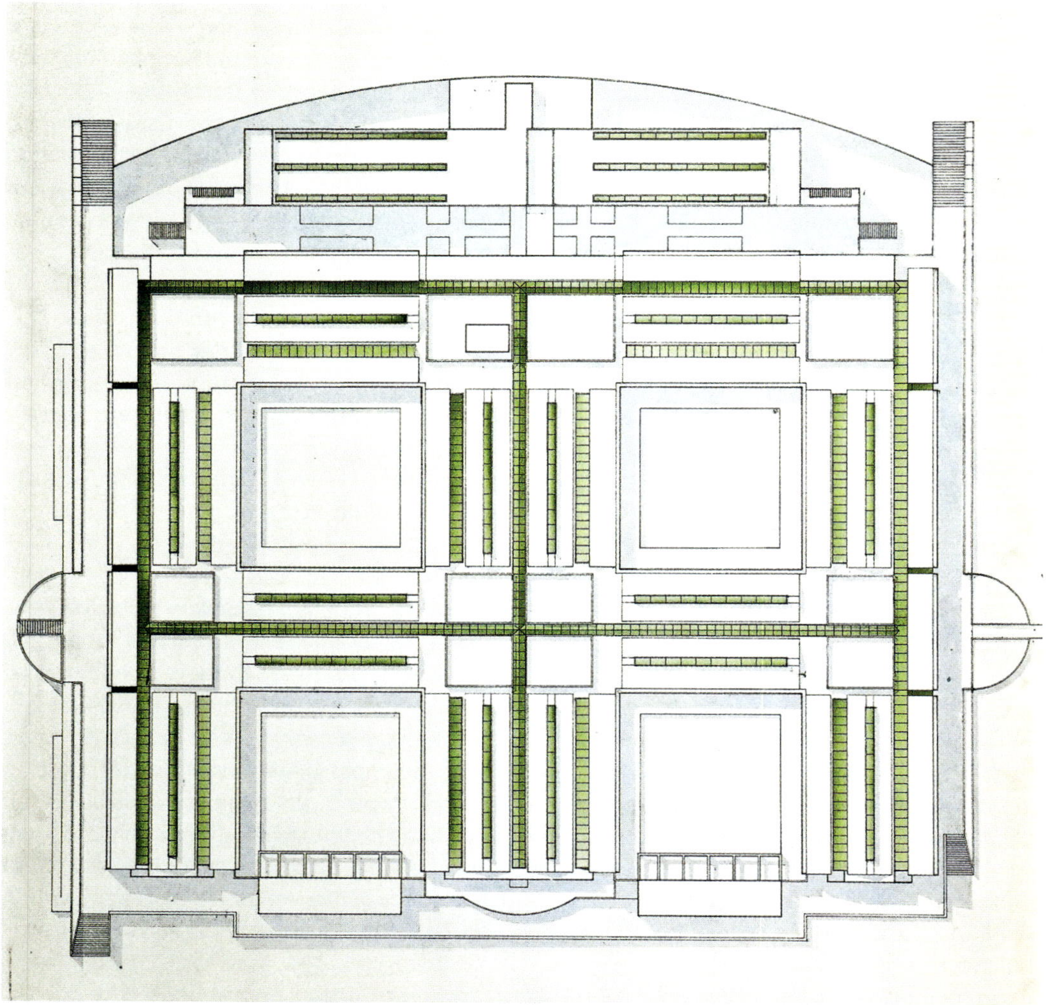

Office of Oscar Tenreiro. National Gallery site plan, preliminary version

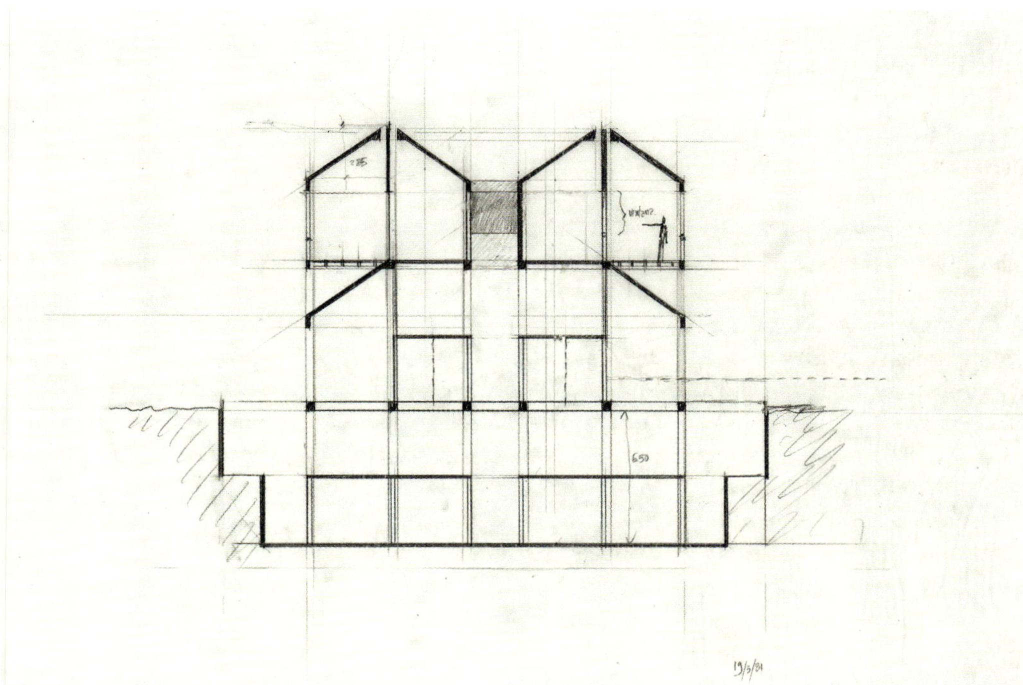

Oscar Tenreiro. National Gallery section sketch of the folded plate structure, 1981

income area to the west and the historic city center. Today it is partially abandoned and even dangerous to visit due to the current political and social context.

When I was starting with the GAN project, I called Dr. Komendant. He asked me to send some drawings. Sketching the sections was very important. We were exploring the structural ideas from the early stages of the project. My initial idea was to use concrete shells similar to Louis Kahn's Kimbell Art Museum [see pp. 268–285], but to turn them upside down, fill with dirt and have a garden on top. Dr. Komendant said that this type of structure would need ribs, and would be too expensive and heavy. He suggested to turn them around or, alternatively, try folded plates instead of curved shells, and that is what I did. That was the key moment for this project.

I told [my structural engineer] Martin Meiser that we had to go see the Kimbell Art Museum because the principle of the [GAN] structure as well as the proportions of the exhibition areas and other design starting points were directly inspired by that building. We first went to visit Dr. Komendant in New Jersey, and from there we went on to see the Kimbell [in Fort Worth, Texas]. We stayed in Dallas for three or four days [and visited the Museum in Fort Worth]. Meiser examined the structure in all its details.

One important structural aspect of the GAN was that the posttensioning cables within the folded plates were to be nonbonded, they would have been placed in plastic tubes with a special grease inside instead of cylindrical metal hose-like ducts. The sections of the gallery wouldn't have allowed ducts because there wasn't enough space for them. In Venezuela, we had never used this kind of cable. It was a new technology. Dr. Komendant was familiar with it. So he thoroughly instructed our local engineers.

Architecturally, the idea of using courtyards or patios immediately strikes the eye. It feels modern and traditional at the same time.

It is curious, Kenneth Frampton was visiting Caracas for a lecture, and I asked him to help with the GAN project. He was always nice, for a British guy. [Laughs] He was relaxed. And he made some sketches that I still have. We talked about the patios. His participation was important because he underlined the importance of having patios, a characteristic tropical architectural element: to have at least one. In the final version we have four.

To have a symmetric structure was in many ways influenced by Kahn's architecture. That's an important aspect of Kahn's architectural legacy—how he treated the organization of a building. The concept of served and servant spaces, to which Dr. Komendant also often referred, was very influential. Before Kahn, this idea wasn't in the "lexicon of modern architecture." It's technical, it's not poetical. In terms of philosophy, it's more about knowledge than metaphysics. I've always kept the idea of served and servant spaces in my mind. It is influential even today. Who discovered it? Lou Kahn.

The idea of using patios is related to the typology of hospitals, military ensembles, monasteries, etc., it comes from architectural history. Apart from that, and as I said before, the basic exhibition unit was taken from the Kimbell. The light concept was also very important: to let natural light into the building. I believe that the design concepts used in this museum, with its patios, controlled natural light, natural ventilation in distribution-circulation areas, etc., had some originality about them, but the project's potential to receive wider international appreciation was never realized because it wasn't built.

How did you get the commission to design the GAN?

At the time I had access to higher [Venezuelan] authorities. I knew the president [Luis Herrera Campins]. He had an adviser, the Governor of Caracas, Enrique Pérez Olivares, an intelligent and cultured person, who helped me get the commission, because he was aware that if they could build this museum, it would be the beginning of a larger urban development providing badly needed public space in the very center of the city.

I presented our design at the National Gallery with all the employees attending. The director was very helpful and supportive. And I was happy because it promised to be the beginning of something very significant, if realized. I think that the GAN is one of the most accomplished projects that I have done.

William Niño was the most active architectural critic in Venezuela at the time. He wrote a very positive article about our project. Everybody seemed happy, except other architects—jealousy is always present among architects—that was the worst part of the experience. Many of them resented that such a young person as I was—aged 42—had such an important commission.

Wasn't there a tradition of organizing architecture competitions for large public buildings in Venezuela?

Architectural competitions have a difficult tradition in Venezuela. In this case that was not even suggested. Sometime after the completion of our project, with the new government, an art critic, Bélgica Rodríguez, was appointed Director of the National Gallery. She knew a lot about art, but she didn't like her office to be in a sector of the city to be renovated. She didn´t view the idea of Parque Cultural positively. So the location became one of the problems I had to deal with. But the architectural concept didn't get much critique. I think there was a sort of consensus that it was a good project.

The Park of Culture master plan included two other public buildings designed by you and on which August Komendant consulted—the Teatro del Oeste dance theater [see pp. 328–333] and the Plaza Bicentenario public square next to the Presidential Palace [see pp. 334–341].

Teatro del Oeste was to be located next to the GAN. Construction started, but the theater was never finished. Another building close by—the School of Arts, designed by my brother Jesús Tenreiro and Henrique Hernández—also remained on paper because with the new President the political situation changed completely. That always happens in Venezuela: political ups and downs continuously.

Office of Oscar Tenreiro. Plaza Bicentenario, gallery section, with the historic Presidential Palace, the Palacio de Miraflores top left

Plaza Bicentenario after the completion of the first construction phase

Plaza Bicentenario was in fact the genesis of the whole operation of Parque Cultural. It was designed and built to commemorate the second centenary of Simón Bolívar's birth. He was born on June 24, 1783. I thought of creating a place where you experience a feeling of the past. That was the idea for the plaza and especially for the public building on its southern side: The Gallery of Reminiscence. Unfortunately, with the new government, only the first phase was completed. There was a very improvised opening in January 1983, after which the new administration, which took over in March, left it abandoned until mid-1984.

The Plaza Bicentenario is three buildings in one: the Gallery of Reminiscence, the parking garage with the public plaza on top of its roof, and a service building for the Presidential Palace. All of its structure is posttensioned concrete. The parking garage has spans of 24 meters—three spans, 72 meters in total—interconnected with posttensioning cables and using elastic joints to provide earthquake resistance. When we started posttensioning, one of the nodes between the beams and the columns broke. I invited Dr. Komendant over from New Jersey. He explained to our engineers and builders what to consider and how to prepare the posttensioning process. Everything went well after that.

How would you describe Dr. Komendant on a construction site?
Oh, he knew how to behave! He tried to connect with the workers, with simple workmen, but they didn't understand him [because they didn't speak English]. He always said that when he went to Lou Kahn's construction sites everybody loved him. But when the architects of Kahn's office came, nobody wanted to talk to them. [Laughs]

We had a small party at my house, Dr. Komendant was staying here. My elder brother Jesús, a well-known Venezuelan architect, was a good talker. With Dr. Komendant they started talking about religion and philosophy. That's when I heard him speak about Steiner. Dr. Komendant was sympathetic to Rudolf Steiner, one of the leading figures of anthroposophy. That is the only hint I had about his philosophical background.

This is surprising, because he always seemed to be more of a science person.
I don't know much about anthroposophy, but I know that it was important to him. He talked freely about his way of seeing things after a couple of drinks. He always recalled their "firsts", drinks that is, with Lou Kahn on the back terrace of Dr. Komendant's New Jersey home where they engaged in long conversations.

Dr. Komendant usually wanted to "fill the room." He had strong ideas about everything, but he wasn't aggressive when he spoke. He also liked to listen, even though he wouldn't change his opinion. I remember them [Dr. Komendant and Jesús] that day on my terrace. My brother, in the same manner as Kahn, talking about "stratosphere" philosophy, and Dr. Komendant insisting on seeing things in a practical way. Nevertheless, they had an enjoyable conversation.

He was so proud of being an Estonian. As was Kahn, even though he was three years old when he came to the United States. The fact that they were from Estonia created a sort of bond between them. Dr. Komendant had this [special] feeling about Estonia. But he was not alienated [despite being an émigré]. His pipe was terrible, though, because he had it with him all the time. [Laughs] Everything smelled of his tobacco. Even our car after we went out together.

August Komendant seems to have been very certain about his competence. He didn't speculate, but proposed, what was in the scope of his knowledge.
Dr. Komendant had the knowledge of how to build. He wanted a good structure with good details. He was a constructor. We, architects, sometimes focus too much on details. But he was different—realistic, pragmatic—and I liked him for that. I also tend to choose the more practical way and not get lost in details. Perhaps that was something that I shared with him. He became a friend and that's why he helped me. He charged me only a fraction of his real fees, because he wanted to help. For me it was a once in a lifetime experience. I learned a lot.

Dr. Komendant's and Kahn's office had a sort of artisan way of working, like an atelier. You don't have that in the United States [nor many other countries] anymore. And that kills architecture. Let's take [the British architect] Norman Foster, he is a very good architect, successful, important etc. But presently he has transformed himself into a corporation. Also [the Italian architect] Renzo Piano, all very talented people, but what have they got to tell us? The buildings might be powerful. They rely heavily on the high-tech industry—everything is stainless steel, glass surfaces, complex geometry etc. Frank Gehry is the epitome of this phenomenon. I recognize talent. But it's a dead end. Zaha Hadid may be in paradise now, but her last building in New York, next to the High Line, is just something to run away from, completely decadent.

Is theory important for architecture as a discipline?
I don't like philosophizing about architecture. It gets you nowhere. Le Corbusier said it clearly, *I am out of any philosophical intention*. Kahn's "philosophy" was poetry. That made a lot more sense. He didn't want to establish knowledge but to suggest and make you think. He wanted to convey a sort of feeling about things.

I don't think there is a theory of architecture, there is no such thing. There cannot be a theory of painting or writing music, or whatever art you are talking about. What you can do is think, and maybe build a body of concepts. But you can't make a theory of architecture.

For you, theory needs to be something which is coherent, logical and applicable?
I have a strong connection with [Ludwig] Wittgenstein's philosophy. I've been influenced by him. What he praises about philosophy is the possibility that through language it is possible to clarify some phenomena. But he denies the possibility of knowledge through philosophy.

Wittgenstein has an inspiring essay, where he speaks about a sense of wonder.[1] Through language, and maybe through architecture and art, it is possible to create these special situations or atmospheres where one may perceive a sense of wonder. Architects and artists cannot have the final word or the final truth, but they can help a wonder to emerge.
I agree. Talking and thinking about architecture help put the focus back on architecture itself and create that wonder. I am very much for a poetic way of describing or talking about architecture.

Did August Komendant speak about Louis Kahn?
He did, many times, always in terms of his friendship. He felt a little painful because they broke up for a period. But then they made up and worked on the Olivetti factory [see pp. 258–267] and other projects. The concept of Olivetti was very interesting, the idea of concrete "umbrellas." The idea of paraboloid umbrellas was in the air all around the world because of Félix Candela and others. The problem was that it became a mannerist approach. But Kahn did something different [with the Olivetti design] and he needed Dr. Komendant's help.

The only thing that Dr. Komendant criticized was Kahn's speculation on forms, like the Dhaka project, in which I think Dr. Komendant was right. But, at the same time, he had difficulties accepting that Kahn's explorations with forms made a great contribution to architecture—this approach became very influential as a consequence of Kahn's work. Kahn started the exploration of ancient forms; he went into the past to see the meaning of the immense vaults in Rome and elsewhere. He opened a window. In that sense, Kahn was modern, in the best sense of the word.

Modern doesn't need to be a bad word, by now it is part of our history. We are rooted in what they did in the beginning of the twentieth century. In Venezuela, a country full of contradictions—you could say a crazy place in the world—as in most of Latin America, modernity is the basis of contemporary culture. When I entered the School of Architecture in Caracas, it was, in many ways, the beginning of architecture here [in Venezuela]. Modern architecture was something natural for me.

Kahn was among the representatives of a different type of modernist architecture. There's the idea of zeitgeist, being aware of your own time, but without demanding the tabula rasa, like the more radical modernists did. On the contrary, in Kahn's case you have to be very conscious of the previous layers of culture.
Kahn had the conditions, he could open that window, and he gave a lot of meaning to research. He wasn't paralyzed by the influence of the stylistic approach to modern architecture [prevalent in the Anglo-American context]. At that time [in the 1950s and 60s], Le Corbusier had already gone in a different direction, and also Alvar Aalto, who had a sort of independence, with his vodka and everything, stating that he didn't care what the world thinks. *I'm a Finnish guy, I can do whatever I want.* [Laughs]

August Komendant and architect Jesús Tenreiro conversing amicably in the living room of Oscar Tenreiro, 1981

And yet, they were all prima donna architects ...
Sure, I remember one anecdote [the Finnish architect and theorist] Juhani Pallasmaa once told me. Whenever a friend of his group started to work for Aalto, they considered him a lost cause. [Laughs] Nowadays he sees Aalto's importance from a different perspective, obviously.

Did you ever meet Louis Kahn?
I did, in 1969. I came to Philadelphia with the intention to meet him. I took a phonebook and called. His wife Esther answered and said, *He has just returned from India, I will put him on the phone*. Kahn said over the phone, *Come to the office tomorrow, we can have lunch*. So I went with a friend, Venezuelan architect Domingo Alvarez. Kahn came and there were two Argentinian architects, and that was uncomfortable. [Laughs] The Argentinians always want to have the last word.

Kahn gave a small lecture on his ideas. I made some notes, and while the Argentinians kept saying flattering phrases to Kahn, I had some questions, populist questions, like what were the social consequences of this or that. [Laughs] Kahn explained his proposals for Philadelphia, the parking structures etc. When I asked my question, Kahn answered that this is question a Russian would ask! [Laughs] He didn't like it. The other question I had was about his relationship with Le Corbusier. He said, I remember very clearly, *Well, we are different persons, like Haydn and Mozart.* Nothing directly about Le Corbusier. My questions and the Argentinians' behavior created an atmosphere where Kahn didn't want to have lunch with us anymore.

In the same way I met [Jørn] Utzon, in Mallorca. He had a summer house there, a beautiful house. We went to his house impromptu, with no previous appointment. And he was just coming from the beach. He was delighted to talk. We had a very good conversation. He was very warm. That was in

1995 or 1996. We talked about different things. His parliament building in Kuwait, about the Sydney Opera House, about Mallorca, a beautiful island, and other things. Dr. Komendant used to say that in the beginning, the structure of the Sydney Opera House was unbuildable, and that it was the office of the structural engineer Ove Arup, and particularly Peter Rice, who made it possible to build.

You've been in contact with several high-profile modern architects.
I went to see Lúcio Costa in Brazil, twice. And I also had a long conversation with Oscar Niemeyer. He always wanted to talk, with anyone, especially the ladies. [Laughs] It was in 1998. We spoke about Brasília [the federal capital of Brazil] and other things. He made some sketches during the conversation and later gave them to me with a dedication. I still have them. He was a soft Communist. He built a lot, millions of square meters. All he did in Brasília would have been impossible for a European architect to achieve. He did the drawings so rapidly and they built [his designs] quickly, within three to four years. I visited Brasília for the first time in May 1961. It had been inaugurated in 1960.

After graduating I had a Venezuelan scholarship. I went to Chile and then to France. I wanted to work for Le Corbusier in the early 1960s. I went to his office in Paris, but I never met him personally. I wrote a letter and applied for a job, but they had no vacancies. Years later I met José Oubrerie from Le Corbusier's office as a consequence of my interest in the project of the Firminy church. José became a good friend of mine even though I haven't been in contact with him in the last few years. I have a very important, essential, relationship with Le Corbusier's legacy, which I describe in the book on my work recently published in Valencia, Spain.

After returning to Venezuela you established your own practice. How large was your office?
We were three architects: my wife Nubia, Francisco Sesto and myself. Those who were helping were mostly students, and for more than thirty years I had a draftsman, Omar Ladera, who was very, very good. In peak times we were twelve to fourteen people. My main partner for many years was Mr. Sesto whose contribution to our work was very positive. Nowadays he is strongly related to the Venezuelan dictatorship. He became a figure of the revolutionary government. He suffered a dramatic change. Power sent him into the mainstream. I cut all connections with him.

Nubia was always a pillar of the office. And, yes, there was this army of students and young architects helping, a result of my professorship at the School of Architecture for more than thirty years; our office was very near to the School. All of them worked with great dedication. In 1999 I had to close my office because of financial problems, and I came here to establish a home office, which has been very active since then. I brought all my archives here and learned CAD to draw with the computer. Ever since, the dynamics of our work changed completely. This house-office was very active up to 2017–2018 when I built the project of a small hotel for my son Esteban, a structural engineer himself. From then on, no work at all, the Venezuelan crisis has had its word. I focused on writing and organizing my documents for publishing. As a result, a book with the title *Todo Llega al Mar* (*Tout arrive à la Mer*) on my work and thought was published in 2019 by the School of Architecture ETSAV in Valencia, Spain.[2] Currently I am preparing a book to be published in 2022, with my texts written over four decades. They are not *theory,* they are *thinking from and towards architecture.*

1 Ludwig Wittgenstein, "A Lecture on Ethics" (1929), *Philosophical Review 74, no. 1* (1965): 3–12.

2 Tenreiro, Oscar, ed. *Todo Llega Al Mar: Pensamiento y obra del arquitecto Oscar Tenreiro*. Valencia: Ediciones ETSAV, 2019.

Architects on August Komendant

Louis I. Kahn
March 23, 1959

Mr. Eero Saarinen
West Long Lake Road
Bloomfield Hills, Michigan

Dear Eero,

Talking with Dr. August E. Komendant last week, he mentioned that your office had been advised of his special abilities.

Komendant combines unusual knowledge and experience with a thoughtful approach to the design and the actual making of concrete structures.

He is one of the rare engineers qualified to guide the architect to develop meaningful form.

Eero, I admire your work. Often I feel we must meet again and talk about Architecture.

Sincerely,
Louis I. Kahn

A letter from Louis I. Kahn to Eero Saarinen, March 23, 1959, typescript copy. Louis I. Kahn Collection, The University of Pennsylvania and the Pennsylvania Historical and Museum Commission

Louis I. Kahn,
March 13, 1968

[August] Komendant is very sensitive to the nature of structures. The fact that he's an actor and a great performer is of no importance. Every time he approaches the problem, he has a very great manner about it. Though your problems are burning ones, he looks at them as though they just came out of an icebox. But he is a wonderful sensor of the validity of certain structures.

He has a weakness, like all men have, of thinking that he's an architect. But he has a lot to give to architecture.

I don't live in concrete, I don't live in steel, I just sense their potentialities.

But he lives in them. He feels the strain of every member. He knows when a thing is pulling away, or when it's staying at rest. He knows repose very well. He's not worried about symmetry, he's just a great balancer. He feels that the thing is out of balance without analyzing it.

His suggestions, when they are referring to the architectural field, are to be disregarded. But when they are purely from an engineering standpoint, they're completely regarded.

Excerpt from Louis I. Kahn's lecture "The Institutions of Man" at Princeton University, Princeton, New Jersey, March 13, 1968. Transcript published in Richard Saul Wurman, ed., *What Will Be Has Always Been* (New York: Access Press Ltd., 1986), 27.

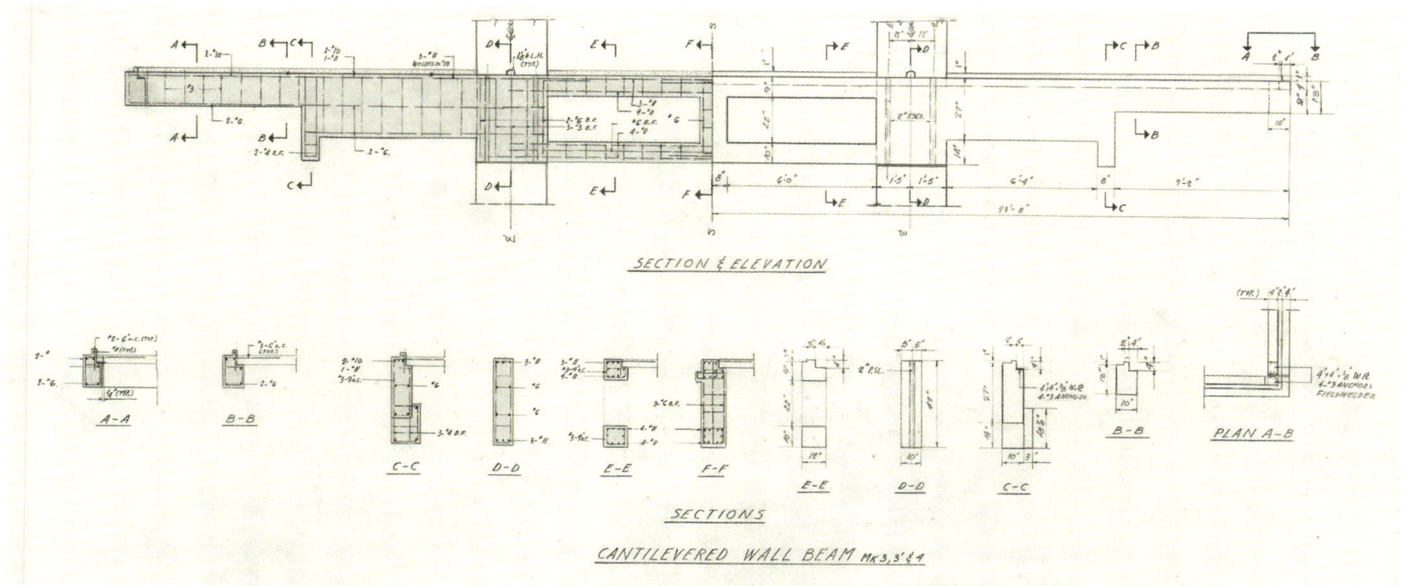

August Komendant. Design for the precast marginal beam of the Richards Medical Research Laboratories, 1958

Installing the precast marginal beams on the construction site of the Richards Medical Research Laboratories

Jaan Holt

September 20, 2019

I met August Komendant while a student at the University of Pennsylvania for my Master of Architecture degree—Dr. Komendant gave a course in Structures and also participated in the master's studio design class. Dr. Komendant was also kind enough to invite me to his residence in New Jersey for several visitations. He spoke Estonian perfectly, and since I spoke it also, we had this automatically in common.

August Komendant was a professional structures engineer, truly knowledgeable about all aspects of structure, especially about concrete structures. He was quite formal but very willing to engage in conversation about the nature of materials and especially concrete.

He was sure of his knowledge and that it was dependable and true—allowing him to undertake efforts that seemed unusual and precise. He believed that reality was not capricious and was a dependable partner in the realization of physical work.

Dr. Komendant loved concrete—and through his deep knowledge, he was able to offer Louis Kahn choices and directions in the use of this material that Kahn would not have had in any other way.

I believe they both realized this after their estrangement over the structure of Salk Laboratories and they therefore reunited—because each saw the other as essential to creating a great work of architecture. August once stated that he "could make concrete better than granite"—he loved this material, and his knowledge was very deep and personal. Without Komendant, there would not have been the Richards Medical Laboratory buildings and the whole professional career of Kahn might have been altered. Their reunion was the realization of the necessity that each felt for the other through love of the finished work. Like Architecture itself—both materiality and poetics are necessary—the measurable must be honored to reach the unmeasurable, and thus August is as essential as Kahn.

I think he realized that the Architect was necessary to complete the partnership that would allow the final result. This is especially true in modern times, when the dance is complex and one individual cannot harbor the entire set of knowledge that needs to be brought to bear—although there must be a conductor of the total set of information, and the architect has played this role. Yet this role of the architect is not a valuation of worth—after all, without any members in the orchestra, there is no realization of the music. I think the reunion of Kahn and Komendant is proof of this reality, the music is the essential thing—both suffered from the loss of the other. It is just like a dance.

They found each other in the realization of Richards Medical Laboratory Buildings on the campus of the University of Pennsylvania—it was the first dance, and it reverberated through the realm of Architecture. Kahn has stated that he discovered the sense of Architecture in Trenton Bath House in New Jersey—but it was the full symphony that was played at Richards Medical Labs. When Kahn and Komendant separated—there was a profound loss to the music that could be played—they both realized this and their reunion was essential for the final work—so much of which was not built; yet is still recognized by the professional world.

At the breakup of the two, when Kahn asked Komendant to alter the structure of Salk and Komendant had already finished the drawings for the folded plates instead of the Vierendeel trusses—Komendant redid the drawings (for free, as far as I know) and stated the Architect had the right to decide, but the Engineer could quit—and that is what happened for a period.[1]

It is profoundly beautiful and a credit to both that they reunited for the achievement of "Architecture as Frozen Music"—as stated by Goethe.

Salk Institute in the final phases of construction

1 Editor's note: There is no indication that Komendant and Kahn had a long-term conflict over the design for the Salk Institute. It was rather the early phases (1964) of the Dhaka project when Komendant decided to cut the strings for a period of time. See August Komendant, *18 Years with Architect Louis I. Kahn* (Englewood, NJ: Aloray, 1975), 80–90.

Service towers and the side facade of the Salk Institute

Ilmar Reinvald
March 7, 2018

I was in Louis Kahn's master's studio at the University of Pennsylvania in 1964–1965, graduating with a degree of Master of Architecture. Dr. Komendant was one of the three other professors that were part of Kahn's studio. The others were Norman Rice, a practicing architect; and Robert Le Ricolais, a French visionary structural engineer.

It was clear to us students that Dr. K was a man of huge accomplishments, particularly in the area of prestressed concrete. He was articulate and very firm in his views relating to engineering and the laws of nature. The impression he left was of his high standard of professionalism and the willingness to pass his knowledge to the students.

One of the areas in concrete construction that Dr. Komendant developed and perfected was the steam-cured finish of precast structural members. This method achieves a very smooth and attractive finish to concrete. To my knowledge, this was first seen in the structure of the Richards Medical Research Building on Penn campus. He was also known for being able to design very efficient structures and structural members with the smallest cross sections, achieving maximum strength.

Once in class he talked about his service during World War II in the German Army as an engineer on the Russian Front.[1] One of his projects was to develop a paving system that can be laid down at a very rapid rate on variable terrain so the German Army can be effective in the Blitzkrieg by moving tanks, etc. into Russia. I have forgotten exactly how fast he said the paving was laid down, but I seem to remember it was something phenomenal in the order of 5–10 km/hr. I suspect the German Reich ran out of materials for this system to be fully operational for the duration of the war.

1 Editor's note: There is no indication that August Komendant ever served the German Army during World War II.

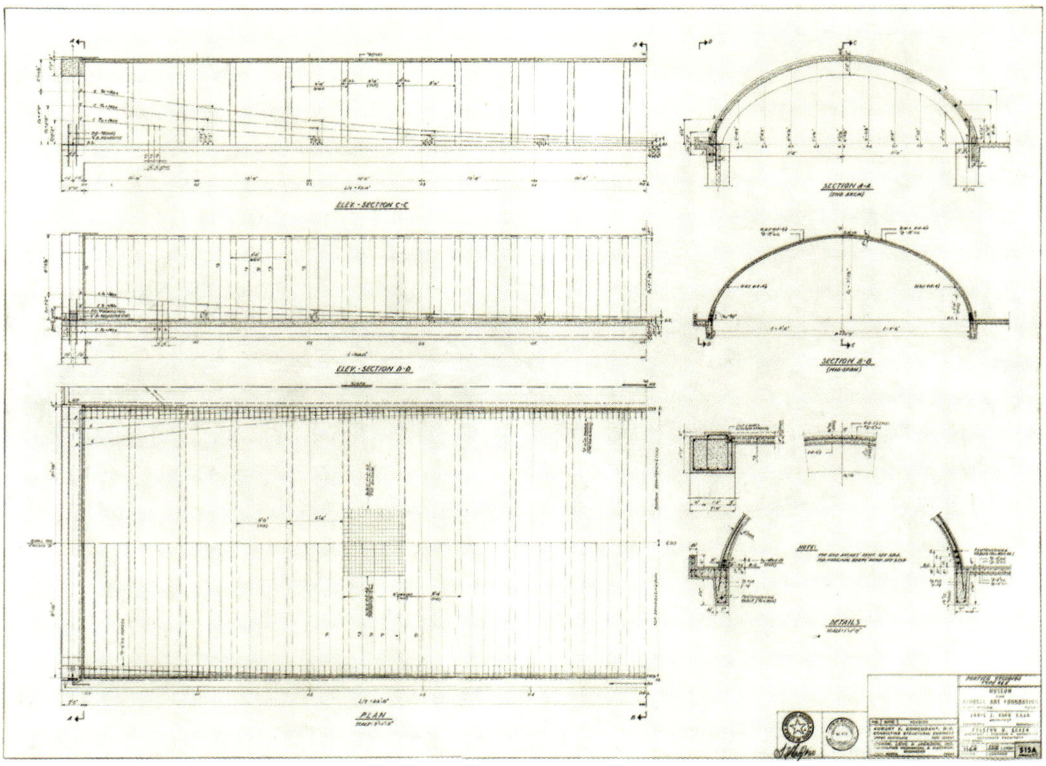

August Komendant. Kimbell Art Museum entrance portico, structure of the cycloid shell, 1970

Frank Sherwood
May 18, 2018

I am ninety-one years old, received a B.S. degree in architectural engineering from the University of Texas at Austin in 1948, joined the firm of Preston M. Geren, Associate Architect with Louis Kahn as project director for the design of the Kimbell Art Museum in Fort Worth in 1969, and since then have had a career consulting with owners in building design and construction.

Not sure of date of first meeting with Komendant, but probably 1970 when Geren agreed to engage Komendant as engineer for the design of the museum's structure from the main floor through the roof. (Geren engineers designed the basement and lower floor.)

Dr. Komendant impressed me as having a strong, assertive personality, with complete self-confidence, and stubborn when his decisions were questioned.

His main accomplishments were his virtual genius in the knowledge of design and to recognize the potential of prestressed concrete, pioneered by French engineer Eugène Freyssinet in 1905, which was still novel in 1969, coupled with his ability to produce complex designs manually, before the age of computers, in a remarkably short time.

He fully recognized the aesthetic quality of Kahn's cycloid concept [for the Kimbell Museum], adding his own improvements to elements such as the shape of the end edge beams with the glass openings.

His professional relationship with Kahn was a genuine friendship, based in the beginning with their mutual birthplace in Estonia.

I was privileged to get to know him through his site visits, when I would convey him and Lou from Dallas Love Field Airport to the building site, and observe his interaction with Tom Seymour, building contractor Thos. S. Byrne's project manager, and with workers on the project.

I treasure his references to me in his book *18 Years With Architect Louis I. Kahn* in which he said:

> *Sherwood was an experienced construction man, inventive and cooperative in many respects. I was regularly informed by Sherwood about what was going on on the site, and he requested my presence when some more complicated work was started or was in progress.*

Kimbell Art Museum entrance portico after completion

Nader Ardalan
August 26, 2019

Of course, Dr. Komendant's reputation as an innovative structural engineer and collaboration with Louis Kahn was world-renowned. In particular, the silvery smooth concrete structures of the Salk Institute and the Kimbell Art Museum that I had personally experienced impressed me greatly.

In 1977 I was in the unique position of being a visiting professor at the Harvard Graduate School of Design, with an office in Boston and major projects contracted from Iran that I thought would interest Dr. Komendant. This emboldened me to have my American office manager place a telephone call to him, introduce me as an international architect who had associated with Kahn in Tehran, and explain the purpose of the call. So when I finally spoke to him, the ground was somewhat set for a serious introductory conversation. From the moment that I heard his friendly, Estonian-English dialect say *Hello*, we commenced a valuable conversation that endured for several years.

I invited Dr. Komendant to Boston to discuss the possibility of his consultation on one or more of the projects that Mandala Collaborative and Mandala International had been commissioned to perform. He chose to take the train from his home in New Jersey to Boston. On the afternoon of our meeting, I went to the South Station Train Terminal in Boston to greet him. Since I had never met him in person, I recognized him from his published photographs, but he looked younger than his photos and more vigorous. Also, I was pleasantly surprised by his kind and gentle, yet direct demeanor. I drove him to his hotel, and we walked to his room, where we had our first long, good conversation.

The conversation allowed me to review my association with Lou Kahn and Kenzo Tange on the Abbasabad City Center Master Plan in Tehran, Iran; Kahn's supportive letter of confirmation to the University of Chicago for the publication of my book, *The Sense of Unity* (1973); and the mutual friendship and collaboration that we shared with Moshe Safdie. Then we got to the heart of our meeting—three world-class projects of national stature in Iran for which I had already developed concept designs, but was waiting for the right person to collaborate with for their innovative structural design and potentially their ultimate, integrated vision.

The first project was the Tehran Center for the Celebration of Music (TCCM), commissioned by the Iran Ministry of Culture, with the focus on the 2,000-seat concert hall, for which the Shah of Iran had selected Maestro Herbert von Karajan to be the musical advisor. The second was the new 100,000-person Nuran-Solar City for the staff and headquarters of the Atomic Energy Organization. The isolated site was located in the valley of two majestic limestone mountains in proximity to the historic, ancient city of Isfahan. The third was the new headquarters of the Mercantile Bank of Iran and Holland, to be one of the first buildings to be built in the new City Center of Tehran, named Shahestan Pahlavi.

From those first in-depth discussions, it became obvious to me that we were going to personally get along fine, that some wonderous architectural creations beckoned to be realized, and that hopefully we would become meaningful friends. Regrettably, the tragic and unexpected Iranian Revolution intervened. Thus, in a short period of about one year from mid-1977 to late 1978, August Komendant nurtured significant ideas, both in terms of structural design and the innovative techniques of their construction that were seamlessly harmonious with my architectural design for the projects. It felt as though we had worked together for years.

It has to be said that even after the revolution stopped all of our creative work and our reimbursements for services duly rendered were not honored by the new Iran government, August continued to provide advice to me and provided the moral support that only a father gives to a son who has suffered a great loss. August was an authentic man who remembered what he had personally gone through during World War II and showed empathy for the painful ordeals that I had to experience.

August Komendant was a graduate engineer, but he learned through his practical World War II experience to build efficient and effective structures with minimum means by the use of pretensioned and posttensioned cast-in-place concrete. Thus August was a leading authority on concrete construction when he began to work with Louis Kahn. August put this previous experience to good use by designing extremely innovative, thin structures that made Lou's architecture sing! The hope of every architect is to collaborate with his engineer in such a manner, but it takes courage to trust in your collaborator in such a manner.

As Steven Fleming has observed of Komendant's roof structure of the Kahn's Kimbell Art Gallery: "The shells that form the gallery roofs are posttensioned curved concrete beams (only five inches thick) [ca. 13 cm], spanning an incredible 100 feet [30.5 m]," which "happened to have been the maximum distance that concrete vaults could be produced without requiring expansion control joints."

Lou dealt with the unmeasurable, while August knew how to build the measurable that inspired the ineffable.

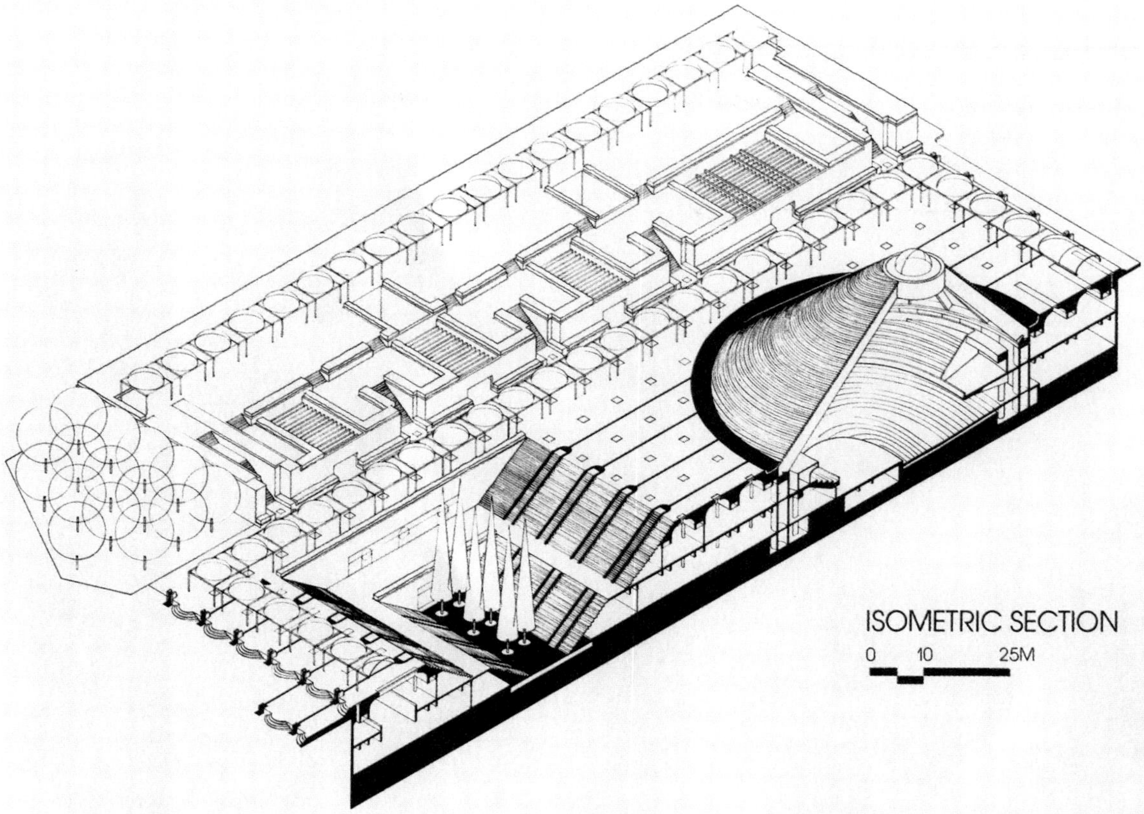

Tehran Center for the Celebration of Music, isometric section, 1978–1979

Nuran—City of Illumination

In the case of this New Town Phase I Housing, the project site lay in a highly seismic valley between two majestic, limestone mountains and the implementation program required that it had to be built in a short period of time, August, after reviewing the limits of site, available technology, and budget, recommended that we consider quarrying stone from the adjacent mountains and initiate an industrialized, cyclopean stone concrete system to construct all the load-bearing walls and on-site precast concrete plank floors. This idea was accepted by my architectural team, as it would generate an aesthetic visually related to the context and adaptive to our sustainability design approach, while the client approved it for its cost savings and rapid construction. It was practical and aesthetically it reminded me of Frank Lloyd Wright's Taliesin West, which I had experienced years before in Arizona, which resembled the Isfahan context.

Mercantile Bank of Iran and Holland

The last project on which August and I collaborated was to be built on the new City Center of Tehran, named Shahestan. It was to be the new headquarters for the Mercantile Bank of Iran and Holland (MBIH).

We Iranians take great pride in our ancient Persian civilizations that date back to the tenth century BC. In terms of iconographic representation, there is no more dominant a theme than Farr, a transcription of the old Persian word meaning divine glory, honor, good fortune. Its symbolic image is a pearl, a circle, a halo. In the time of Cyrus the Great (550 B.C.), the plan view was carved in stone as the center of a lotus flower in the Apadana of Persepolis.

I wanted to design the new headquarters as a cluster of four cylinders around a central elevator core. The exposed ceiling structure of each cylinder would be in silvery smooth concrete in the form of a lotus flower—thereby allowing the bank to bring the ancient symbolic gift of Farr to the new city center. As esoteric as it may sound, August worked with me to realize in concept such a dream. The result was a "halo" of cast-in-place posttensioned concrete floor, a structure that integrated mechanical, electrical, and plumbing in a modular coffered ceiling, at the center of which was a shaft of natural light.

Selected Works of August Komendant

Ülemiste Airport after completion

(*previous page*) Construction site of the Kimbell Art Museum: (*from the left*) architect Preston M. Geren, August Komendant, architect Frank Sherwood, ca. 1970

Ülemiste Airport

Tallinn, Estonia
Konstantin Bölau, Johannes Pikkov, August Komendant et al.
1934–1936 (partly extant)

As a young engineer, August Komendant helped design and supervise the construction of the first international airport in Estonia. The Ülemiste Airport in Tallinn consisted of two parts: the seaplane harbor on the banks of Lake Ülemiste, and a large repair hangar, customs building and runways on the land side. Komendant designed the landing bridge of the seaplane harbor and headed the dredging works on Lake Ülemiste. He was also involved in the construction of runways, taxiways, the airport railway and the plumbing system, as well as the hangar and the customs building.

August Komendant (*left*) on the construction site of the seaplane landing bridge

Concreting of the taxiway
(*next spread*) View toward the newly completed airport ensemble from Lake Ülemiste

Hangar after completion, ca. 1936

Military Aircraft Hangar

Tartu, Estonia
August Komendant
1935–1936 (extant)

The concrete aircraft hangar was August Komendant's first major project after graduating as a structural engineer in Germany in 1934. He was soon hired by the Estonian Ministry of Roads and became responsible for several important infrastructure projects. The hangar in Tartu is strikingly modern not only in its structural design but also in its architectural features. It is probably the earliest structure in Estonia where prestressing of concrete was implemented. The main part of the hangar's structure consists of six concrete frames. The horizontal tie rods on the floor level, which help brace the frames together, were manually pretensioned with wrenches and then cast into the concrete floor.

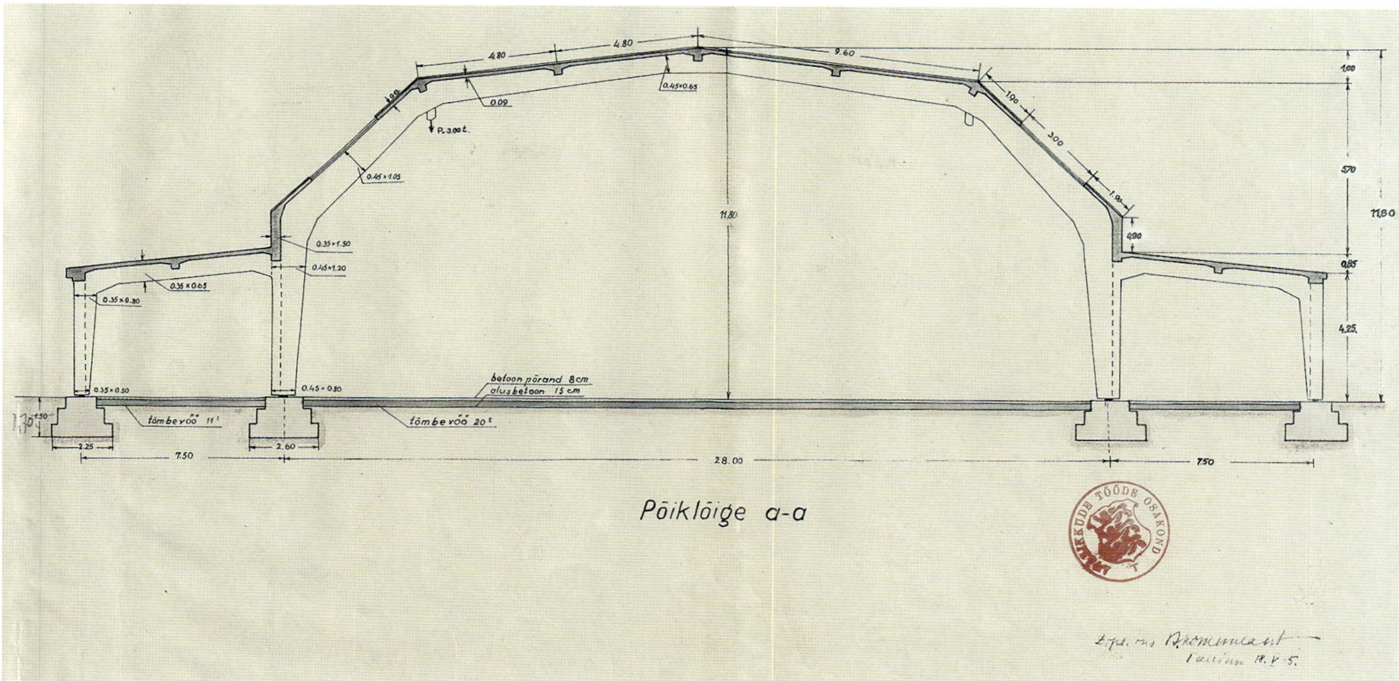

August Komendant. Hangar design, cross section, 1935

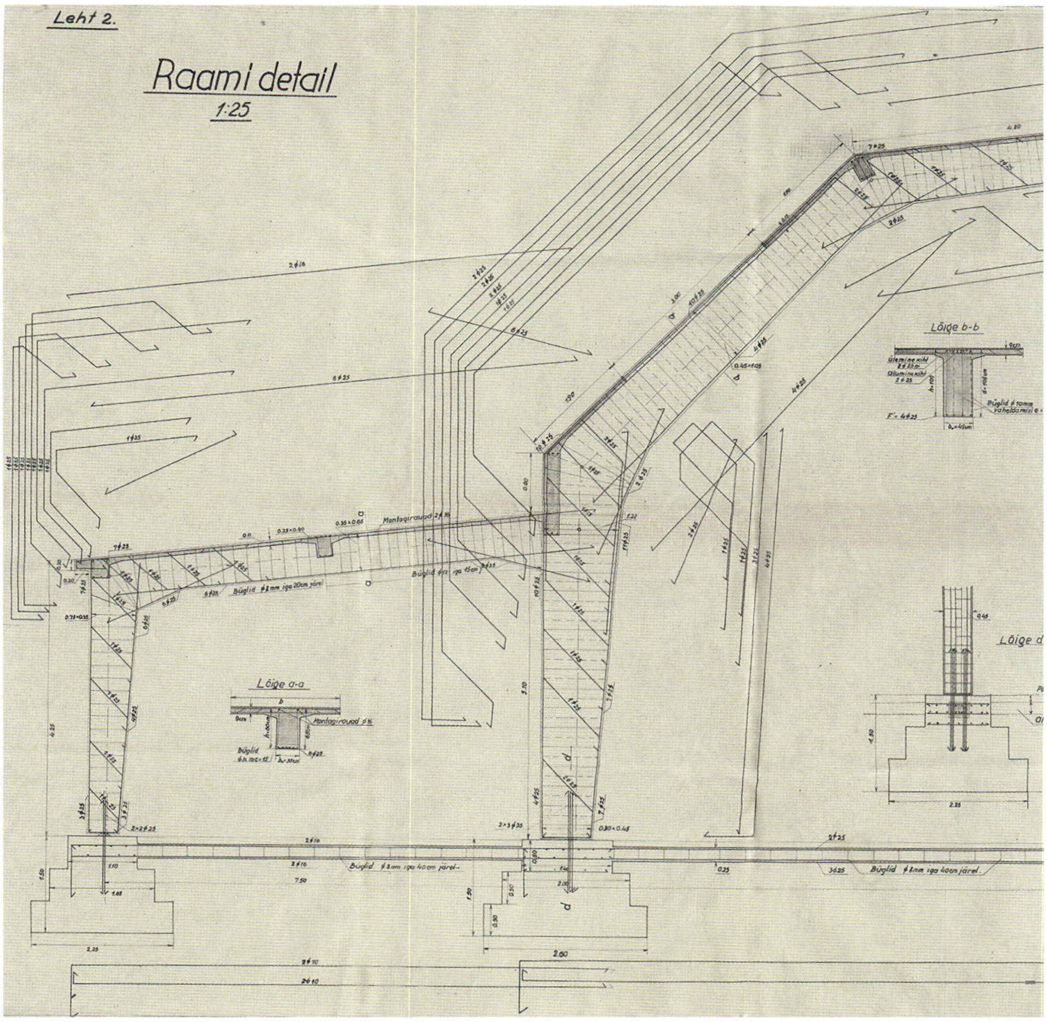

August Komendant. Concrete frame structural design, detail

Installing the roof plate reinforcement before concreting

Hangar during construction
(***next spread***) **Interior and skylights during the final phases of construction**

National Archives building after completion

National Archives and Library

Tallinn, Estonia
architect August Tauk,
structural engineer August Komendant
1935–1937 (extant)

The office building with a simple appearance but a modern structure was built between the medieval walls of Toompea Castle. August Komendant designed the monolithic reinforced concrete structure consisting of columns and floor slabs.

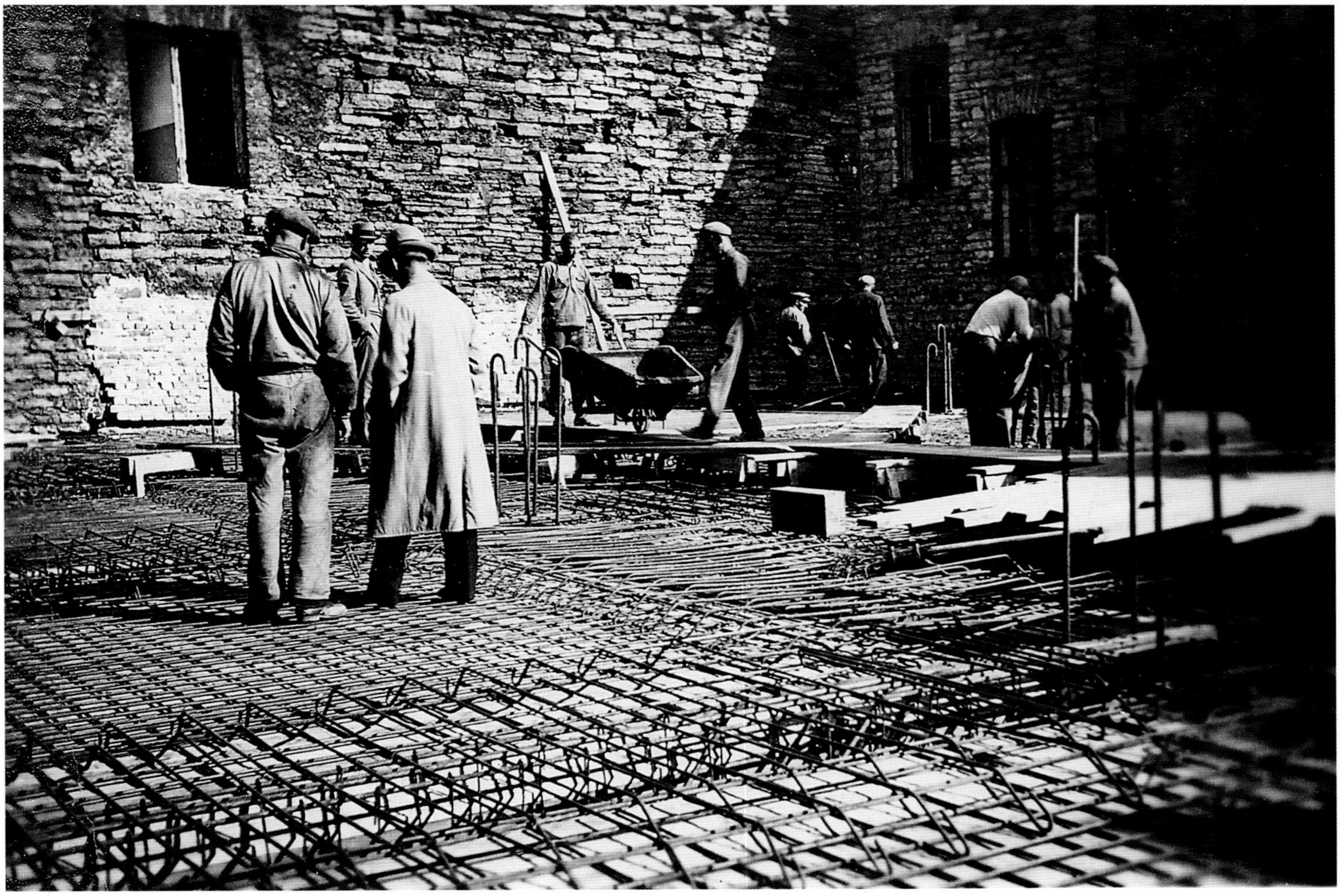

Installing floor slab reinforcement before concreting

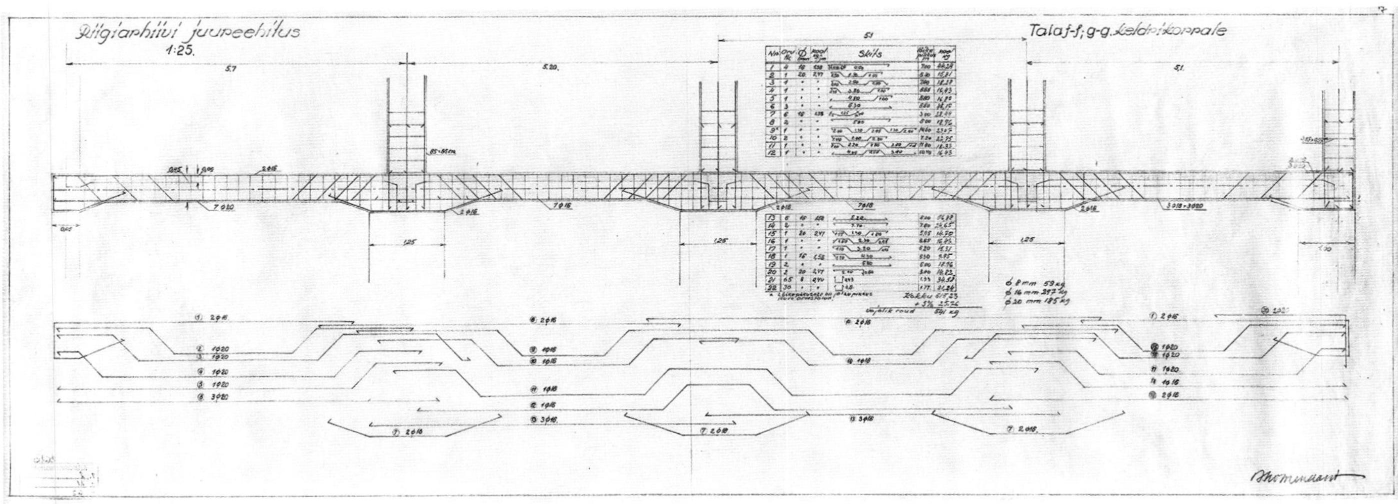

August Komendant. Reinforcement of the basement ceiling beam

Grandstand after completion, ca. 1938

Kadriorg Stadium Grandstand

Tallinn, Estonia
architect Elmar Lohk,
structural engineer August Komendant
1936–1938 (extant)

The grandstand at Estonia's premier stadium is a symbol of local sporting life and a great architectural achievement, daring in both form and structure. Elmar Lohk followed developments in world architecture, and the building has a strong affinity with the architecture of the Helsinki Olympic Stadium (Yrjö Lindgren, Toivo Jäntti, 1934–1938).

The grandstand is comprised of 26 parallel reinforced concrete frames, of which the 12 middle ones support the 12.8-meter cantilevered roof. The roof plate is 12 centimeters thick. The grand-stand is 112.3 meters long and initially had 3,500 seats, of which 2,000 were under the roof.

Elmar Lohk. Grandstand design, cross section, 1936

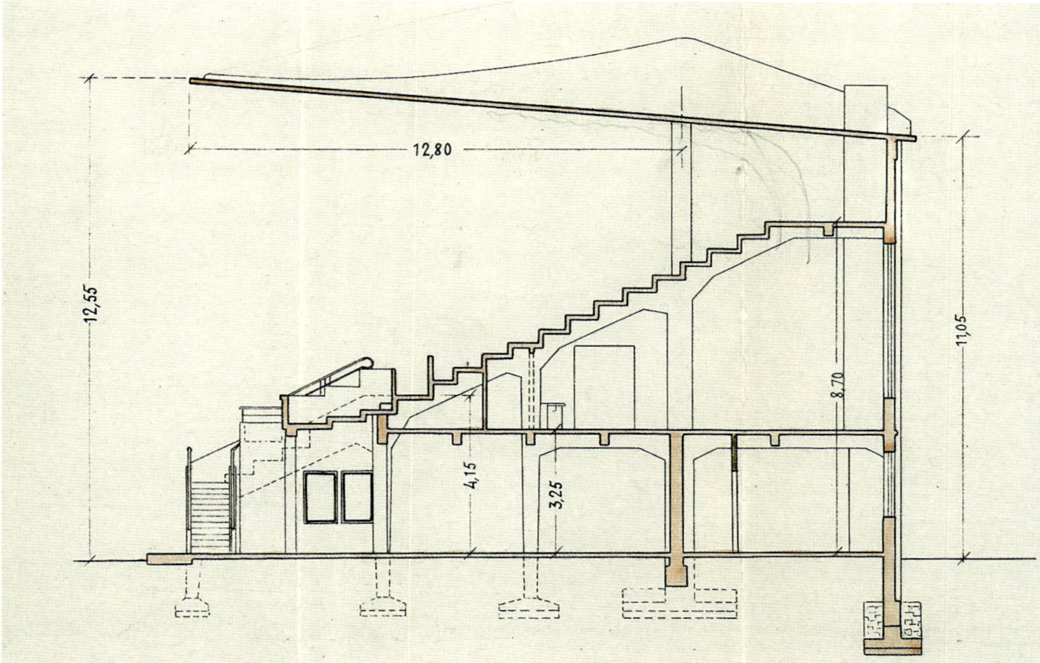

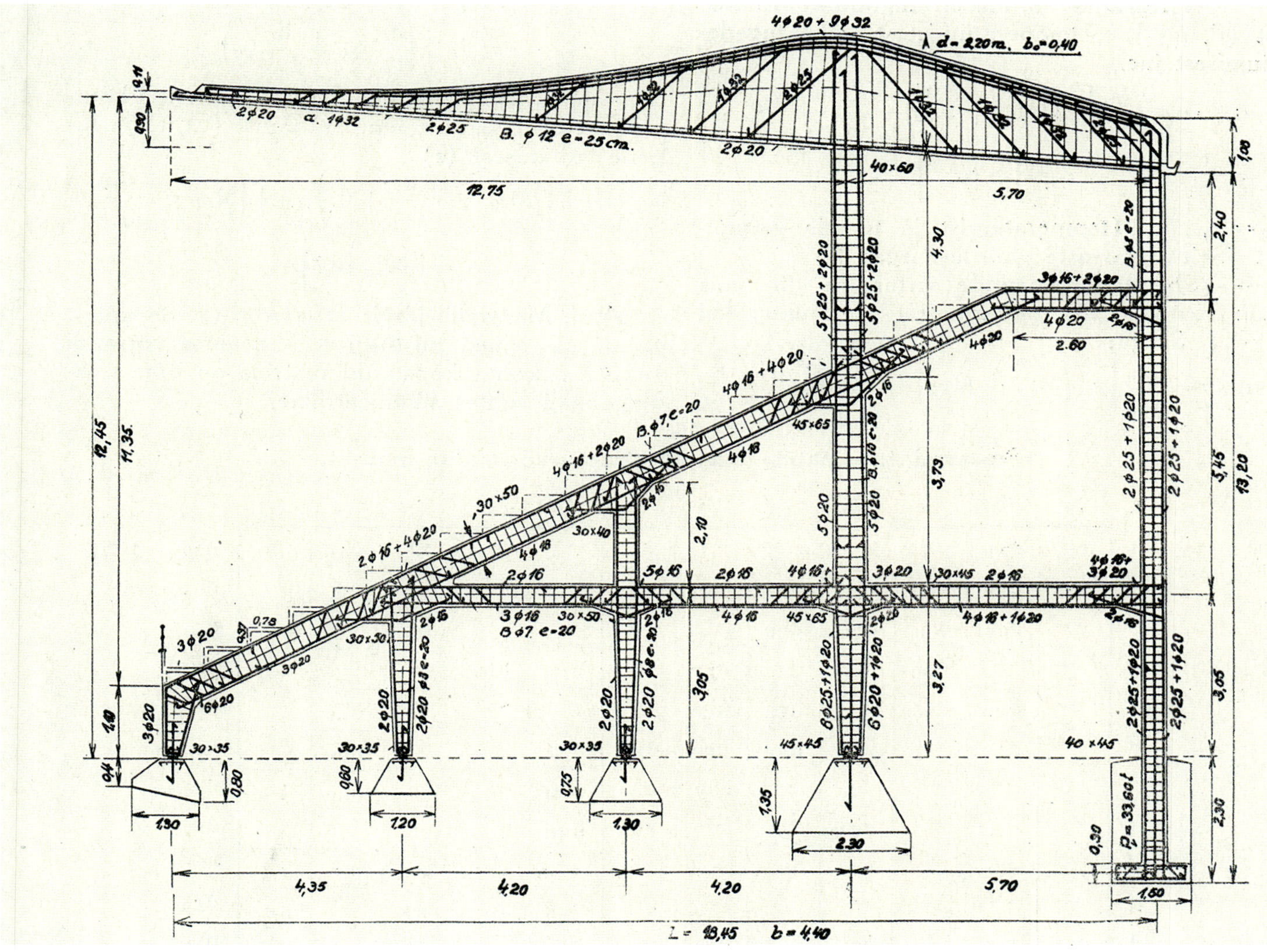

August Komendant. Cantilever roof reinforcement scheme, 1937

Grandstand construction, 1937

Elmar Lohk. Grandstand design, cross section, 1936

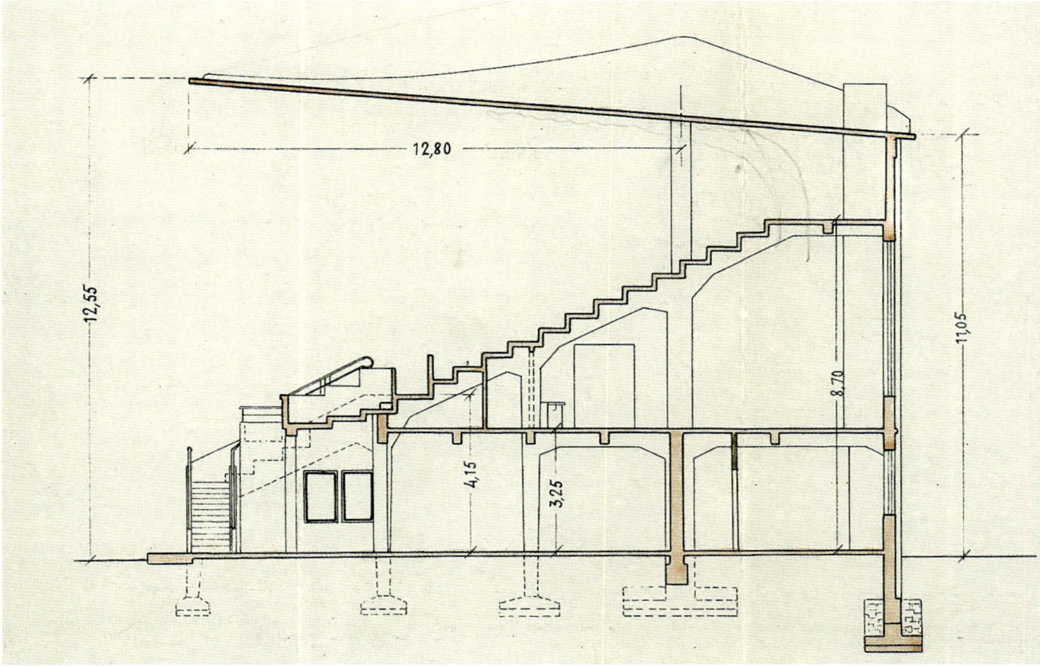

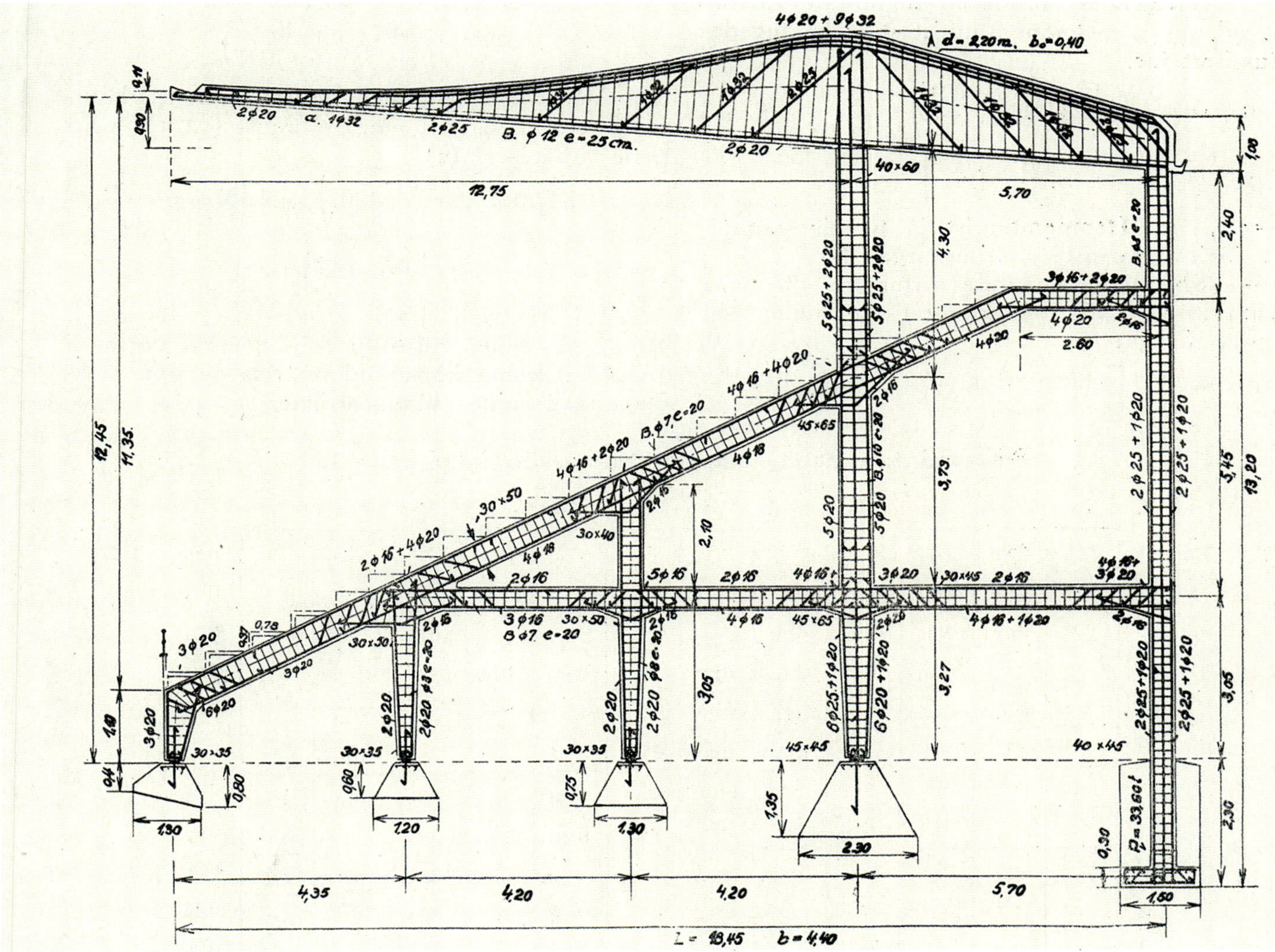

August Komendant. Cantilever roof reinforcement scheme, 1937

Grandstand construction, 1937

Opening ceremony of the new grandstand, with Olympic champion Kristjan Palusalu carrying the Estonian flag, May 15, 1938

Track and field competitions, 1940

2nd Estonian Games, 1939

After completion, ca. 1940

(*right*) Passageway below the grandstand and concrete columns
(*next spread*) View of the grandstand, 2016

Pulp and paper mill ensemble after completion, 1938

Kehra Pulp and Paper Mill, Glauber Salt Silo

Kehra, Estonia
August Komendant
1937–1938 (demolished)

August Komendant produced several designs for the nationally important factory complex. The most impressive of these was a reinforced concrete storage unit with a circular floorplan and 20-centimeter-thick walls more than 17 meters tall. Glauber Salt, or sodium sulphate, is a key ingredient in sulphate-based cellulose production.

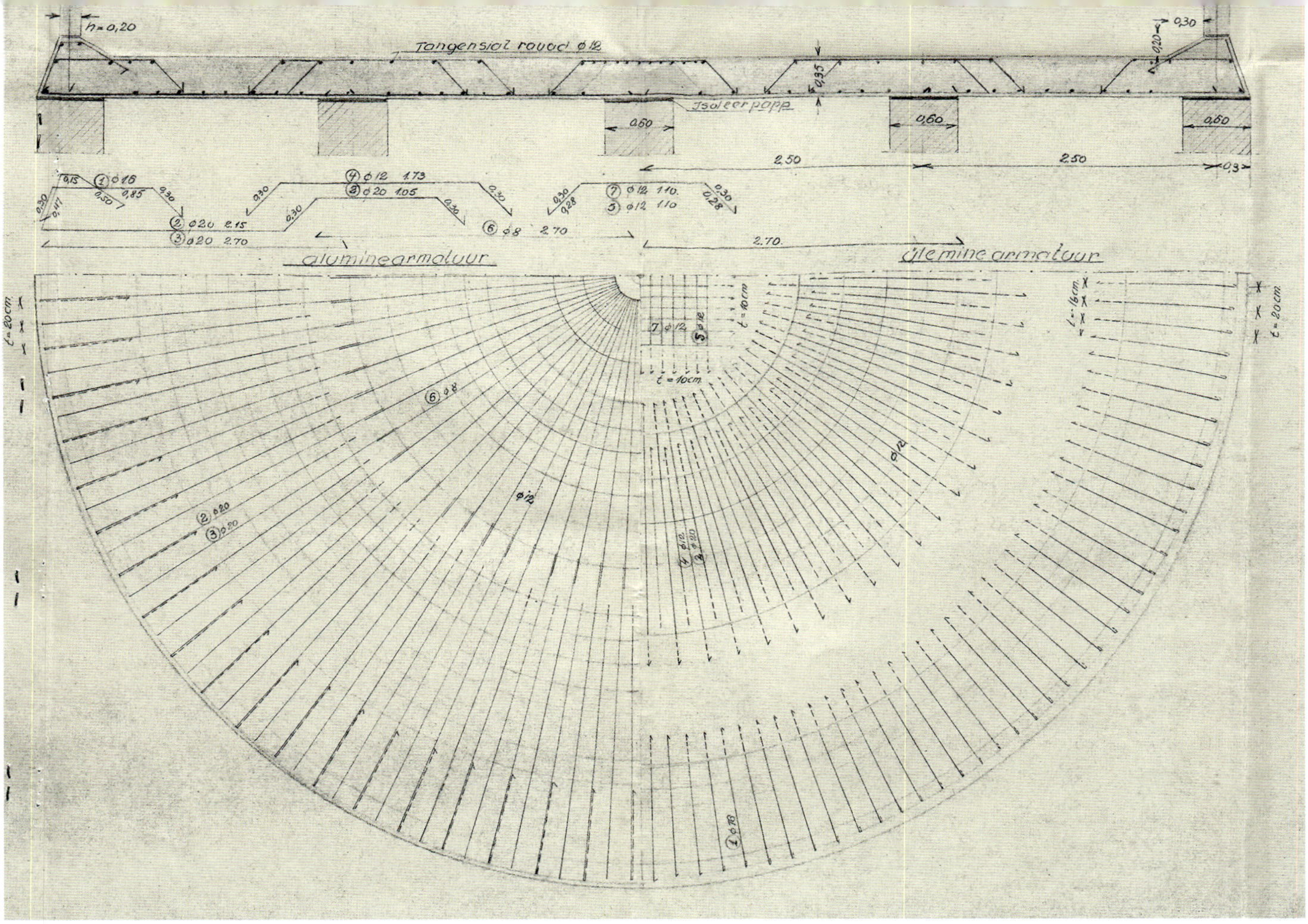

August Komendant. Glauber salt silo design, with reinforcement of the floor slab, 1937

Silo floor slab before concreting, 1937

Silo concrete wall's formwork under construction, 1937

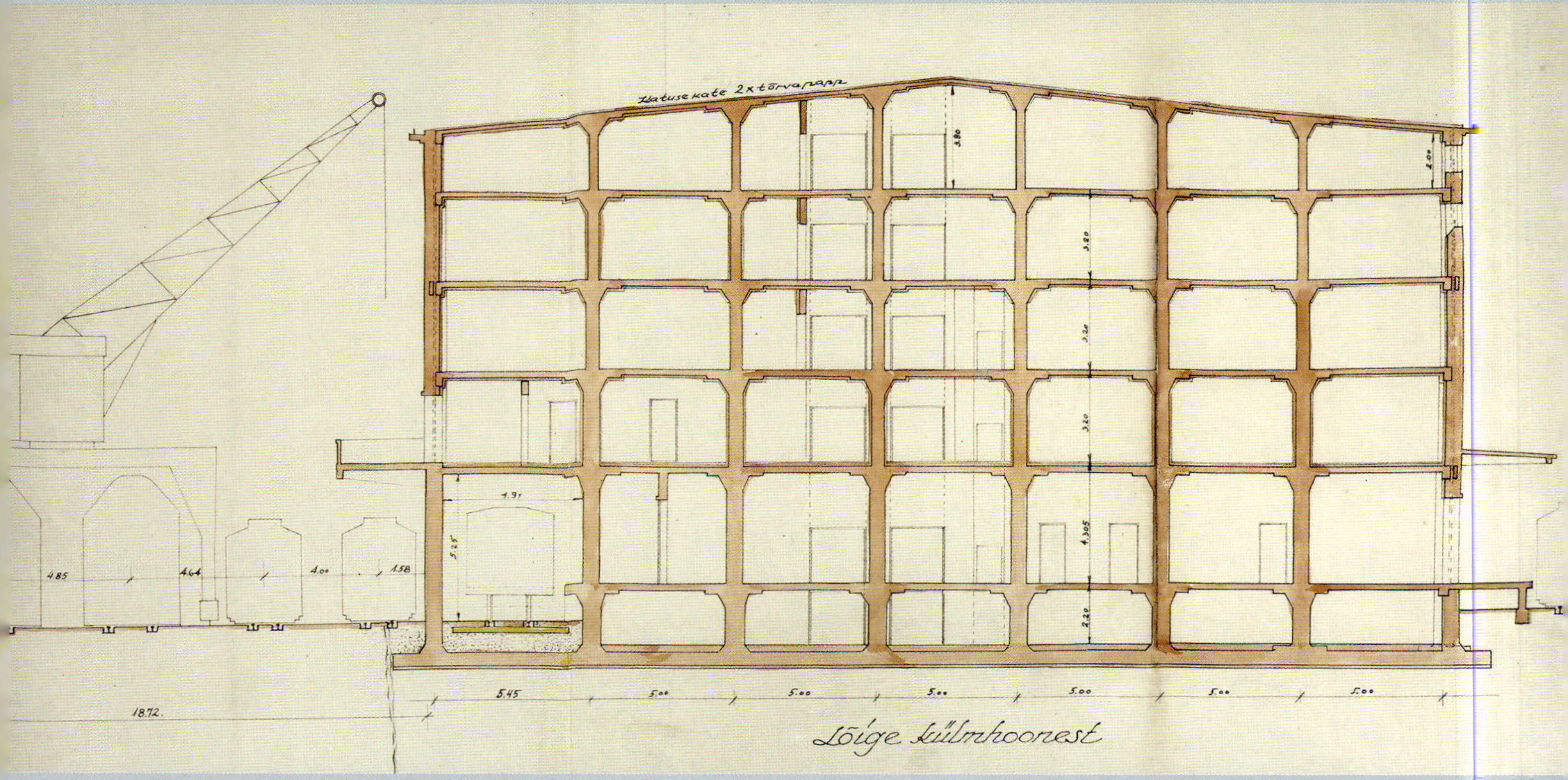

Roman Koolmar. Cold storage design, cross section, 1937

National Cold Storage, Port of Tallinn

Tallinn, Estonia
Preliminary design AS Franz Krull, architect Roman Koolmar, structural engineer August Komendant
1937–1941 (destroyed)

The large and modern warehouse complex was designed for cold storage for Estonian food product exports. Behind the limestone-clad office block was a six-story cold store for keeping butter, cheese, eggs, and other products. The reinforced concrete warehouse had a structure of flat slabs supported by mushroom columns, and was built on a 30-centimeter-thick slab foundation, which was in turn supported by more than 250 timber piles. The main structure of the complex was completed, but installing the equipment ceased due to World War II. The cold storage was destroyed during the war.

Cold storage under construction, with the limestone-clad machinery building (*middle*) and office block (*right*) in the foreground, ca. 1939

Floor slab reinforcement

National Grain Silo in Tartu, perspective drawing, postcard

National Grain Silo

Tartu, Estonia
August Komendant, Ernst Kesa
1939–1941 (extant, altered)

The modernist-looking grain silo was designed in collaboration with architect Ernst Kesa. The facility is special because of the mushroom ceiling between the basement and the ground floor, as well as the construction method of the silos, whereby modern sliding formwork helped save both time and materials. Attempts were made to destroy the structure during World War II; and the stairway tower collapsed, but the monolithic block of 15 silos merely tilted to one side. The silos were straightened in 1947 and are still being used for storing grain today.

August Komendant visiting the construction site, 1940

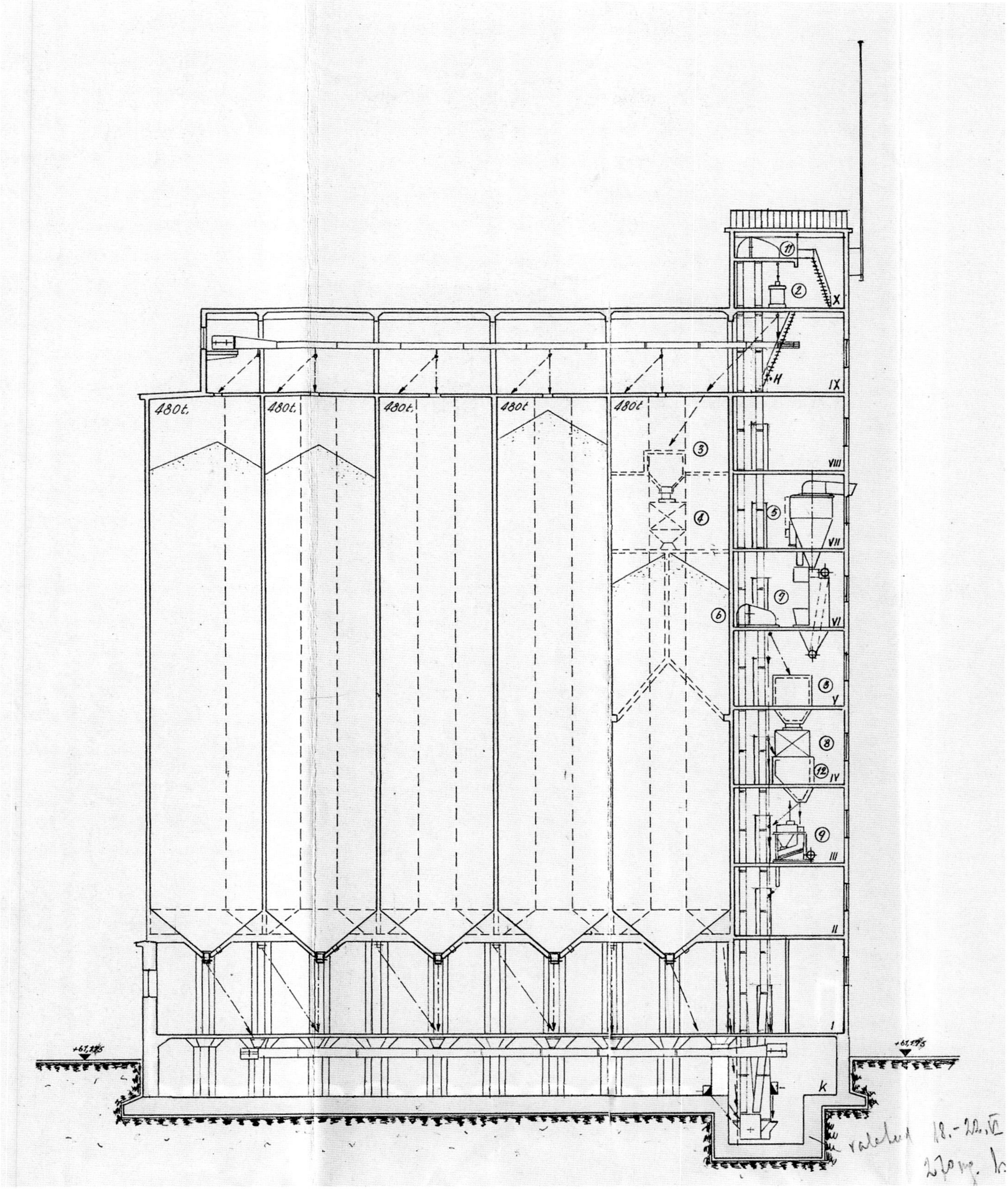

August Komendant. Grain silo design, longitudinal section, 1939
(*next spread*) Construction workers and installed reinforcement, 1940

Grain silo after completion, 1941

(*left*) Construction of silos using sliding formwork, 1940

Grain silo was reconstructed after the war using an altered design, 1956

(*left*) Grain silo tilted to one side after a failed attempt to blow up the building during World War II, 1946

Enrichment plant during the Soviet era, 1966

Estonian Phosphorite Ltd.

Maardu, Estonia
architect Eugen Saarelinn (Sacharias),
structural engineer August Komendant
1940–1941, completed after World War II (partly extant)

This is a large industrial complex of national importance near Tallinn. The planned annual production capacity was 100,000 tons of enriched phosphorite, most of which was intended for the production of fertilizers for export to Germany. However, due to the outbreak of World War II, construction of the factory was put on hold. The central building of the complex is an enrichment plant designed by architect Eugen Saarelinn (Sacharias), as were the screening plant and pre-crushing plant. The buildings have limestone facades with massive reinforced concrete load-bearing structures designed by August Komendant. Komendant also independently designed a number of smaller facilities for the factory: ramps, bridges, a sediment basin and a tippler building.

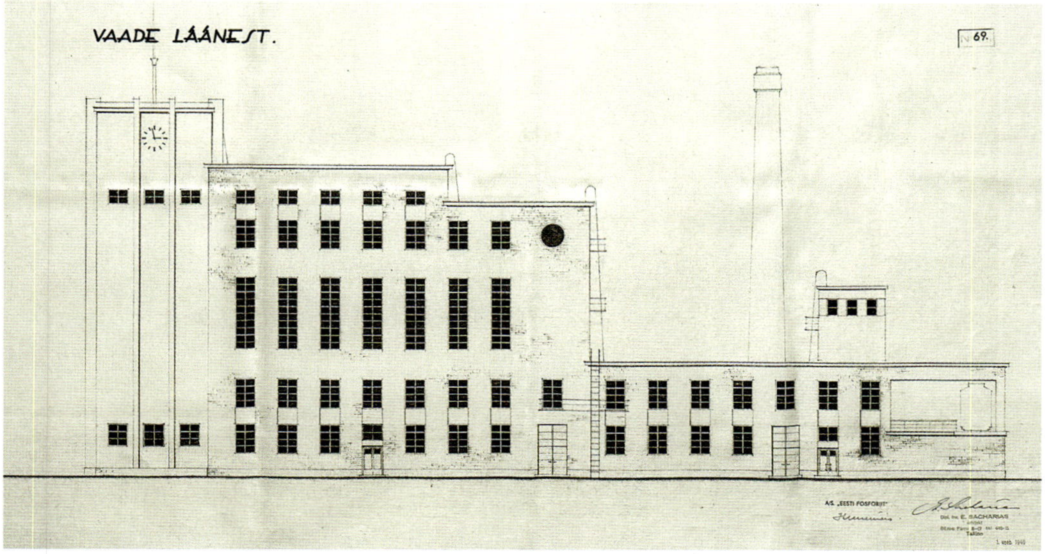

Eugen Saarelinn (Sacharias). Enrichment plant design, side elevation, 1940

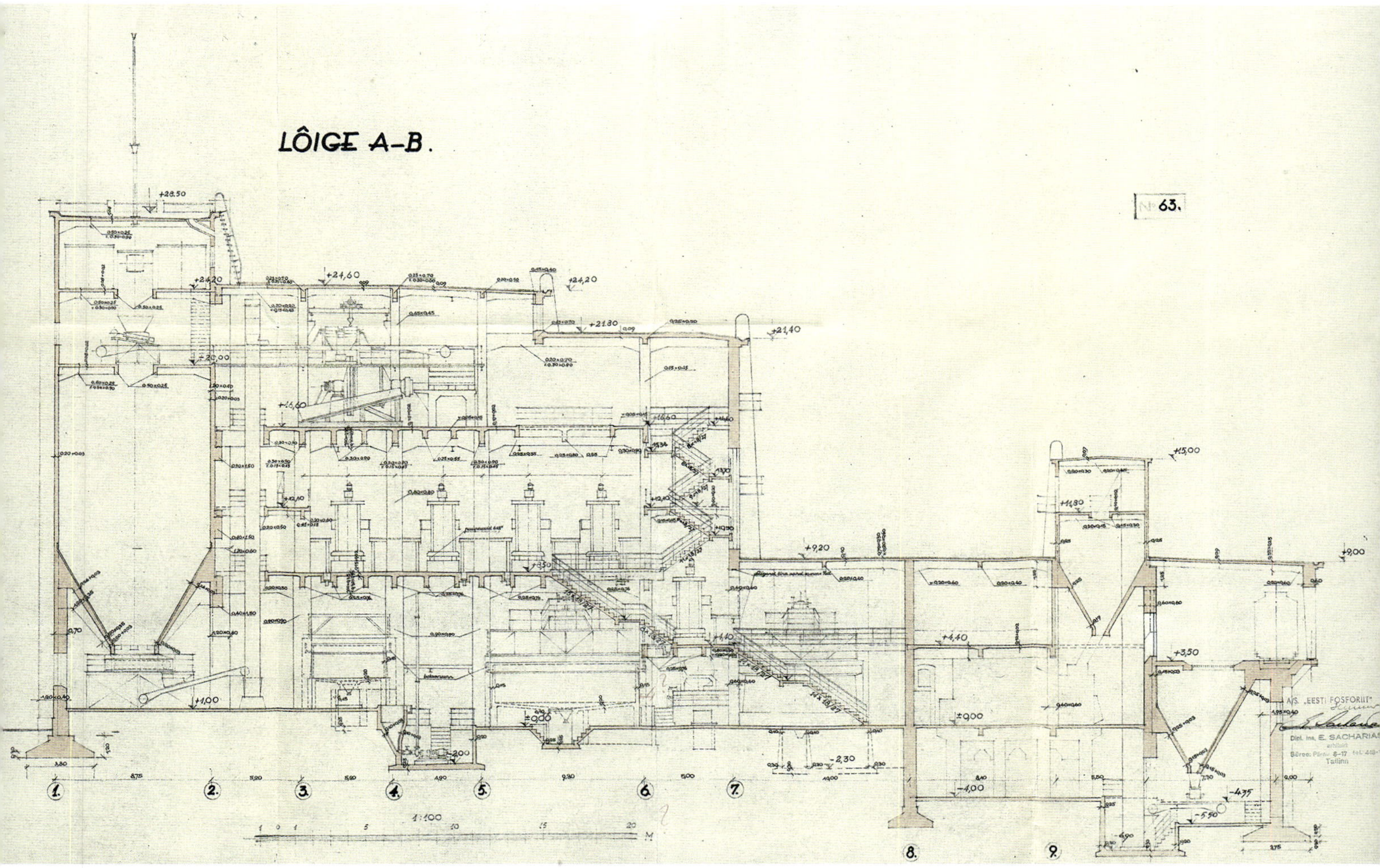

Eugen Saarelinn (Sacharias). Enrichment plant design, longitudinal section, 1940

Interior of the former enrichment plant, 2019
(*right*) Trestles for transporting the phosphorite ore, 1945
(*next spread*) Interior of the former enrichment plant, 2019

Management of the Lakewood concrete plant, and August Komendant on the left

Lakewood Prestressing Company, Inc. Concrete Plant

Howell, New Jersey, USA
August Komendant
1956–1958 (extant, altered)

August Komendant designed several precasting plants during the 1950s. The first was the Lakewood Prestressing Company, Inc. (1956–1958) established by local Estonians. Unfortunately, due to inexperienced managers, the company never got its feet firmly on the ground and went bankrupt. Being not only a consulting engineer but one of the shareholders, Komendant also lost his investment. Komendant also collaborated with the Atlantic Prestressed Concrete Co., which manufactured the precast elements for both the Richards Medical Research Building [see pp. 150–165] and the cold storage of the Merchants Refrigerating Co. [see pp. 180–183]

Heavy machinery at the Lakewood concrete plant

Prestressed concrete girder in the casting bed at the Lakewood concrete plant

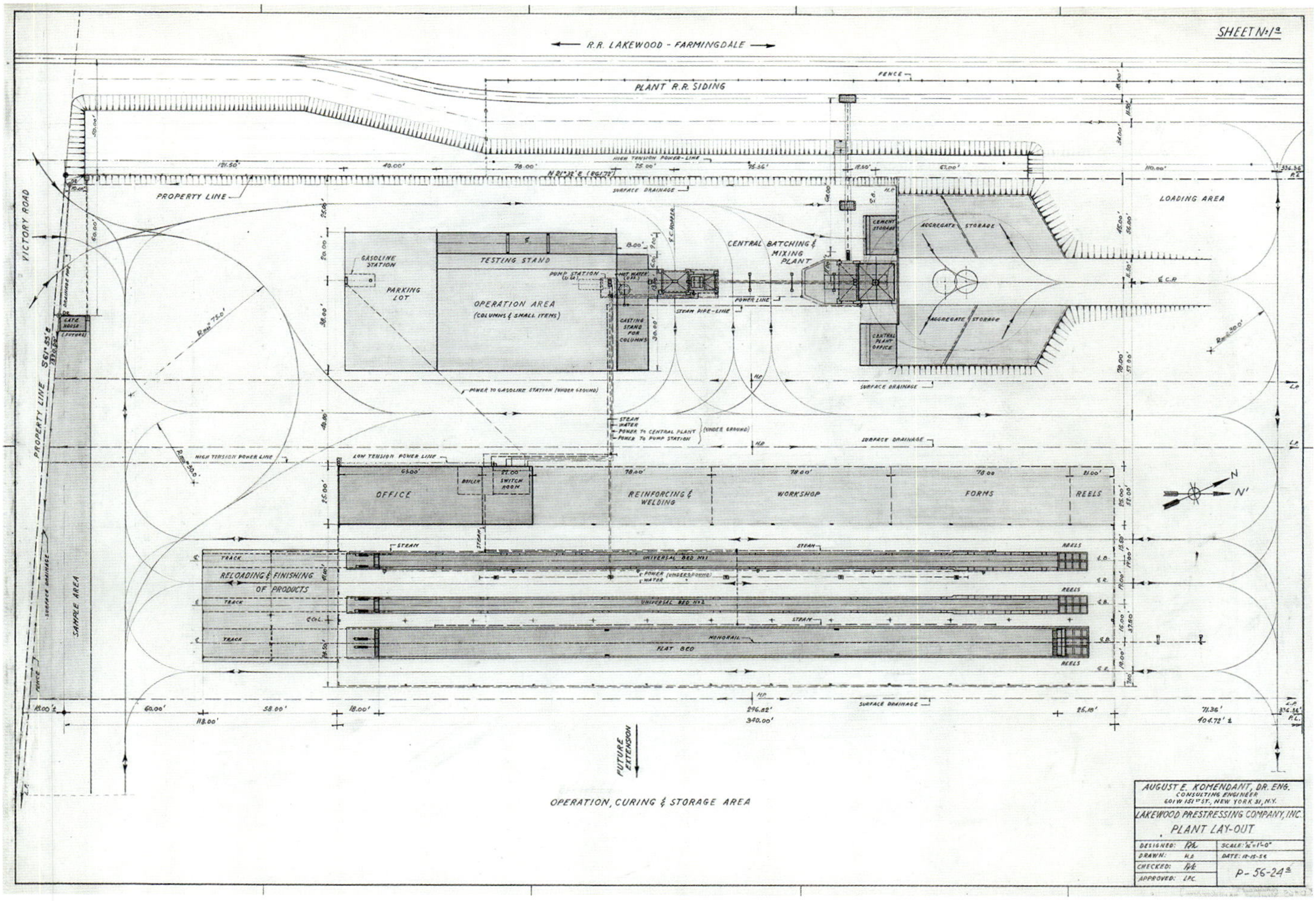

August Komendant. Lakewood concrete plant design, site plan, drafted by Helmi Aren, 1956

Louis Kahn. Community building cross section

Trenton Jewish Community Center, Community Building

Ewing Township, New Jersey, USA
architect Louis Kahn,
structural consultant August Komendant
1957–1958 (not built)

Louis Kahn had already completed the bathhouse that belonged to the center by the time he met Komendant (1956), but the central community building which would house the hall, childcare, gym and other facilities, had not yet been built. Kahn was interested in using factory-produced concrete elements. Several of Komendant's drawings with various solutions survive (pyramidal precast roof modules; large span box girders), but they were not used—the project went through several phases over the years but was never implemented by the client.

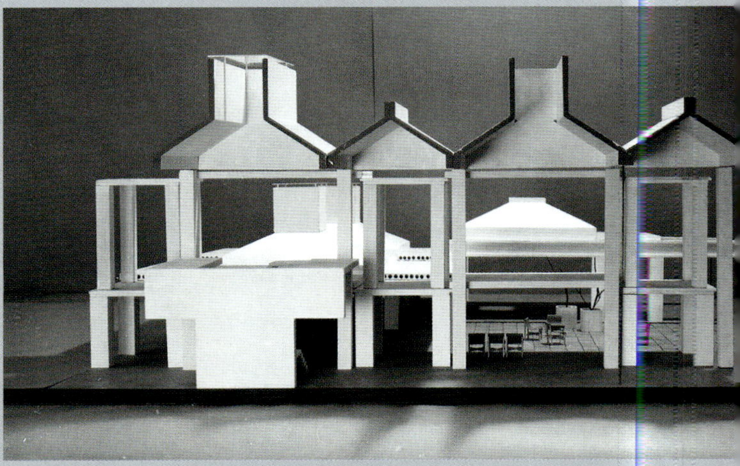

Community building sketch model

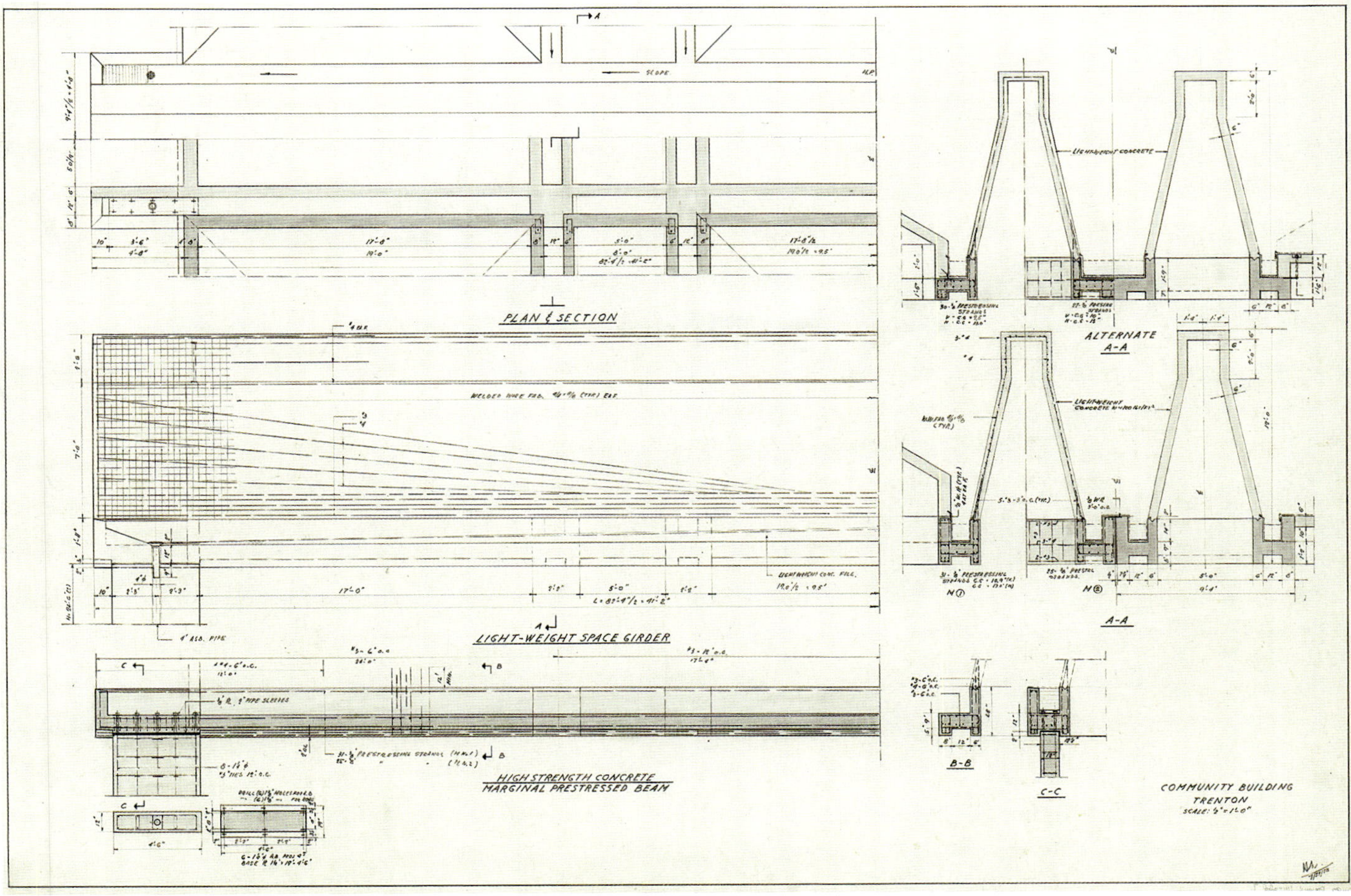

August Komendant. Community building roof structure, prestressed folded plates, and edge members, 1958

Medical laboratories after the completion of the first construction phase

Alfred Newton Richards Medical Research Building and Biology Building

Philadelphia, Pennsylvania, USA
architect Louis Kahn, structural engineer August Komendant
1957–1965 (extant)

The Richards laboratory complex is one of the symbols of twentieth-century architecture. It was the first large project that Kahn and Komendant collaborated on and provided the impetus for the further careers of both men. The structural solution of the building supports the architectural idea that envisions laboratories as studios for researchers. The floor slab system worked out by Komendant is striking and economical. It is comprised of precast Vierendeel trusses and marginal beams which, after being lifted into place by a crane, were connected and posttensioned into unity with steel cables.

Louis Kahn. Site plan sketch, 1957

Structure of the laboratory tower, preliminary version, model 1:50, 1957

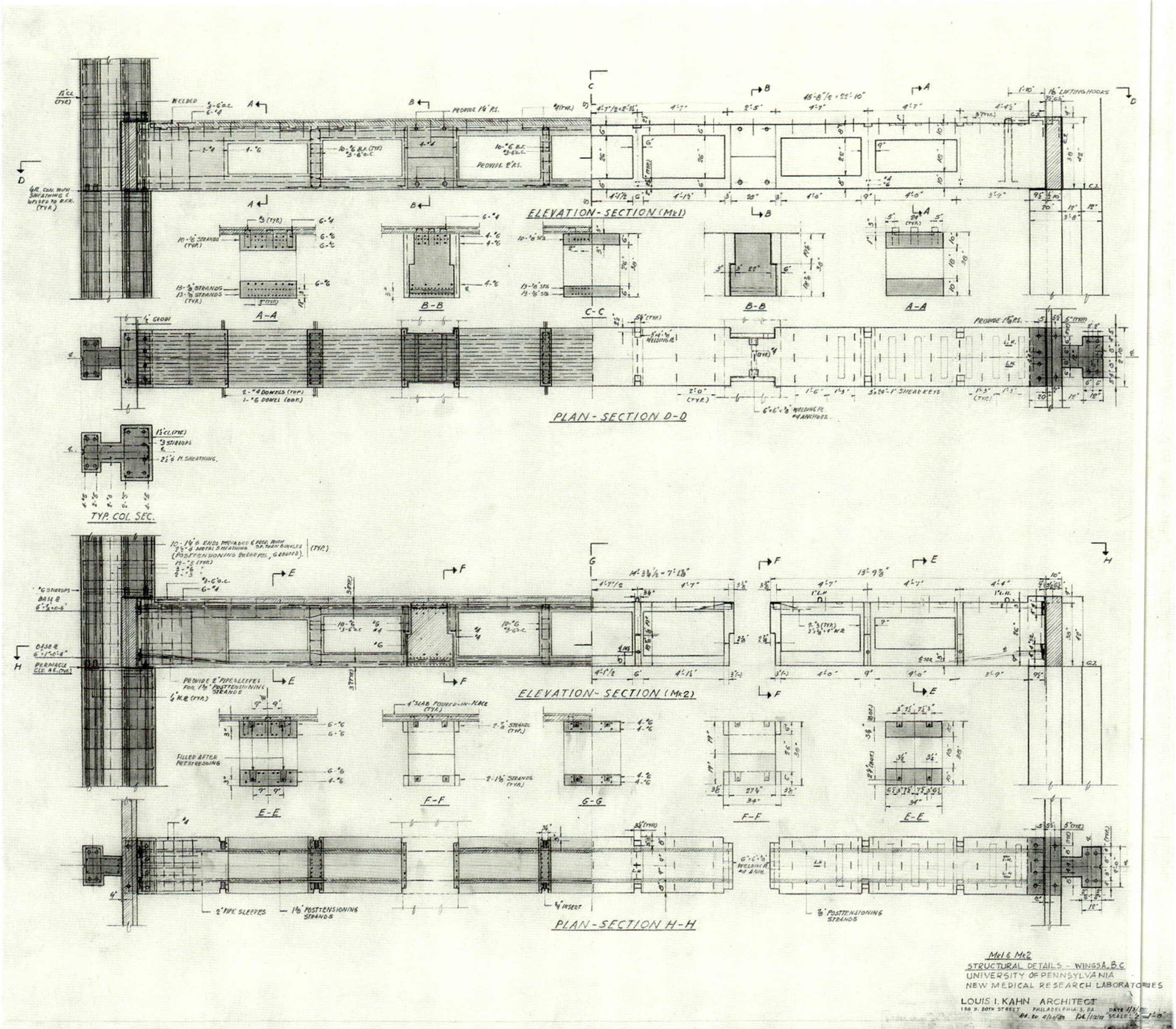

August Komendant. Preliminary design for the Vierendeel truss, 1958

The Vierendeel truss on the construction site

Installing the precast marginal beams on the construction site

Construction of the floor slab

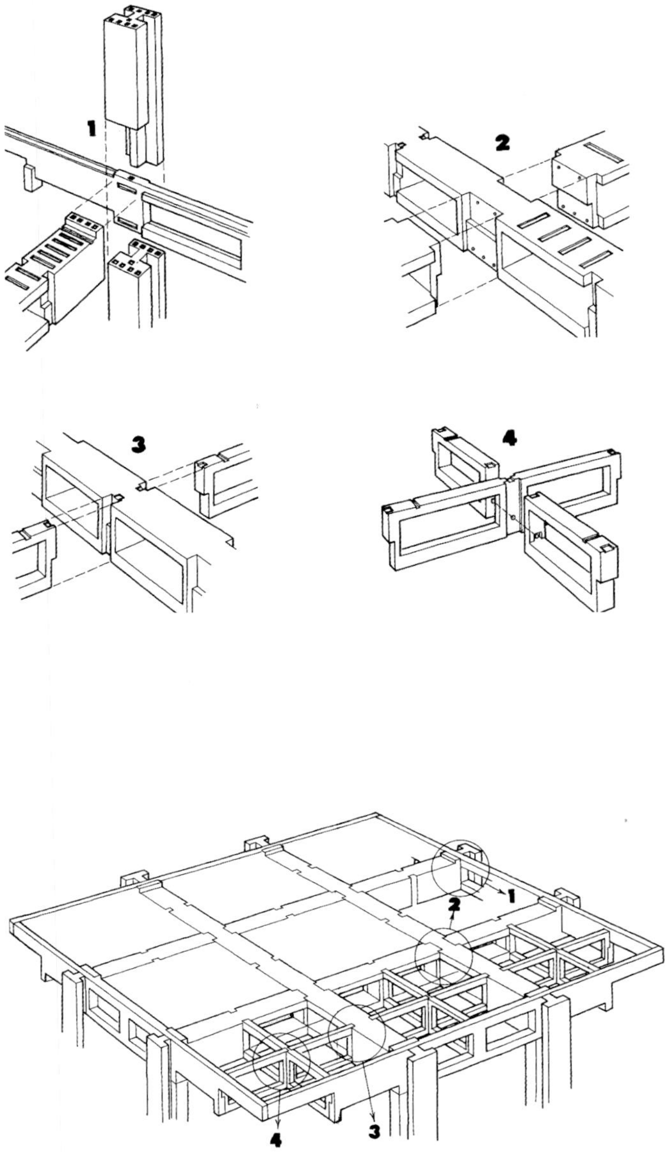

Posttensioning of the steel cables with hydraulic jacks

Structural system of the precast elements

Floor slab before concreting

Construction workers having a break

The laboratory towers were built of precast elements and the central service tower of monolithic poured-in-place concrete

The first phase of construction nearing completion

(*right*) Service towers clad in brick

Laboratory towers after completion

Windows of the research laboratories

Interior of a research laboratory

Medical research laboratories after the completion of the first construction phase

Main entrance facade of the Tribune Review building

Tribune Review Publishing Company Building

Greensburg, Pennsylvania, USA
architect Louis Kahn, structural engineer August Komendant
1958–1962 (extant, altered)

This was one of six collaborative projects completed by August Komendant and Louis Kahn. The building housed a regionally significant newspaper printing house and office space. Kahn used simple, ascetic materials, natural light and a serene distribution of volumes. The most impressive components of the structural system proposed by Komendant are prestressed roof beams that span approximately 15 meters. These girders, which don't have intermediate supports, helped to create rooms with a spacious and uplifting atmosphere for both the printing house and the offices.

Louis Kahn. Perspective drawing of the future building, with the public entrance to the left, and the service entrance to the right side

Side facade with the service entrance

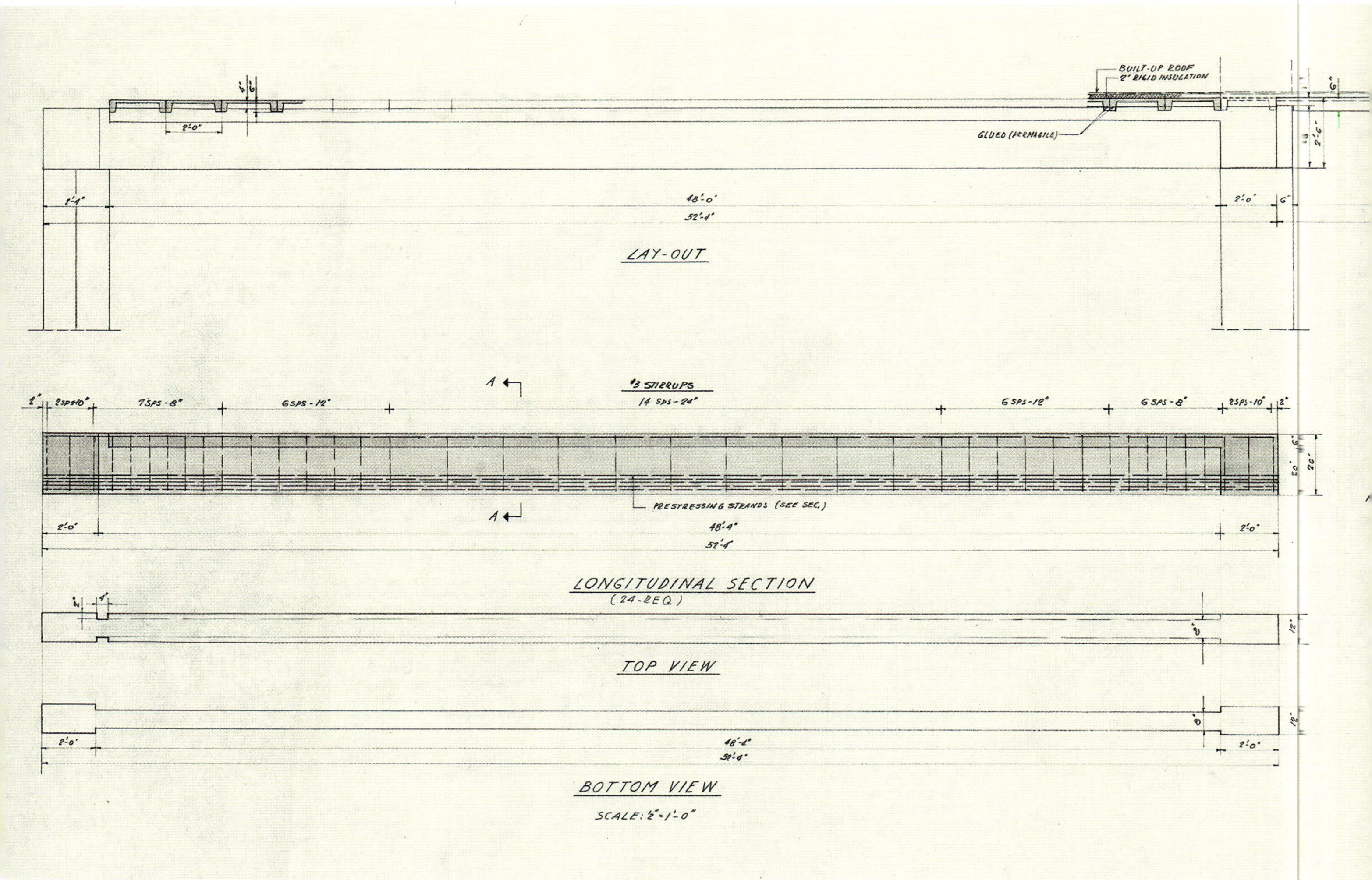

August Komendant. Prestressed concrete beam, 1959

Outer corner and marginal beam

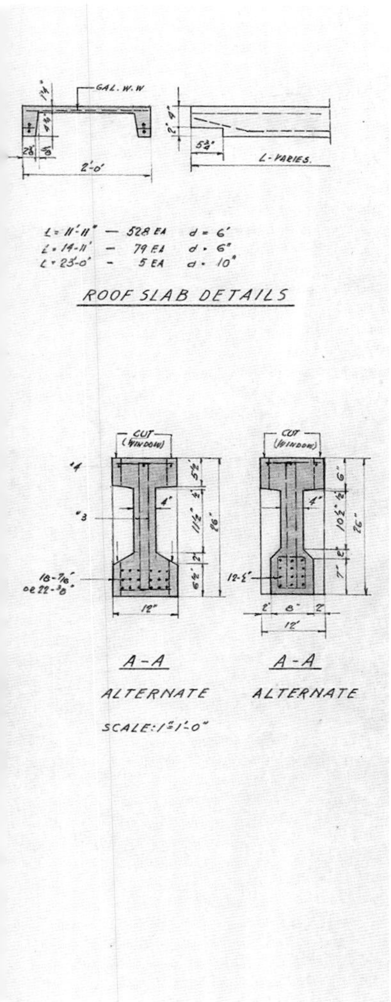

Offices

(***next spread***) **Interior—simple materials, natural light, expressive structure**

Henry Klumb. Perspective drawing of the church, 1959

Parroquia Nuestra Señora del Carmen—Parish Church of Our Lady of Mount Carmel

Cataño, Puerto Rico
architect Henry Klumb,
structural engineer August Komendant
1959–1960 (not built)

Architect Henry Klumb, who collaborated with Frank Lloyd Wright and Louis Kahn during the 1930s, met August Komendant in the 1950s. The Parish Church of Our Lady of Mount Carmel, also known as the Del Carmen church, was their first major collaboration and is unique because of its structural system. It consists of precast elements (the so-called stability rings) and sections of thin reinforced concrete shells, which were meant to be built with gunite—sprayed concrete, also known as shotcrete.

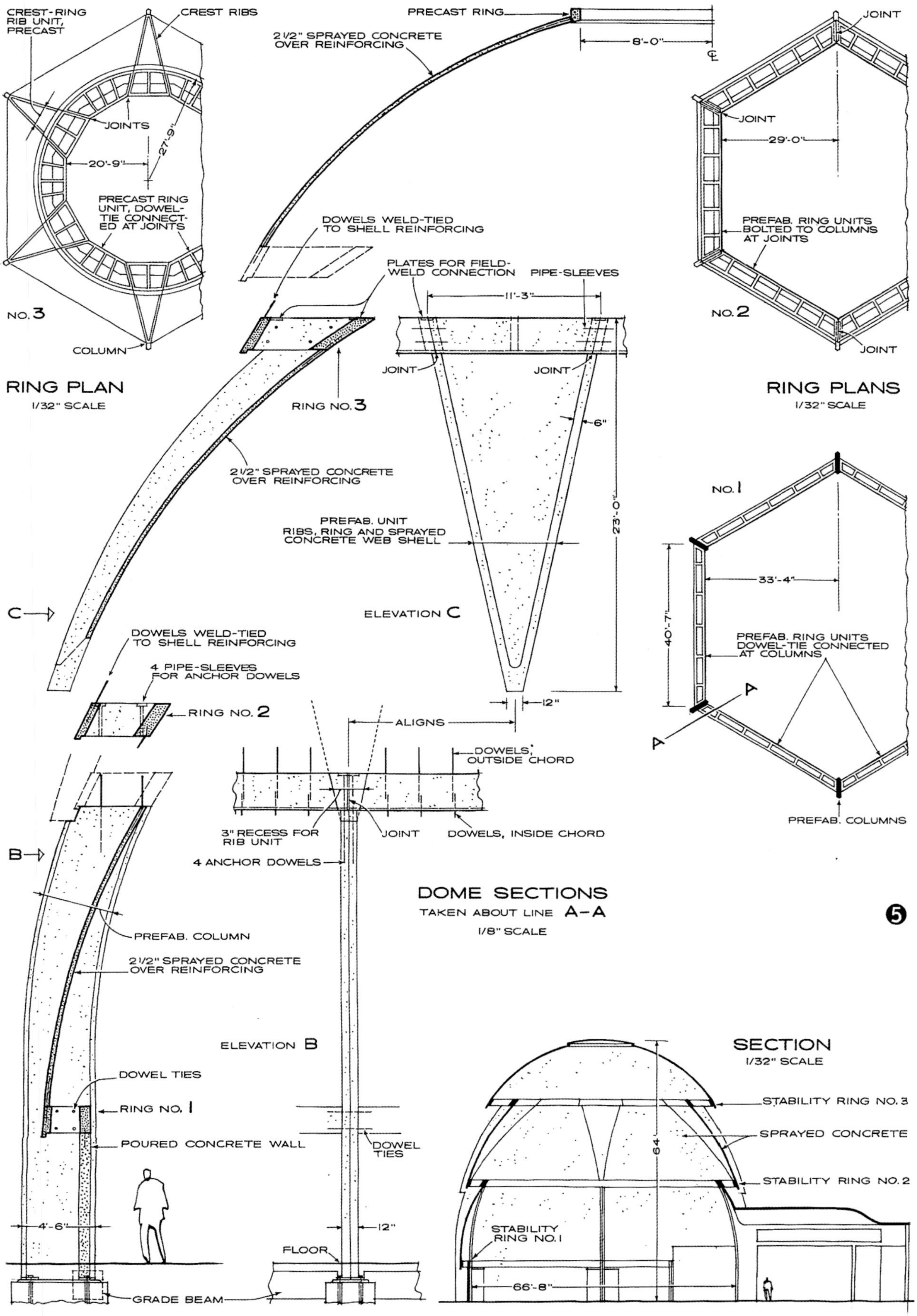

Structural system for the church building

Courtyard and dining hall of Ezra Stiles College

Dining Halls of the Ezra Stiles and Samuel Morse Colleges, Yale University

New Haven, Connecticut, USA
architect Eero Saarinen,
structural consultant August Komendant
1960–1961 (extant)

This is the sole collaboration between the well-known Finnish-American architect Eero Saarinen (1910–1961) and August Komendant. Using both materials and light, Saarinen aspired to create a dialogue with the existing Gothic Revival architecture on the campus. For the dining halls, Komendant helped Saarinen's structural engineer, Henry Pfisterer, design an ambitious fan-shaped roof structure using reinforced concrete Vierendeel trusses.

Office of Eero Saarinen (Newton). Perspective drawing of the dining hall, 1959

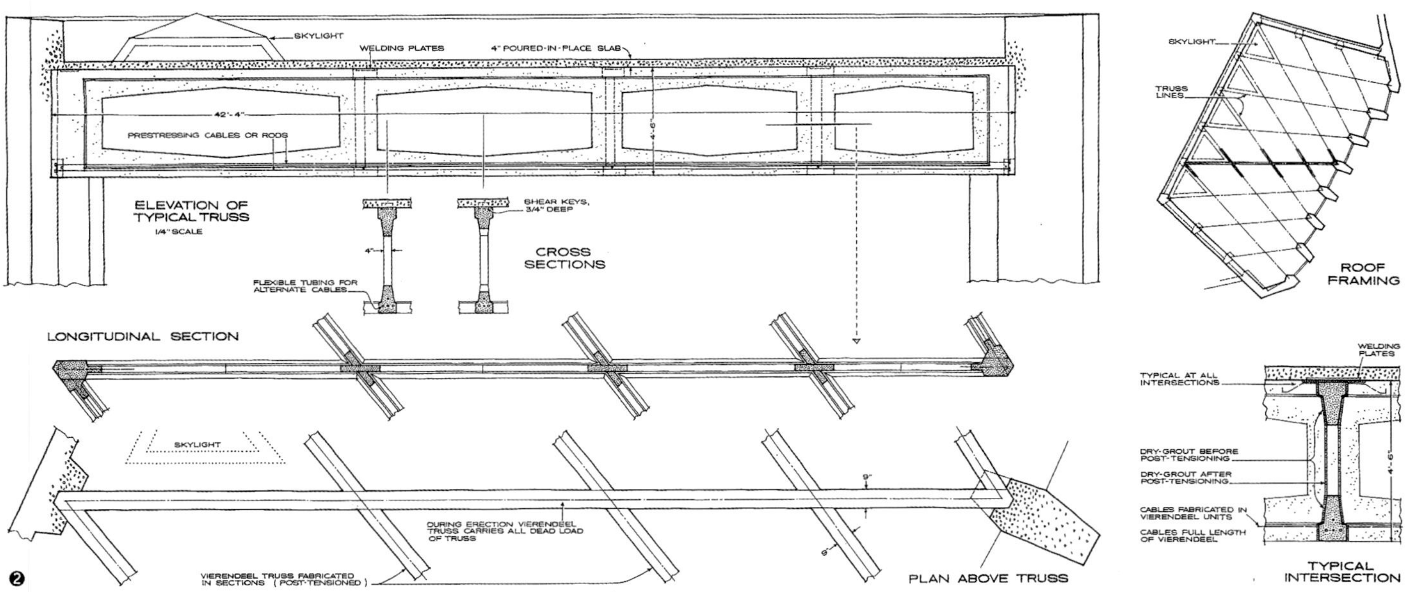

❷

Structural system for the dining halls' roofs

Interior of the dining hall

Henry Klumb. Perspective drawing of the gymnasium, 1960

Colegio San Ignacio de Loyola Gymnasium Building

San Juan, Puerto Rico
architect Henry Klumb,
structural engineer August Komendant
1960 (not built)

Architect Henry Klumb designed several buildings for the Jesuits in Puerto Rico. One of them was a sports building for the San Ignacio de Loyola college, named after the founder of the order. The architect wanted to use an expressive structure, the main components of which were trussed frames. August Komendant completed the preliminary calculations and drawings, but the gymnasium was not built.

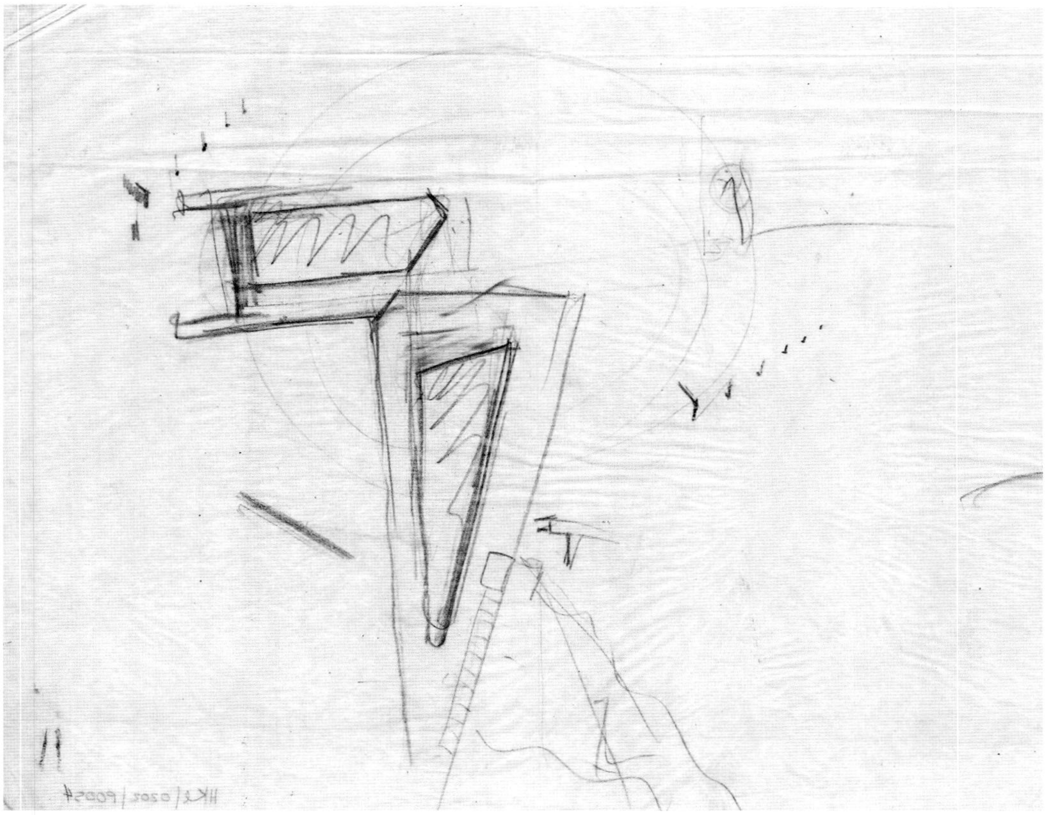

Henry Klumb. Roof structure tie sketch

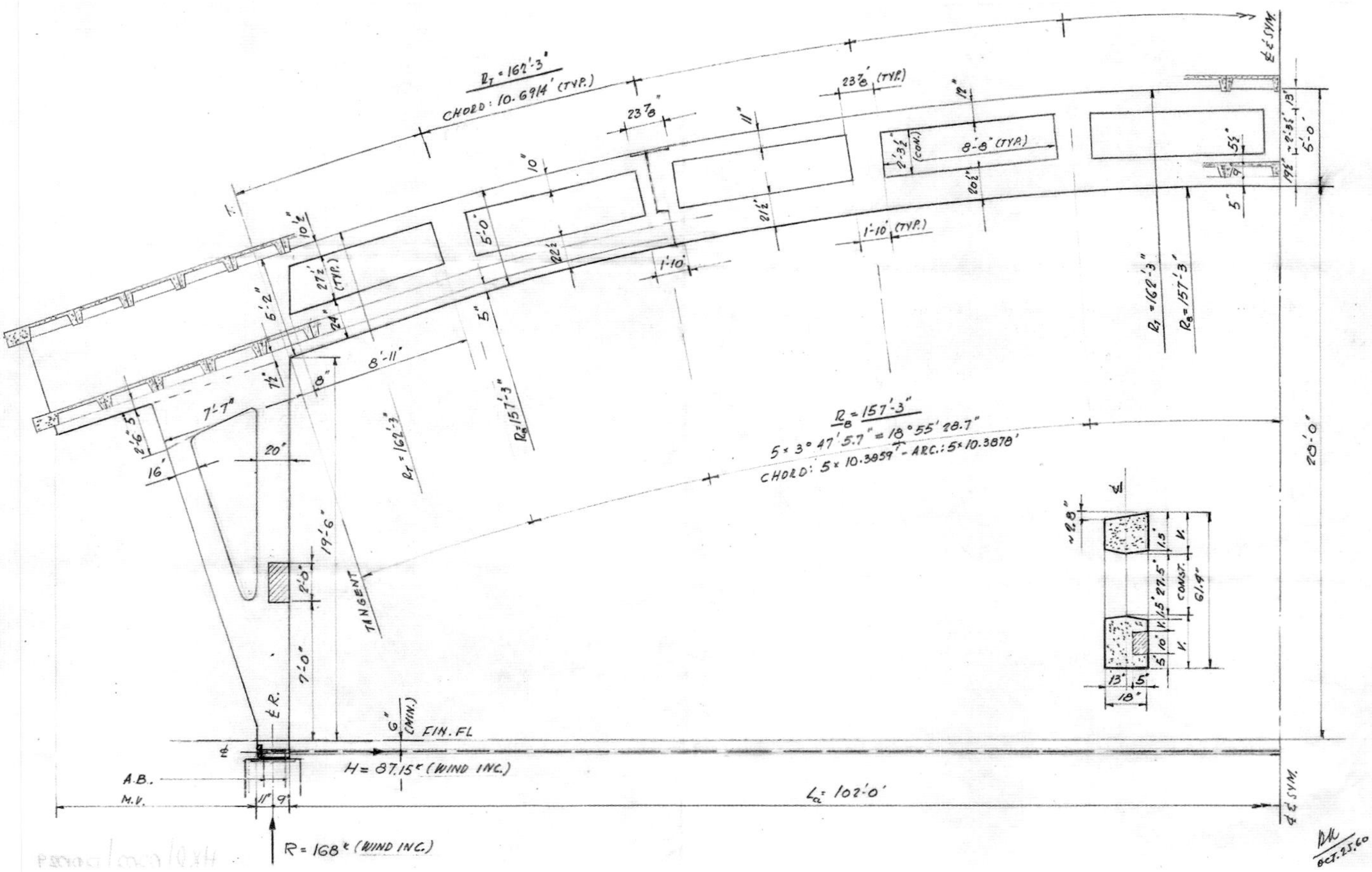

August Komendant. Preliminary design of the roof structure

Test-loading of the precast truss at the Atlantic Prestressed Concrete Co.; standing among others are structural engineers Harald Laupa (*second from the left*) and August Komendant (*fifth from the right*)

Cold Storage and Distribution Center, Merchants Refrigerating Co.

Secaucus, New Jersey, USA
architects Abbott Merkt & Co.,
structural engineer August Komendant
1960–1961 (demolished)

For the large cold storage structure, August Komendant designed an impressive and economical structure made up of concrete elements. The precast, pretensioned Vierendeel trusses (about 12 meters long) were tied together into a 130-meter-plus continuous truss system in which the spans between columns exceeded 24 meters. Expansion joints, typical of reinforced concrete structures, were not used—the volume changes caused by fluctuation in temperature were absorbed by semielastic joints, which allowed the members to move.

Installing the precast elements on the construction site, 1960

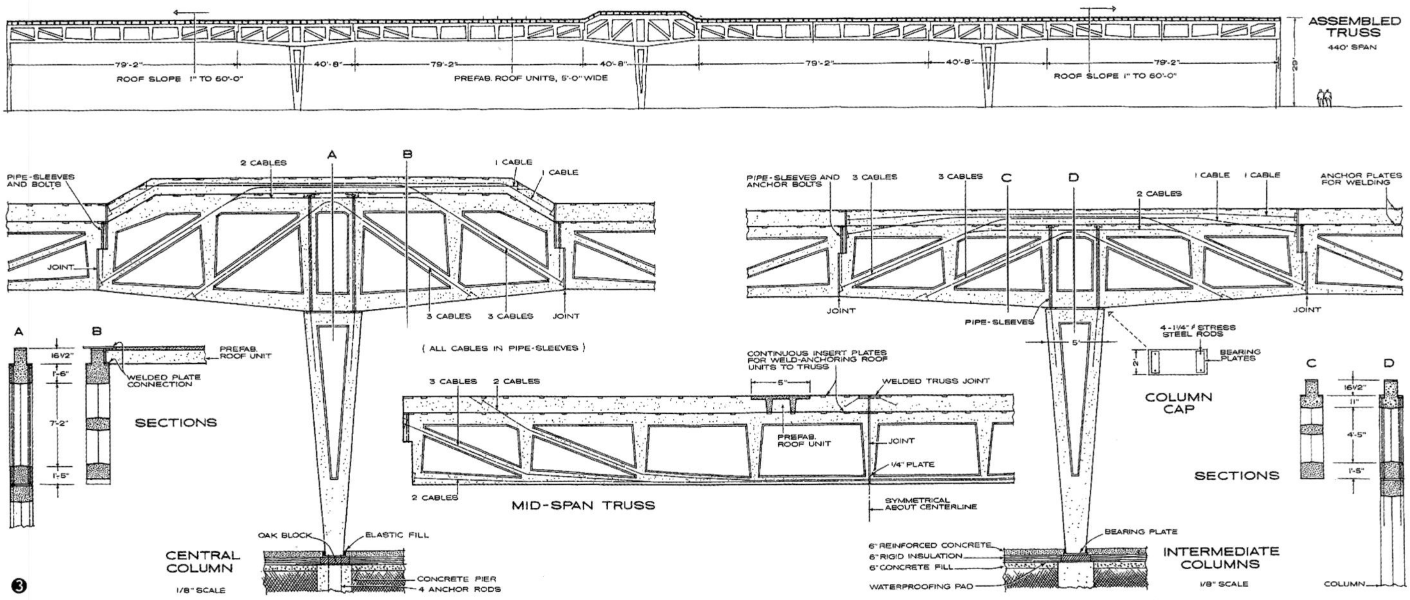

❸

Structural system for the cold storage

(*next spread*) The combined long-span truss was assembled from multiple precast, prestressed trusses, 1960

CONNELL & CO. INC.
CONTRACTORS
WOODBURY, N.J.
TI-5-0490

Installation of the facade panels, 1961

Philadelphia Police Administration Building

Philadelphia, Pennsylvania, USA
architects Geddes Brecher Qualls Cunningham,
structural engineer August Komendant
1959–1963 (extant)

For the Philadelphia Police Administration Building, August Komendant, together with the architects, developed an integrated and economical system of precast concrete elements. The load-bearing facade panels and floor panels were cast in a concrete factory and were partly prestressed. The geometry of the panels was optimized to reduce the number of different elements in production. On the construction site, the panels were installed with a crane and tied together with steel cables that were posttensioned.

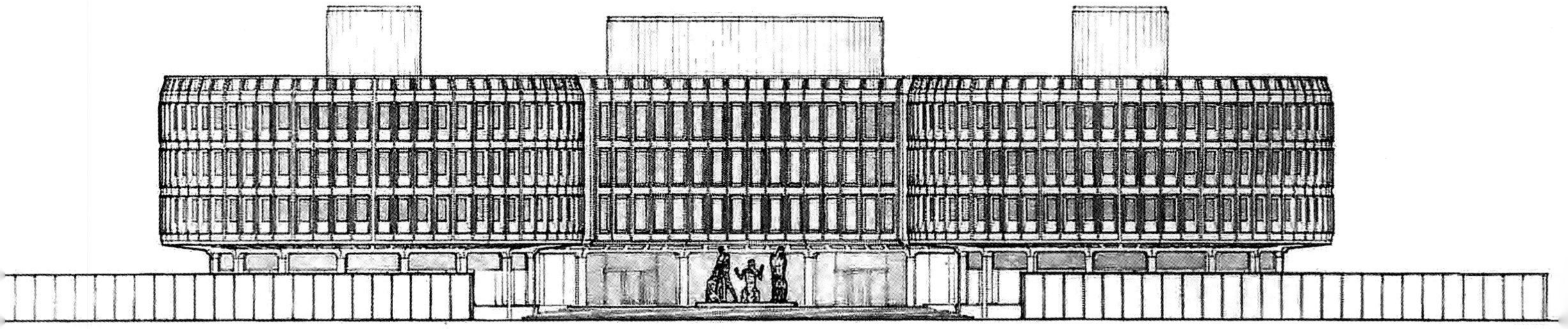

Street Elevation

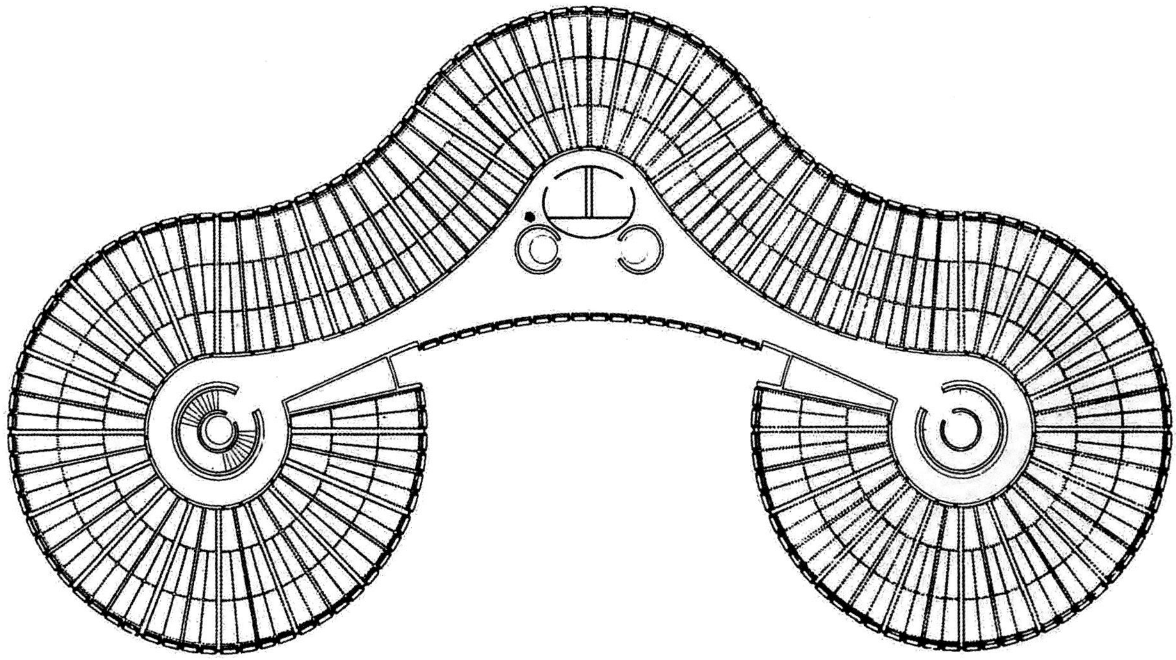

Schematic Office Floor Plan

Geddes Brecher Qualls Cunningham. Front elevation (*top*) and schematic office floor plan with a reflected ceiling of precast panels

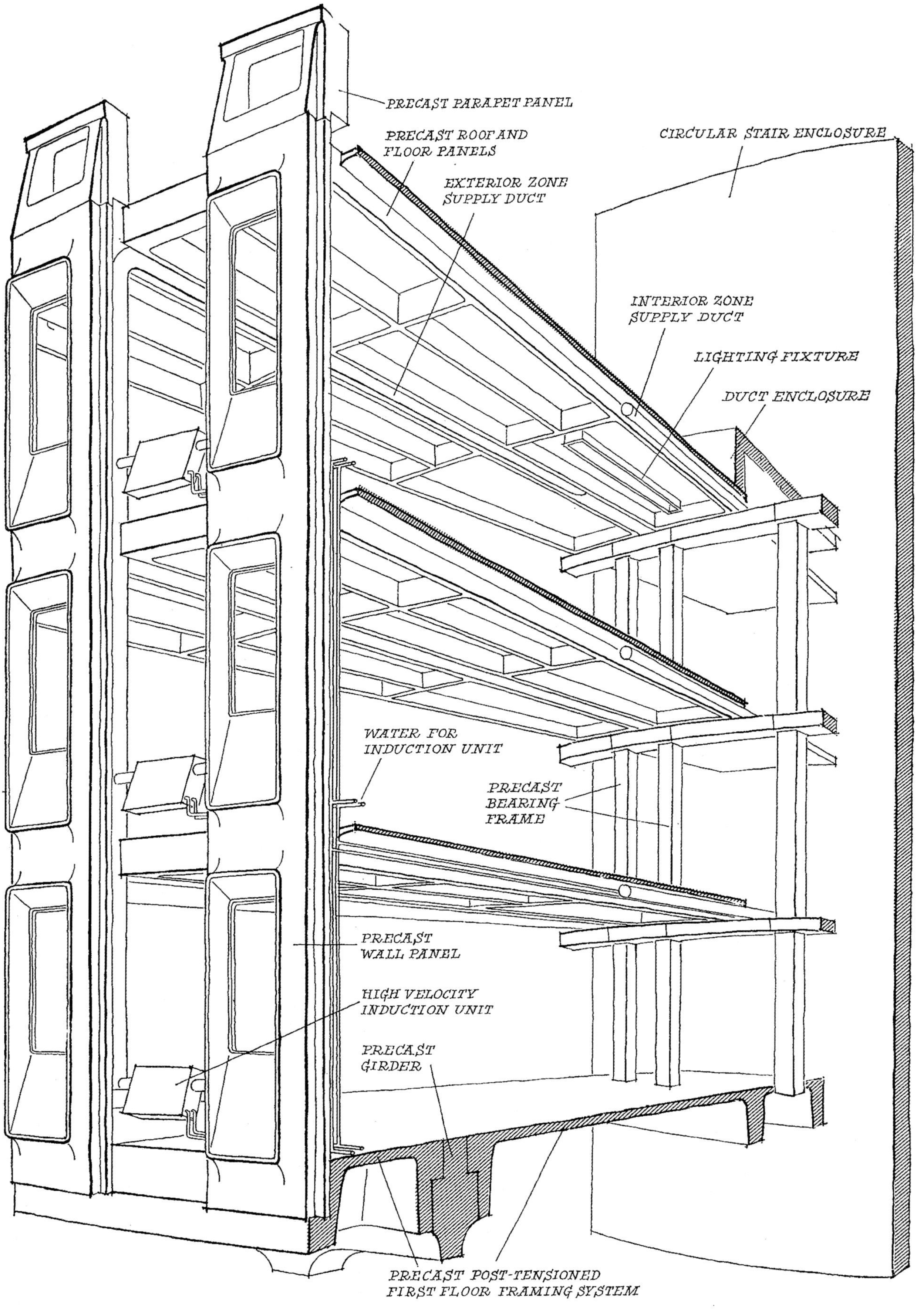

Structural system of the building

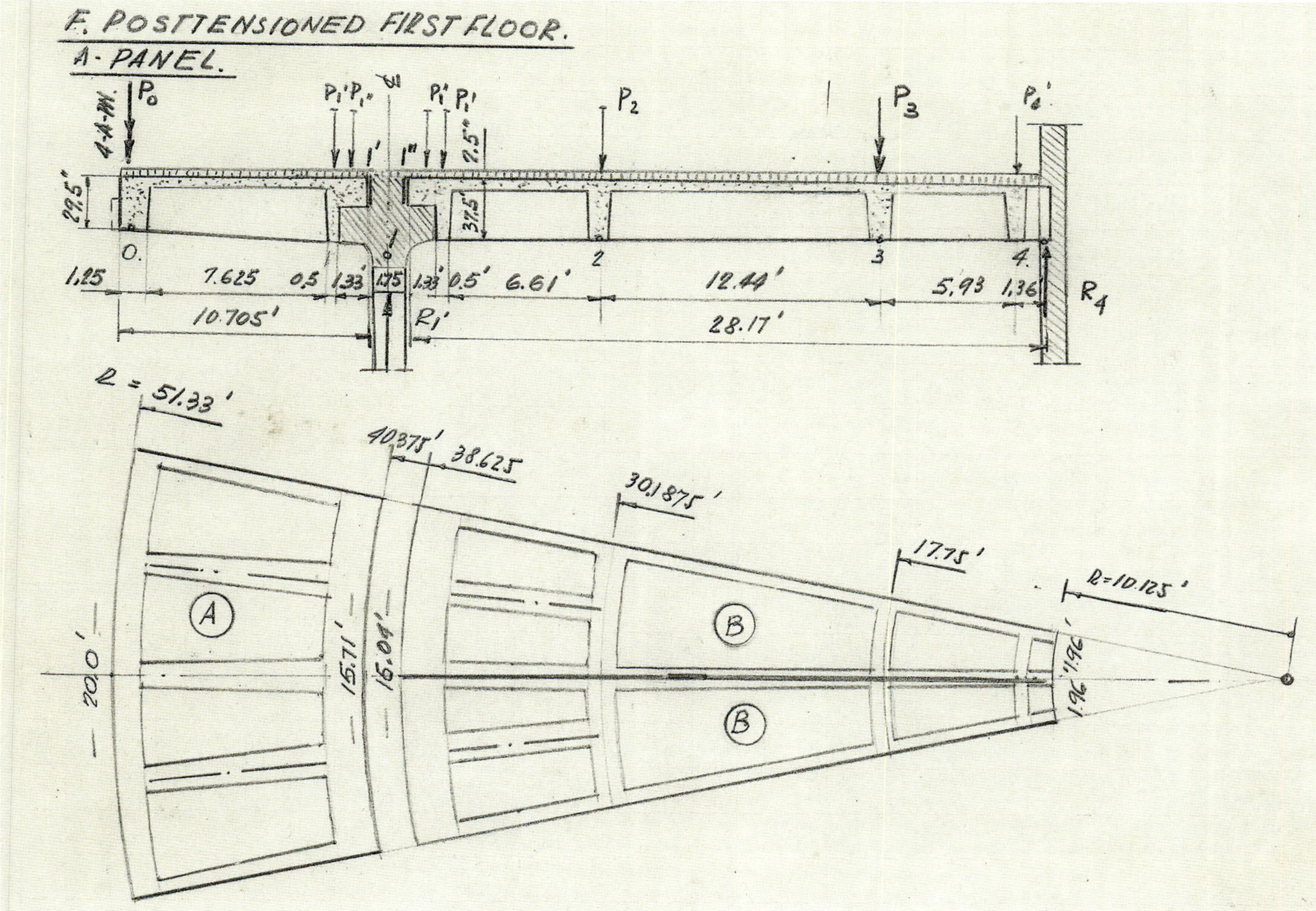

August Komendant. Static calculations of the building, posttensioned floor panels, 1960

Posttensioning of the facade panels

Police Administration Building under construction
(*right*) August Komendant visiting the construction site

Police Administration Building in the final phases of construction, 1962

ARCHWAY
CLOTHING

Post-construction inspection of the police building, 1962

Courtyard of the Salk Institute, view toward the Pacific Ocean

Salk Institute for Biological Studies

La Jolla, California, USA
architect Louis Kahn,
structural engineer August Komendant
1959–1965 (extant)

Dr. Jonas Salk, founder of the Salk Institute for Biological Studies, wanted to create a research center for the world's top scientists. The beautiful location on the hillside near the Pacific Ocean in La Jolla, California, inspired Kahn's sensitive design for the ensemble, in which aesthetics and technology are blended. Along with ensuring the complex could withstand an earthquake, another important structural challenge was posed by the long spans of the spacious laboratories. The initial structural proposal was comprised of box girders and folded plates. However, in the completed building, the main components are large Vierendeel trusses, which form separate mechanical floors.

Louis Kahn. Early site sketch, view to the ocean

Louis Kahn. Early site sketch, view of the cliffs
(*right*) Salk Institute in the landscape

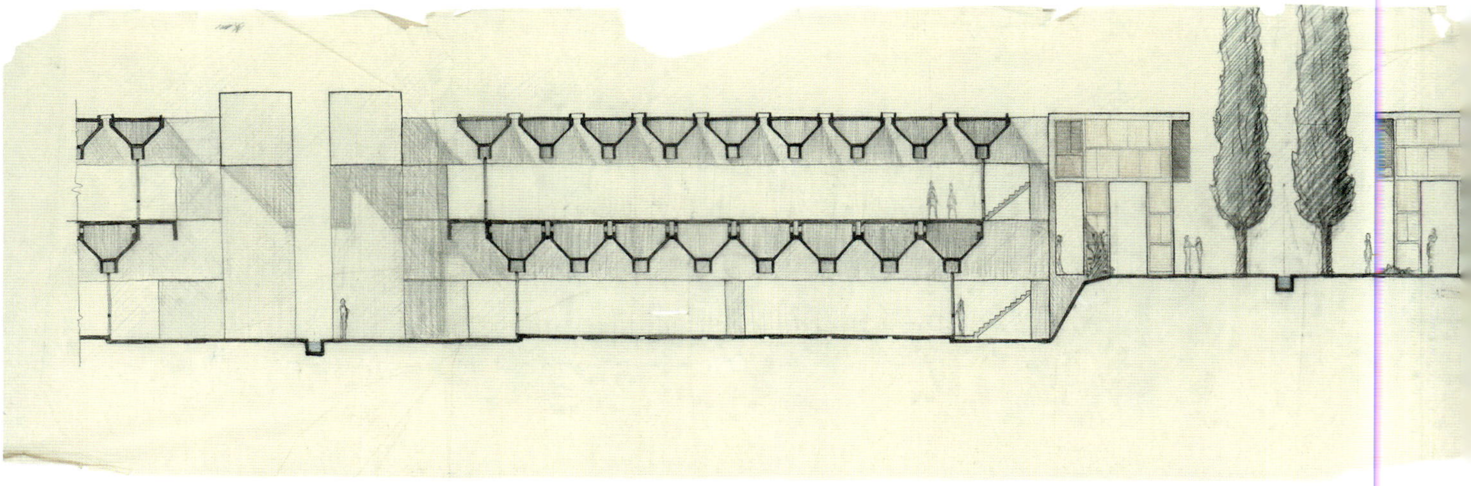

Office of Louis Kahn. Preliminary structural system, cross section

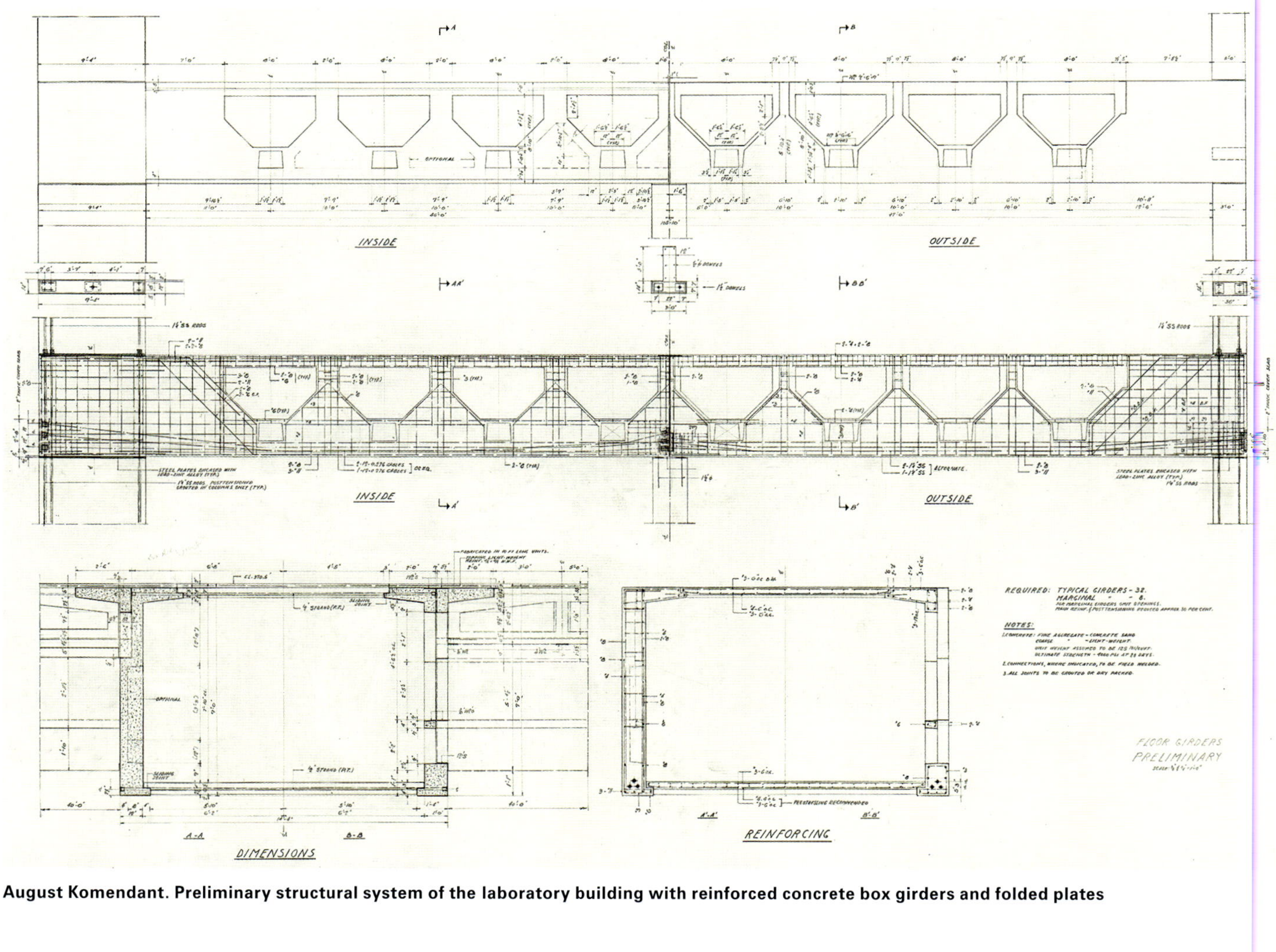

August Komendant. Preliminary structural system of the laboratory building with reinforced concrete box girders and folded plates

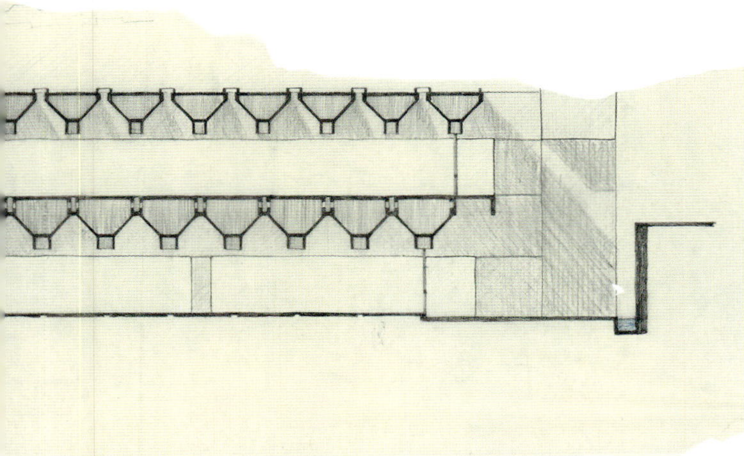

Model of the preliminary structural system

Louis Kahn. Proposed garden in the courtyard between the laboratory buildings, perspective drawing, 1962

Office of Louis Kahn. Aerial view of the Salk Institute, perspective drawing

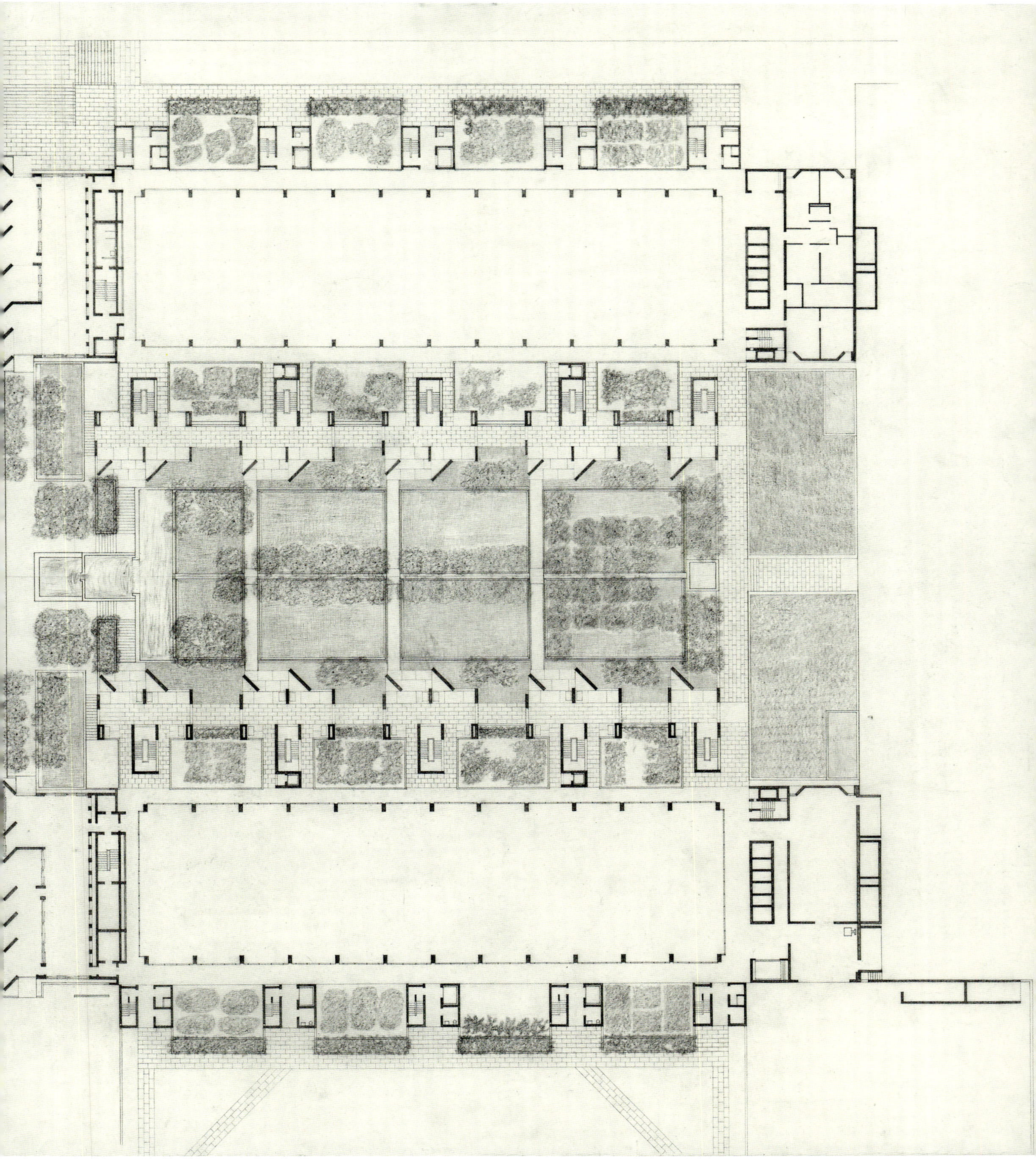

Office of Louis Kahn. Site plan

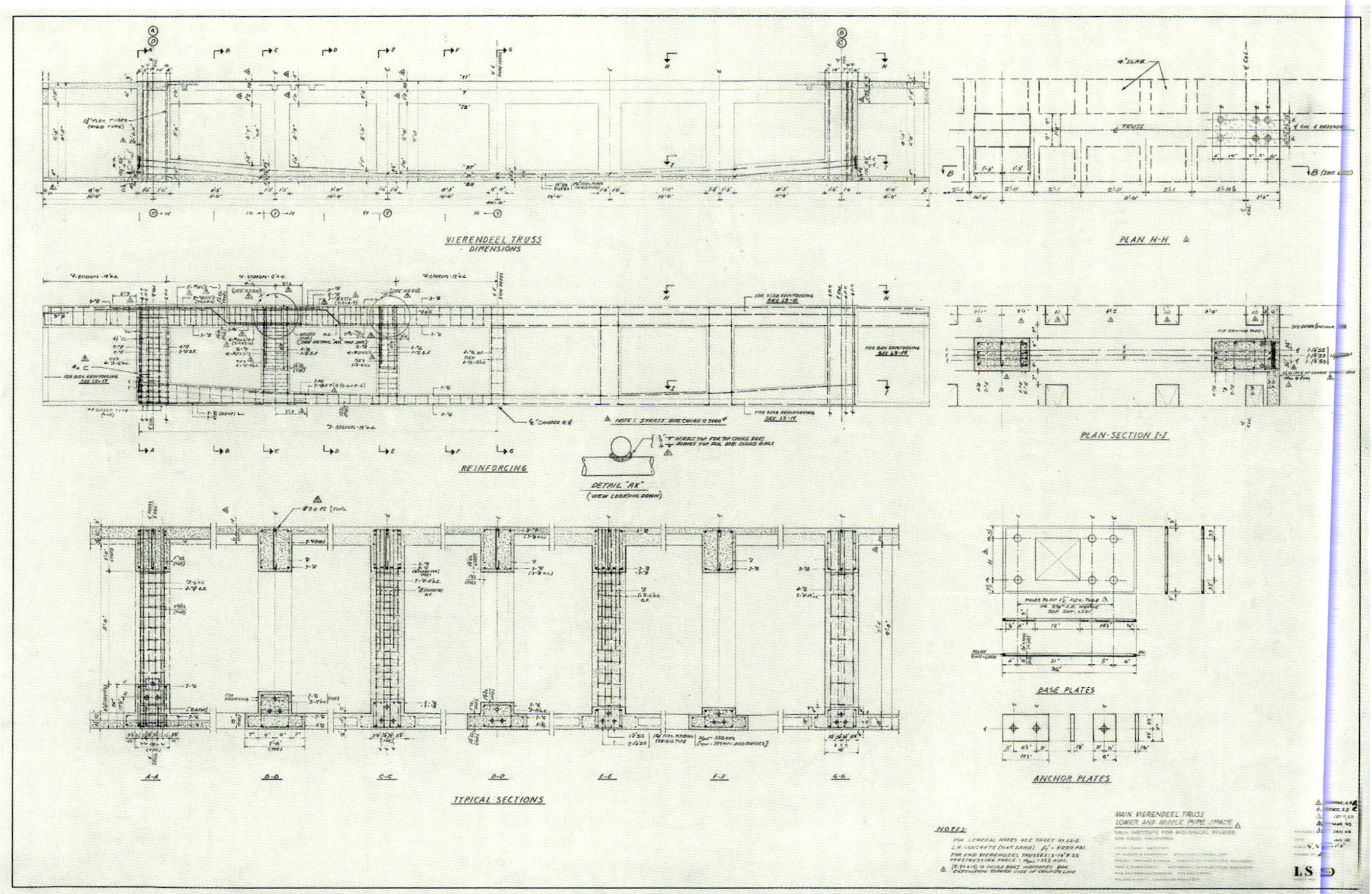

August Komendant. Final structural system for the laboratory building with reinforced concrete Vierendeel trusses

Floor slab construction for the laboratory building

Floor slab construction for the laboratory building, 1964

Laboratory floor before furnishing

Work spaces for researchers under construction and after completion

August Komendant visiting the site in the final phases of construction

Salk Institute in the final phases of construction

Clean concrete surfaces
(*right*) Service towers and the side facade
(*next spread*) Side view to the service towers

Church exterior in the final phases of construction

First Unitarian Church

Rochester, New York. USA
architect Louis Kahn,
structural engineer August Komendant
1959–1969 (extant)

A modern church building, where sensitive use of natural light is skillfully combined with an impressive structure. Light wells with skylights are in the corners of the church hall. The hall is dominated by a reinforced concrete folded plate roof that seems to be floating in the air.

Louis Kahn. Facade sketch

Church exterior during construction

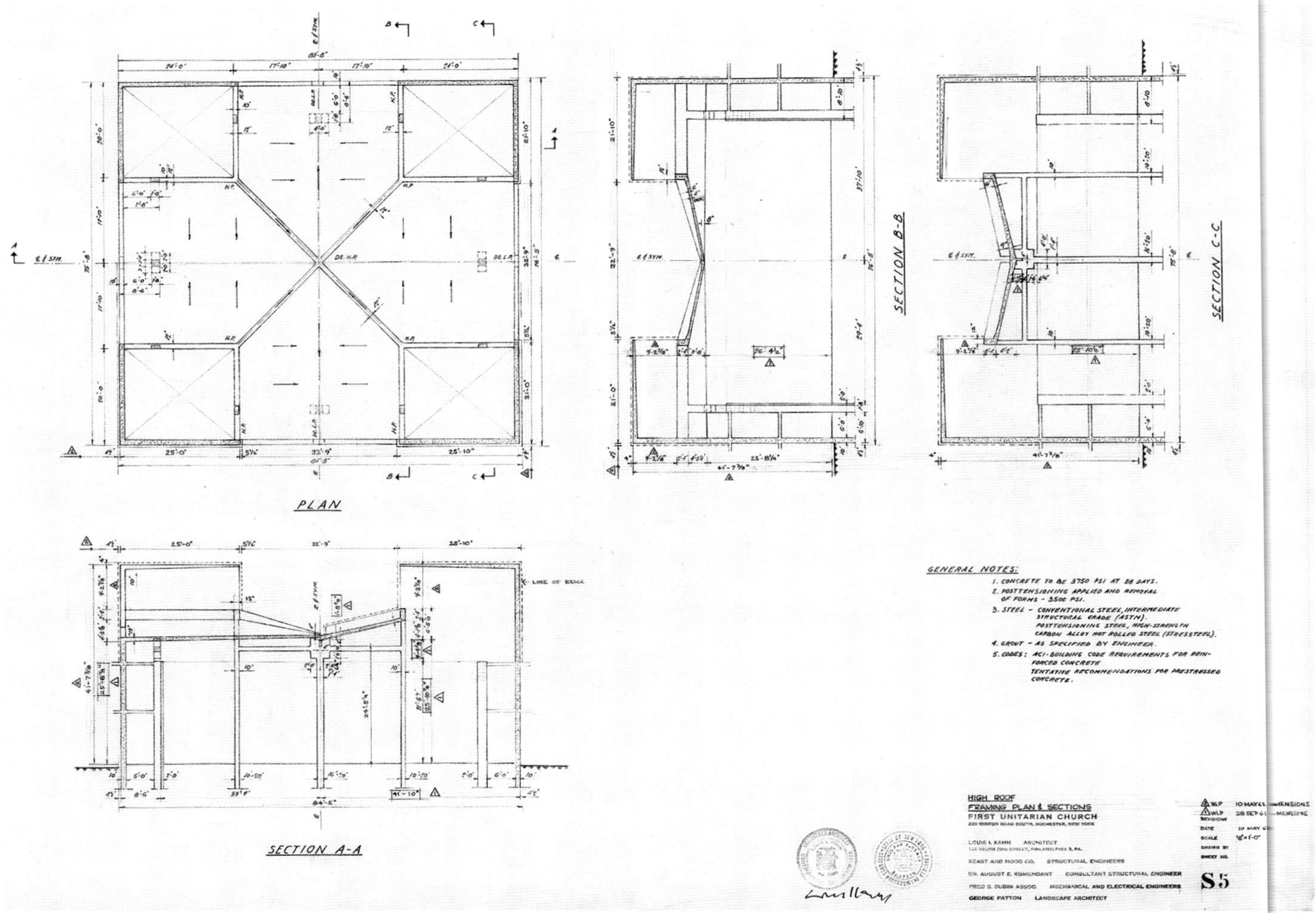

August Komendant. Structural system of the church hall, 1961

Roof under construction

Interior under construction

Church hall after completion

Brick walls and a skylight
(*right*) **Church interior and the folded plate roof structure**

Habitat '67 on the bank of the St. Lawrence River

Habitat '67

Montreal, Quebec, Canada
architect Moshe Safdie, associate architects David, Barott, Boulva, structural engineer August Komendant
1964–1967 (extant)

The residential complex built for Expo 67, the World Fair held in Montreal in 1967, symbolizes the social optimism and technological advances of the 1960s. Moshe Safdie wanted to create a modular urban ensemble which provides the comforts of private houses—spacious balconies, plenty of light, and sufficient privacy. August Komendant helped with not only providing the structural solution but also with organizing the production and construction process. All of the housing units (354) and the smaller details were produced in the temporary concrete factory installed next to the building site. The concrete modules were put in place by crane and then connected and posttensioned into unity with steel cables. The static calculations were challenging due to the large number of cantilevered surfaces.

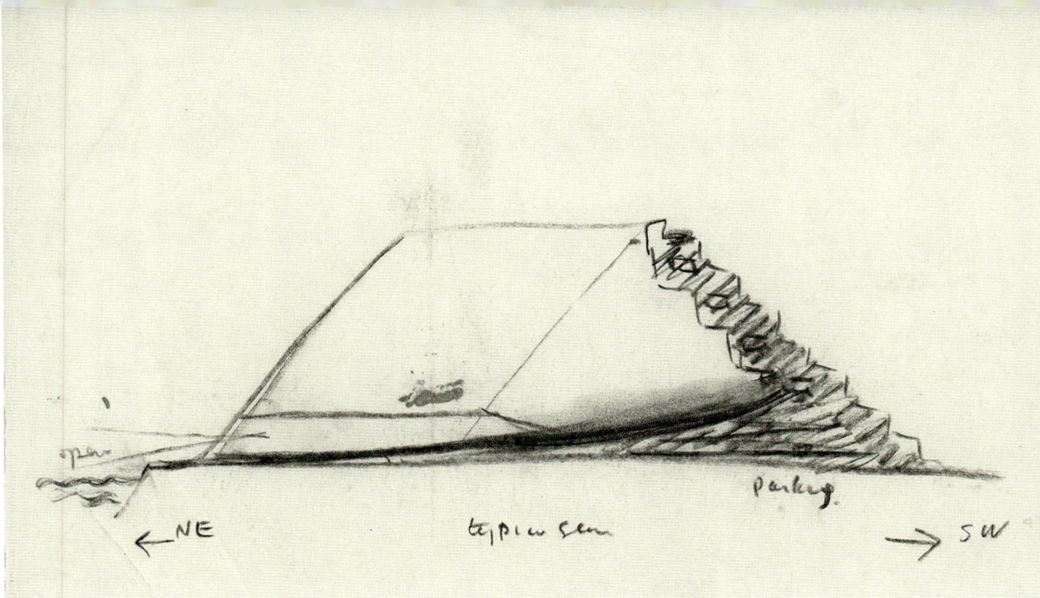

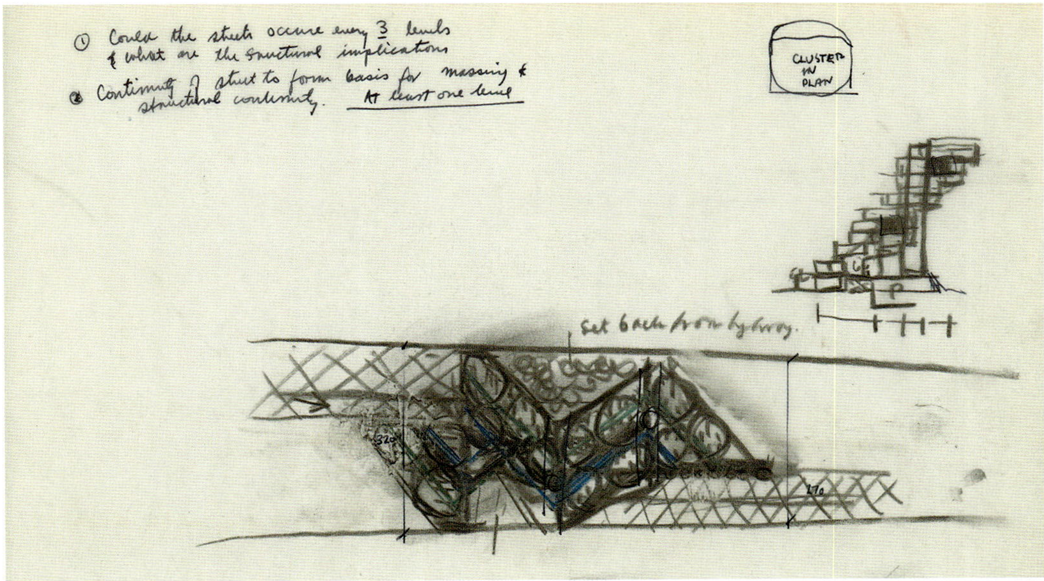

Moshe Safdie. Early sketches and a conceptual model

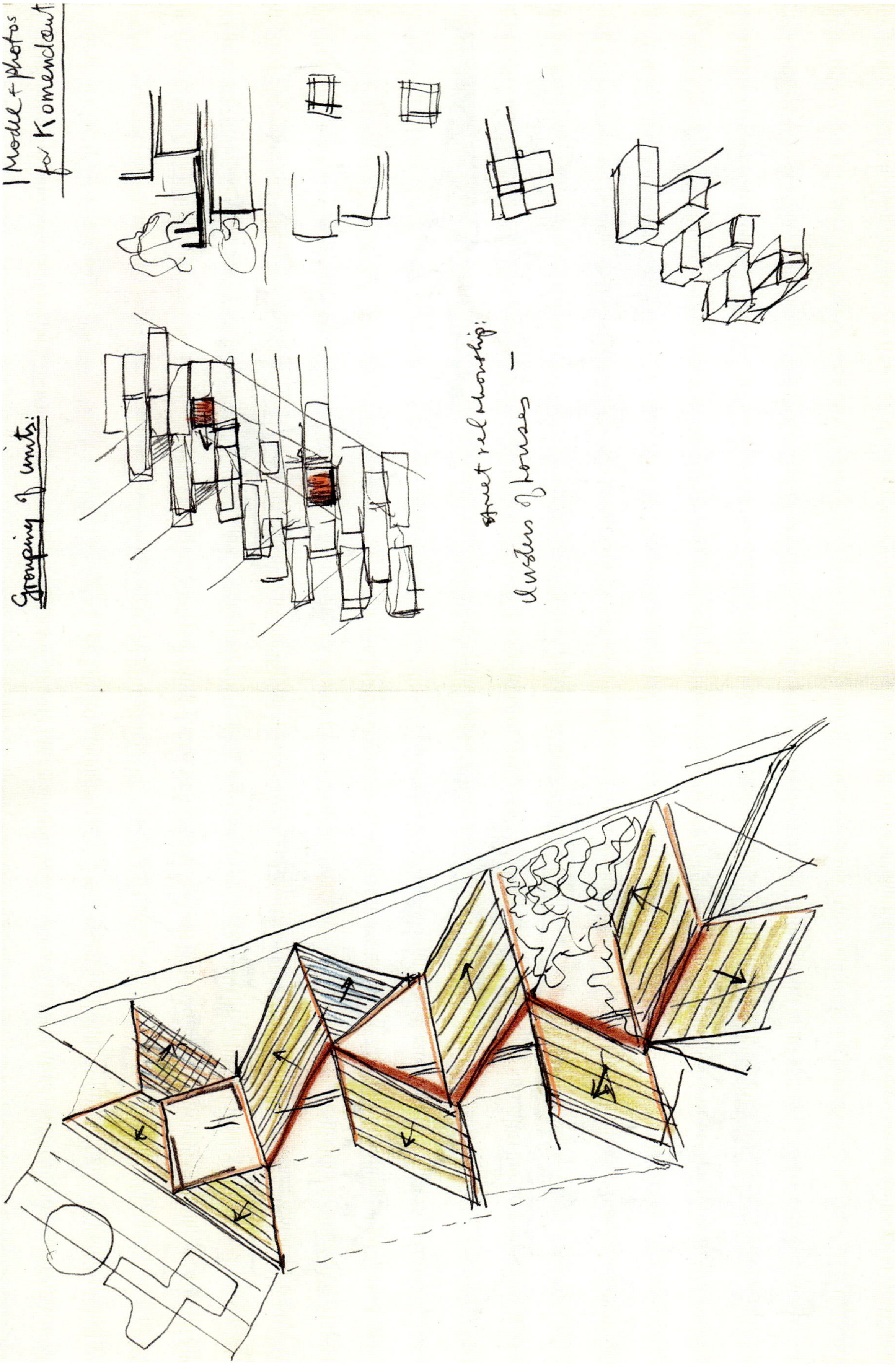

Moshe Safdie, Early sketch

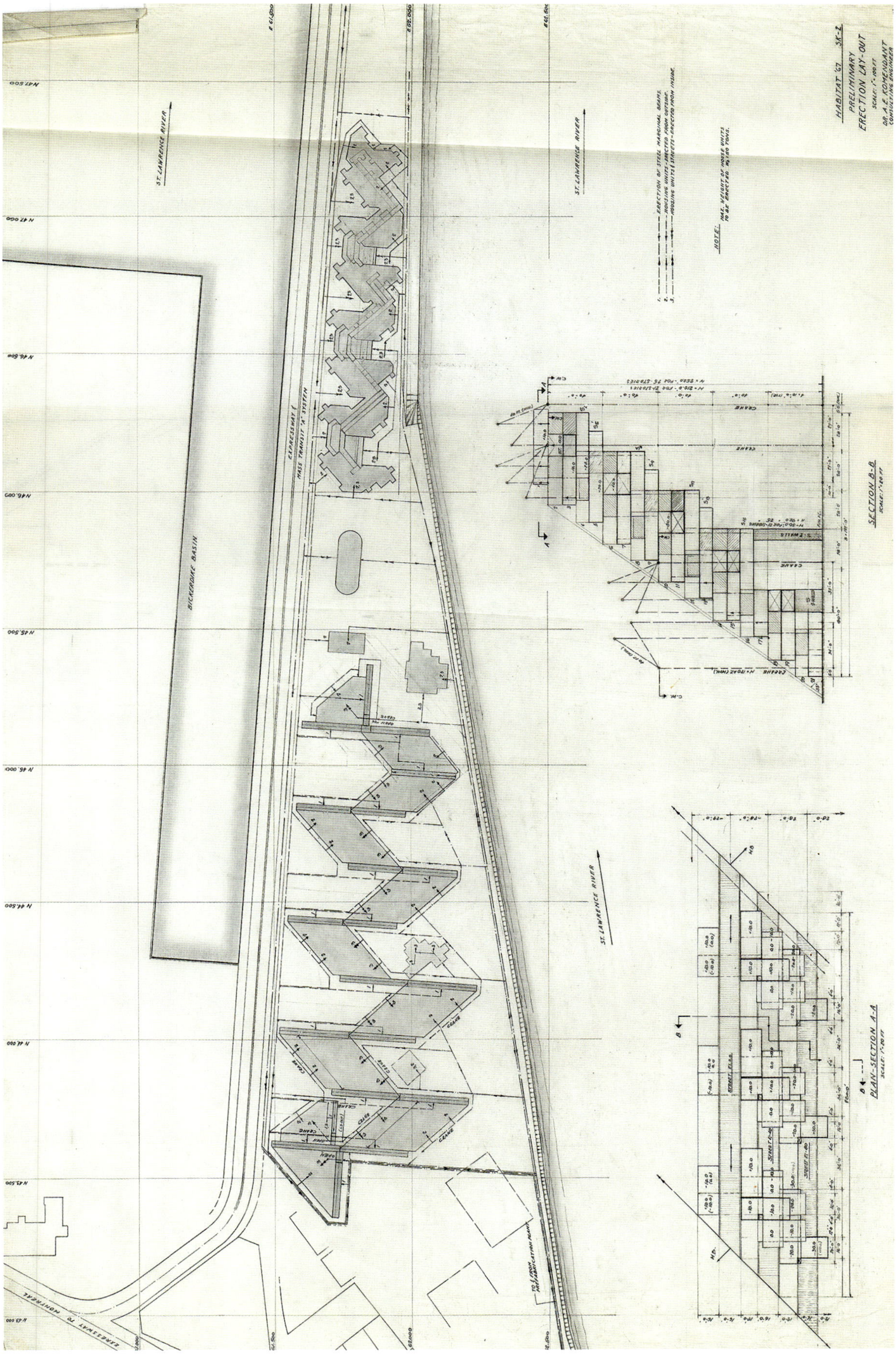

August Komendant. Preliminary site and erection layout, 1964

Sketch model

Office of Moshe Safdie (David Rinehart). Early color perspective

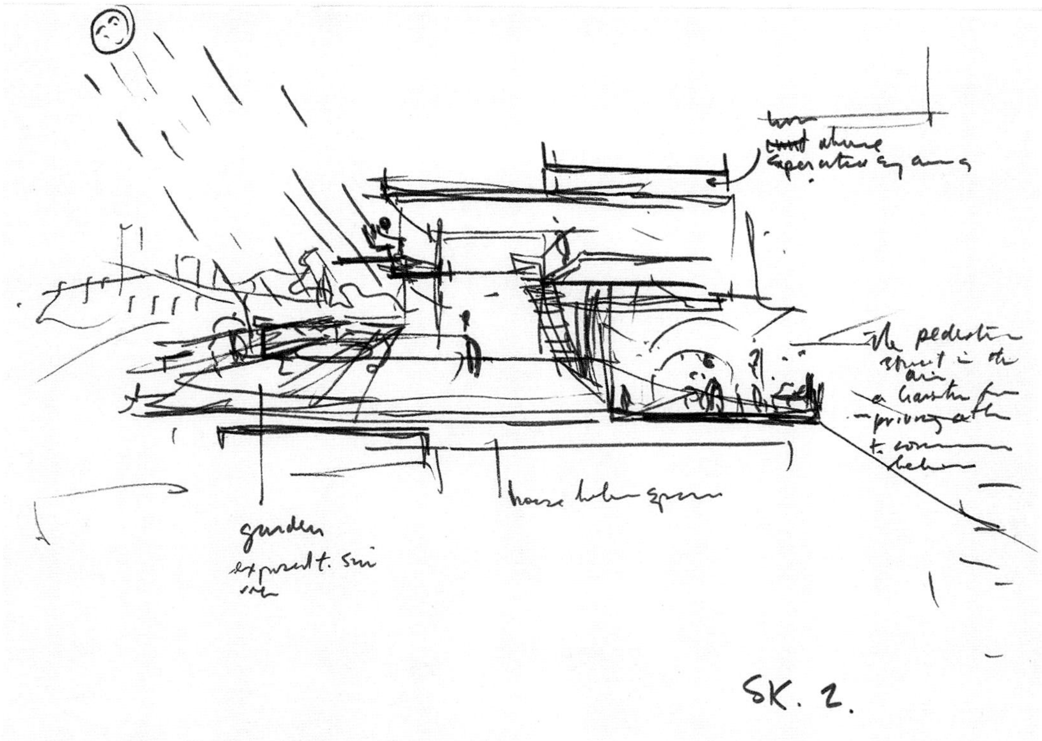

Moshe Safdie. Early section sketch

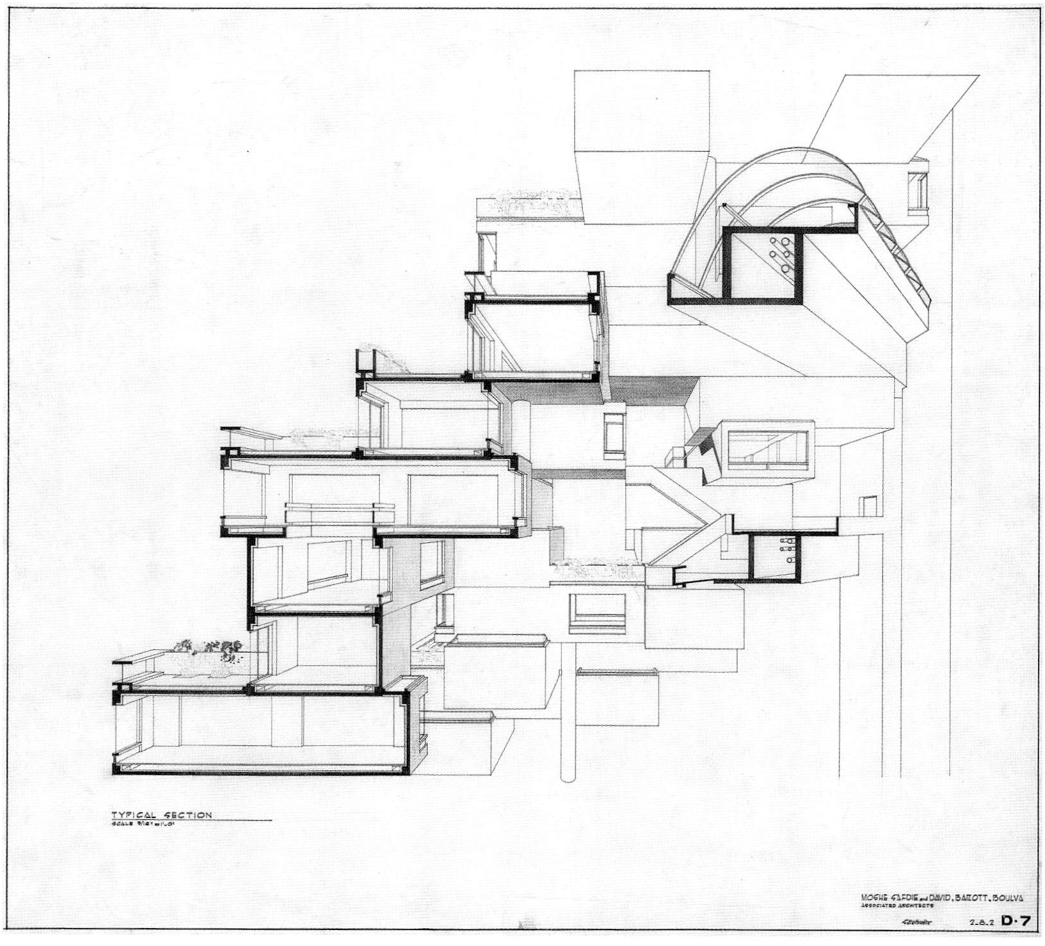

Office of Moshe Safdie (Satterthwaite). Perspective section

Precast elements of one apartment

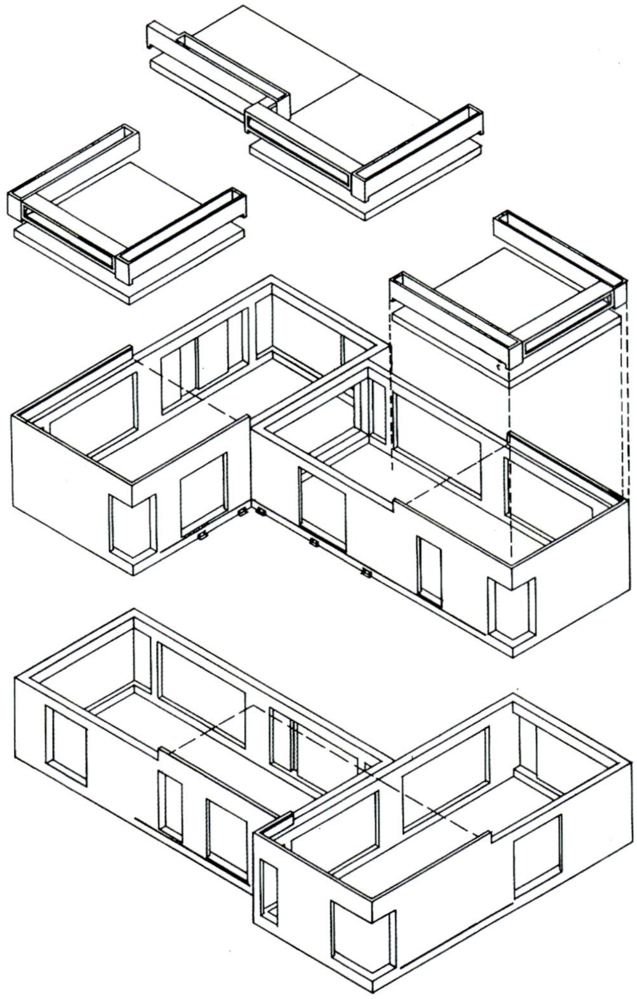

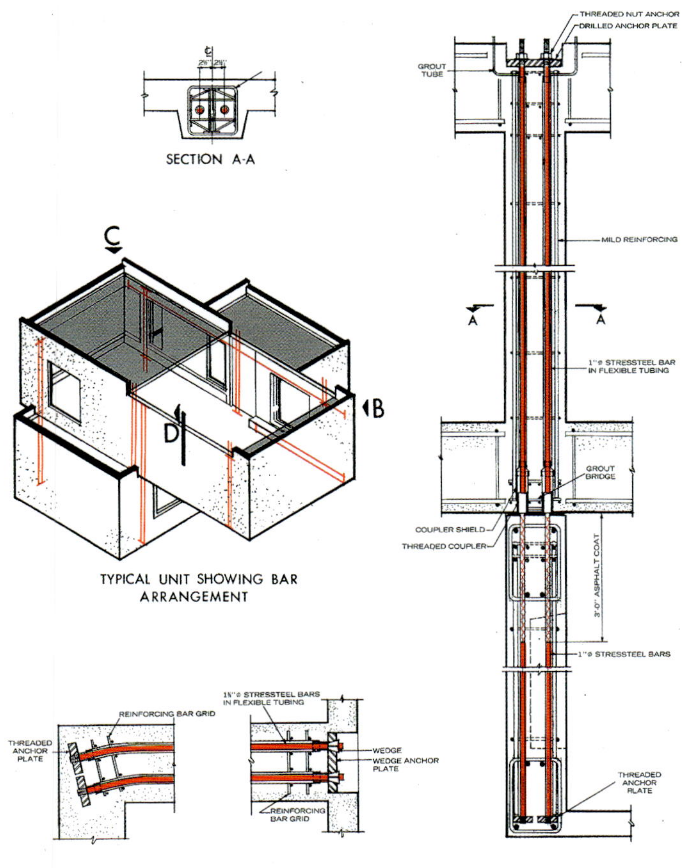

Posttensioning of concrete modules with steel cables

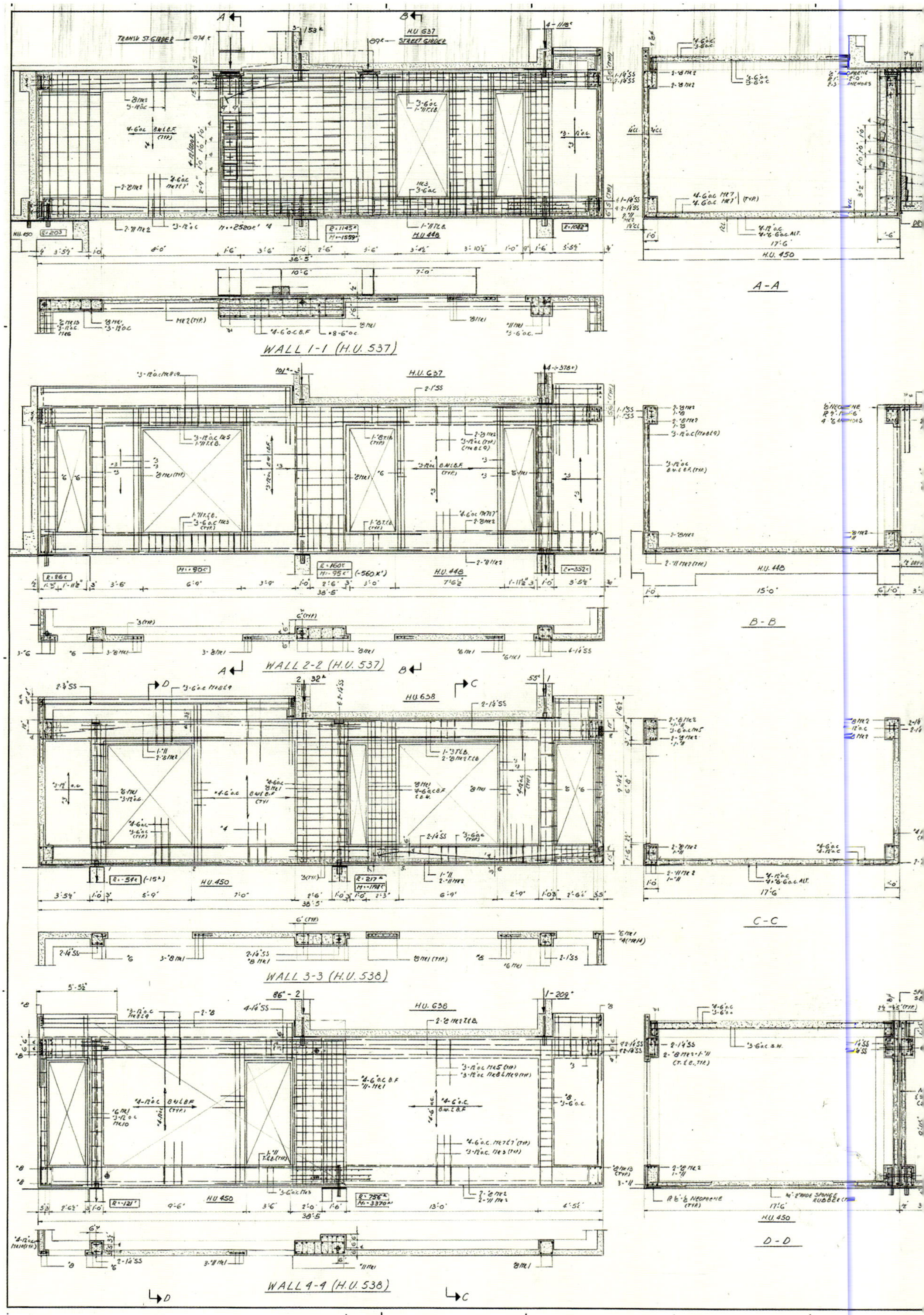
WALL 1-1 (H.U. 537)
A-A
WALL 2-2 (H.U. 537)
B-B
WALL 3-3 (H.U. 538)
C-C
WALL 4-4 (H.U. 538)
D-D

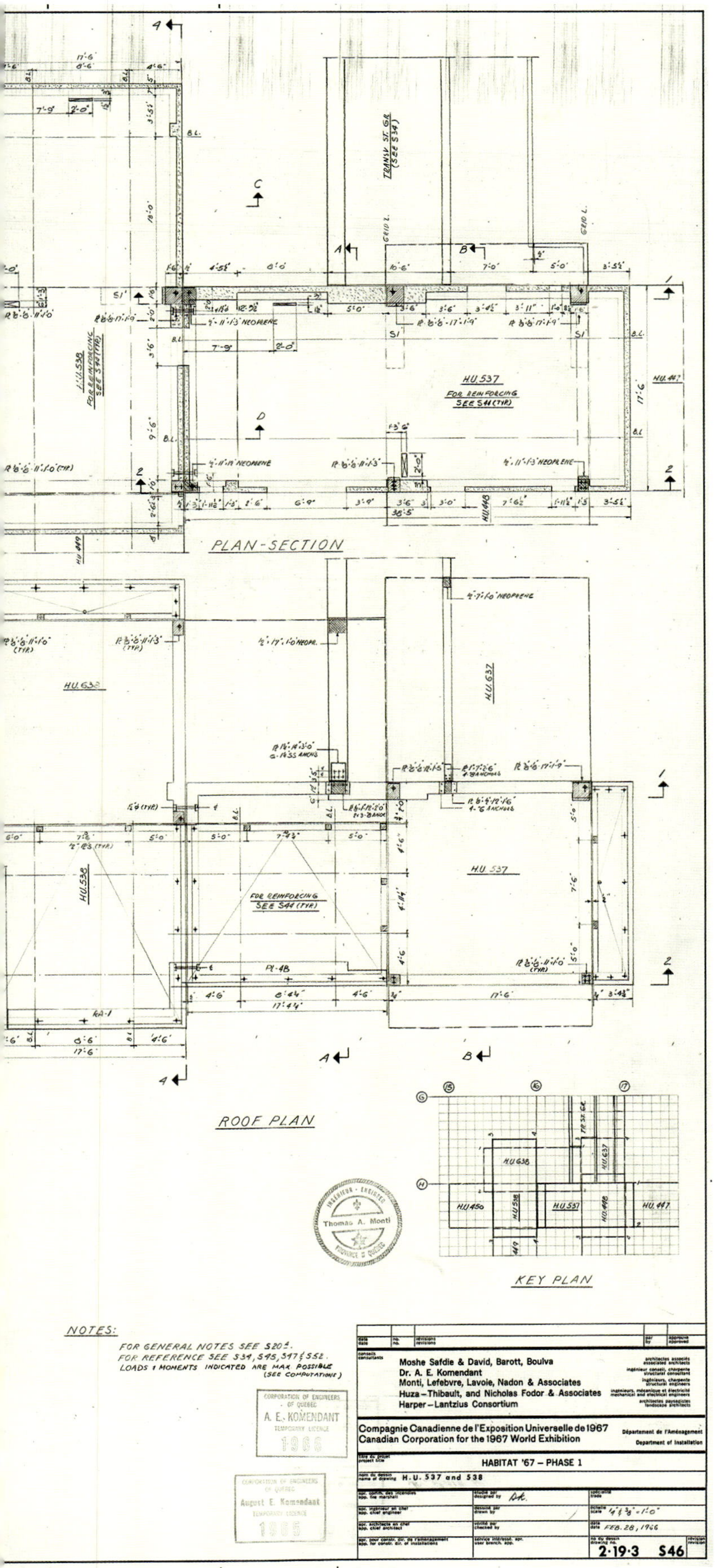

August Komendant. Housing modules nos. 537 and 538, 1966

Production of the housing modules

Transporting the housing modules to the construction site

Construction worker unhooking a housing module

Installing the housing modules with a large crane

August Komendant (*third from the left*) visiting the construction site

Installing the housing modules

(next spread) **Installing the horizontal girders, which contain the mechanicals and serve the inhabitants as "streets in the air"**

BRIDGE
ALLIED
CRANE SERVICES INC.
1967

A street in the air

Connecting routes and accesses to the apartments

Courtyard milieu

(*next spread*) Construction in full swing

SECANT
NO HELP REQUIRED
AUCUNE AIDE
DEMANDÉE

Higher floors and a shared terrace

Spacious terraces decked with wood
(*next spread*) **Habitat '67 after completion**

Synagogue after completion

Temple Beth Hillel

Wynnewood, Pennsylvania, USA
architect Norman Rice,
structural engineer August Komendant
1964–1968 (extant)

This is a synagogue with a community center in a modernist architectural style. In terms of both its architecture and structure, the most striking part is the main sanctuary of the synagogue, above which rises a grand, pyramidal monolithic concrete roof. Architect Norman Rice and August Komendant were colleagues at the University of Pennsylvania. This is the only known building they designed together.

Synagogue interior

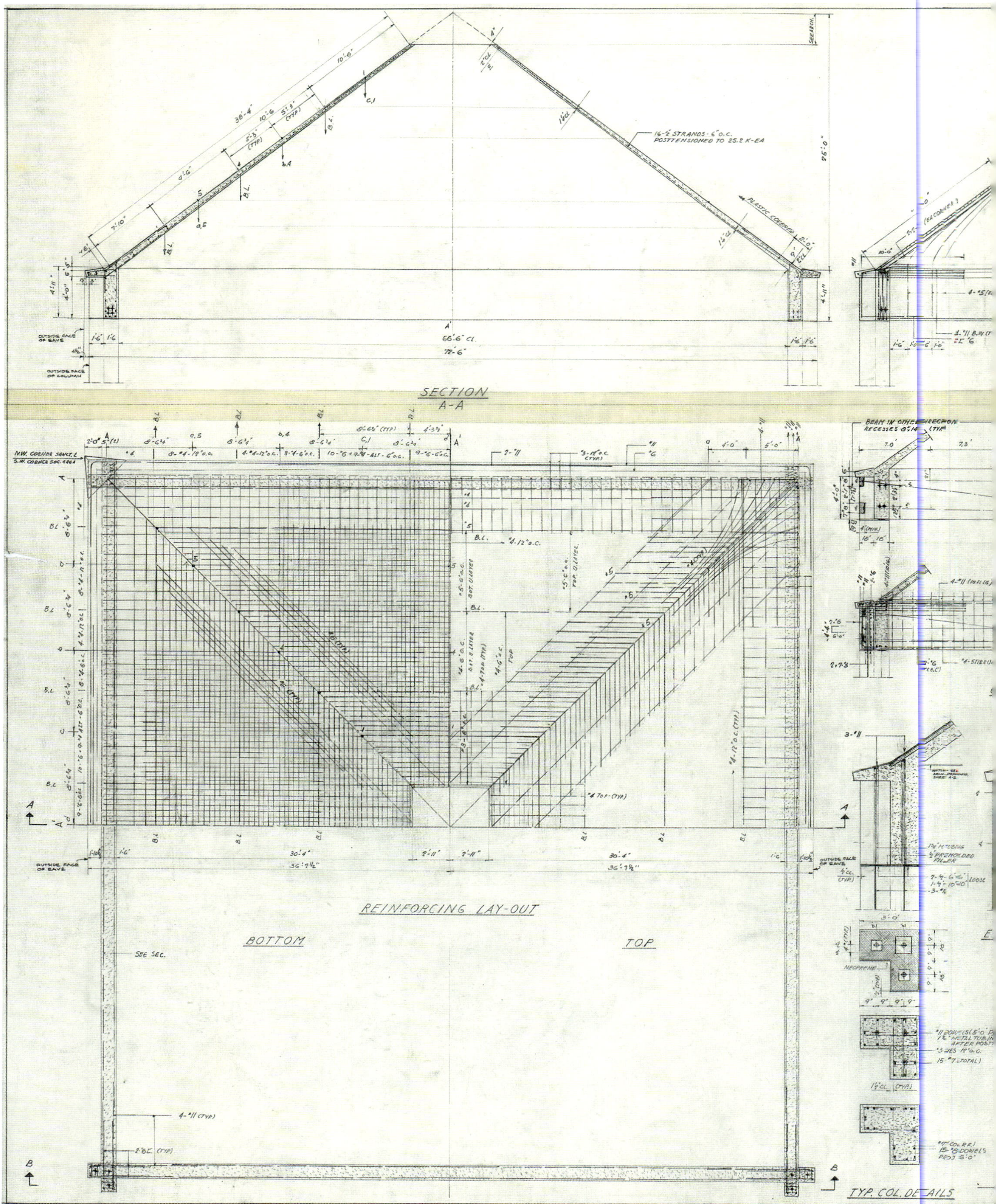
SECTION
A-A
16-½ STRANDS - 6" o.c.
POSTTENSIONED TO 25.2 K-EA
PLASTIC COVERED
OUTSIDE FACE OF EAVE
OUTSIDE FACE OF COLUMN
66'-6" C.L.
72'-6"
REINFORCING LAY-OUT
BOTTOM
TOP
SEE SEC.
30'-4"
36'-7½"
NEOPRENE
TYP. COL. DETAILS

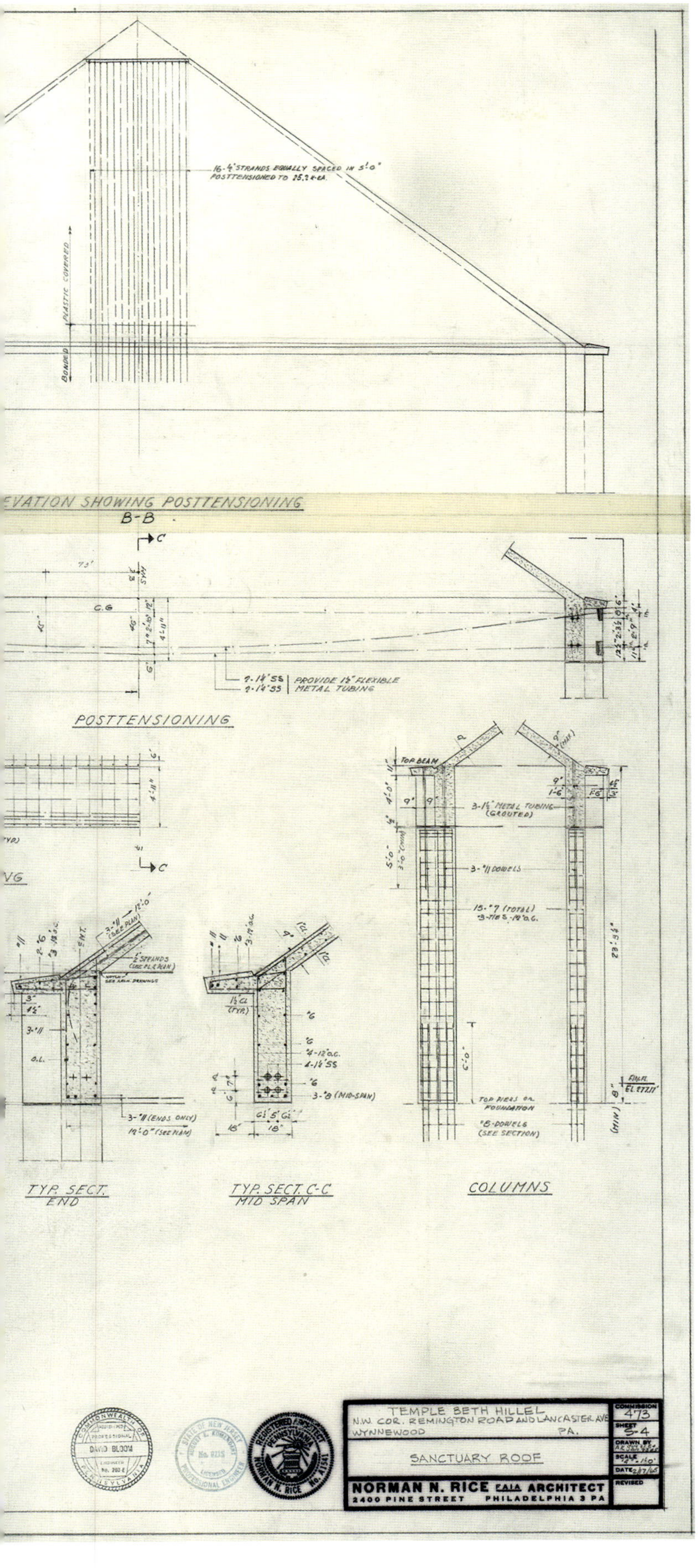

August Komendant. Structure of the pyramidal roof, 1965

Parking garage after completion

Parking Garage No. 2, University of Pennsylvania

Philadelphia, Pennsylvania, USA
Mitchell/Giurgola Architects,
structural engineer August Komendant
1966–1969 (extant)

The design of the six-story garage in the immediate vicinity of the historical campus had to consider a height restriction and dignified neighboring buildings. Together with architect Romaldo Giurgola, August Komendant designed an original concrete structure for the building consisting of single-ribbed floor panels, marginal beams, and column segments.

Mitchell/Giurgola Architects. Elevation sketch

Mitchell/Giurgola Architects. Perspective view, 1967

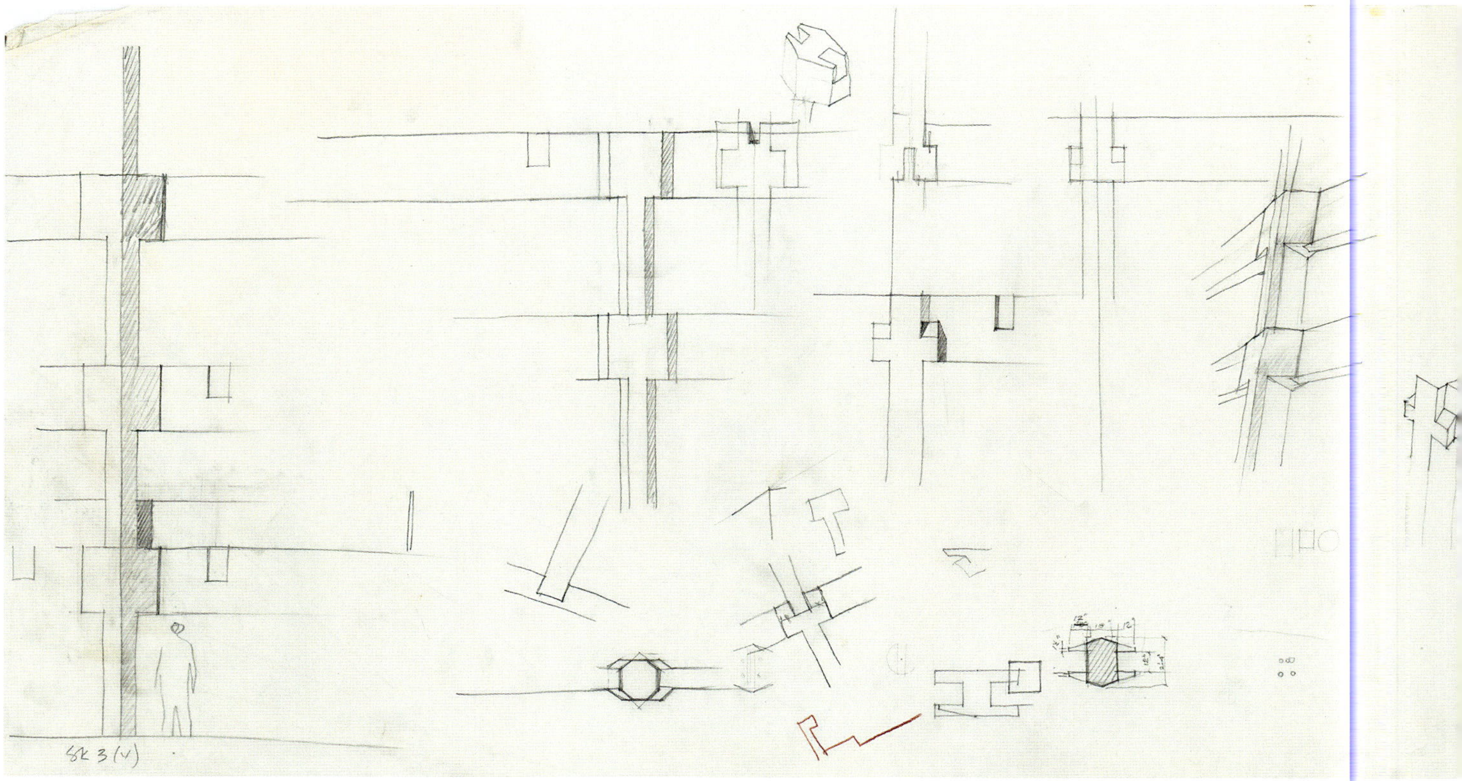

Mitchell/Giurgola Architects. Sketches of the structural system

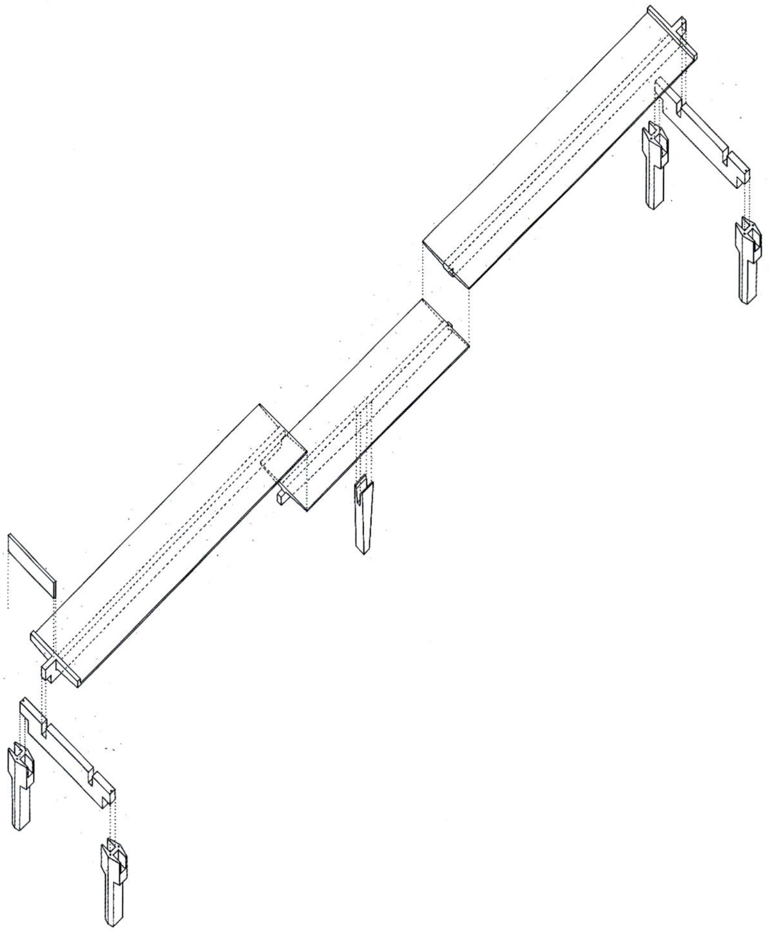

The structural system and its components

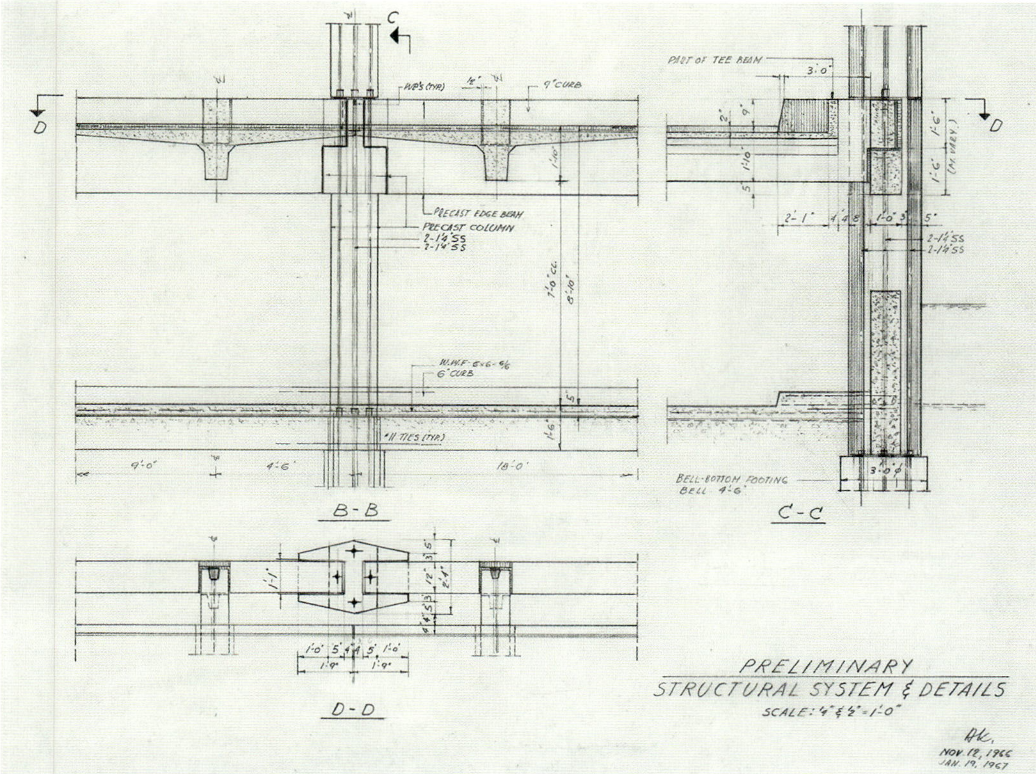

August Komendant. The structural system of the building, detail, 1966

Early phases of construction

MC HUGH
BROS.

Installing the precast elements

Installing the concrete column segments
(***next spread***) **The parking garage after completion**

Parking Garage No. 2, University of Pennsylvania

Casting the concrete modules

Olivetti-Underwood Factory

Harrisburg, Pennsylvania
architect Louis Kahn,
structural engineer August Komendant
1966–1970 (extant, altered)

The factory building for the Italian typewriter manufacturer consists of large reinforced concrete modules reminiscent of inverted mushrooms or umbrellas. One module, supported by a single column, is 17 meters wide and 8.7 meters high. To create a unified structure, the "mushrooms" were tied together with posttensioning cables. To allow natural light into the production facilities, skylights were placed on top of the openings that form in the corners of the concrete modules.

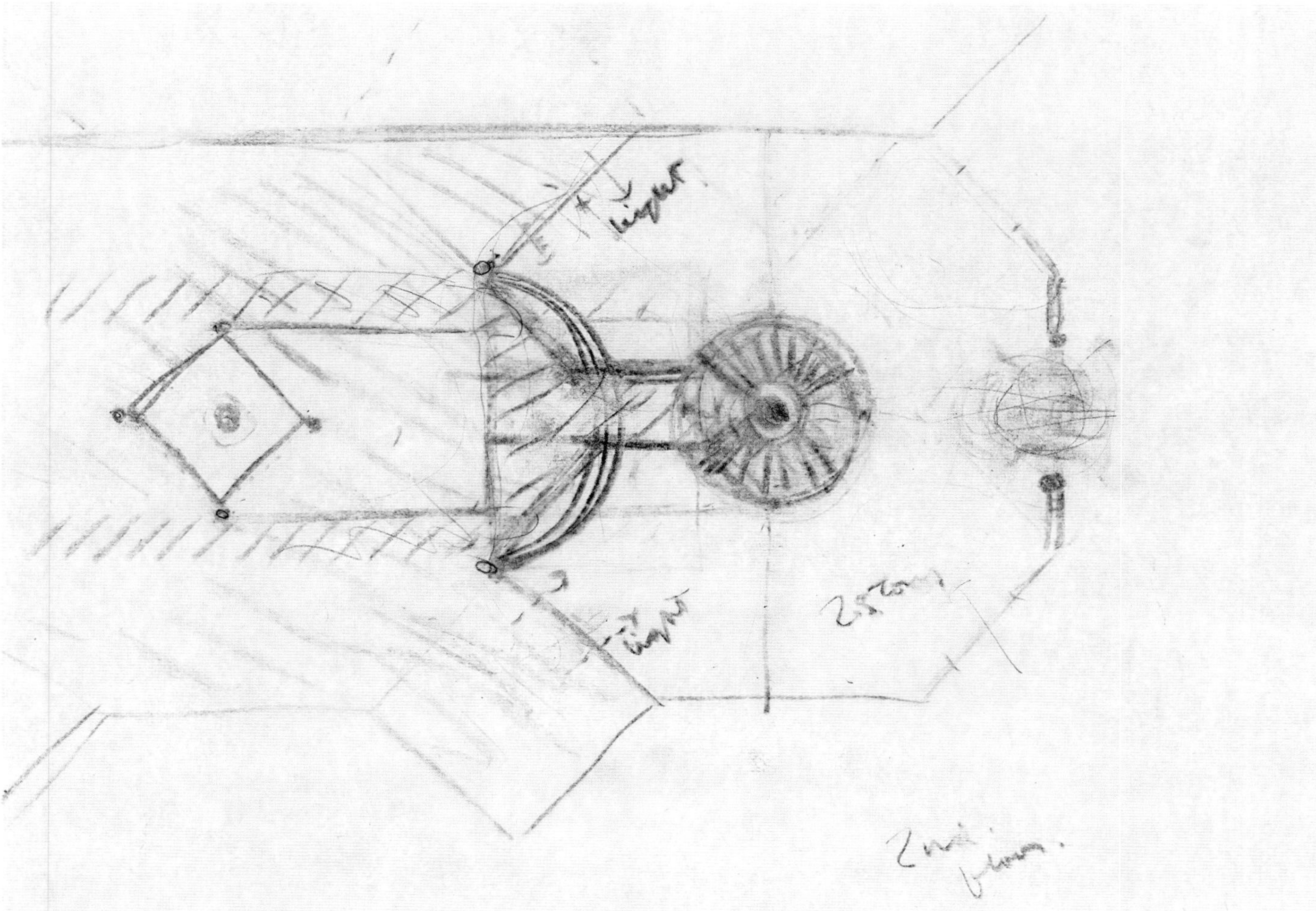

Louis Kahn. Early sketch of the factory building

Study model

(*next spread*) August Komendant. Concrete module, 1967

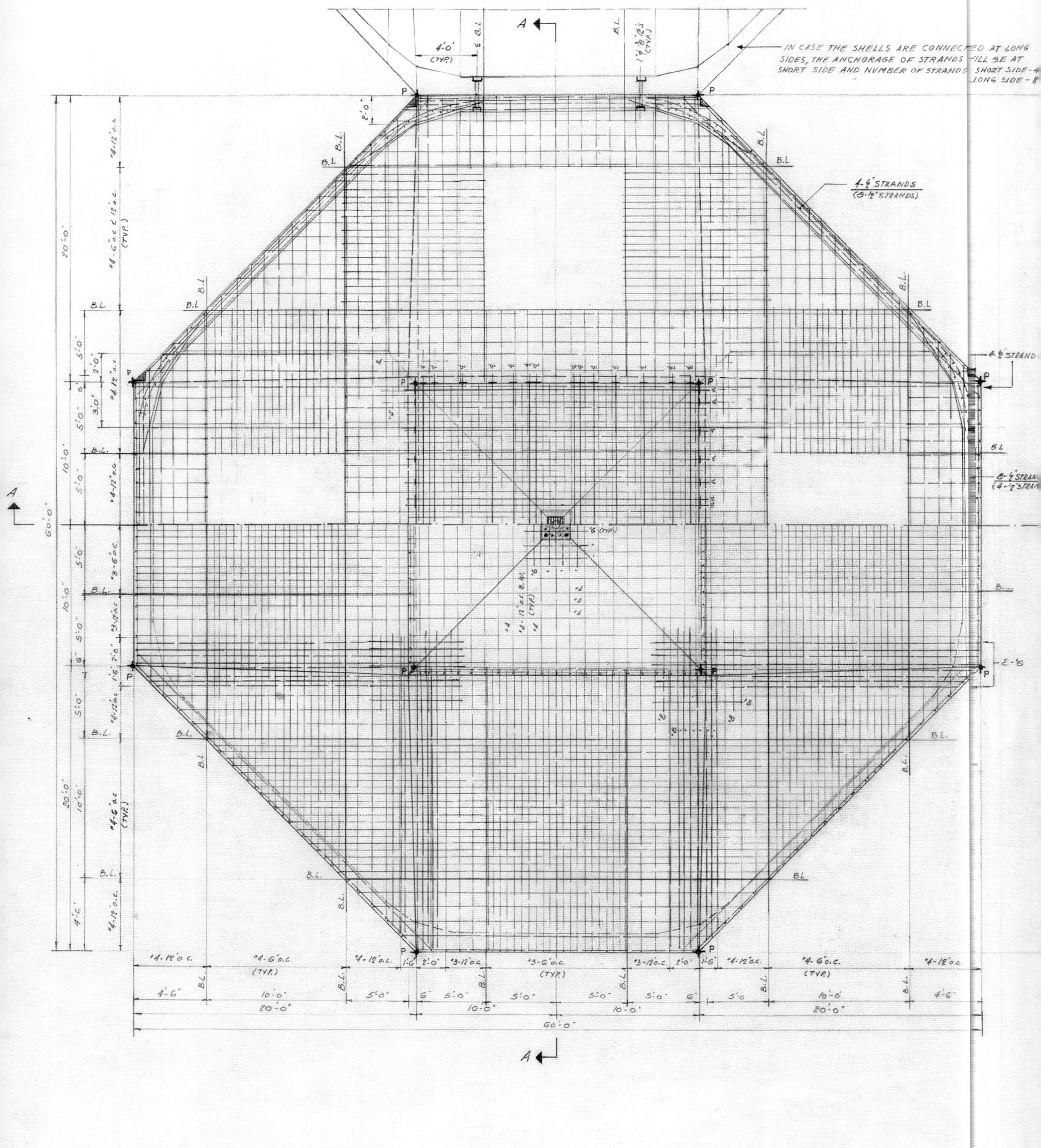

NOTES:

1. CONCRETE: 3750 PSI AT 28 DAY
" 5000 " " "
" 6500 " " "

2. REINFORCING: f_S = 20000 PSI -

3. SS - f_{ULT} = 50000 "

4. STRANDS - f_{ULT} = 250000 "

5. CONSTRUCTION IN TWO STAGE
1ST - COLUMN DISTRIBUT
POSTTENSIONED AFT
2ND - SHELL & TENSION R
POSTTENSIONED AFT

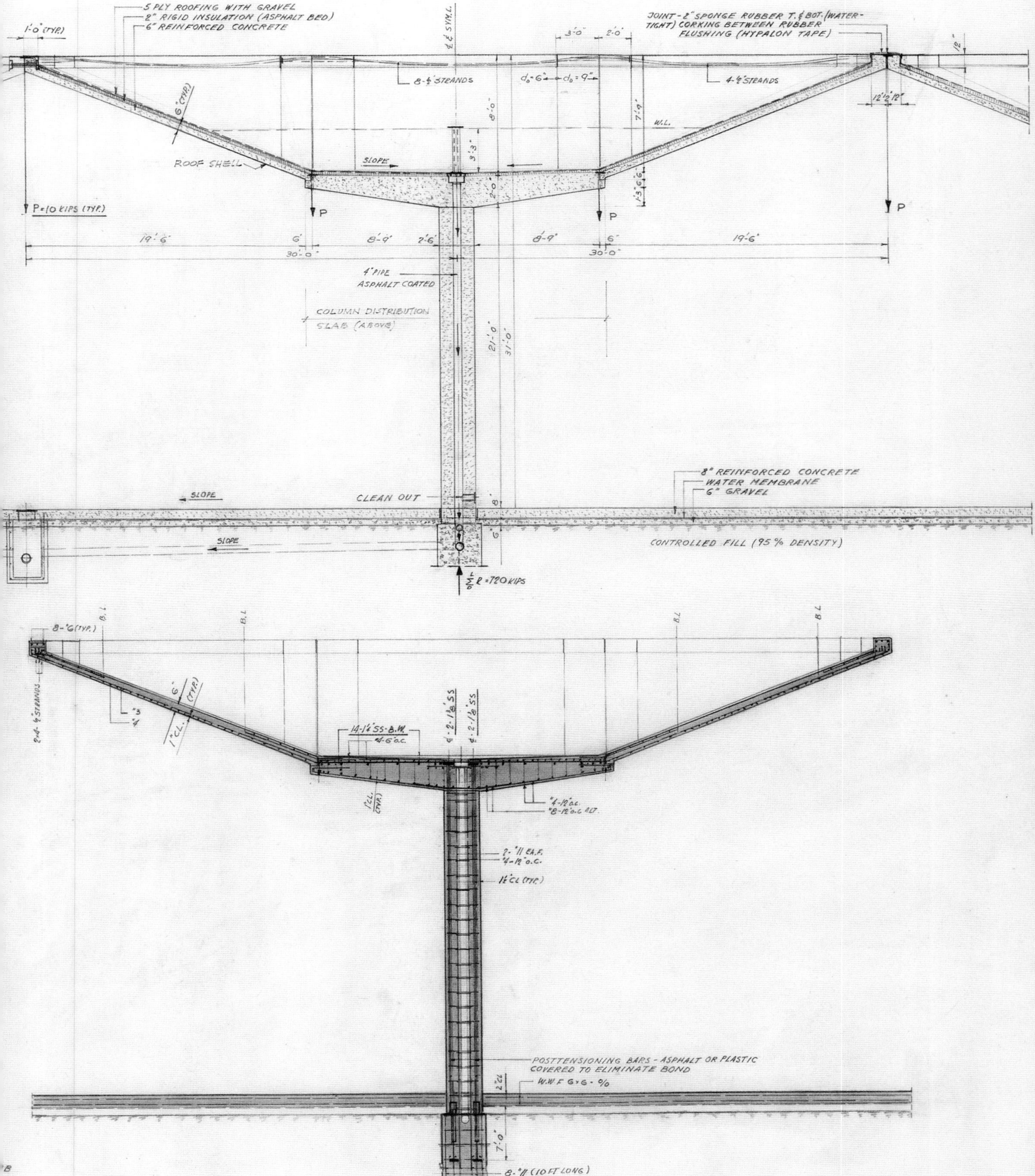

SECTION & REINFORCING A-A

Casting the concrete modules; August Komendant (*middle and top*) visiting the construction site

Construction workers installing the reinforcement

Rooftop during construction

August Komendant (*left*) visiting the construction site
(*next spread*) The factory after completion

Interior of the Kimbell Art Museum

Kimbell Art Museum

Fort Worth, Texas, USA
architect Louis Kahn, associate architect Preston M. Geren,
structural engineer August Komendant
1966–1972 (extant)

The Kimbell Art Museum is a temple of art built for an extraordinary private collection, and a museum building that is unique in the world. Louis Kahn paid special attention to the use of natural light and dignified materials—concrete, travertine, wood, glass, and polished metal. Kimbell could be considered a culmination of a collaboration between a mature architect (Kahn) and his consulting engineer of many years (Komendant). The central part of the structure is comprised of cycloid shells that delicately disperse light. The cycloid shape was proposed by Marshall Meyers, the project architect from Louis Kahn's office. The shells are built of monolithic reinforced concrete, are posttensioned with steel cables, and carry the marginal beams with spans of more than 30 meters.

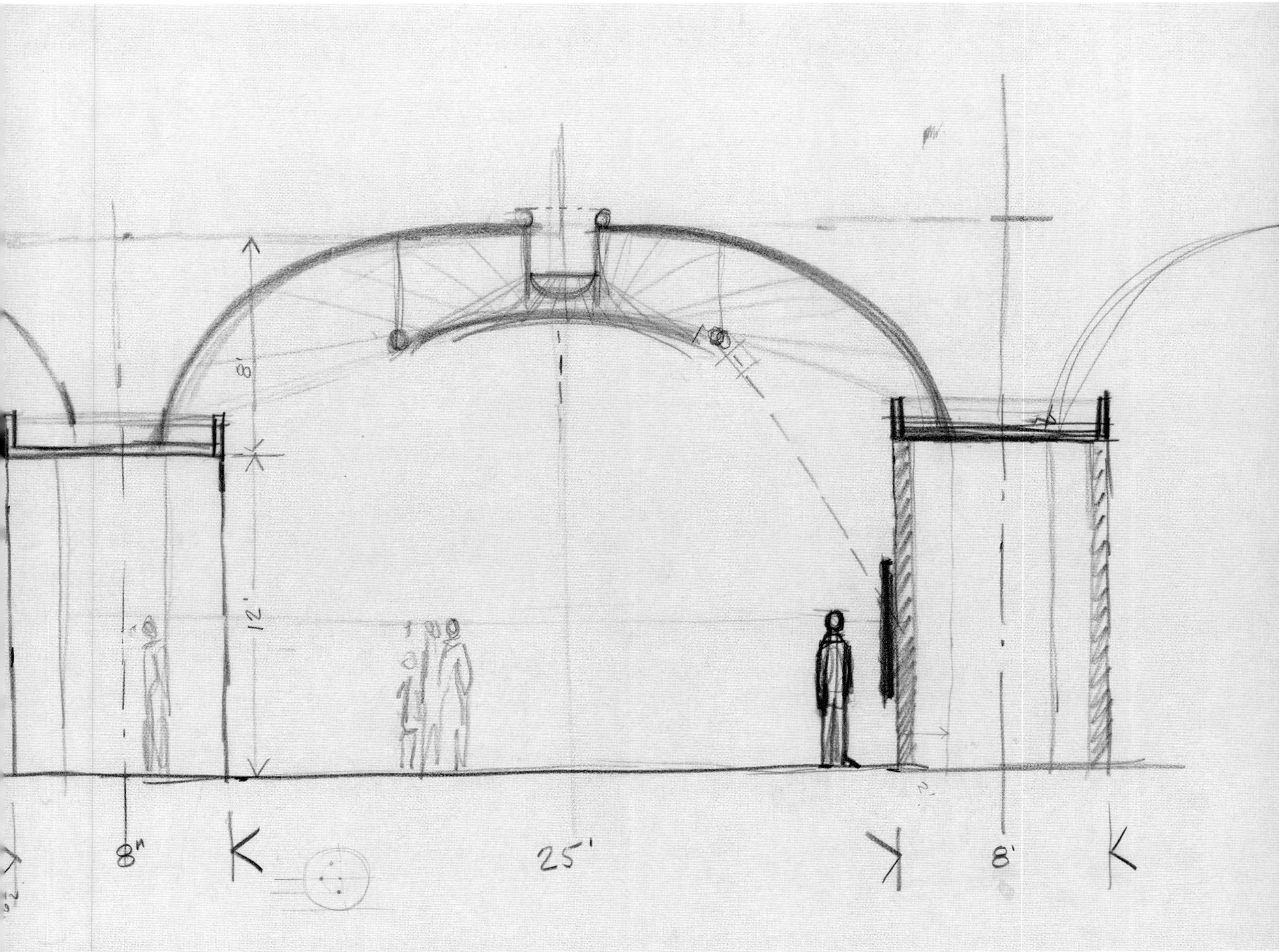

Office of Louis Kahn (Marshall D. Meyers). Early sketch, gallery cross section

Louis Kahn. Museum in the landscape, early perspective drawing, 1967

LIK 9-22-67
Kimbell Museum

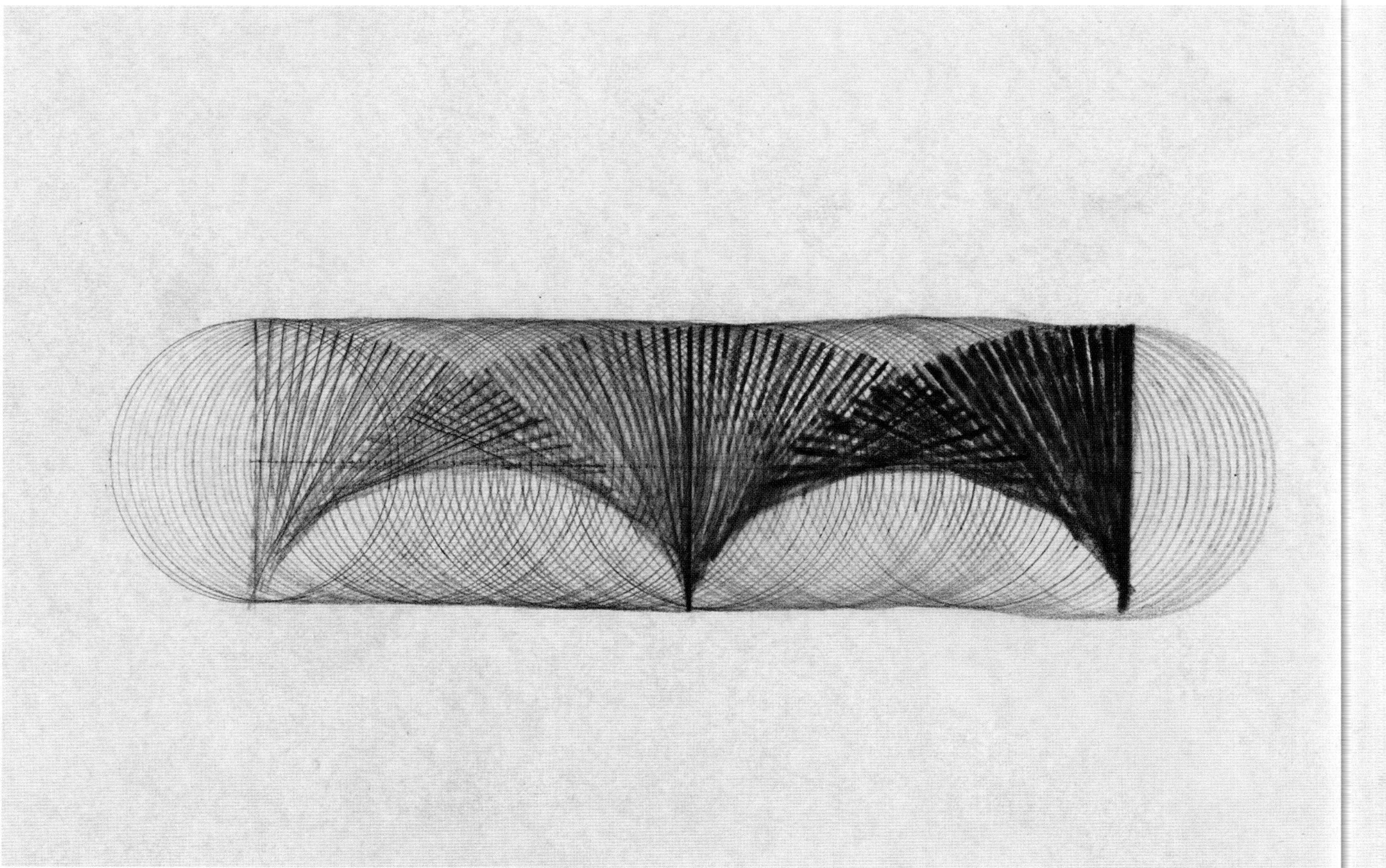

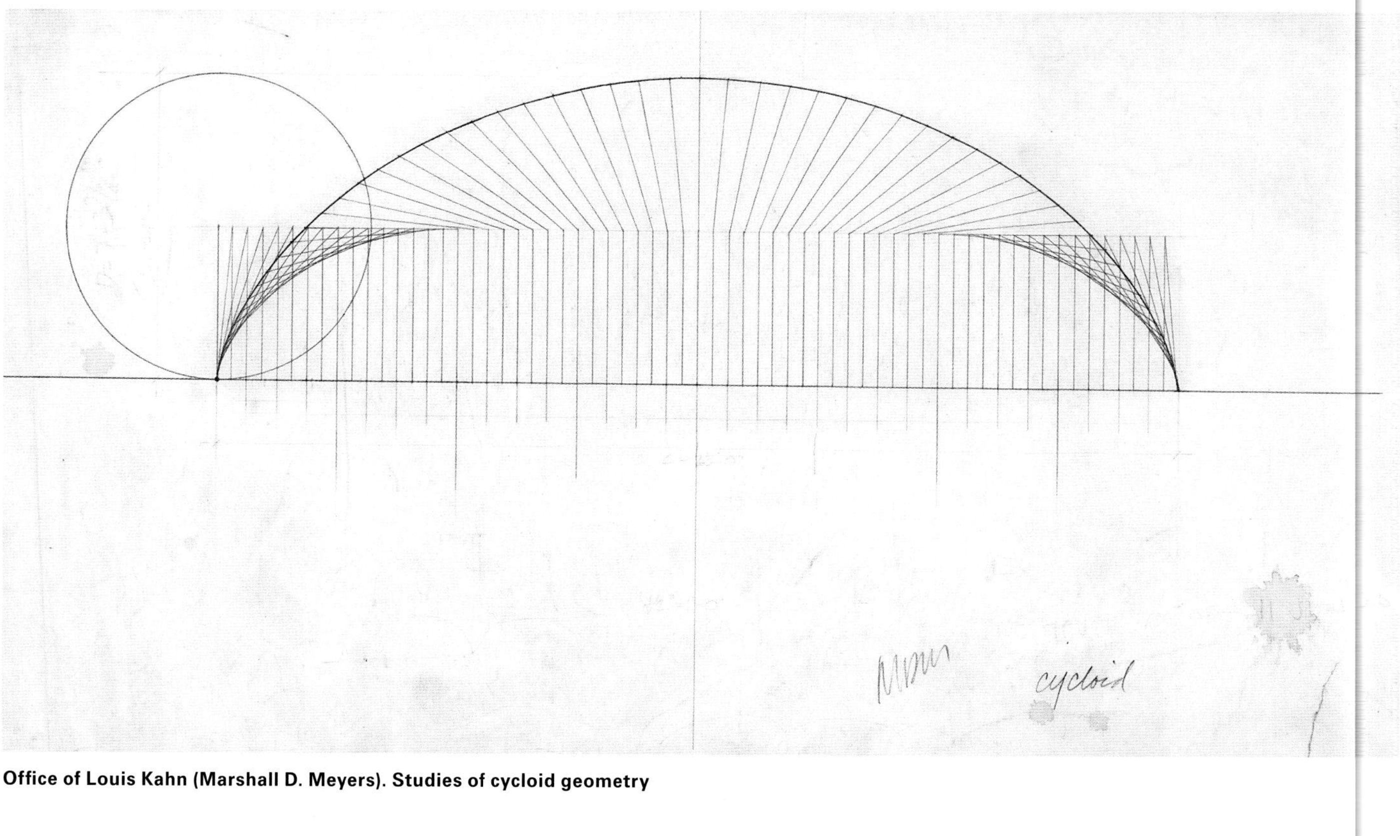

Office of Louis Kahn (Marshall D. Meyers). Studies of cycloid geometry

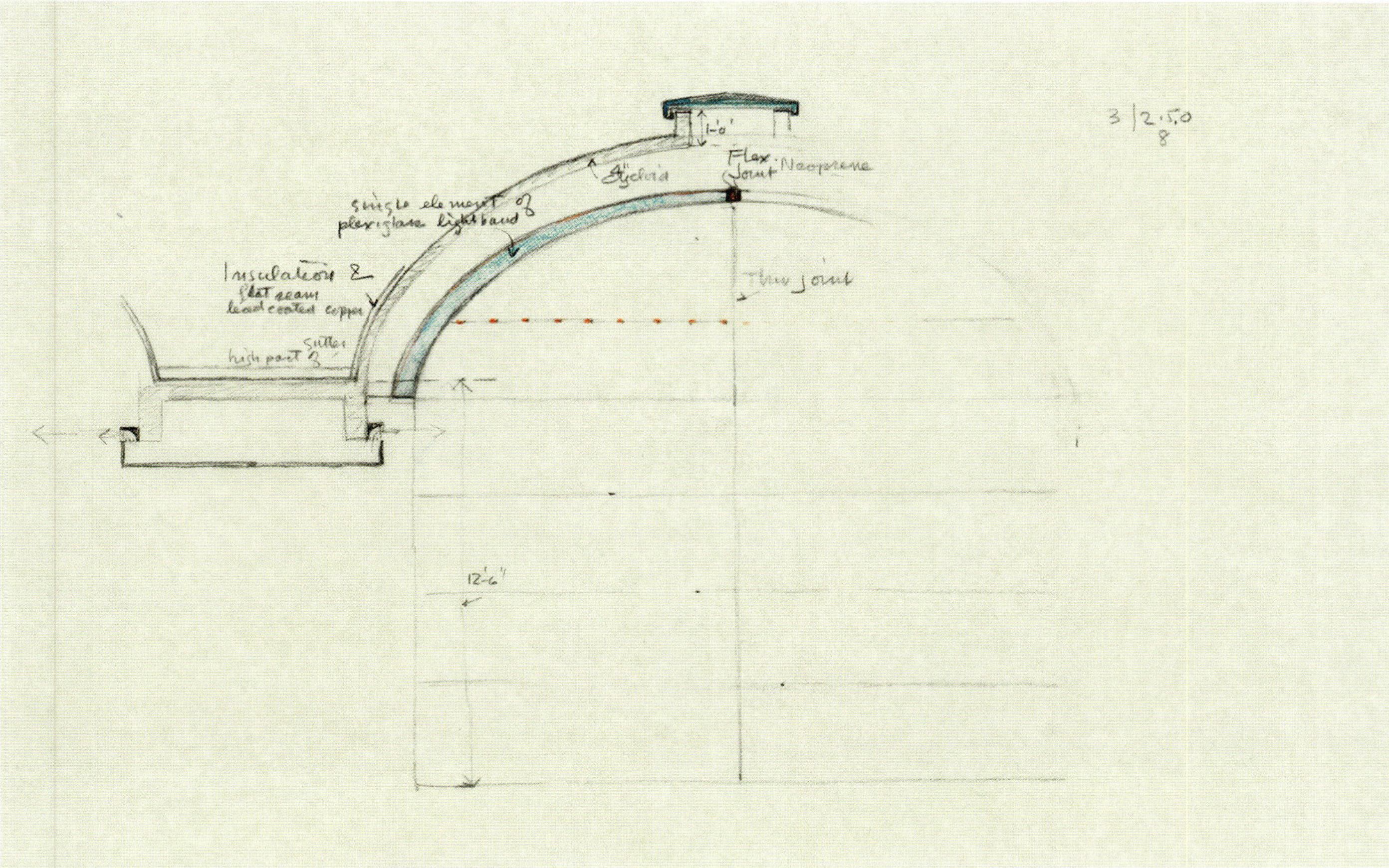

Louis Kahn. Cycloid shells and profile of the end window

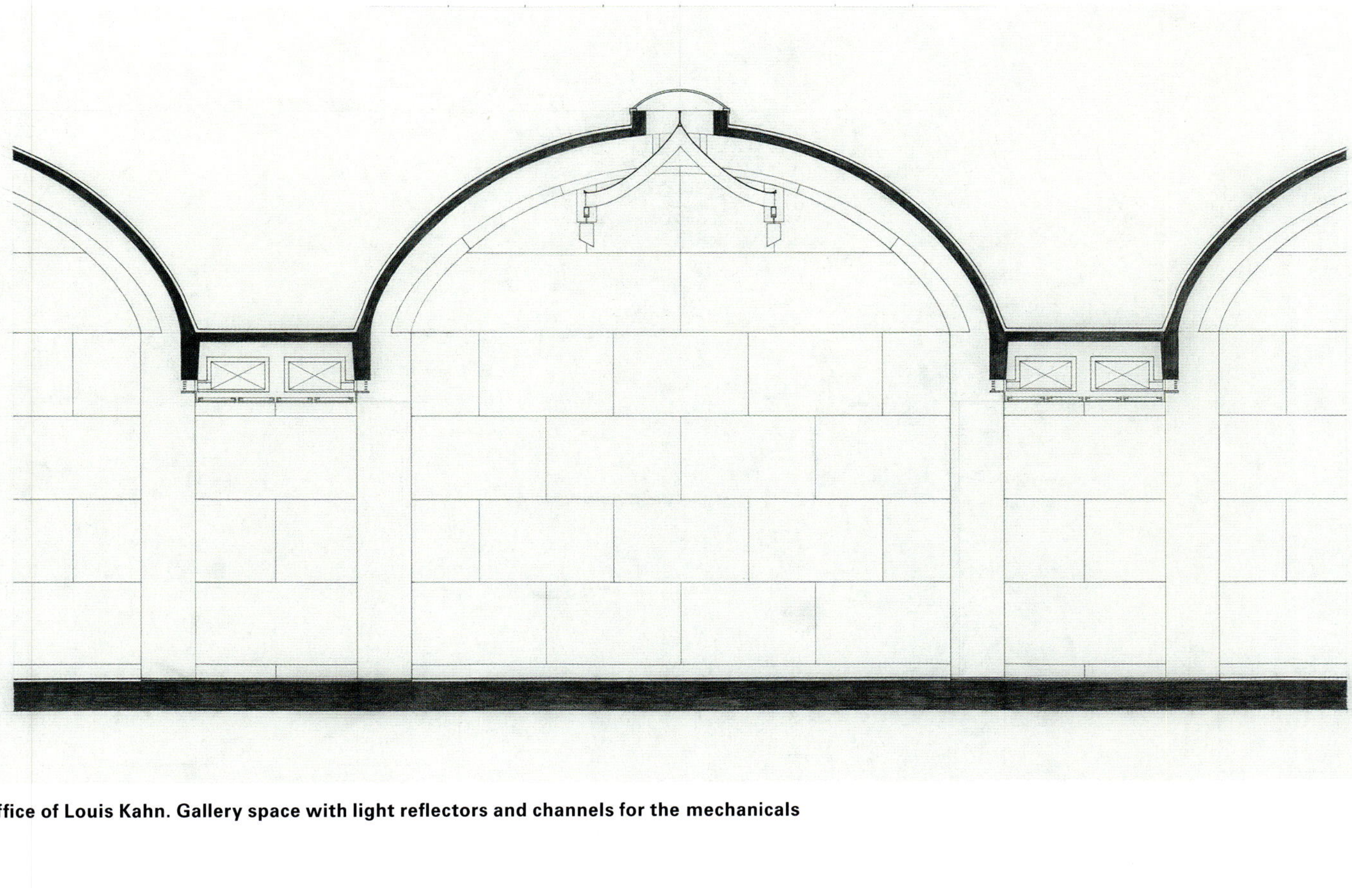

Office of Louis Kahn. Gallery space with light reflectors and channels for the mechanicals

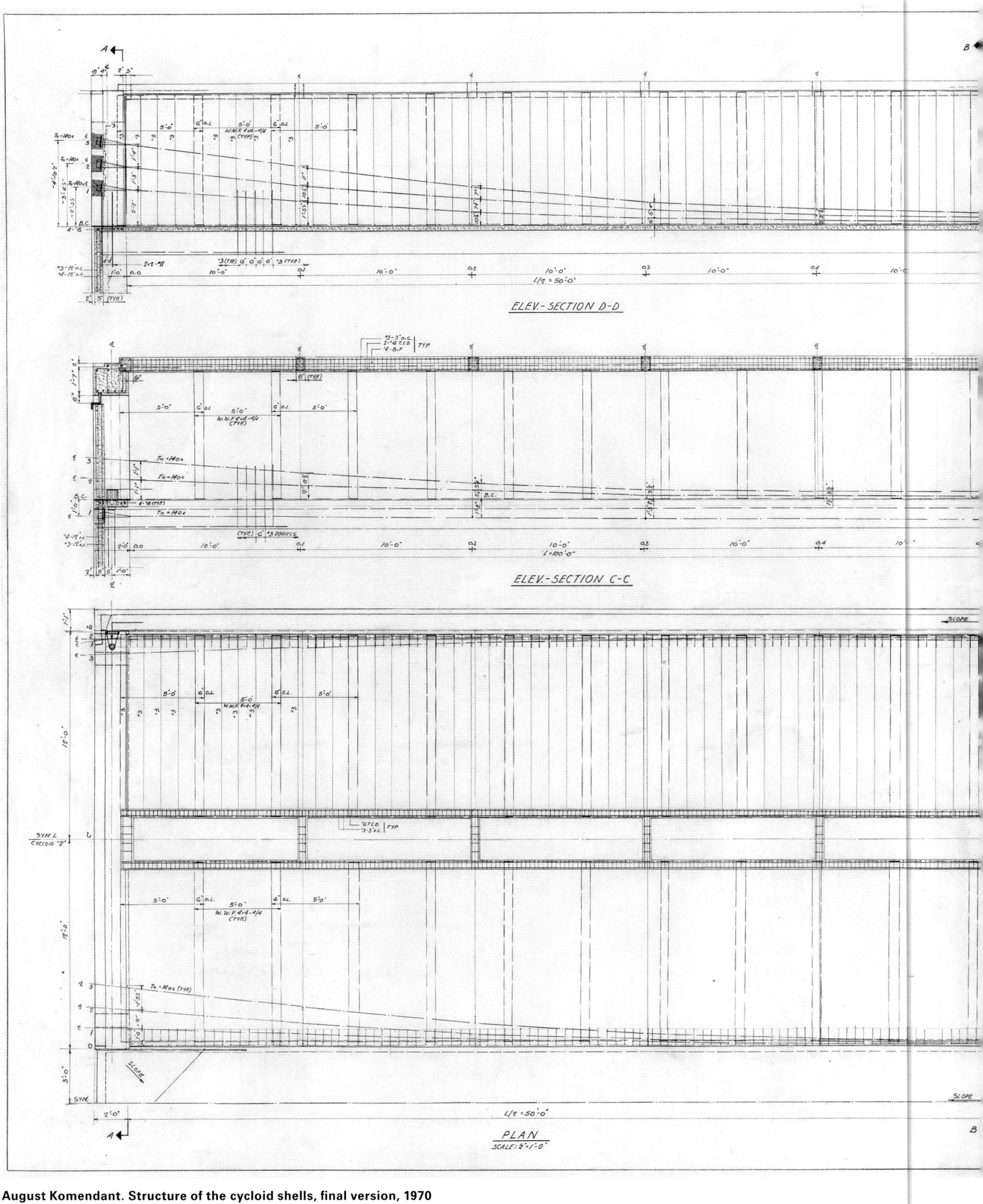

August Komendant. Structure of the cycloid shells, final version, 1970

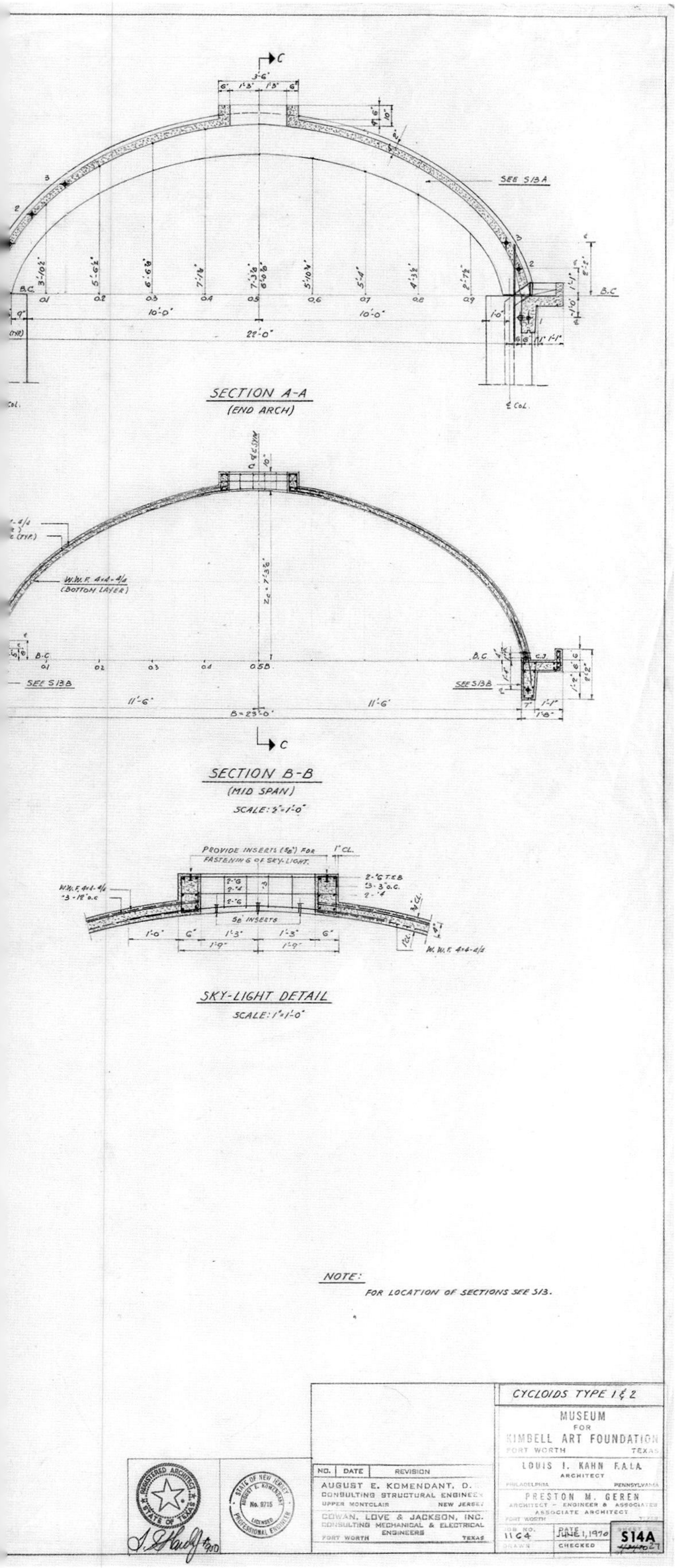

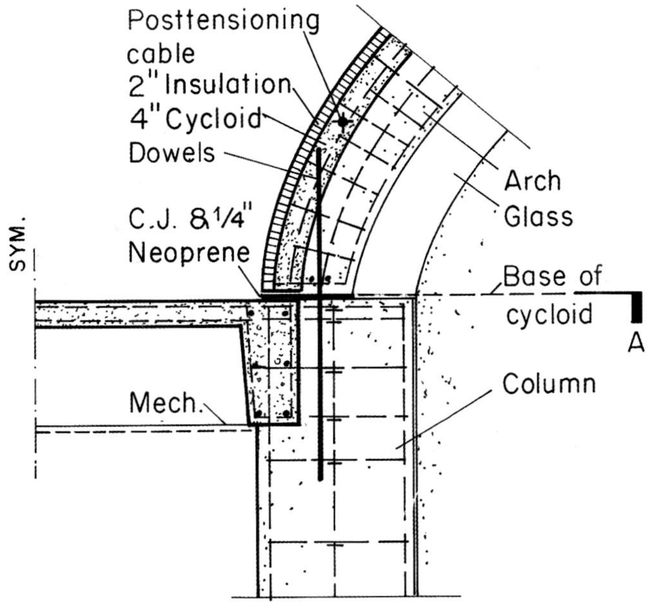

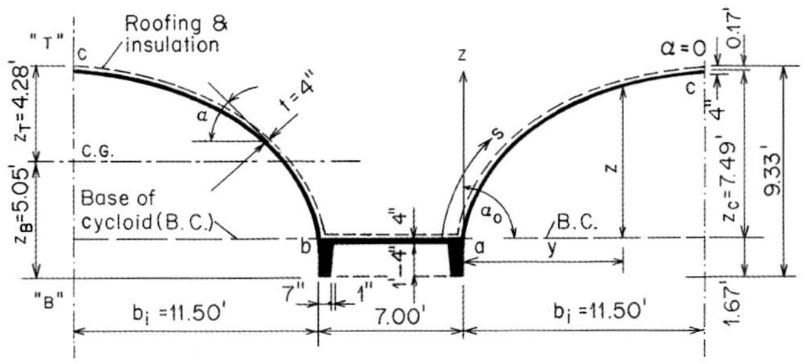

Primary components, dimensions and geometry of the structural system

Cycloid shell before concreting, with posttensioning cables winding between the reinforcement

Final phases of construction

Architect Louis Kahn (*left*) on the construction site

(*next spread*) Cycloid shell by the main entrance of the museum in the final phases of construction

Museum after completion

Cycloid shells in the sunshine

The interstitial space allows natural light into the building

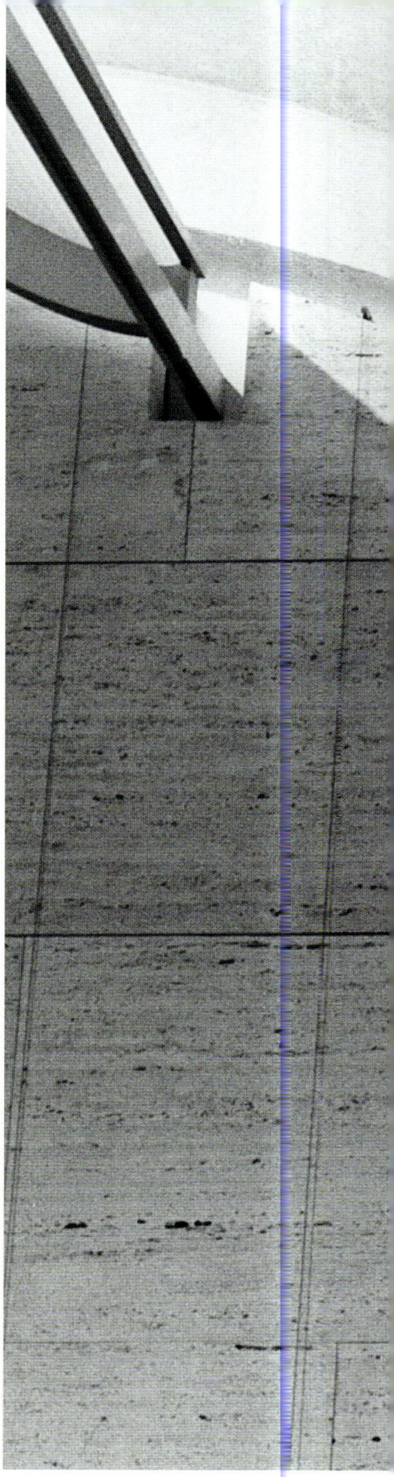

High-quality detailing

The end window creates a dialogue between different materials and structural components
(*next spread*) Garden of the Kimbell Art Museum

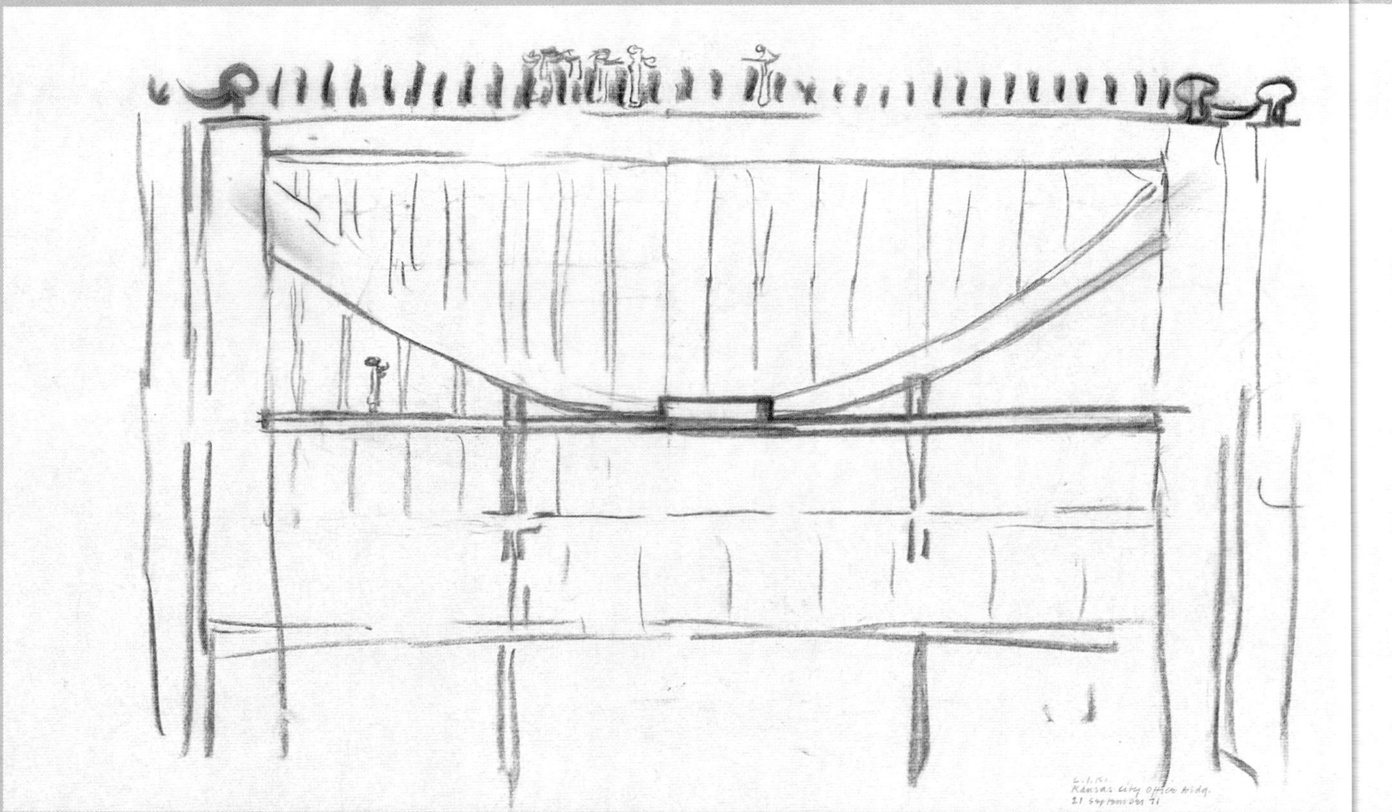

Louis Kahn. Sketch of the upper part of the office building

Kansas City Office Building

Kansas City, Missouri, USA
architect Louis Kahn,
structural engineer August Komendant
1967–1974 (not built)

This was among the last major collaborations between Louis Kahn and August Komendant. Its revolutionary construction method—without the use of cranes and without closing the neighboring streets—would have enabled a quicker and more economical build compared to more conventional skyscraper construction. Komendant suggested Kahn use a construction sequence which, after completing the elevator and mechanical cores, would have allowed them to pour floor slabs starting from the top of the building and moving down to the bottom. The higher floors would have been completed and available for interior installation and furnishing to commence, while construction continued on the lower levels.

Structural model

Louis Kahn. Perspective view, 1971

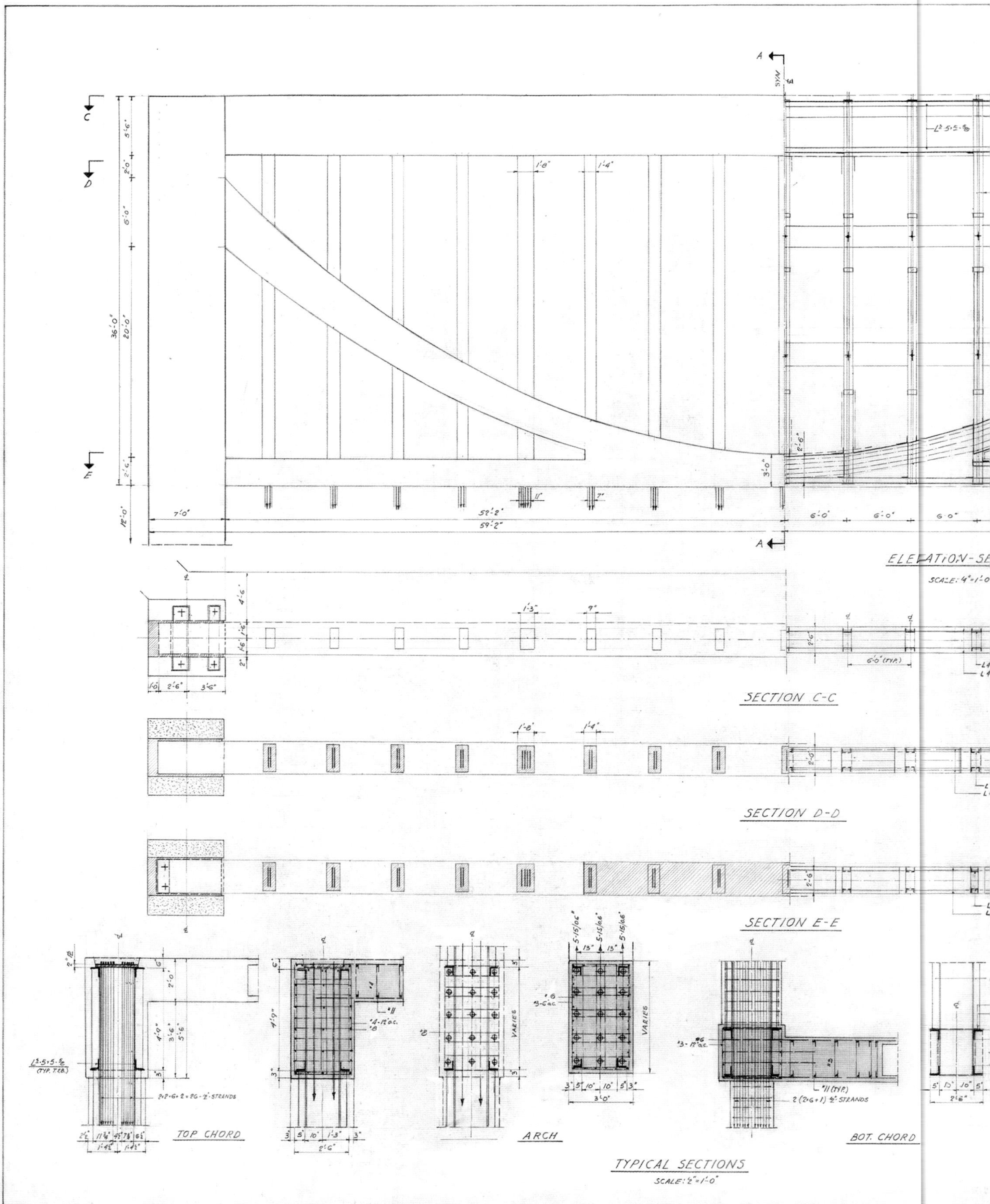
ELEVATION-SE
SCALE: 4"=1'-0
SECTION C-C
SECTION D-D
SECTION E-E
TOP CHORD
ARCH
BOT. CHORD
TYPICAL SECTIONS
SCALE: ½"=1'-0"
36'-0"
20'-0"
6'-0"
5'-6"
59'-2"
57'-2"
7'-0"
12'-0"
VARIES
2(2-6+1) ½" STRANDS

August Komendant. Structural system of the upper part of the office building, 1971/1973

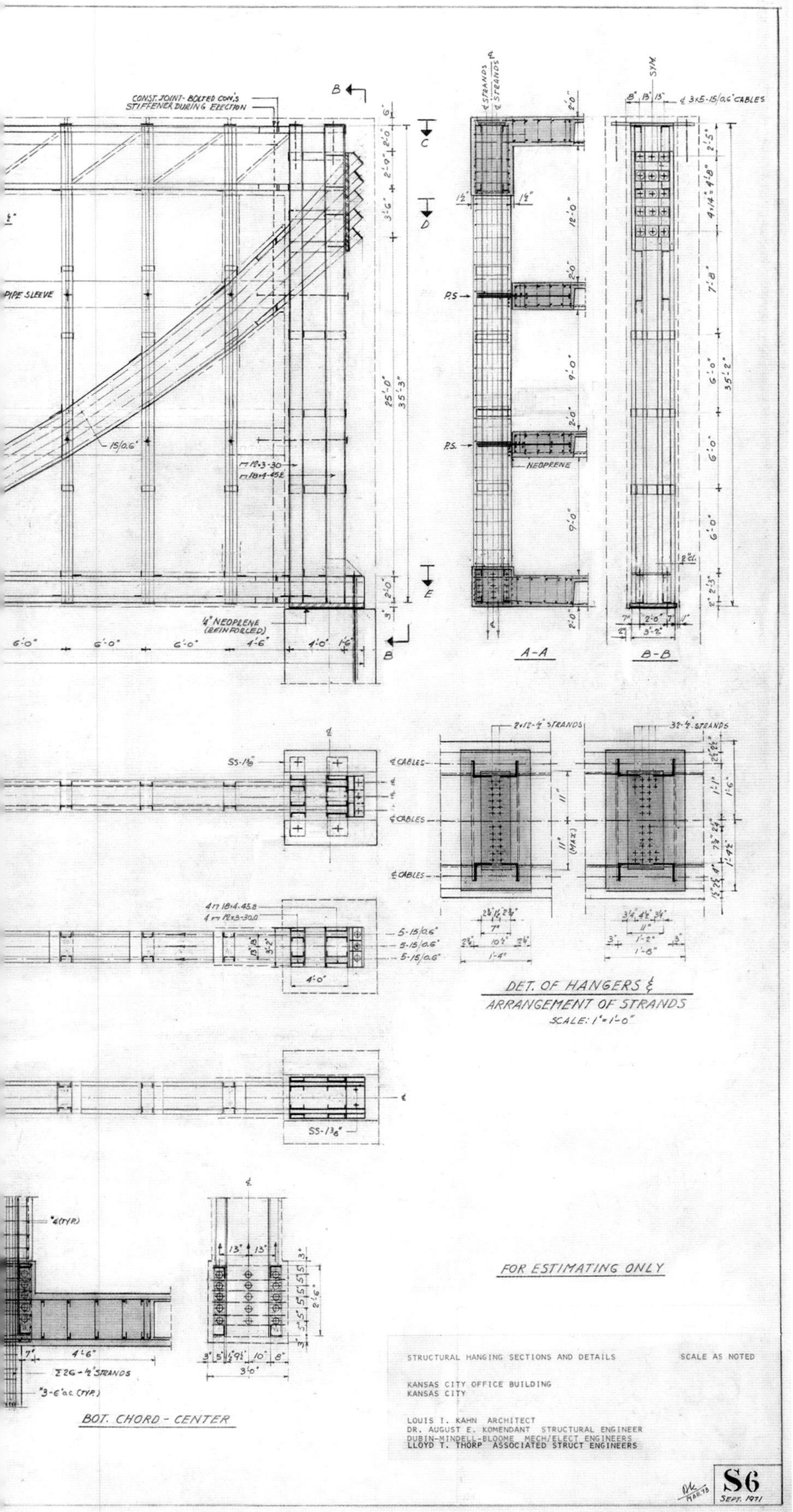

The building as part of the ensemble of national pavilions at the Venice Giardini, site model

Palazzo Dei Congressi

Venice, Italy
architect Louis Kahn,
structural engineer August Komendant
1968–1974 (not built)

The Government of Venice in 1968 commissioned Louis Kahn to design a new Palazzo Dei Congressi. The initial site proposed for the public building was among the national pavilions at the Biennale Giardini, but this was rejected in favor of another site at the Arsenale that spanned a small canal and inspired a new design. Based on Kahn's early sketches, August Komendant proposed a structural system able to span nearly 116 meters and consisting of two large reinforced concrete box girders and a suspension system.

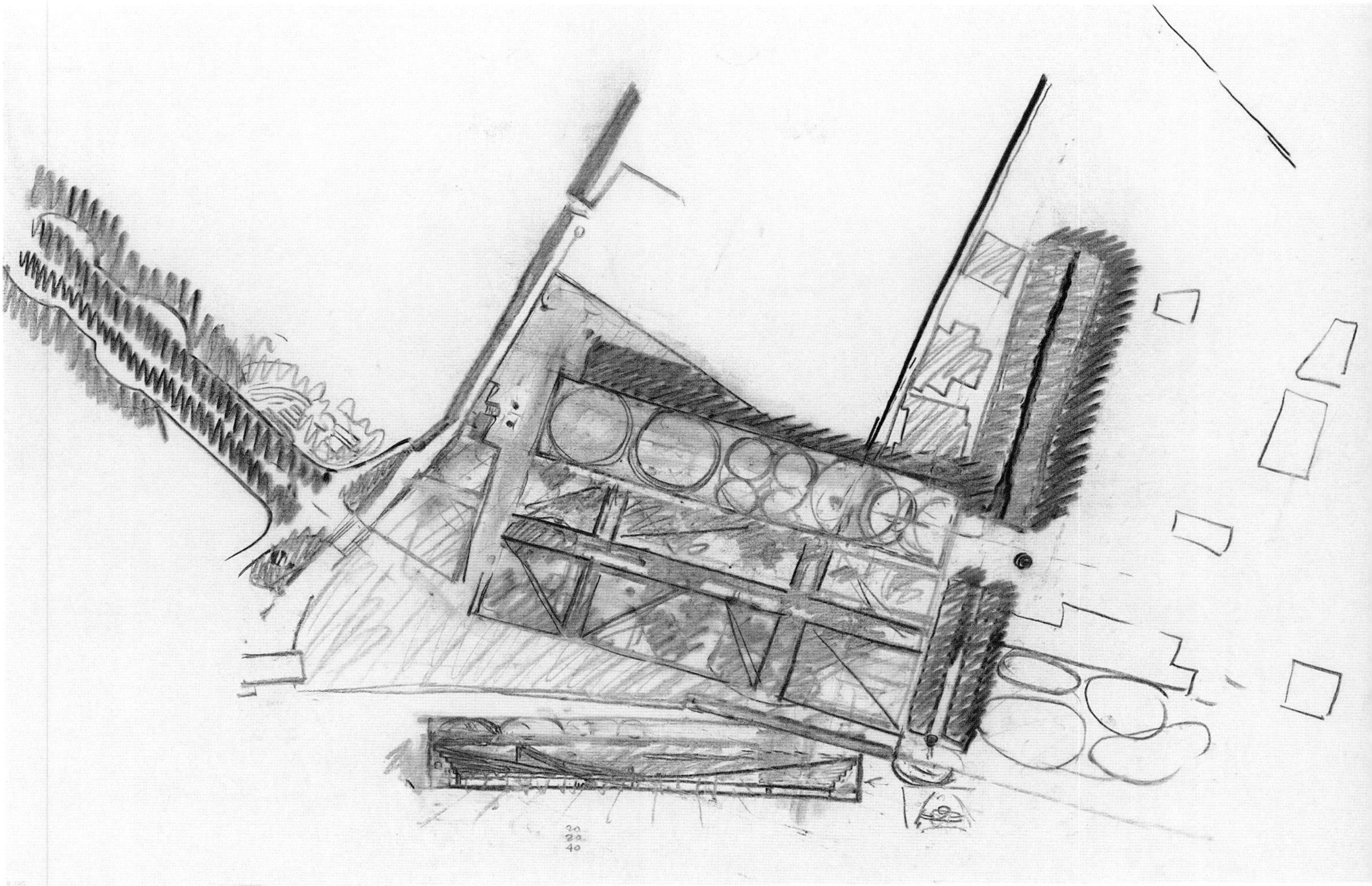

Louis Kahn. Early site plan sketch

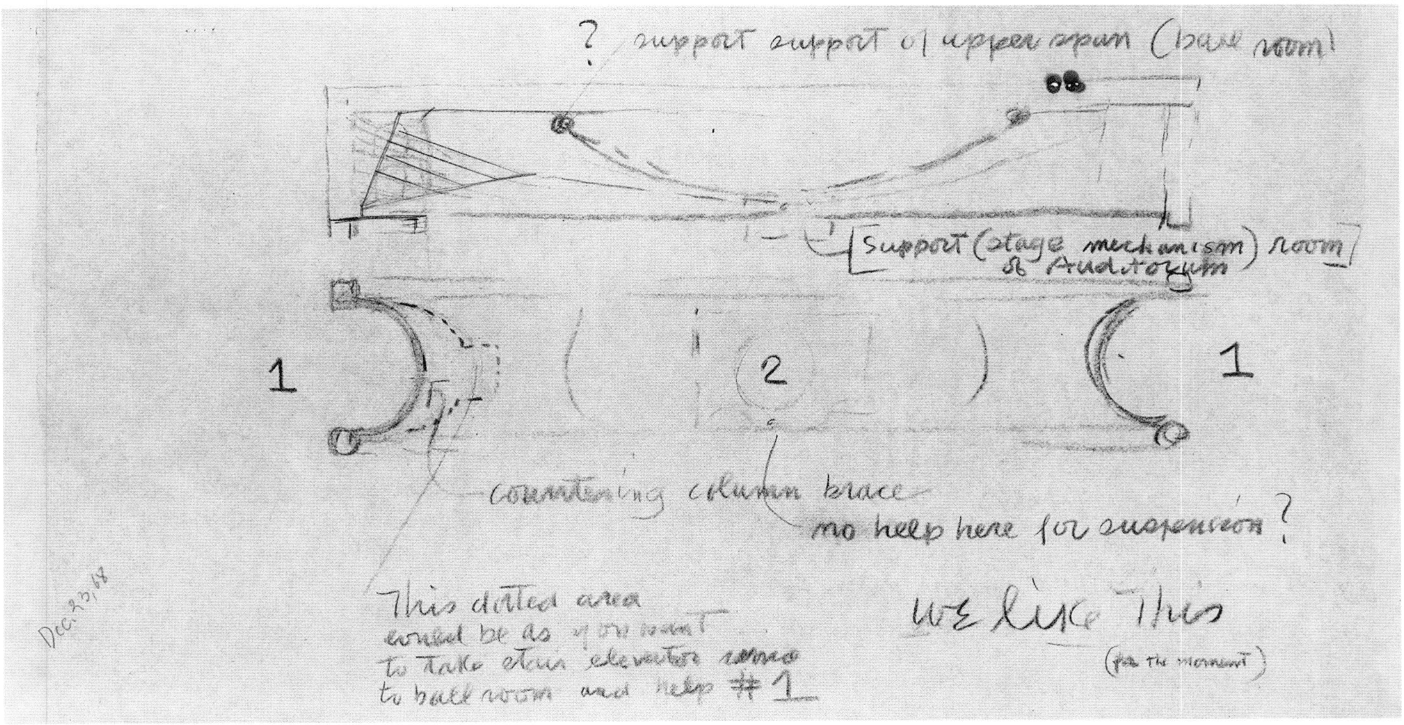

Louis Kahn. Early structural sketch with Kahn's comments sent to August Komendant

Louis Kahn. Early sketch, longitudinal section and plan

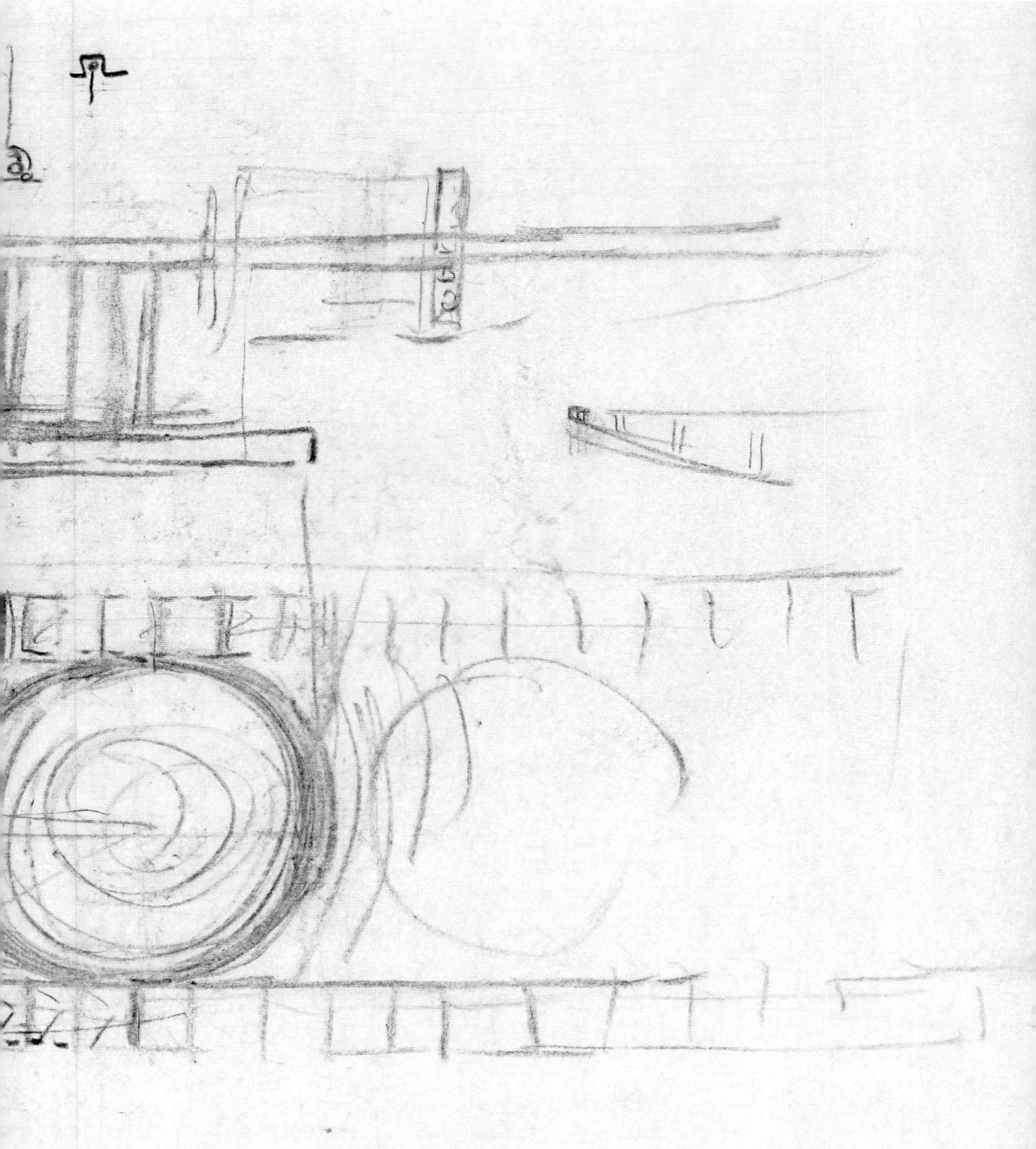

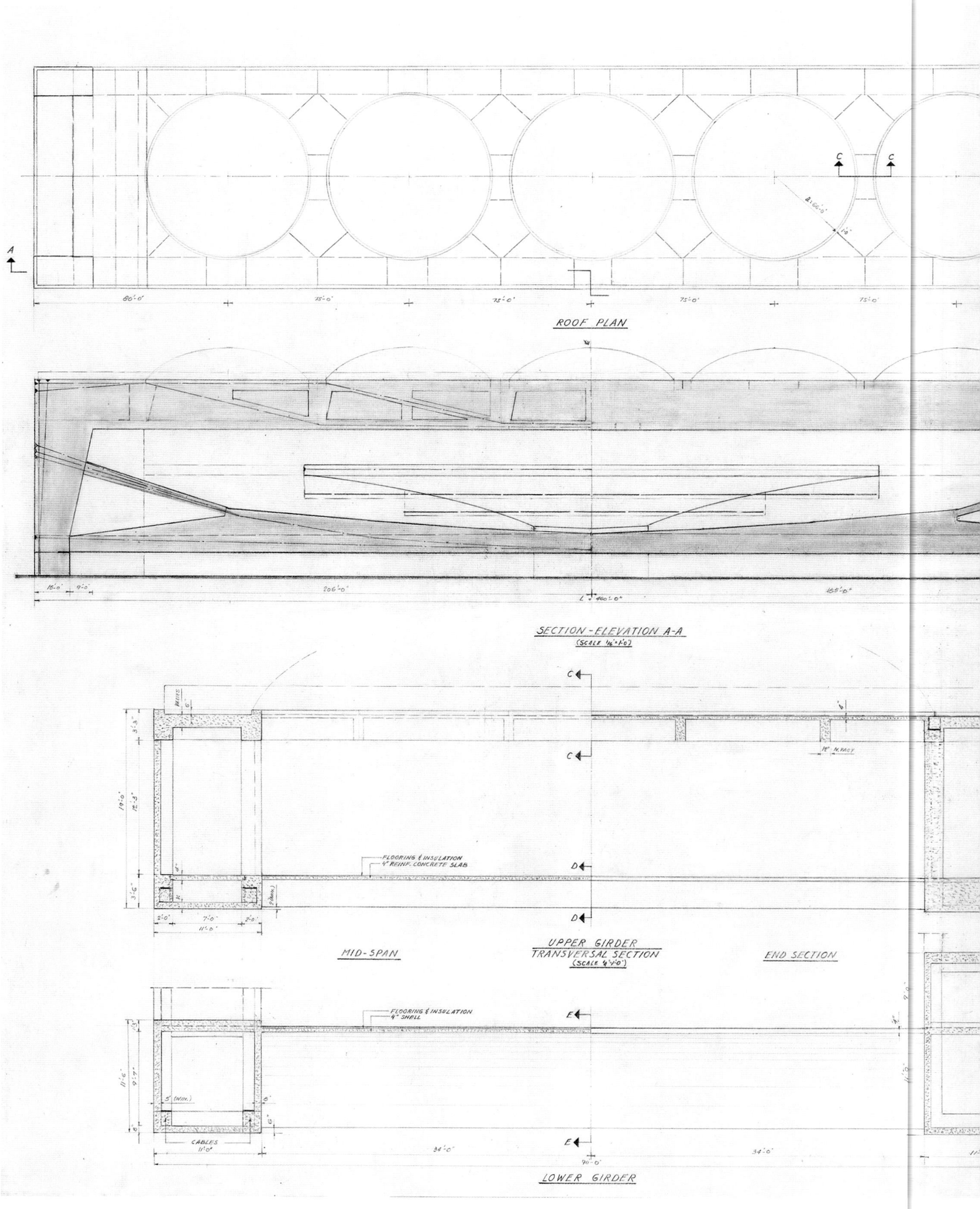
ROOF PLAN
SECTION-ELEVATION A-A
FLOORING & INSULATION
4" REINF. CONCRETE SLAB
MID-SPAN
UPPER GIRDER
TRANSVERSAL SECTION
END SECTION
FLOORING & INSULATION
4" SHELL
CABLES
LOWER GIRDER

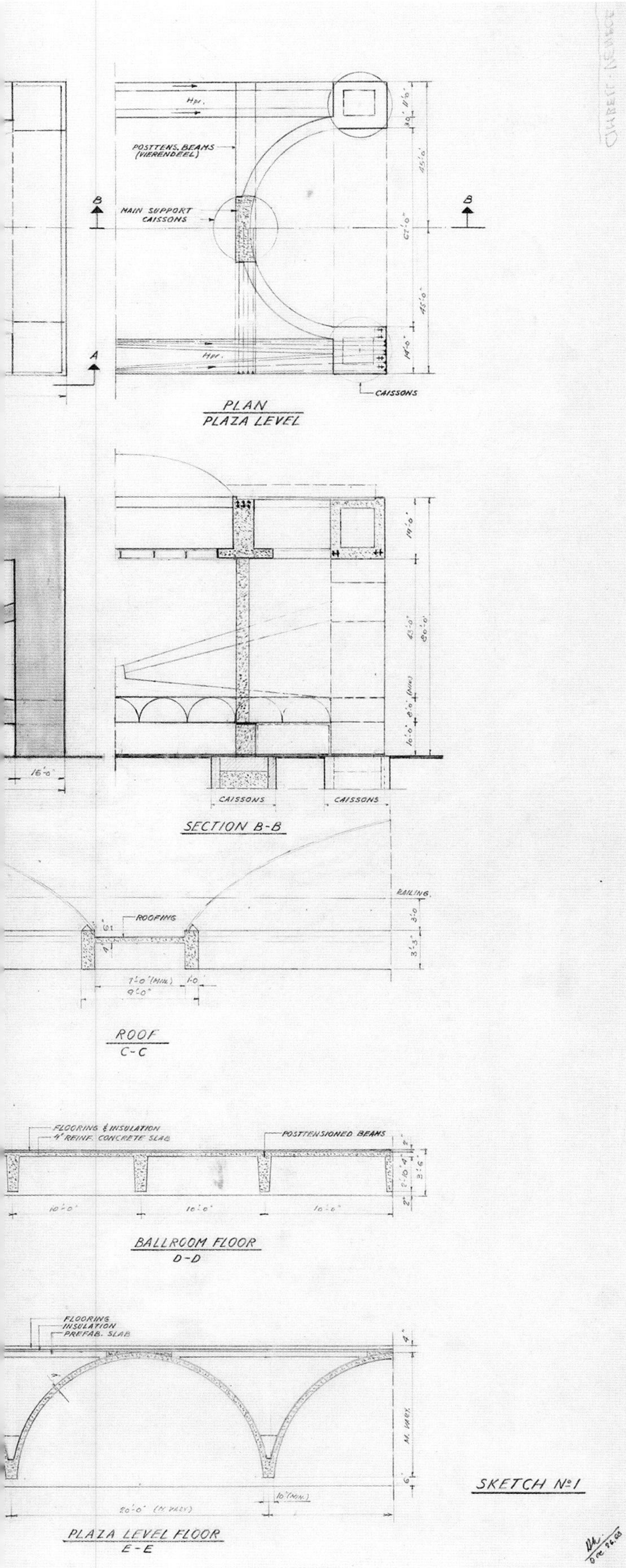

August Komendant. Preliminary structural system, 1968

Advanced version of the structural system without the central support

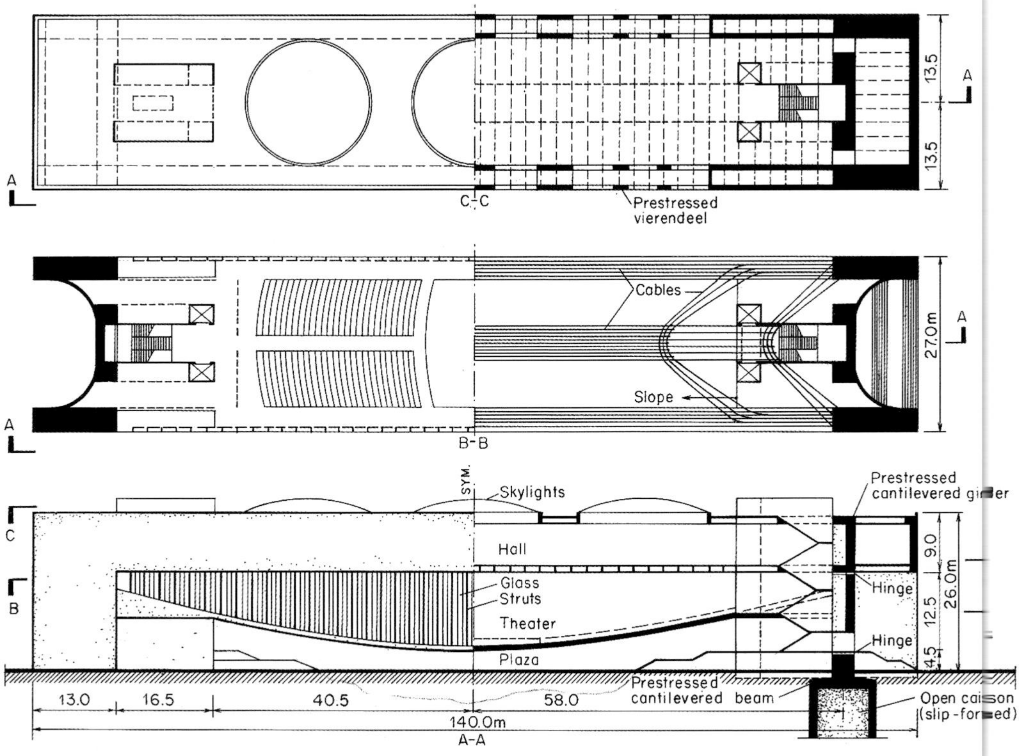

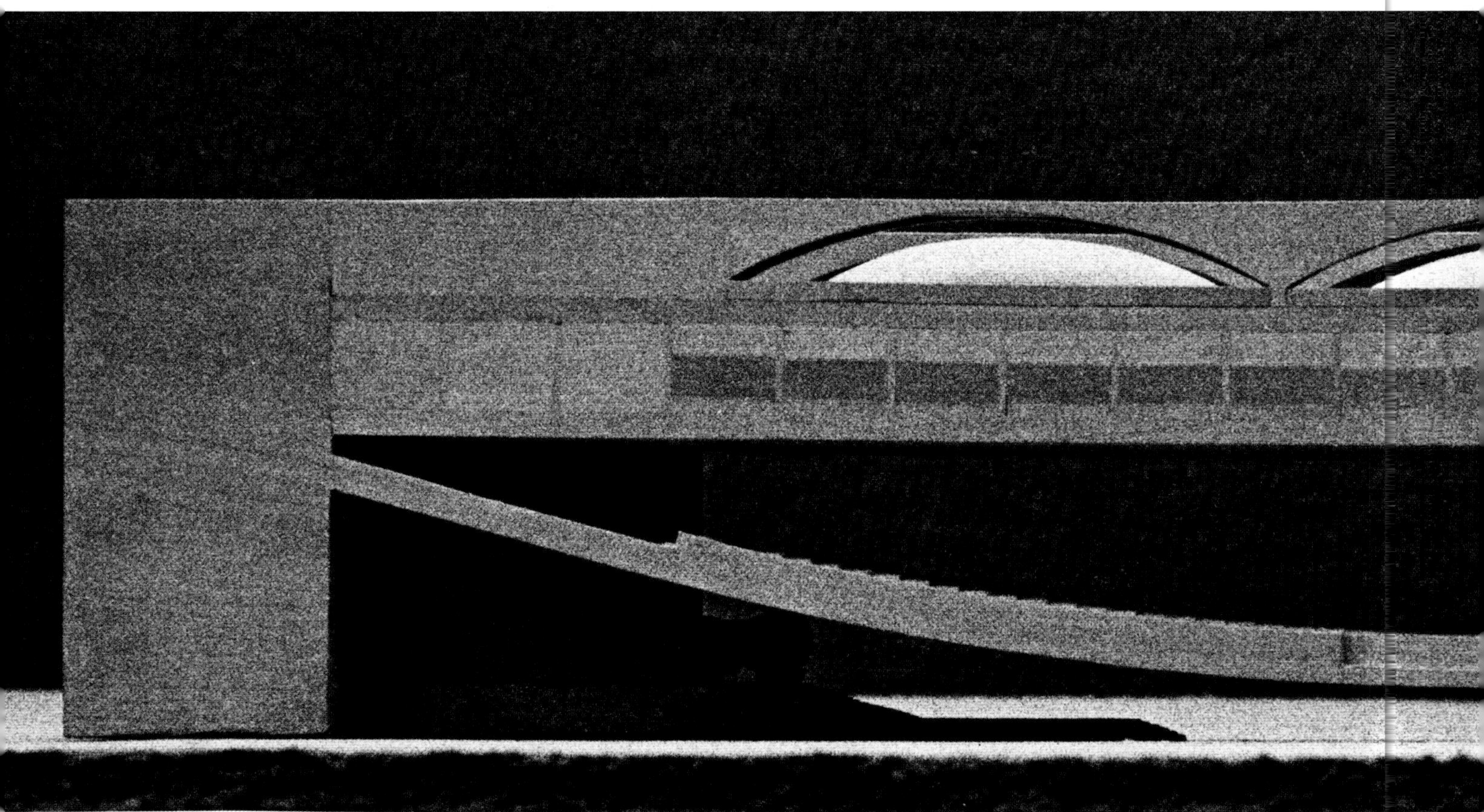

Sectional sketch model

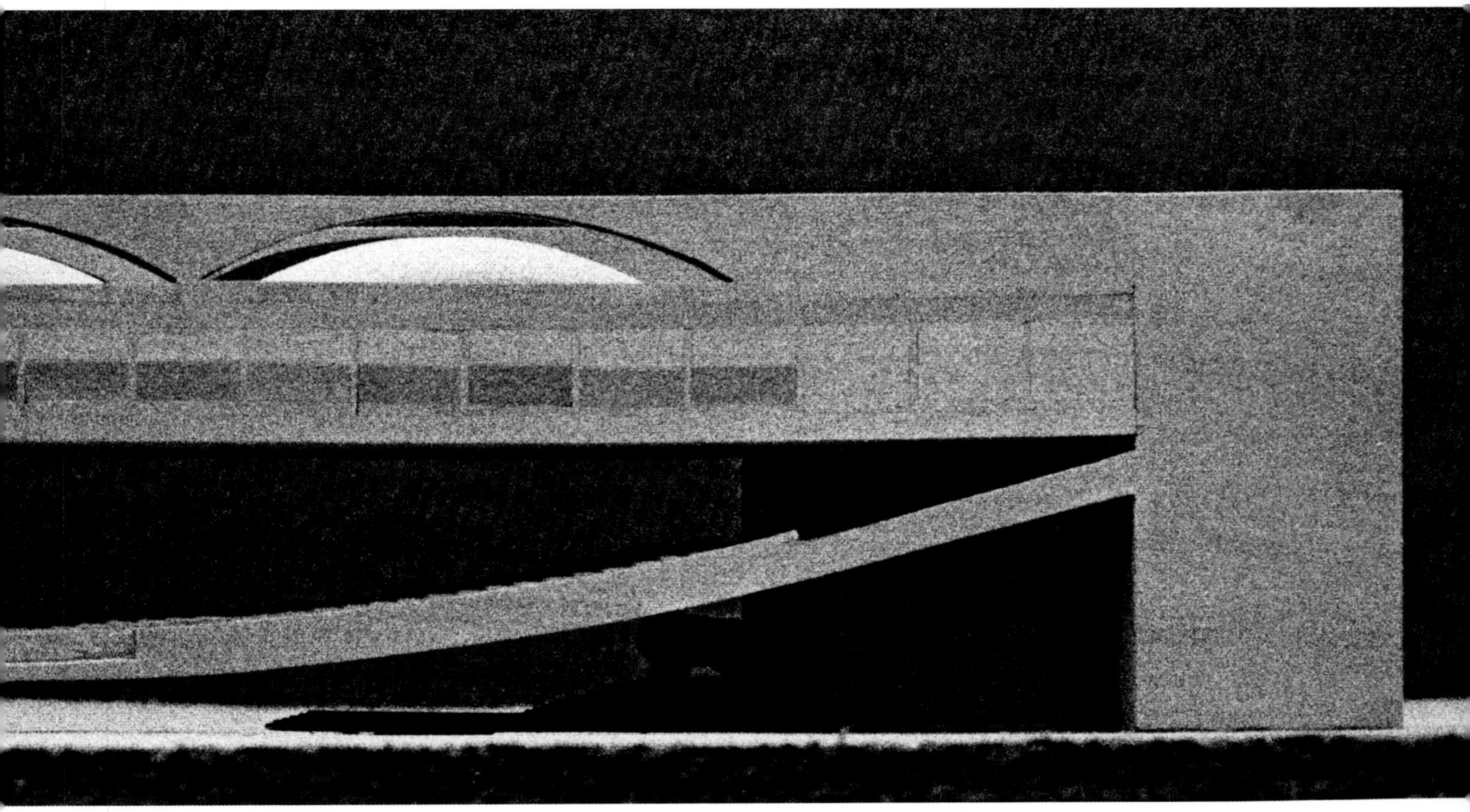

Caracas Bus Terminal, presentation model

Caracas Bus Terminal

Caracas, Venezuela
architect Oscar Tenreiro,
structural consultant August Komendant
1976–1977 (not built)

This was the first major collaboration between architect Oscar Tenreiro and August Komendant. It was intended for a huge modernist infrastructure facility with an ambitious structural system, the core of which is comprised of long-span posttensioned reinforced concrete trusses.

12

OSCAR R. TENREIRO DEGWITZ
ARQUITECTO C. A. V. - C. I. V.

this is the general distribution of the different functions taking place in the complex.

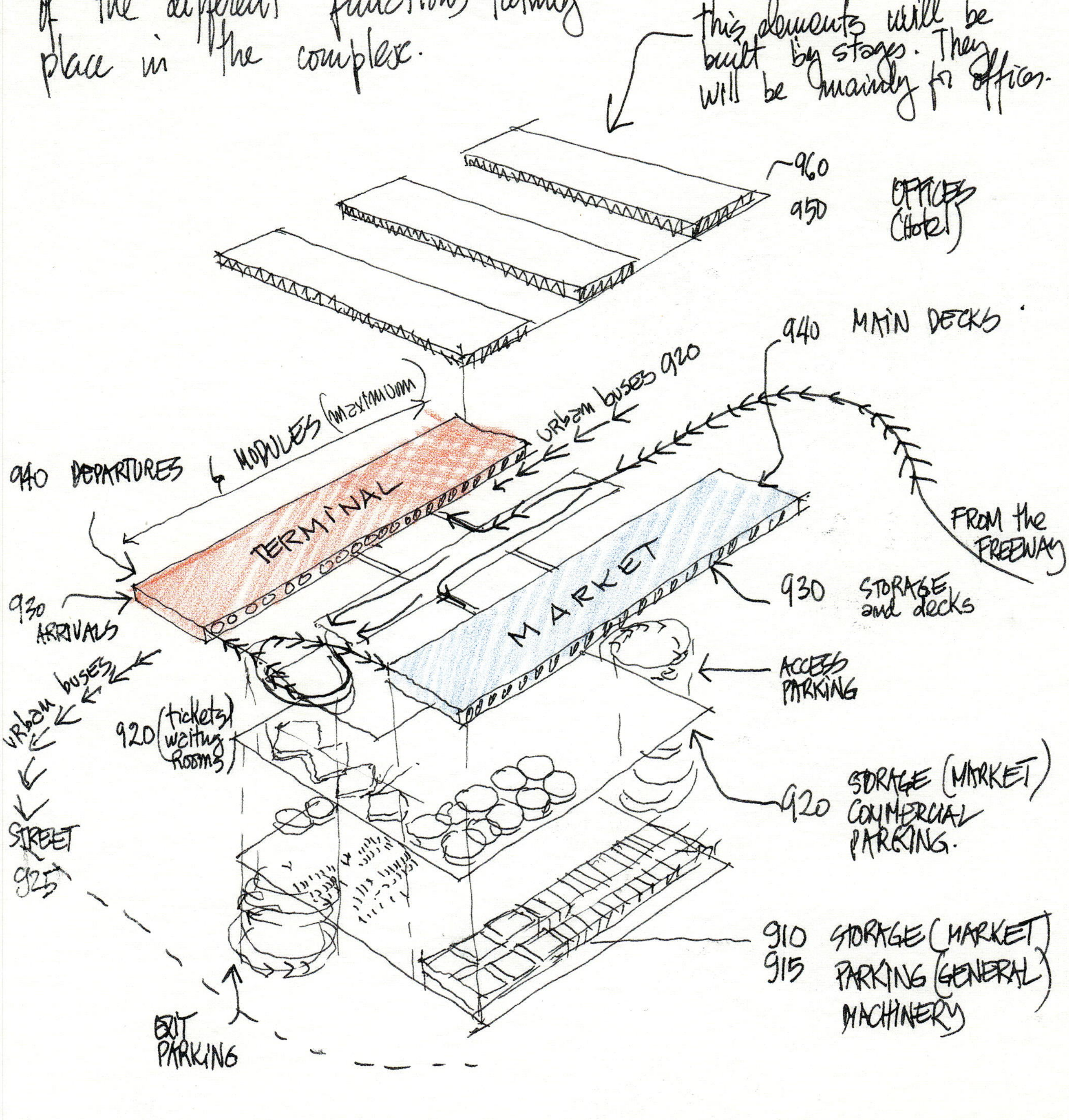

CENTRO COMERCIAL SANTA MONICA - P. H. 504 - SANTA MONICA - CARACAS - VENEZUELA - TELEFONOS

A letter from architect Oscar Tenreiro to August Komendant explaining the general distribution of functions, 1976, excerpt

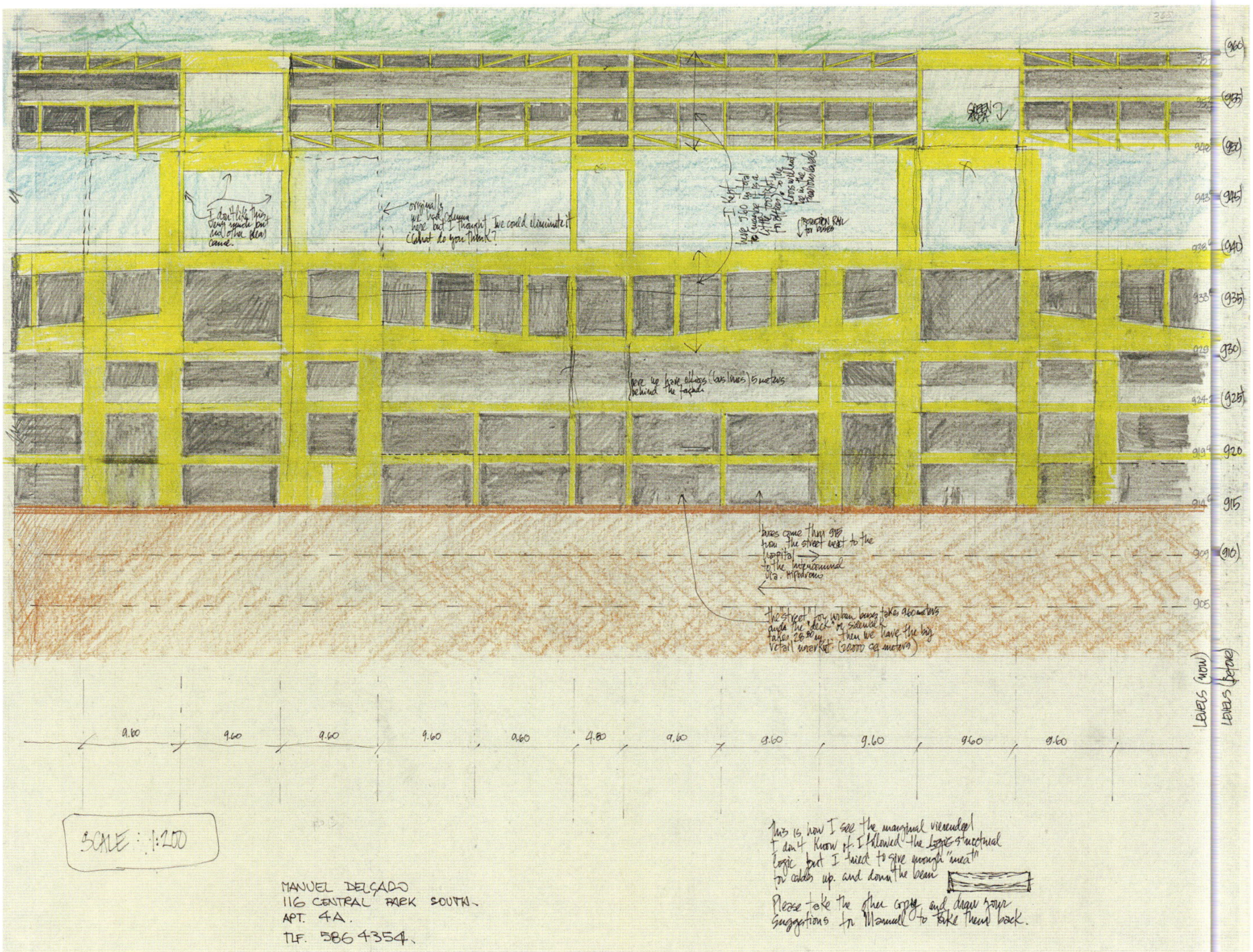

Oscar Tenreiro. Exterior sketch sent to August Komendant with comments about the structural system

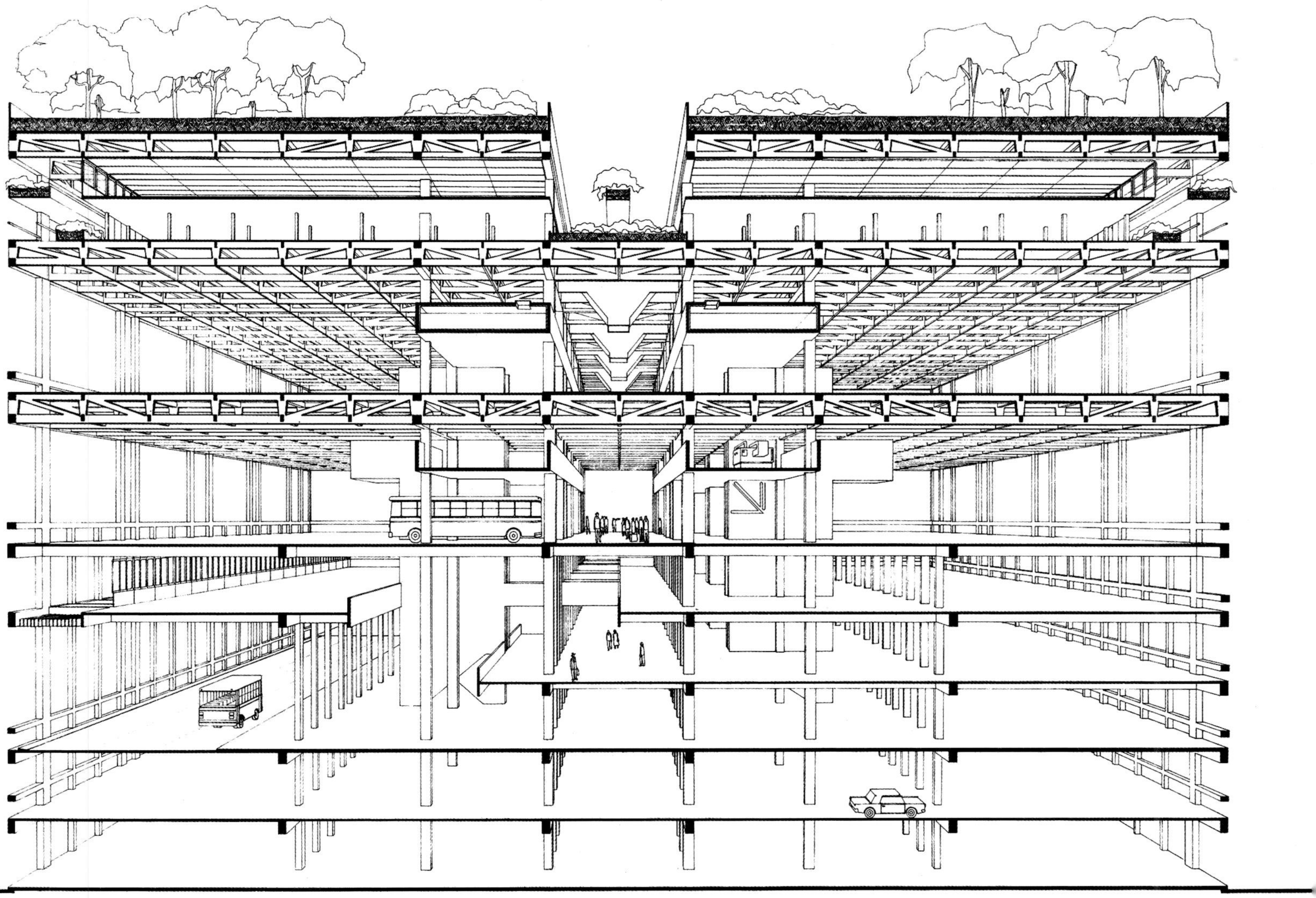

Perspective section

Oscar Tenreiro. Elevation sketch

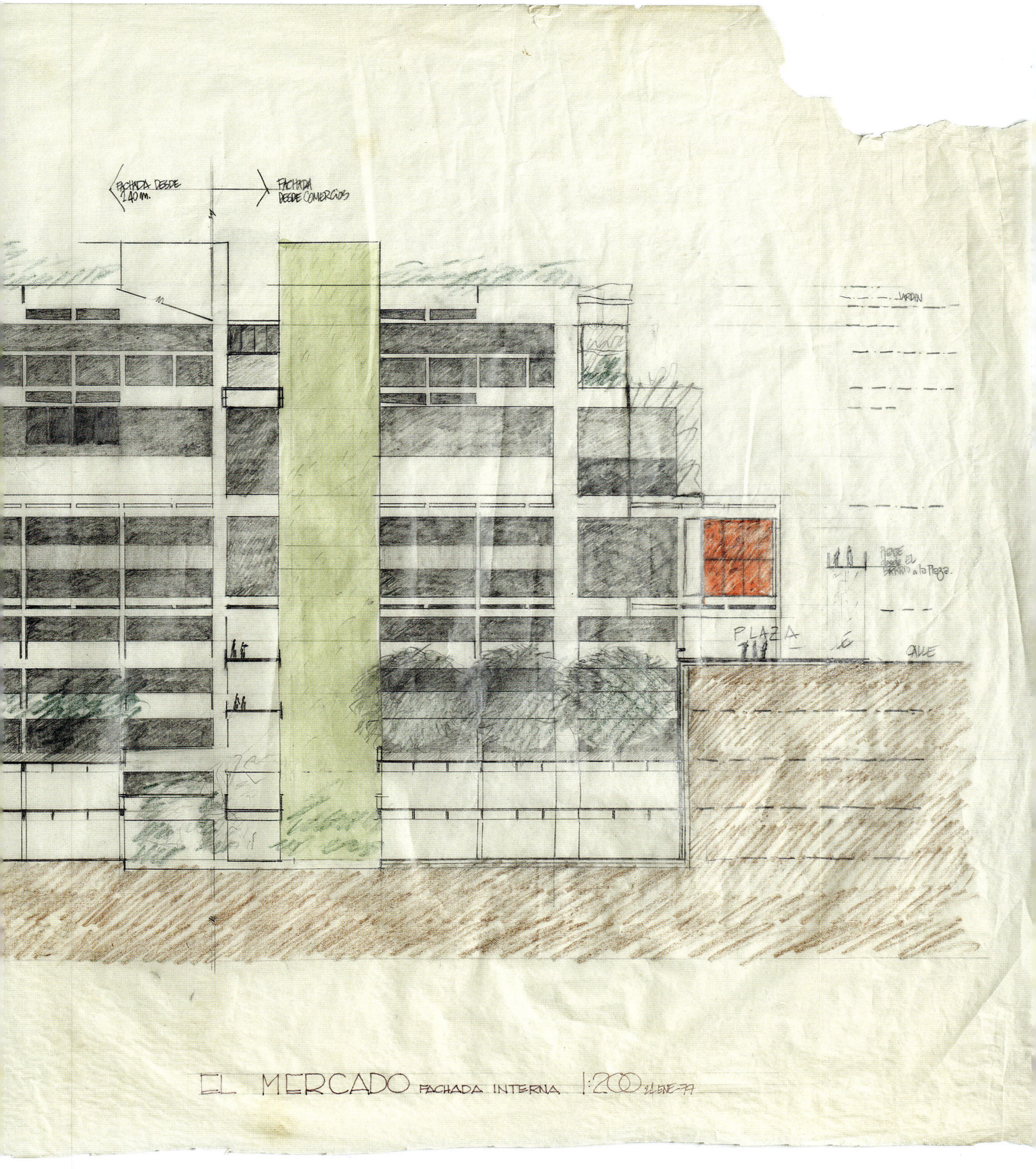

FACHADA DESDE 2.40 m.
FACHADA DESDE COMERCIOS
JARDIN
PLAZA
CALLE
EL MERCADO FACHADA INTERNA 1:200 24-ENE-77

K-System apartment building, presentation model

K–System Apartment Building

Juangriego, Isla de Margarita, Venezuela
architect Oscar Tenreiro,
structural engineer August Komendant
1977–1978 (not built)

In 1977 architect Oscar Tenreiro approached August Komendant to find an economical solution for both the structure and construction of an apartment building. For the project, and in close dialogue with Tenreiro, Komendant further developed his ideas related to the Kansas City and Broadway office buildings, which Louis Kahn had designed but were never built. First, the elevator and mechanical cores would be cast and connected and the upper floor built. Then a sliding formwork would be used to pour the floor slabs starting from the top and progressing to the bottom.

Oscar Tenreiro. Elevation sketch of the upper part of the building

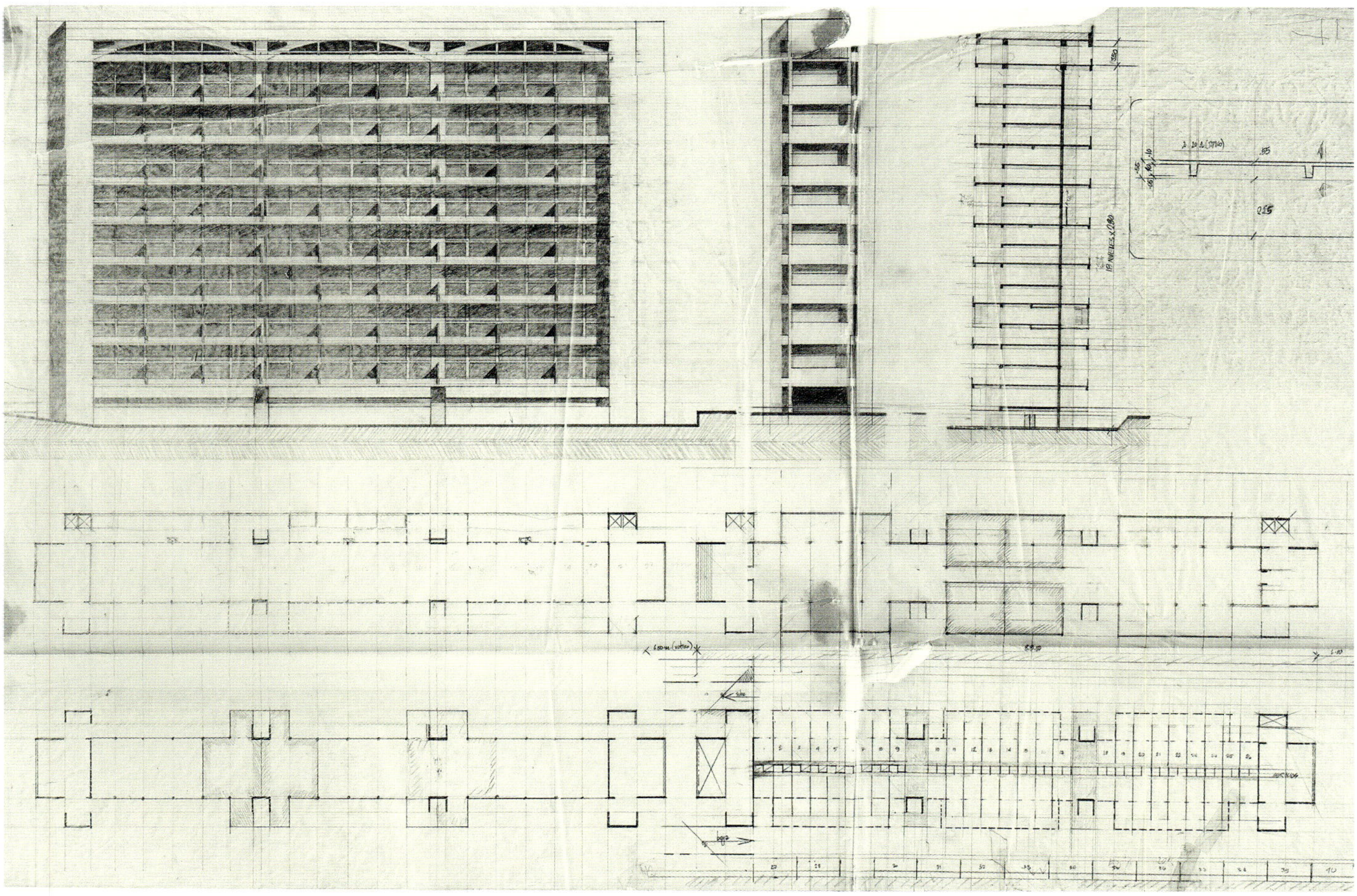

Oscar Tenreiro. Preliminary design for the apartment building

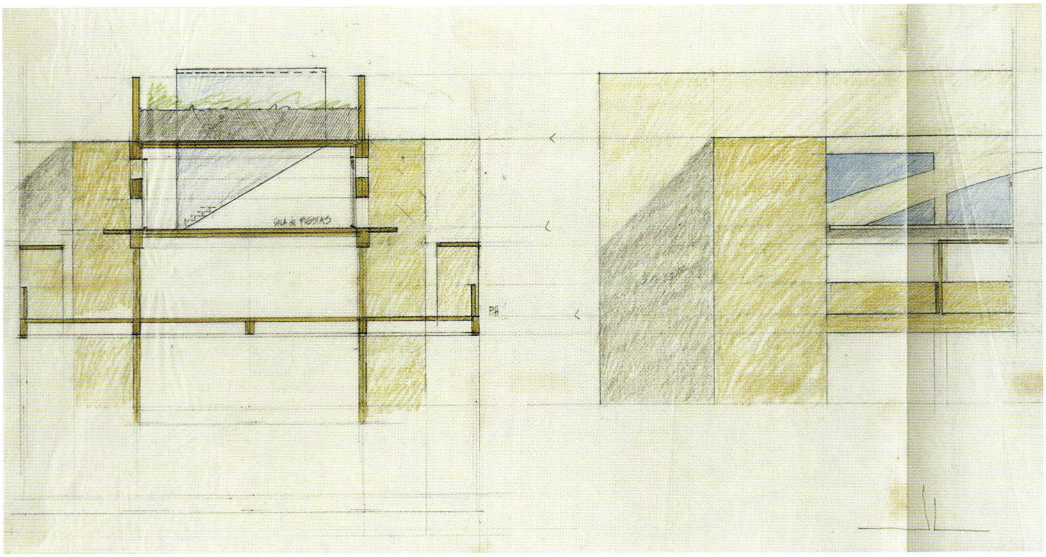

Oscar Tenreiro. Sketches of the upper part of the building, section and elevation detail

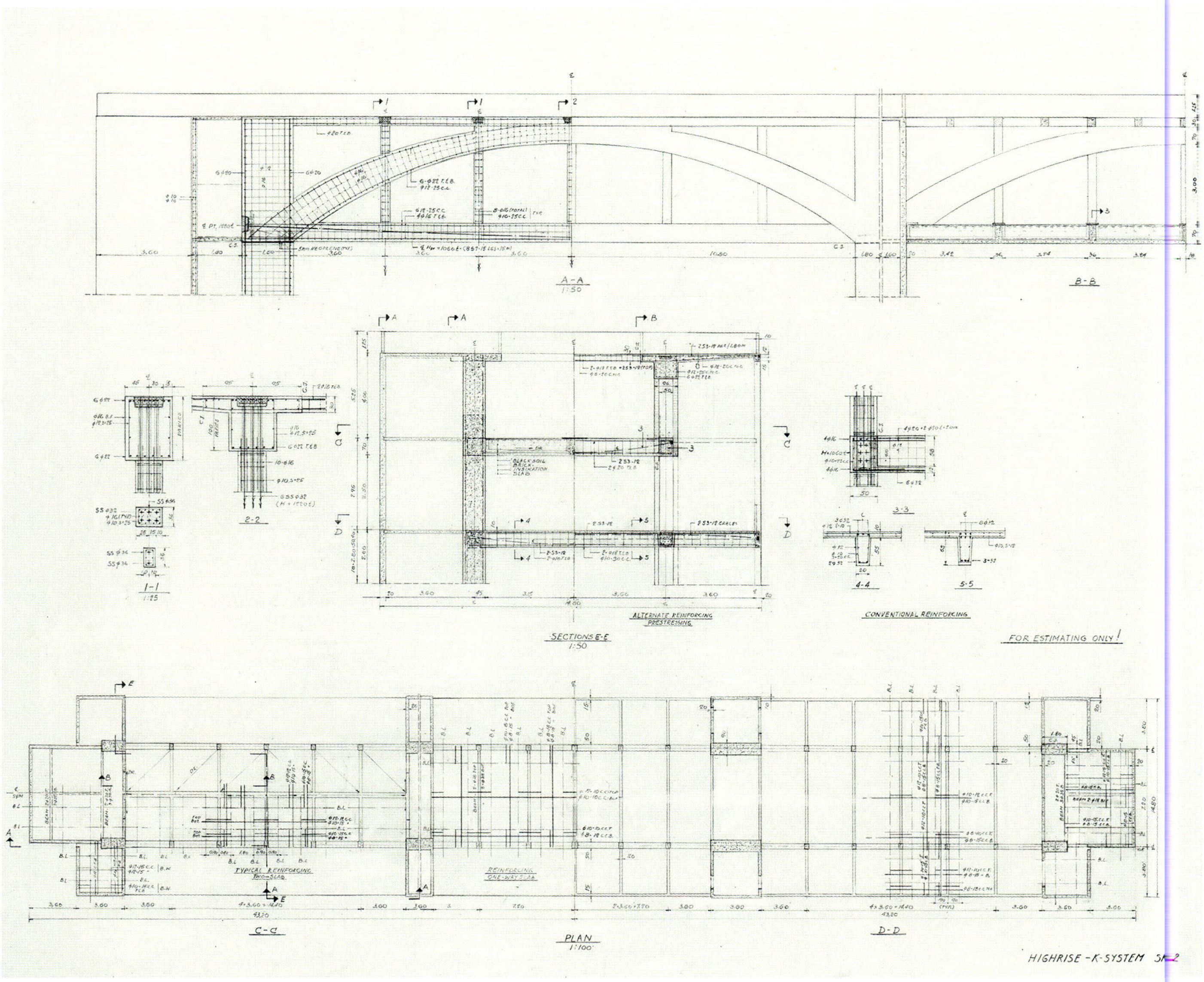

August Komendant. Structure for the upper part of the apartment building, 1978

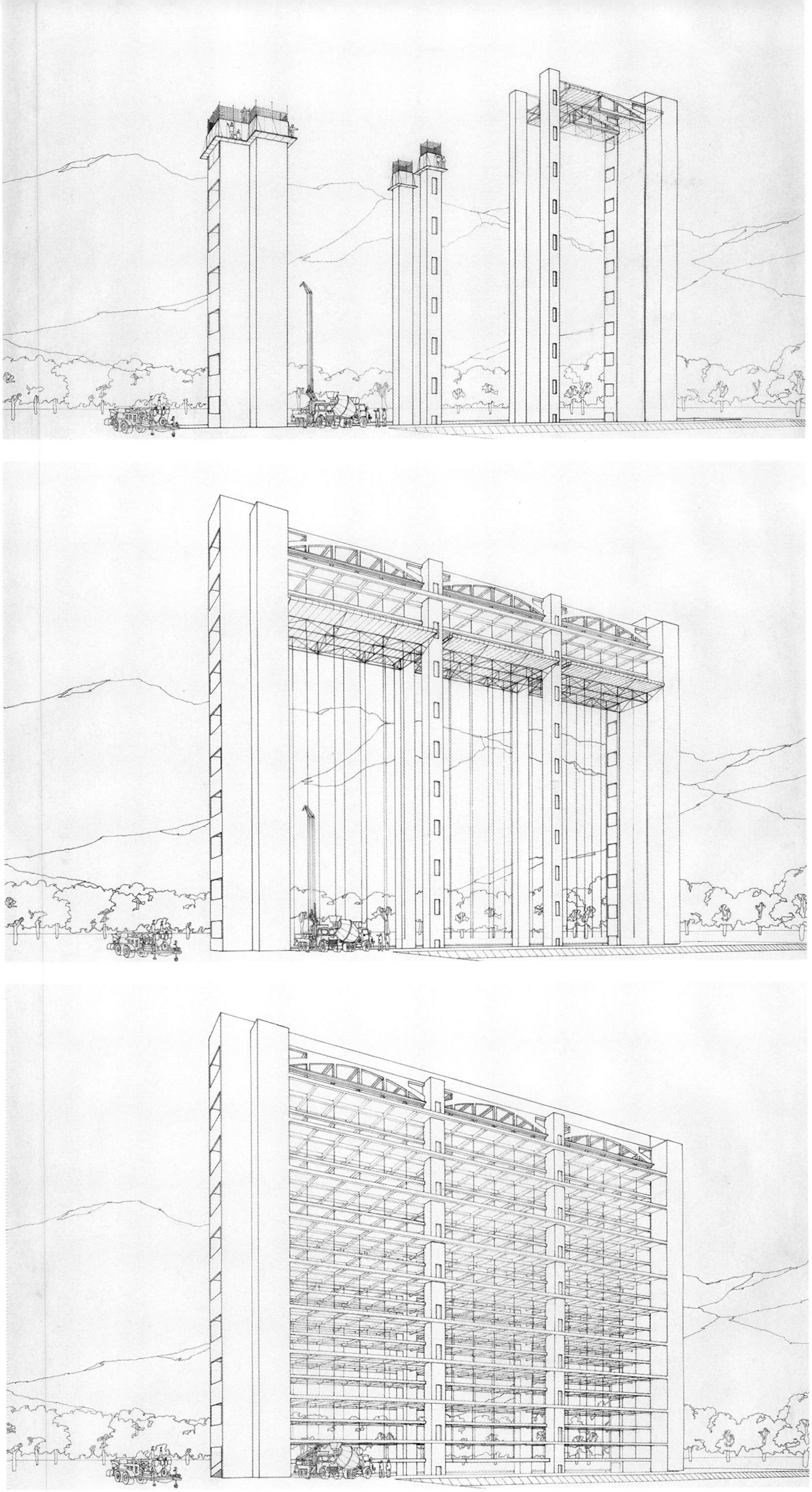

Office of Oscar Tenreiro (Vladimir Pereda Feliú). Construction sequence: First the elevator and mechanical cores are cast, then the upper floor is built, and the sliding formwork is installed for pouring the lower floors

Merike Komendant Phillips. Possible use of the K-System, perspective view

K-System Modular Building System

August Komendant
1977–1980

Primarily based on his Habitat '67 experience, August Komendant developed a modular construction system for multifloor buildings. Patented in 1980 (US4195453A), the system consists of precast concrete modules, "semi-boxes" without tops or bottoms. The modules, lifted into place with a crane, are arranged between horizontal concrete slabs and later posttensioned into unity with steel cables.

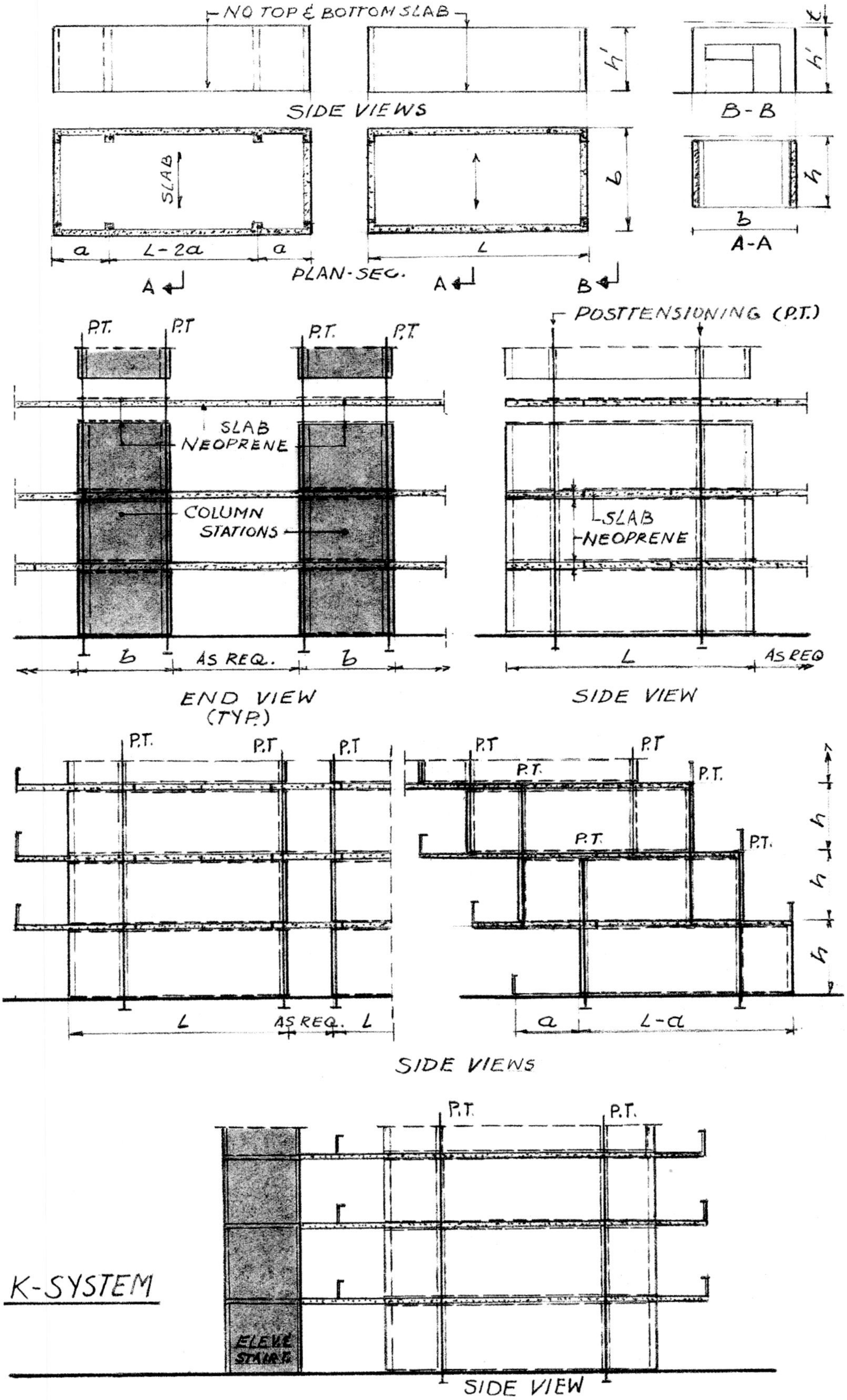

August Komendant. Static calculations of the K-System, structural system

(*next spread*) Merike Komendant Phillips. Possible use of the K-System, perspective view

Merike Phillips 80

The National Gallery with large courtyards, presentation model

GAN—Galeria de Arte Nacional

Caracas, Venezuela
architects Oscar Tenreiro, Francisco Sesto,
structural engineer August Komendant
1980–1986 (not built)

The National Gallery complex was planned for the vicinity of the presidential palace. It was to be a central building in the ensemble of new plazas, parks, and cultural institutions. The galleries of the monumental museum were organized around four spacious courtyards. Natural light, directed by screen walls and skylights, was designed to dominate the interior. The structure of the building was developed with Tenreiro and Komendant in close dialogue. They intended to use long-span posttensioned folded plates, separated by skylight ribbons. Joints elastically controlled with sponge rubber were to be used to provide earthquake resistance.

Oscar Tenreiro. Early volume sketch

Oscar Tenreiro. Early site plan sketches

Axonometric site plan, preliminary version

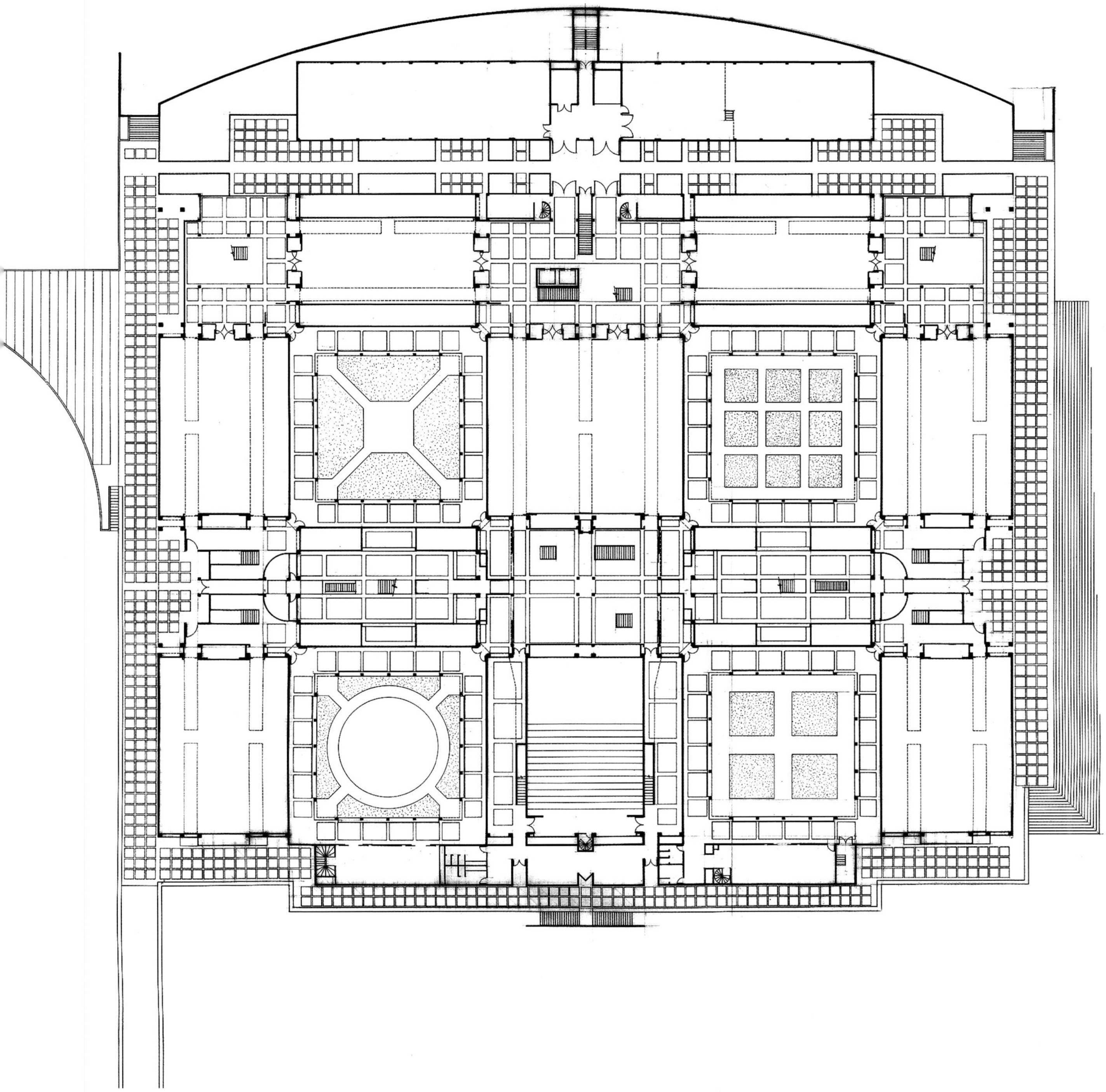

Ground-floor plan

Oscar Tenreiro. Detail of the folded plates structure with a human figure

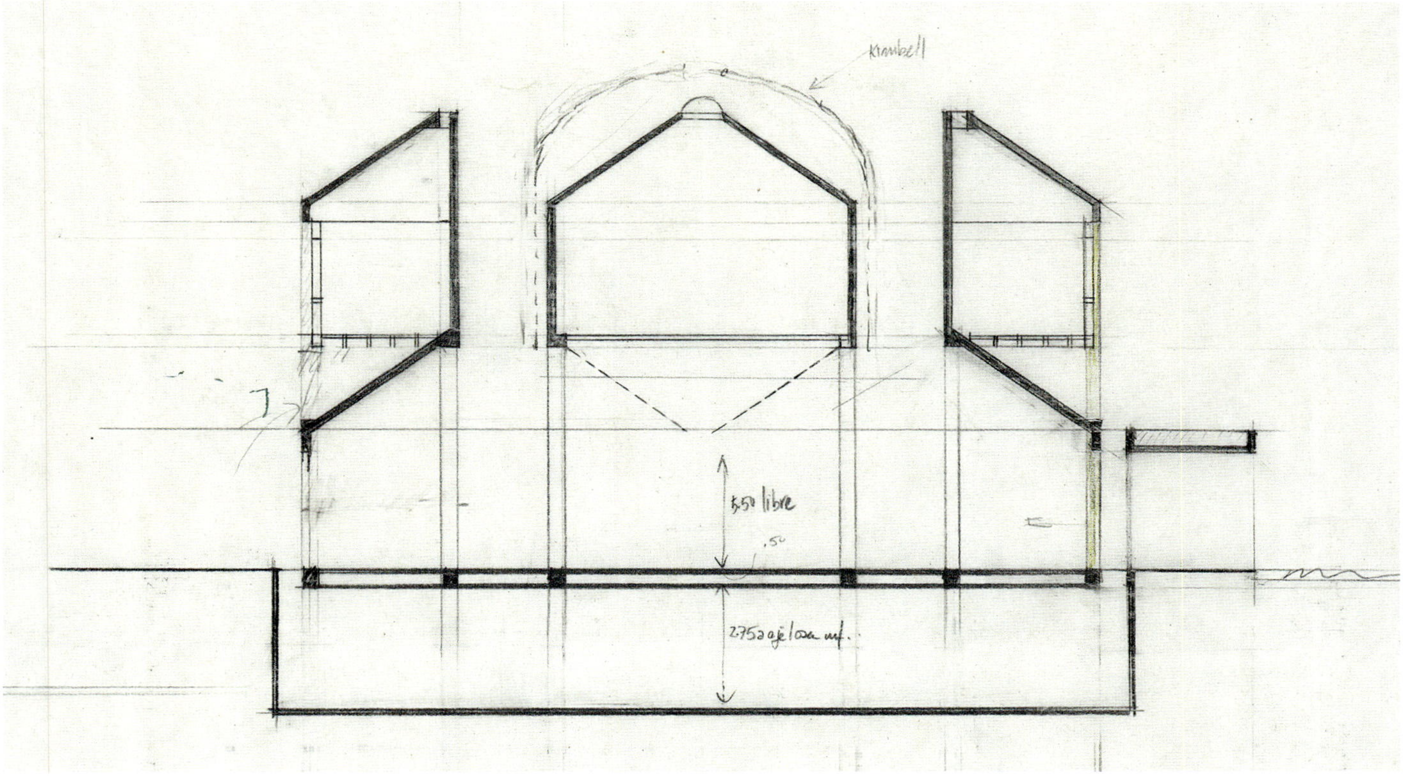

Oscar Tenreiro. Section sketch of the folded plates structure, with Kimbell Art Museum's profile marked on the central volume

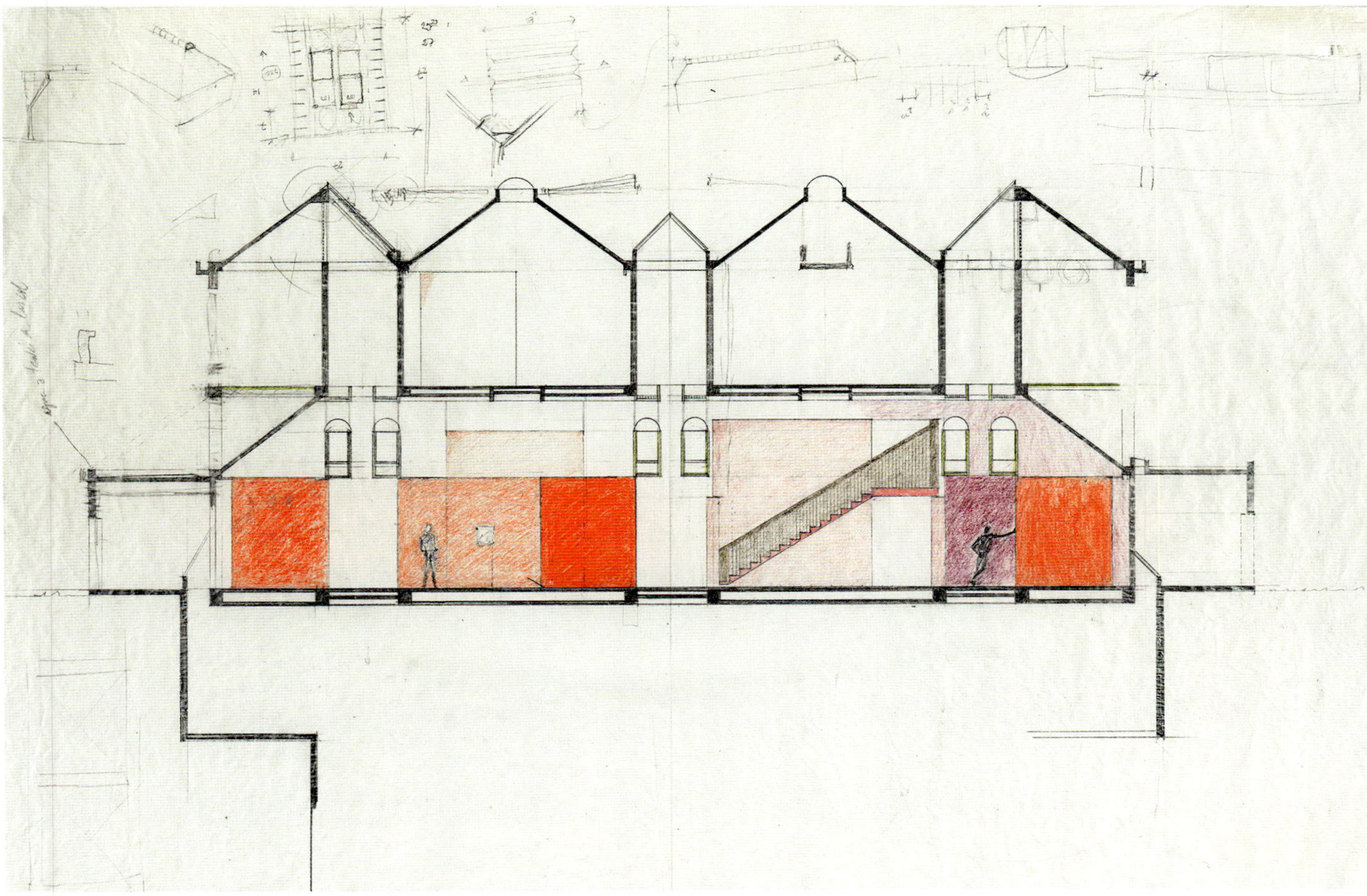

Oscar Tenreiro. Section sketch of the folded plates structure from the main gallery

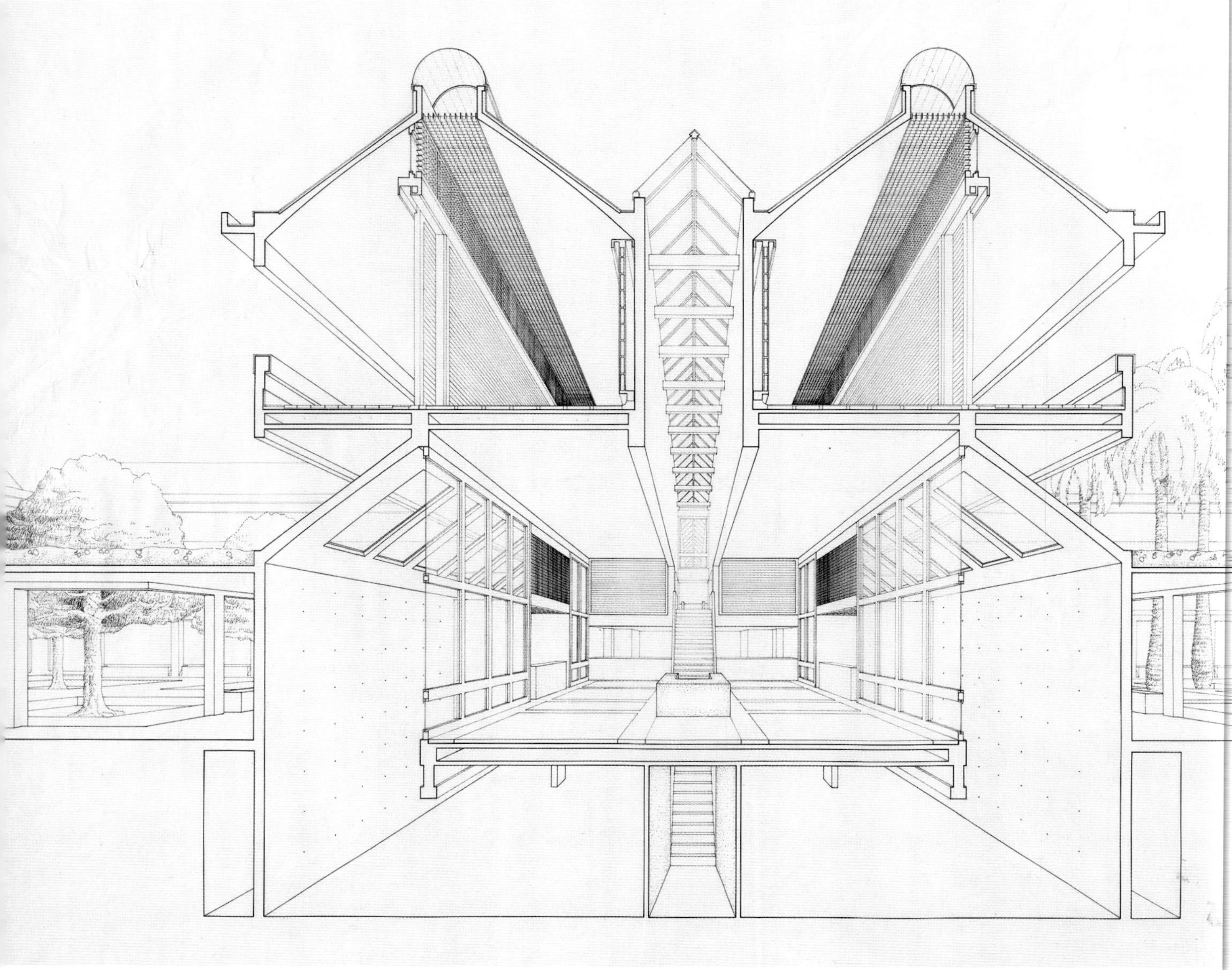

Perspective section through the museum lobby, patios, exhibition halls, and library

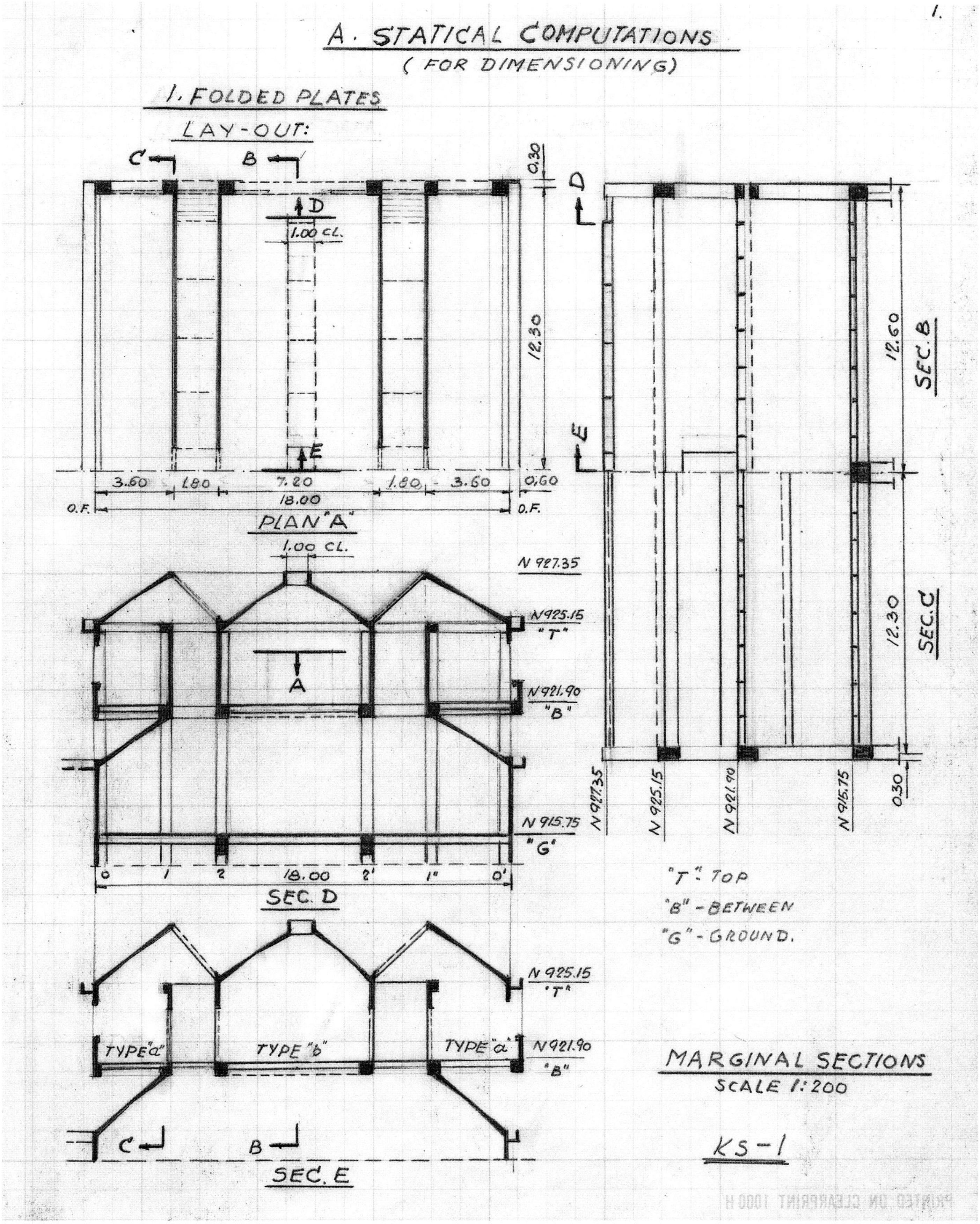

August Komendant. Static calculations of the building, structural system

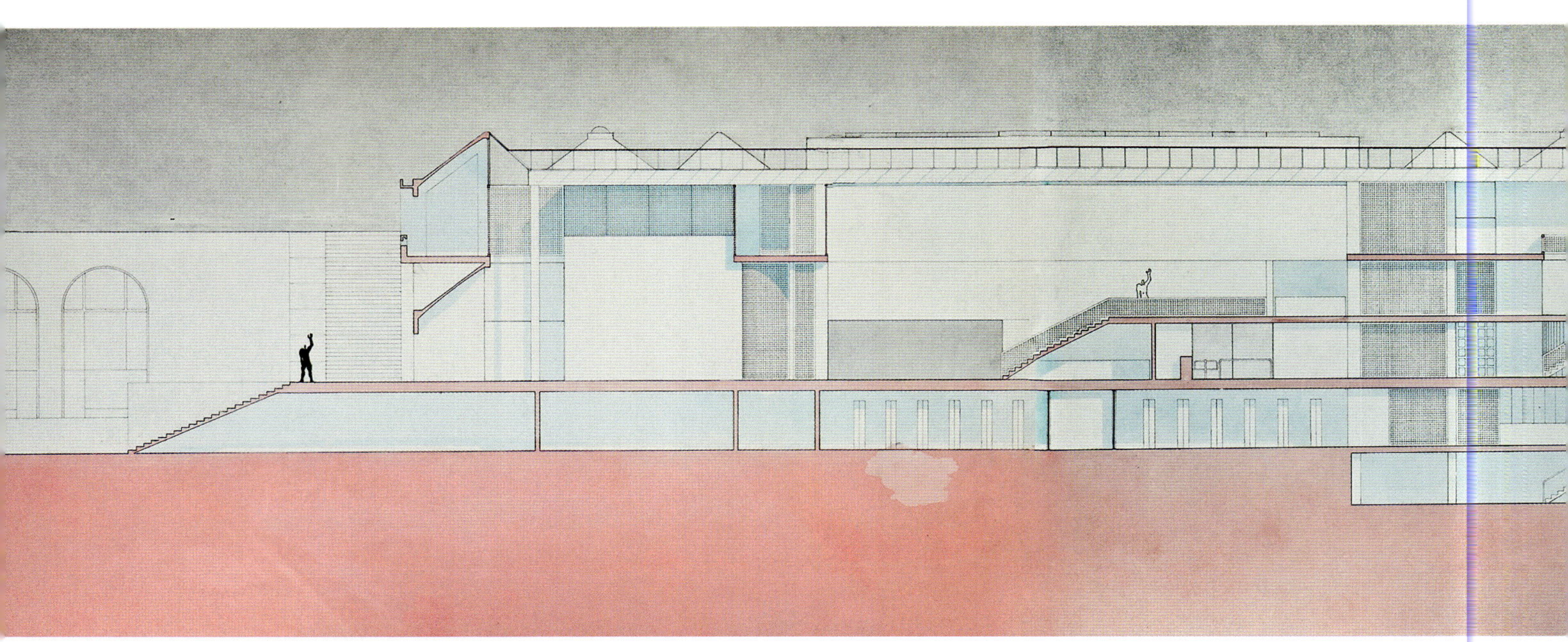

Oscar Tenreiro. Illustrated section of the museum building

Side entrance (*top*) and spacious courtyards

The main entrance to the Medical Research Building

Ciba-Geigy Pharmaceutical Company

Summit, New Jersey, USA
The Office of Henry Klumb, K.S.K. Associates (Henry Klumb, Salvador Soltero, Richard Klumb), structural engineer August Komendant
1981–1986 (demolished)

The facility was designed to house a chemistry laboratory, a scientific information center, and a medical research building for the international pharmaceutical company. In addition to architectural quality, particular emphasis was put on modern technology, energy efficiency, and noise absorption.

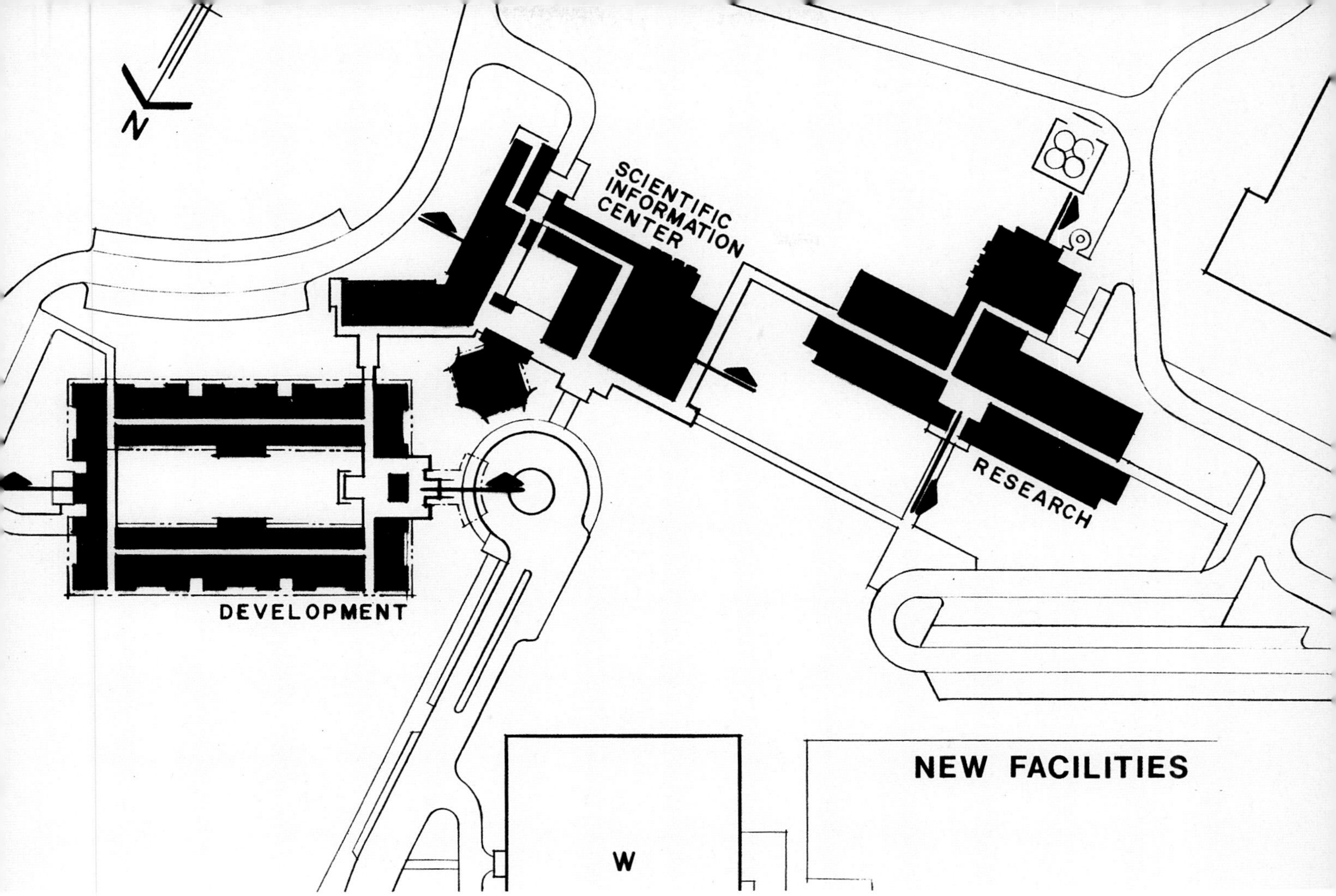

Site plan

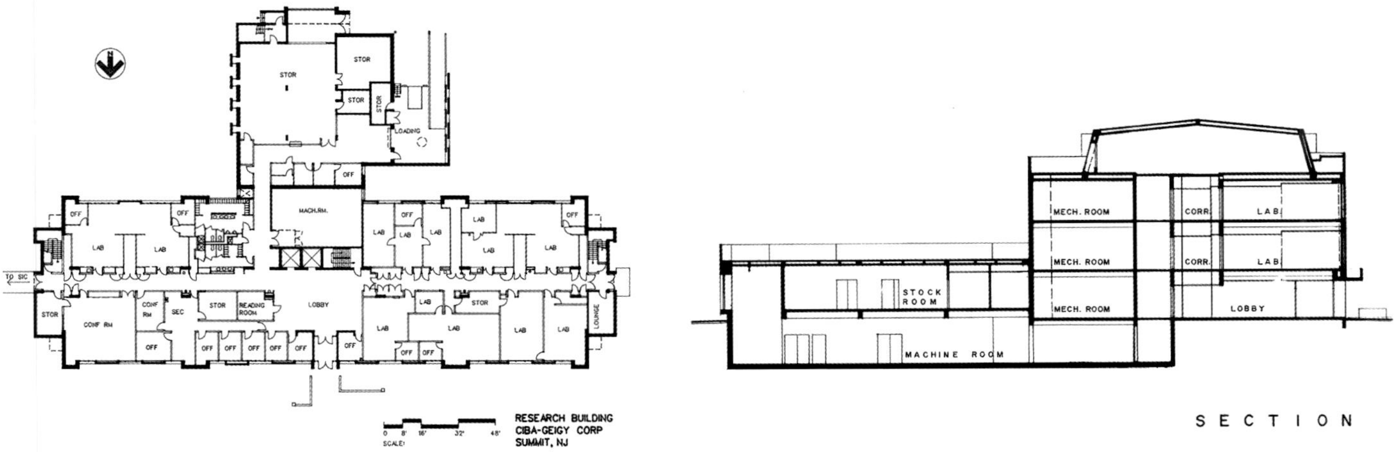

Chemistry building, ground-floor plan (*left*) and section

(*next spread*) Ensemble of buildings after completion, with the chemistry building in the foreground

Aerial view of the unfinished dance theater

Teatro del Oeste Dance Theater

Caracas, Venezuela
architect Oscar Tenreiro,
structural consultant August Komendant
1982–1983 (not finished)

The Teatro del Oeste was part of a plan to build new cultural buildings and green spaces in the heart of Caracas. In addition to the dance theater, the author of the plan, architect Oscar Tenreiro, also designed the ensemble of the Plaza Bicentenario [see pp. 334–341] and the National Gallery GAN [see pp. 312–323]. Of these, only the Plaza Bicentenario was completed, though only through the first phase. Work on the Teatro del Oeste dance theater progressed until the main structure was almost complete, but due to financial difficulties, construction was put on hold, and the unfinished concrete structure has been left to decay for more than three decades. Posttensioning of the concrete was used in the construction of the monolithic structure, including Vierendeel trusses in the main hall.

Expressive concrete structures under construction
(*next spread*) Perspective section of the dance theater, seats of the main hall in the middle, stage on the left-hand side

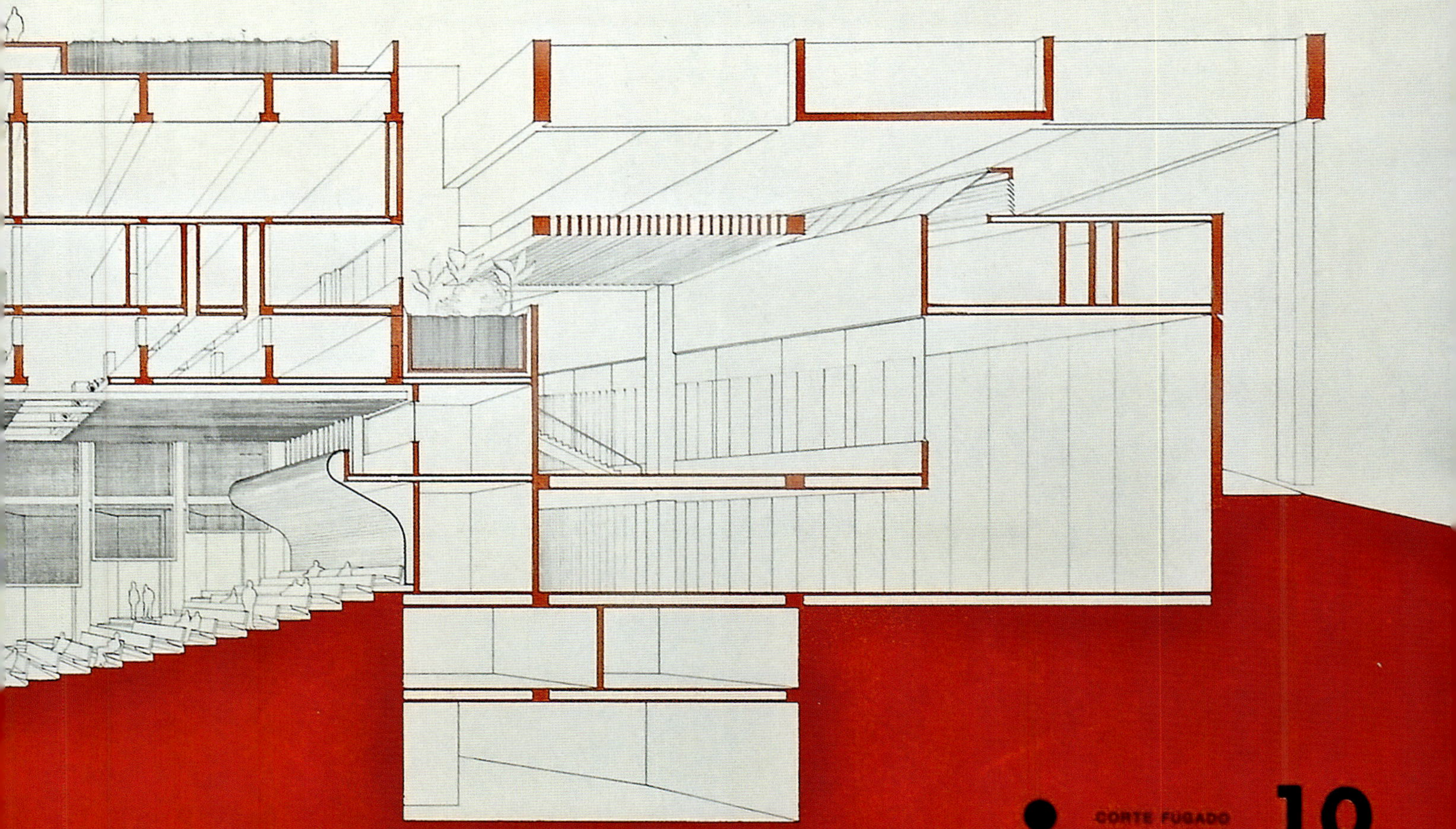

● CORTE FUGADO **10**

Posttensioning cables and steel reinforcement

Current view of the unfinished dance theater

Ramp heading to the square

Plaza Bicentenario and the Presidential Palace Extension

Caracas, Venezuela
architect Oscar Tenreiro,
structural consultant August Komendant
1982–1987, first phase completed (extant)

Built next to the Presidential Palace of Venezuela, the Palacio de Miraflores, the plaza was part of a master plan to construct a number of cultural venues and open public areas in central Caracas. The author of the master plan, architect Oscar Tenreiro, designed not only the Plaza Bicentenario but also the National Gallery GAN [see pp. 312–323], and the Teatro del Oeste dance theater [see pp. 328–333]. Only the plaza was completed, and even that was only through the first phase of construction. There are parking spaces underneath the plaza and galleries and office spaces on the edges of the site. Most of the load-bearing structures are of reinforced posttensioned concrete, designed in collaboration with August Komendant.

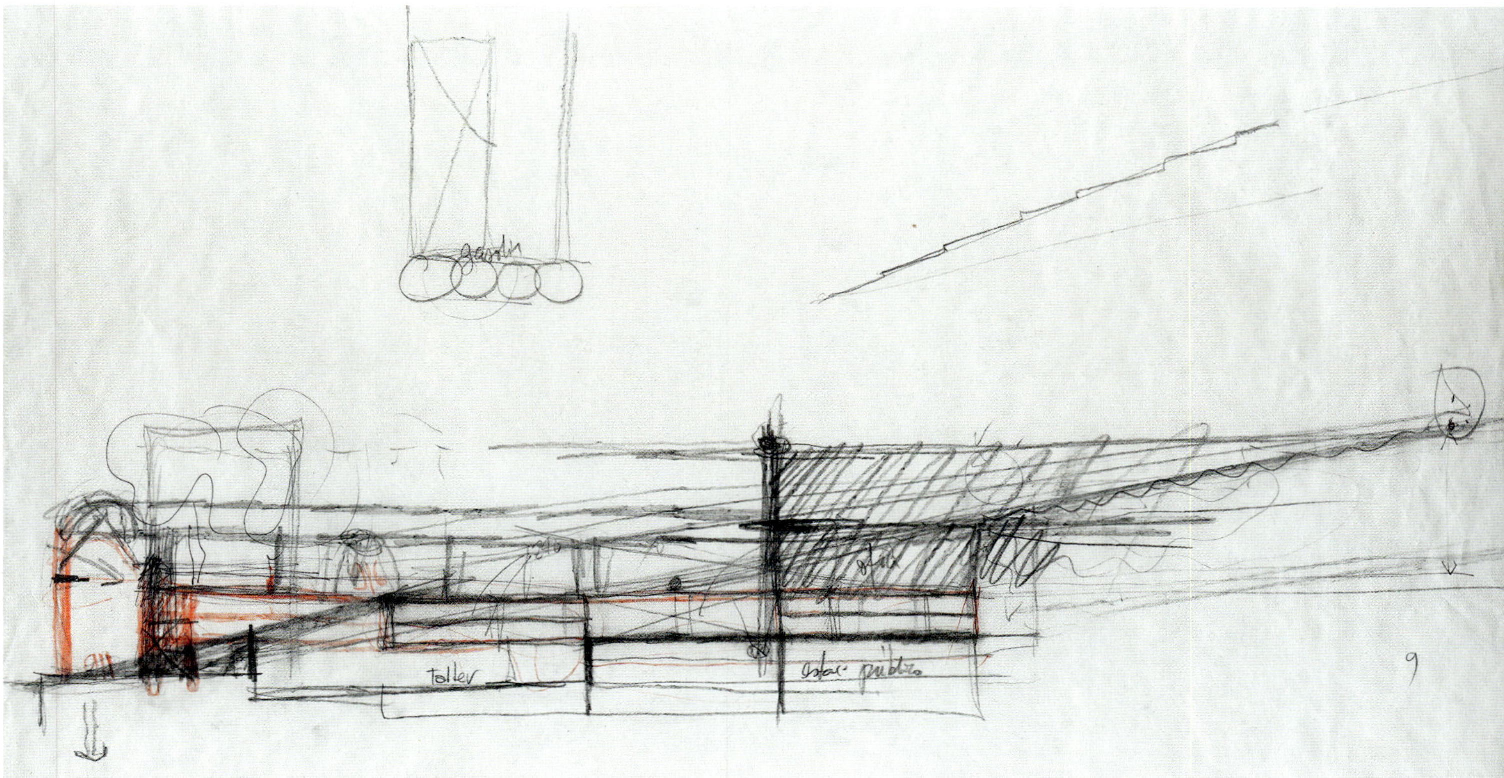

Oscar Tenreiro. Site plan (*top*) and section of the square, early sketches

Plaza Bicentenario, presentation model
(*right*) Final phases of construction

Plaza Bicentenario after the completion of the first construction phase
(*next spread*) Aerial view of the plaza after completion, with the Presidential Palace, the Palacio de Miraflores, on the left, 1986

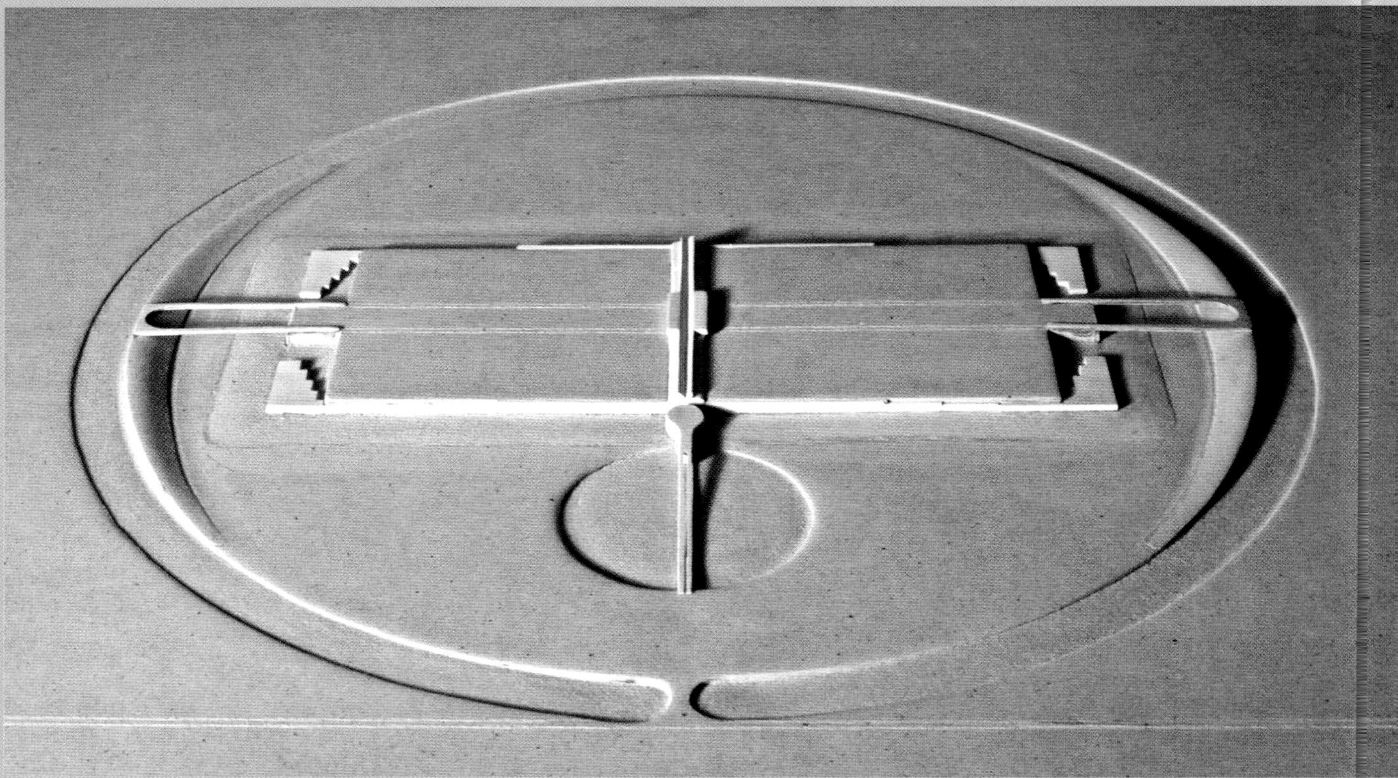

Site model of the future factory

General Motors 21st-Century Manufacturing Facility

architect Oscar Tenreiro,
structural consultant August Komendant
1987, design research competition

This was a vision of a twenty-first-century car factory with an ambitious spatial program. Architect Oscar Tenreiro's competition work was completed in collaboration with architecture students from the University of Kentucky. Tenreiro was in close contact with August Komendant during the project. The experienced engineer gave detailed advice on, among other things, the use of large-span Vierendeel trusses.

Vierendeel trusses exposed on the side facade

Sectional model illustrating the Vierendeel trusses as part of the structural system

Biography

Catching the horizon, 1960s
(*previous page*) On the Great Wall of China, ca. 1986

Biography

August Eduard Komendant
1906–1992

1906	born to farmers Hans and Leena Komendant in Nurmsi village, Järva County, Estonia
1927	graduated from Paide Co-educational Secondary School
1934	graduated from the Technical University of Dresden as a certified engineer
1936	established his own design office
1944	to escape the war, fled with his family to Germany
1945	worked for five years as a consulting engineer for the US armed forces in Europe
1950	emigrated to the United States
1953	became an active member of the New York Academy of Sciences
1956	met architect Louis Kahn
1957	received his engineering license in the State of New Jersey
1961	built his home near New York City
1967	designed the Habitat '67 housing complex together with architect Moshe Safdie
1978	received the American Institute of Architects' Medal
1980	elected to be a permanent member of the American Society of Civil Engineers
1992	died in Upper Montclair, New Jersey

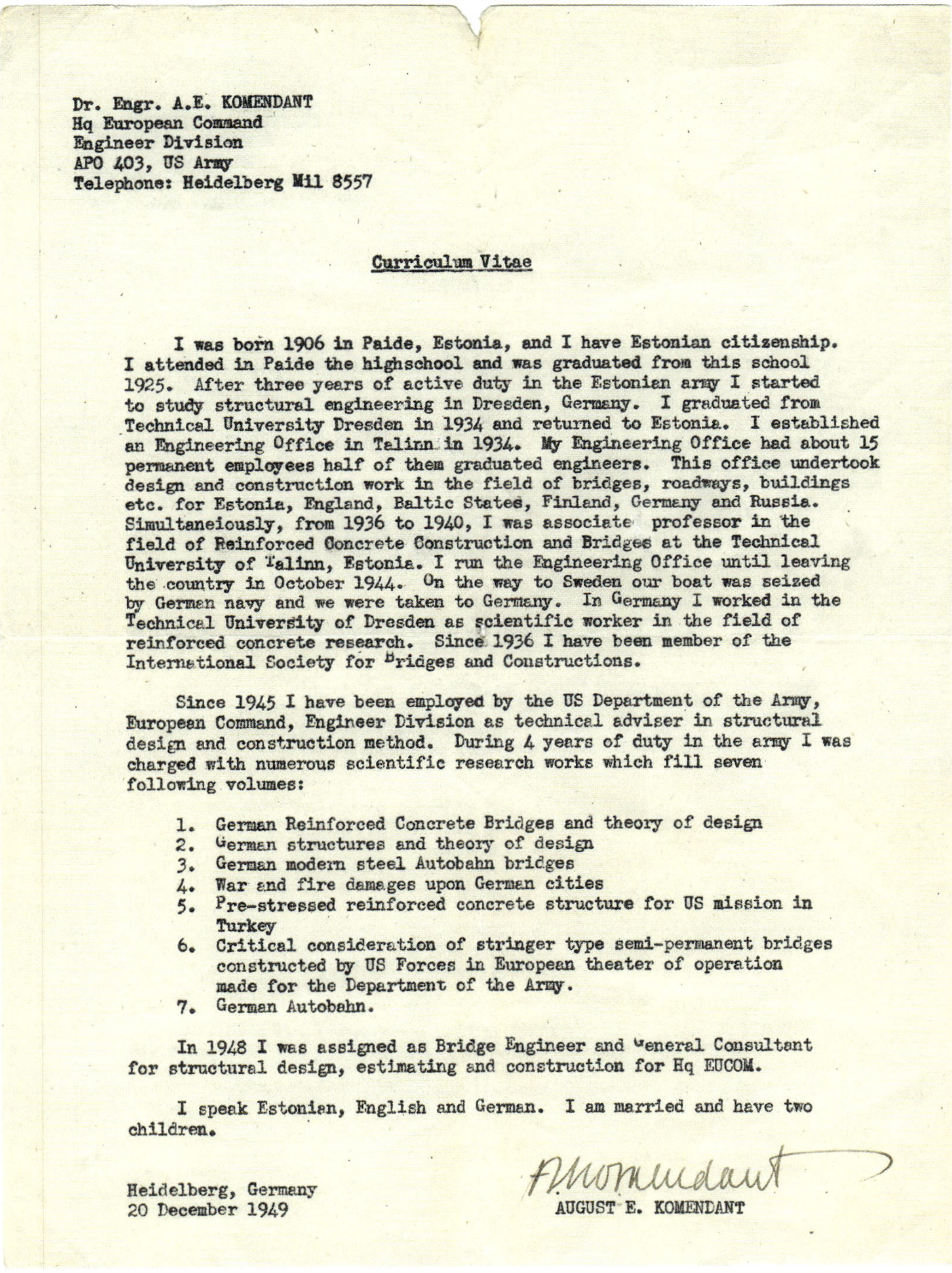

Dr. Engr. A.E. KOMENDANT
Hq European Command
Engineer Division
APO 403, US Army
Telephone: Heidelberg Mil 8557

Curriculum Vitae

I was born 1906 in Paide, Estonia, and I have Estonian citizenship. I attended in Paide the highschool and was graduated from this school 1925. After three years of active duty in the Estonian army I started to study structural engineering in Dresden, Germany. I graduated from Technical University Dresden in 1934 and returned to Estonia. I established an Engineering Office in Talinn in 1934. My Engineering Office had about 15 permanent employees half of them graduated engineers. This office undertook design and construction work in the field of bridges, roadways, buildings etc. for Estonia, England, Baltic States, Finland, Germany and Russia. Simultaneiously, from 1936 to 1940, I was associate professor in the field of Reinforced Concrete Construction and Bridges at the Technical University of Talinn, Estonia. I run the Engineering Office until leaving the country in October 1944. On the way to Sweden our boat was seized by German navy and we were taken to Germany. In Germany I worked in the Technical University of Dresden as scientific worker in the field of reinforced concrete research. Since 1936 I have been member of the International Society for Bridges and Constructions.

Since 1945 I have been employed by the US Department of the Army, European Command, Engineer Division as technical adviser in structural design and construction method. During 4 years of duty in the army I was charged with numerous scientific research works which fill seven following volumes:

1. German Reinforced Concrete Bridges and theory of design
2. German structures and theory of design
3. German modern steel Autobahn bridges
4. War and fire damages upon German cities
5. Pre-stressed reinforced concrete structure for US mission in Turkey
6. Critical consideration of stringer type semi-permanent bridges constructed by US Forces in European theater of operation made for the Department of the Army.
7. German Autobahn.

In 1948 I was assigned as Bridge Engineer and General Consultant for structural design, estimating and construction for Hq EUCOM.

I speak Estonian, English and German. I am married and have two children.

Heidelberg, Germany
20 December 1949

A. Komendant
AUGUST E. KOMENDANT

Curriculum Vitae, 1949

Triple portrait, 1978

Family portrait, seated (*from the left*): Erna, Merike, Jüri, ca. 1948

Home and Family

In 1935 August Komendant married Erna "Cutu" Gutmann (1911–2014). A daughter, Merike (1939), and a son, Jüri (1942), were born to the family. They lived in Tallinn. To escape the war the family went to Germany (1944). Soon after they moved on to the United States (1950). The family separated upon arriving in the US. The children went to live with their mother on Long Island, while August Komendant went to live in New York City in Manhattan. Having met as refugees in Germany, Helmi Aren (1906–2006) became Komendant's life partner. In 1961 the construction of their home, with offices on the lower floor, was completed near New York. There was a wonderful view of Manhattan from the upper floor.

Home in Upper Montclair, New Jersey, 1960s

Helmi Aren and August Komendant, 1960s

Sunny morning after a party

A brother's kiss, August and Verner, 1976

On the balcony at home with daughter Merike, 1973

With grandson Erik in the garden, 1981

Shoveling snow from the front door at home, ca. 1984

With a new car, 1984

Beautiful nature and majestic structures of North America, 1966–1984

(*next spread*) August Komendant and Helmi Aren, visiting the newly completed Habitat '67 housing complex at Expo in Montreal, July 14, 1967

Board of the Paide Co-educational Secondary School sports club, August Komendant in the middle, 1926–1927

Education

In 1927 August Komendant graduated from the Paide Co-educational Secondary School. After his military service, he was sent to the school for noncommissioned officers, and from there to the military school for his post-graduate studies. He left the military as a junior officer (1929) and went to study in Germany. He graduated from the Technical University of Dresden as a certified structural engineer specializing in the statics of reinforced concrete (1934). In the whirlwind of World War II, Komendant was not able to defend his PhD, but his fellow faculty members and colleagues always called him Dr. Komendant. His friends simply called him Doc.

A conscript, 1927

Students of the school for Noncommissioned Officers, August Komendant on the left, 1928–1929

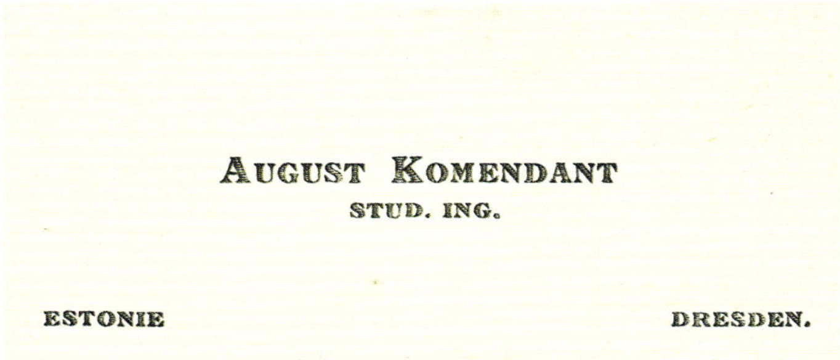

AUGUST KOMENDANT
STUD. ING.

ESTONIE DRESDEN.

Student name card

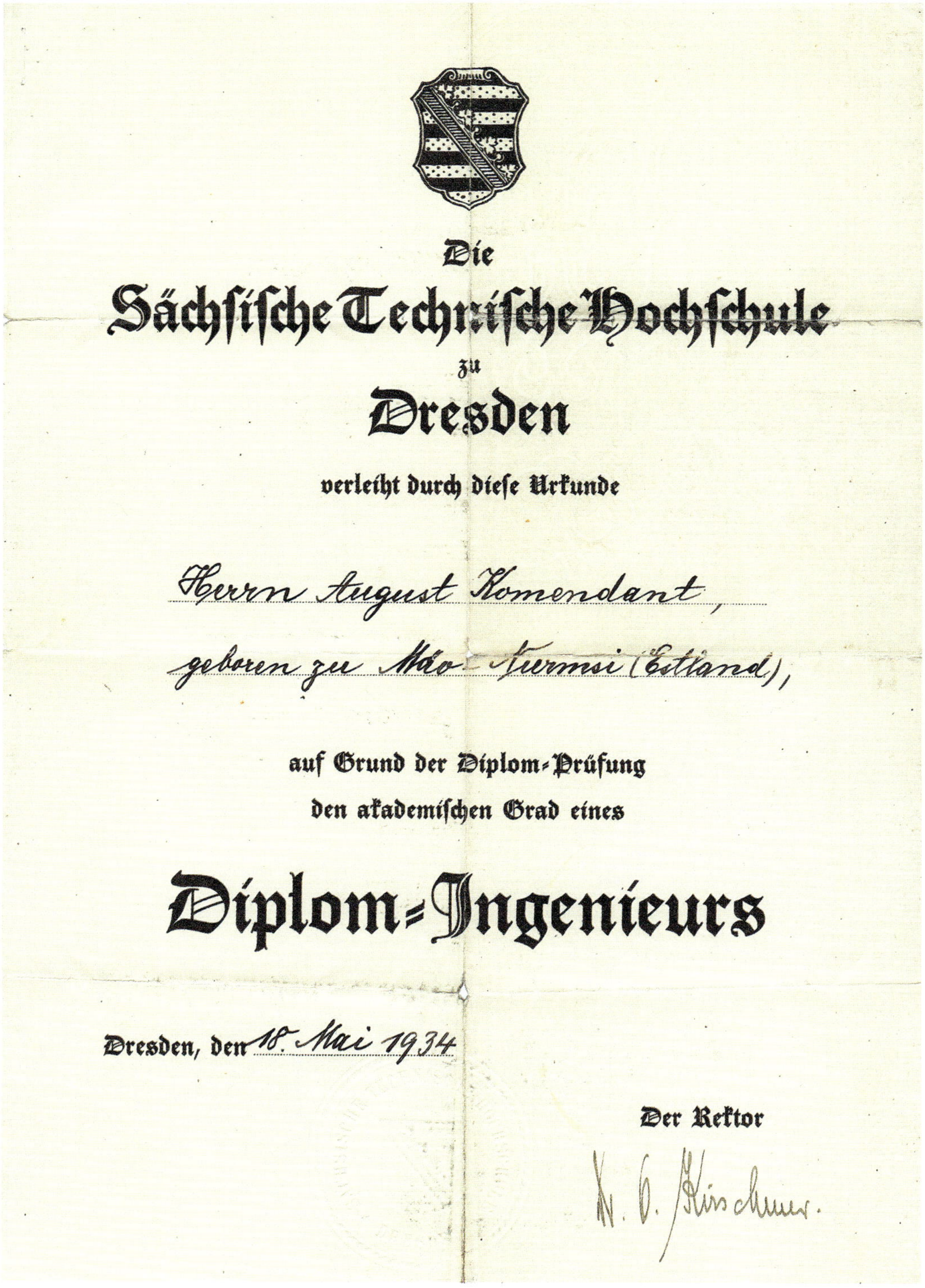

Die
Sächsische Technische Hochschule
zu
Dresden
verleiht durch diese Urkunde

Herrn August Komendant,
geboren zu Ado-Nurmsi (Estland),

auf Grund der Diplom-Prüfung
den akademischen Grad eines

Diplom-Ingenieurs

Dresden, den 18. Mai 1934

Der Rektor

Diploma from the Technical University of Dresden, 1934

As a student at the Technical University of Dresden, August Komendant is seated, ca. 1930

Behind the drafting table with engineer Ervin-Aksel Sööt, late 1940s

At Work

Throughout his career August Komendant played a variety of roles in the construction industry. In the 1930s he was construction supervisor and entrepreneur, and in the second half of the same decade, he was a faculty member and structural designer. After World War II, he was primarily a consulting engineer. He felt just as comfortable on building sites as he did at the drawing table, and rumbling concrete mixers were just as familiar to him as graphite pencils and slide rules. Before the computer age, all drawings and calculations were done by hand. This required great concentration and precision. During his career, Komendant prepared thousands of drawings and hundreds of calculations. He had many assistants, including his life partner, Helmi Aren, who was talented in music and mathematics as well as technical drawing.

Inspecting bridges in Germany with engineer Jaan Lamp, second half of the 1940s

War-damaged highway bridge and a warehouse (*right*) in Germany, second half of the 1940s

Home office in Upper Montclair, New Jersey

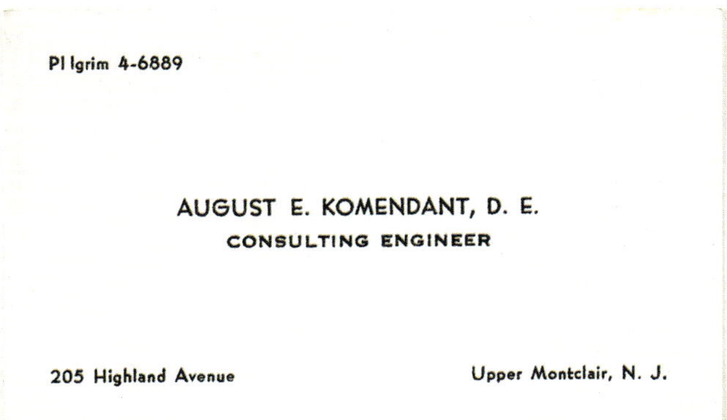

A business card and a rubber stamp

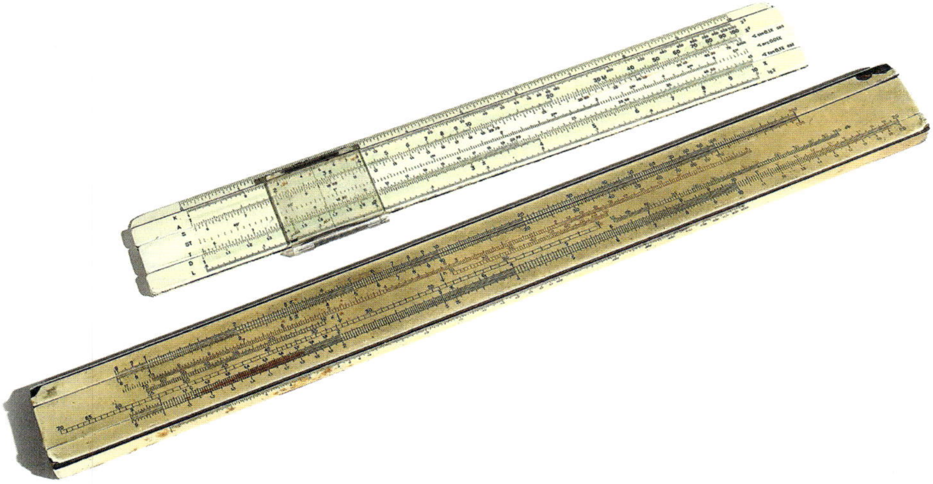

Slide rules—August Komendant's "computers"

Drafting supplies

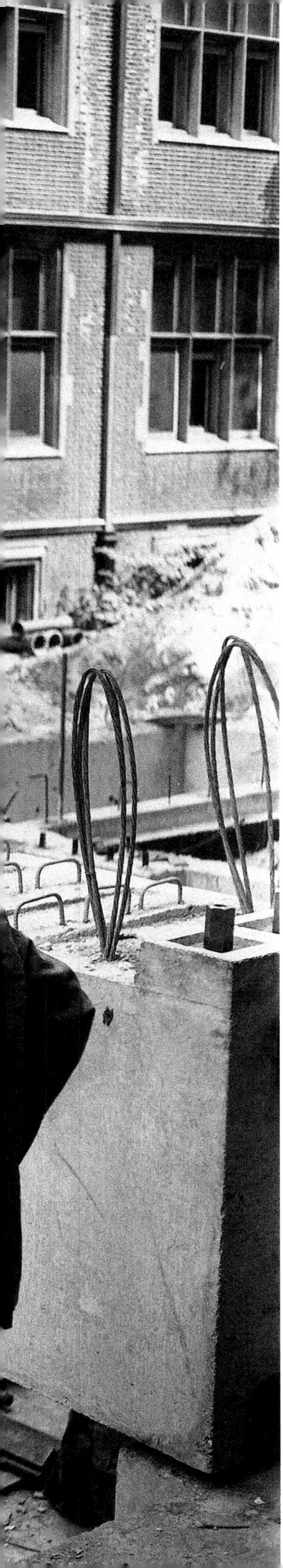

On the construction site of the Richards Medical Research Laboratories, 1959

Site visit to the Kimbell Art Museum construction, 1970

On the stairs of the Salk Institute, 1967

Visiting the Plaza Bicentenario construction site, 1983

THE AMERICAN INSTITUTE OF ARCHITECTS

Elmer E. Botsai, FAIA
President

January 11, 1978

Dr. August E. Komendant
205 Highland Avenue
Upper Montclair, New Jersey

Dear Dr. Komendant:

This will confirm our telegram of December 8. May I again congratulate you upon being selected the recipient of an AIA Medal.

Your AIA Medal is awarded to individuals or organizations who have inspired and influenced the architectural profession. Past recipients of the Medal are Peter Blake, FAIA, Gemini G.E.L., and the Walker Art Center.

Presentation of your Medal will be made at the AIA national convention to be held in Dallas, Texas, May 21-24, 1978. The Awards Presentation will be held at 2:00 PM, Sunday, May 21 at the Dallas Music Hall.

As soon as you notify us of your intention to be present, we shall make a reservation for you at the Fairmont Hotel, which has been designated the headquarters hotel. Much as we would like to reimburse you for your travel expenses, budget restrictions will permit us to reimburse you only for your hotel room costs. Transportation, meals and personal expenses for your trip must be borne by the individual recipient. Upon departure, you should send us a copy of your receipted hotel bill and a reimbursement check covering your room charges will be sent to you immediately.

The release date on your Medal is February 10, 1978. Please provide Laura K. Baker, Public Relations Department, here at headquarters, with a list of any special news media which should receive the press release.

Again, our warm congratulations.

Sincerely,

Elmer E. Botsai, FAIA

1735 NEW YORK AVENUE, N.W. • WASHINGTON, D. C. 20006 • (202) 785-7300

American Institute of Architects' official announcement to August Komendant of the AIA Medal, 1978

American Institute of Architects (AIA) Medal Acceptance Speech

August Komendant
AIA National Convention A Time to Learn
Dallas, Texas
21 May 1978

Thank you!

I appreciate this honor! It was a surprise, because architects usually do not honor engineers – the necessary evil to many architects. To be honest, in accordance with my own experience, some of the engineers can truly be "pain in the neck", especially to anyone who dares to propose a novelty or advanced design. But evil or not, engineering is an integral part of contemporary architecture.

Since the theme of this convention is A Time to Learn my advice to you is – learn a little more engineering and to engineers – be more concerned about esthetics. At present, divided as we are, we very often disrespect each other and ignore our related problems. We carry out orders from politicians, real estate operators and others – orders which are very often against our own better professional judgment.

Let us close ranks for the same aim in view – sound and beautiful building or structure and better environment.

This honor I am receiving today seems to me a proper start in this direction.
Once more, I thank you very much!

Medal of the American Institute of Architects, 1978

(*next spread*) AIA president Elmer Botsai and August Komendant, medal ceremony, May 21, 1978

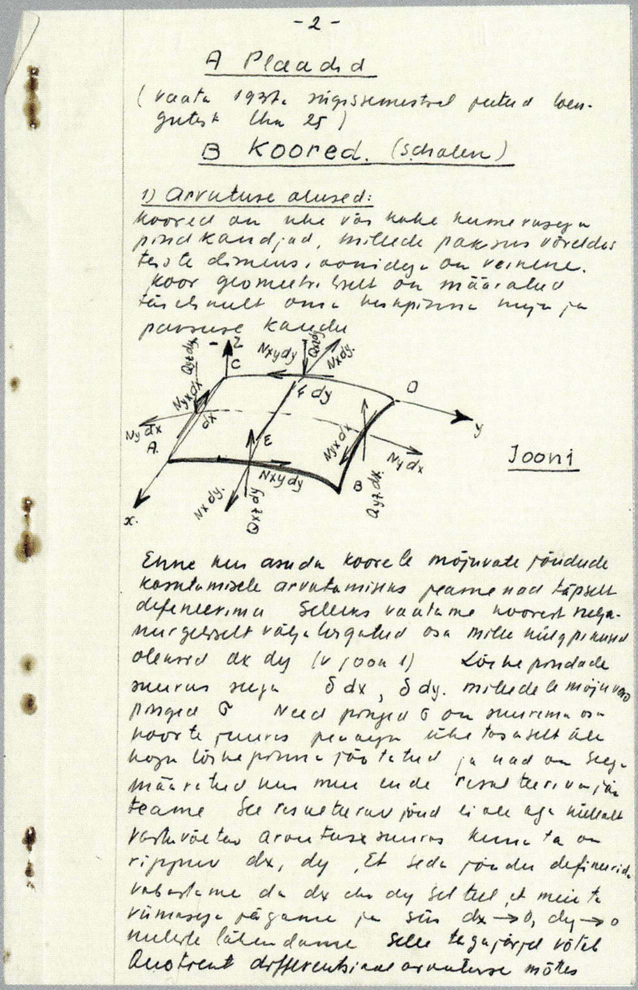

-2-

A Plaadid

B Koored. (Schalen)

1) Arvutuse alused:

Jooni

Notes for the Tallinn University of Technology lectures, 1938–1939

University

August Komendant was a successful educator. As a young engineer, he gave lectures on concrete structures at the Tallinn University of Technology (1937–1939). After having emigrated to the United States, he became a visiting professor at the University of Pennsylvania, where, together with Louis Kahn, he primarily taught architectural students. In the 1970s Komendant taught a course in the philosophy of technology at the renowned Pratt Institute in New York. The students appreciated Komendant's knowledge, experience and directness. He was convinced that a good education did not mean acquiring lots of facts but learning how to think.

Design crit at the University of Pennsylvania: (*from the left*) Norman Rice, Louis Kahn, Robert Le Ricolais, August Komendant, autumn 1970

A humorous gift from students

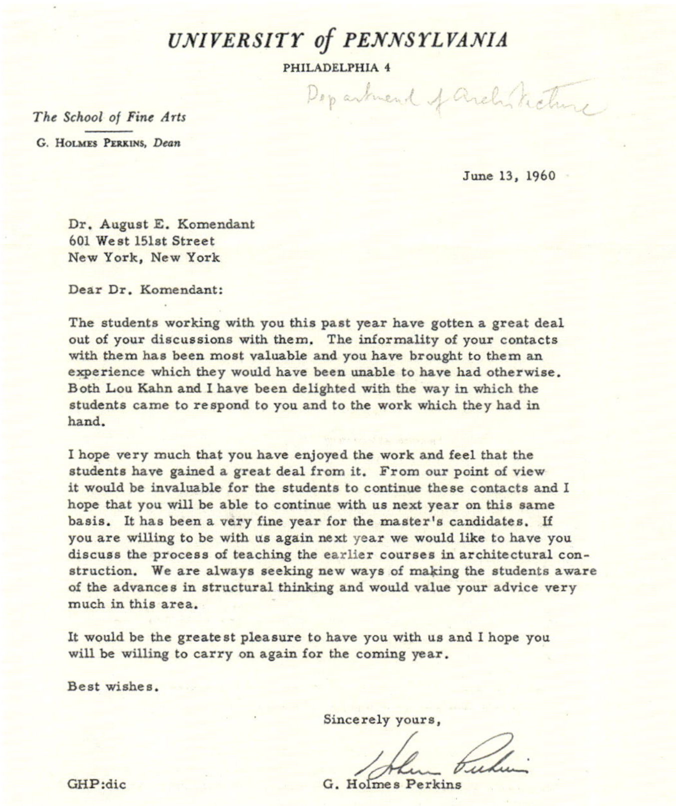

UNIVERSITY of PENNSYLVANIA
PHILADELPHIA 4

Department of Architecture

The School of Fine Arts
G. Holmes Perkins, *Dean*

June 13, 1960

Dr. August E. Komendant
601 West 151st Street
New York, New York

Dear Dr. Komendant:

The students working with you this past year have gotten a great deal out of your discussions with them. The informality of your contacts with them has been most valuable and you have brought to them an experience which they would have been unable to have had otherwise. Both Lou Kahn and I have been delighted with the way in which the students came to respond to you and to the work which they had in hand.

I hope very much that you have enjoyed the work and feel that the students have gained a great deal from it. From our point of view it would be invaluable for the students to continue these contacts and I hope that you will be able to continue with us next year on this same basis. It has been a very fine year for the master's candidates. If you are willing to be with us again next year we would like to have you discuss the process of teaching the earlier courses in architectural construction. We are always seeking new ways of making the students aware of the advances in structural thinking and would value your advice very much in this area.

It would be the greatest pleasure to have you with us and I hope you will be willing to carry on again for the coming year.

Best wishes.

Sincerely yours,

G. Holmes Perkins

GHP:dic

Letter from Dean Holmes Perkins of the School of Fine Arts, University of Pennsylvania, 1960

Prestressed Concrete Structures, 1952

Books

August Komendant was a productive writer. During his lifetime he wrote four books of which the most famous is his retrospective *18 Years with Architect Louis I. Kahn* (1975). The other three are technical works. *Prestressed Concrete Structures* (1952) was his first book published in the United States, and it introduced Komendant to local architects and engineers. A curious fact: unbeknownst to its author, the book was translated into Russian in the USSR (1959). In addition to books, Komendant wrote scientific articles for technical publications as well as popularizing texts for the general public.

18 Years with Architect Louis I. Kahn, 1975

Russian translation of *Prestressed Concrete Structures*, 1959

Estonian translation of *18 Years with Architect Louis I. Kahn*, 2019

(*next spread*) August Komendant in front of the Habitat '67 housing complex in Montreal, ca. 1980

The Exhibition

Miracles in Concrete. Structural Engineer August Komendant

Estonian Museum of Architecture
Rotermann Salt Storage
January 10—July 26, 2020

Curator Carl-Dag Lige, Estonian Museum of Architecture
Exhibition design Tomomi Hayashi, Andrea Ainjärv, HGA
Graphic design Marje Eelma, Tuumik Stuudio

Dialoog
Kodu ja perekond
Haridus

Töö juures
kool
Raamatud
Ühine hüve

Modernsus
Modernity
Esteetika

Modernsus
Modernity

Dialoog

Moodu
Dialoog

Elulugu
Töö juur

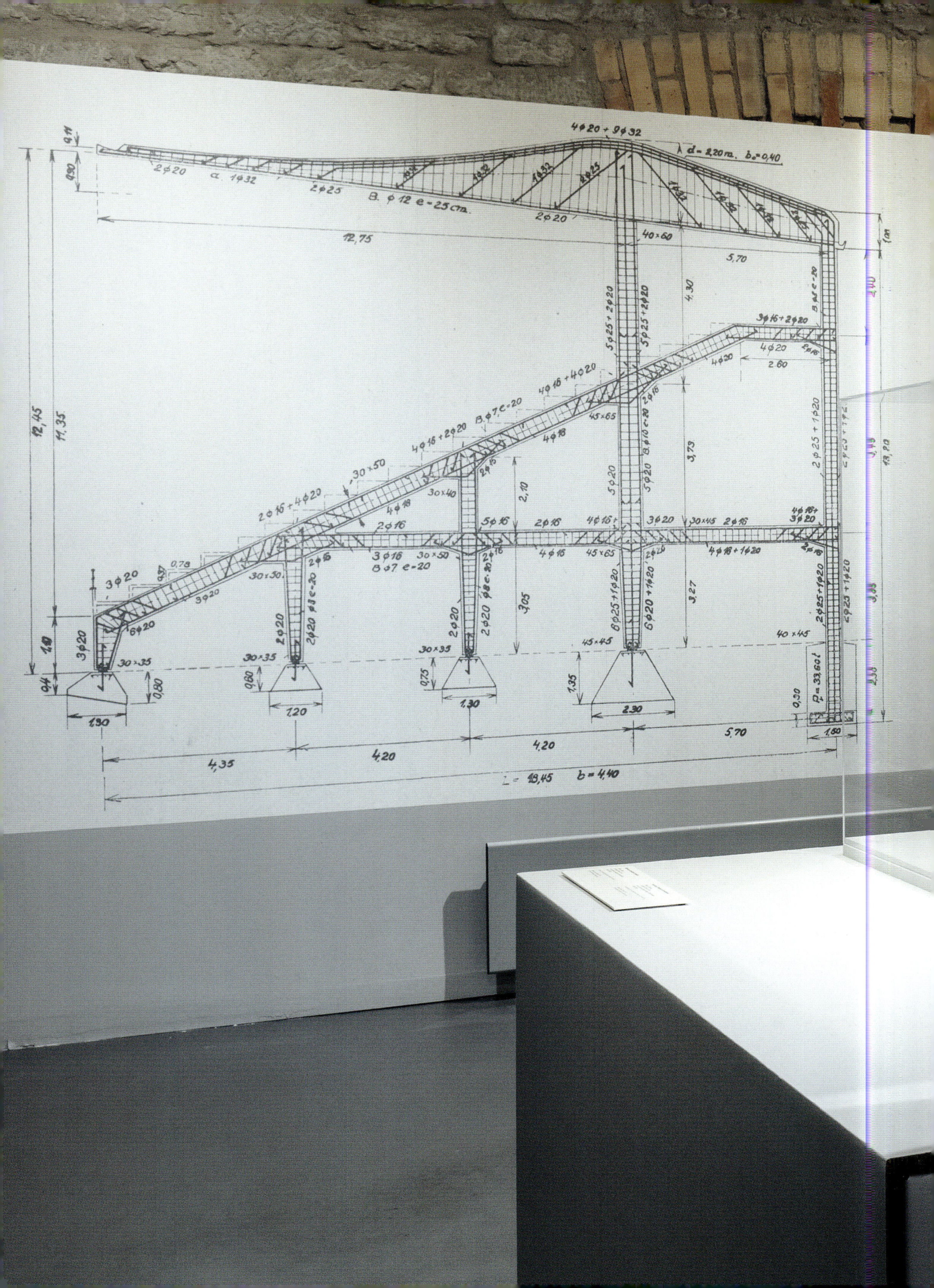

Betoon

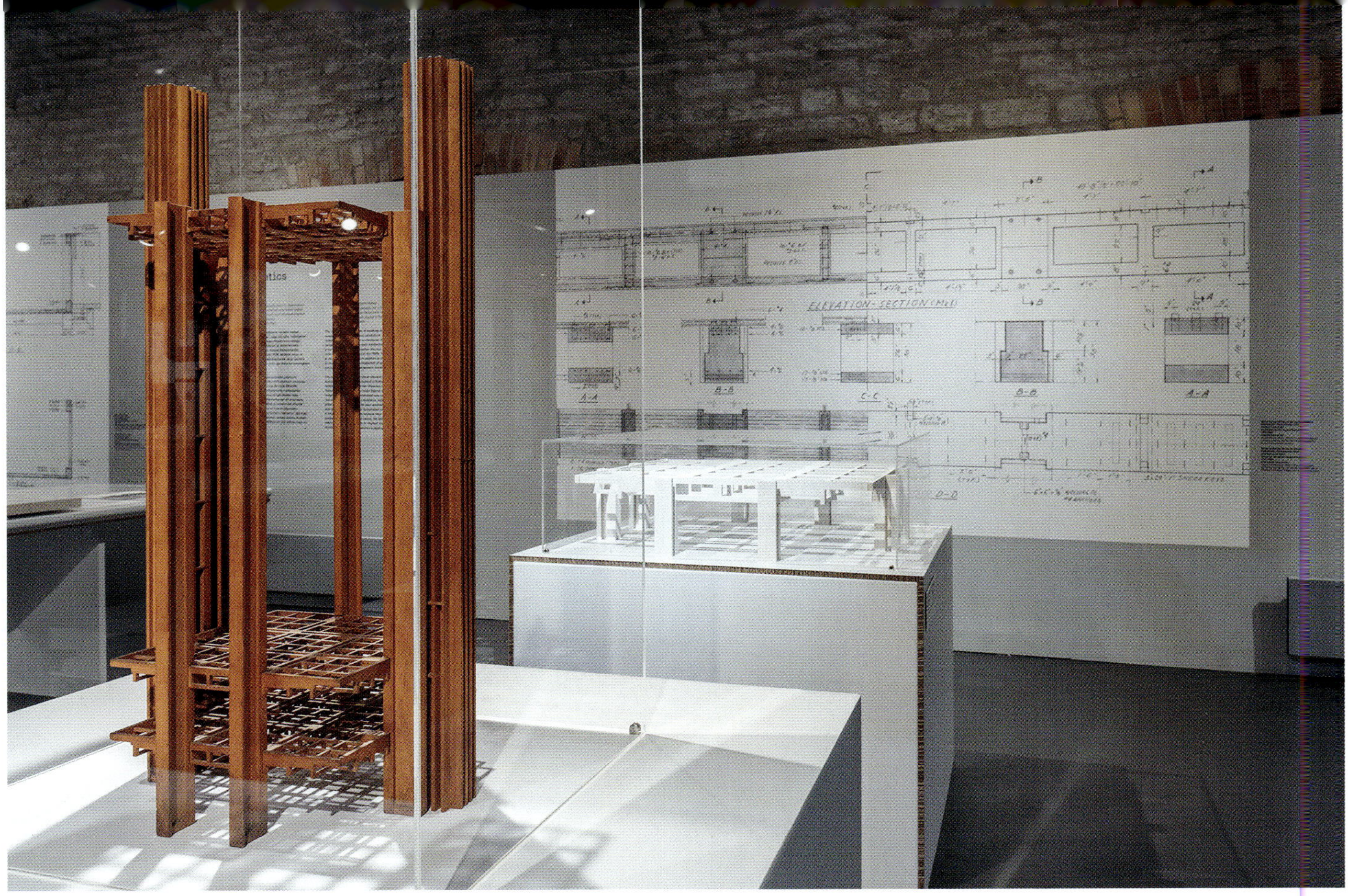

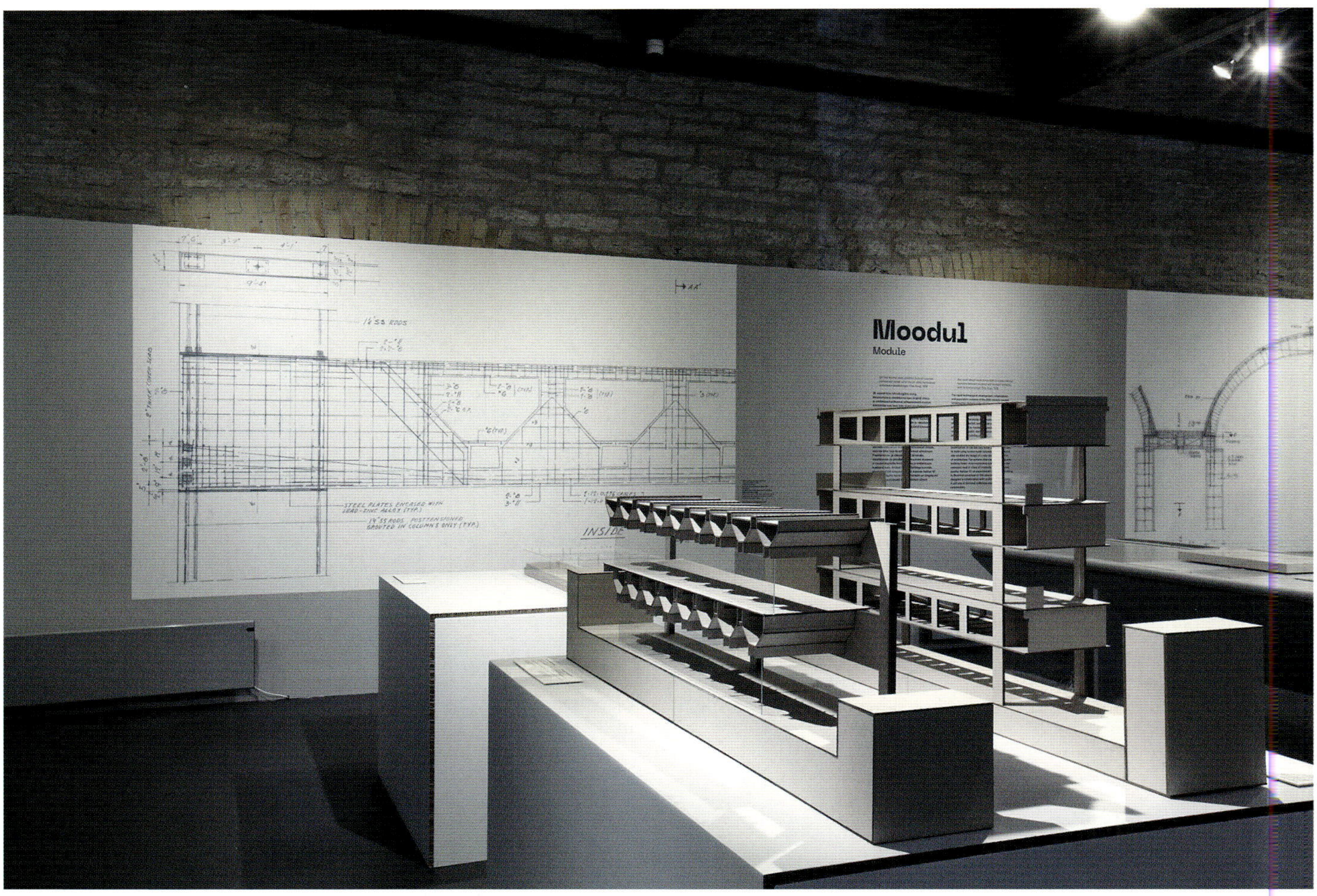
Moodul
Module

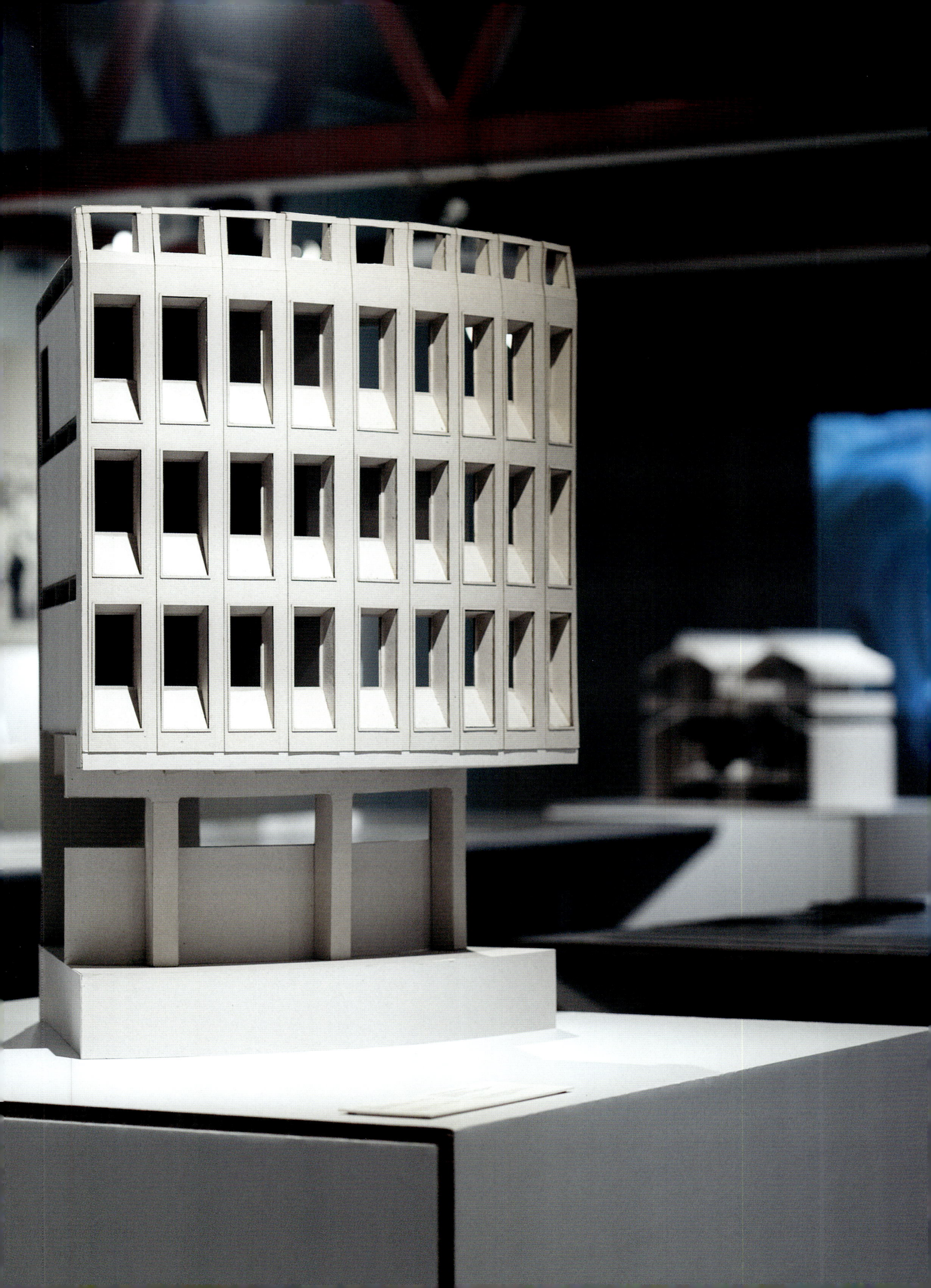

Kodu ja perekond
Home and Family
Haridus
Education

Kodu ja perekond
Home and Family
Haridus
Education

Ülikool
University
Raamatud
Books

KIMBERLY
REFILL
Drawing Leads
HB
TURQUOISE
DRAWING
LEADS
3H
STAEDTLER MARS
Turquois

Louis Kahni soovituskiri, 1973
© Pennsylvania ülikooli arhitektuuriarhiiv
Louis Kahn's letter of recommendation, 1973
© The Architectural Archives, University of Pennsylvania
Kaitsekiiver
© Eesti Arhitektuurimuuseum
Safety helmet
© Museum of Estonian Architecture

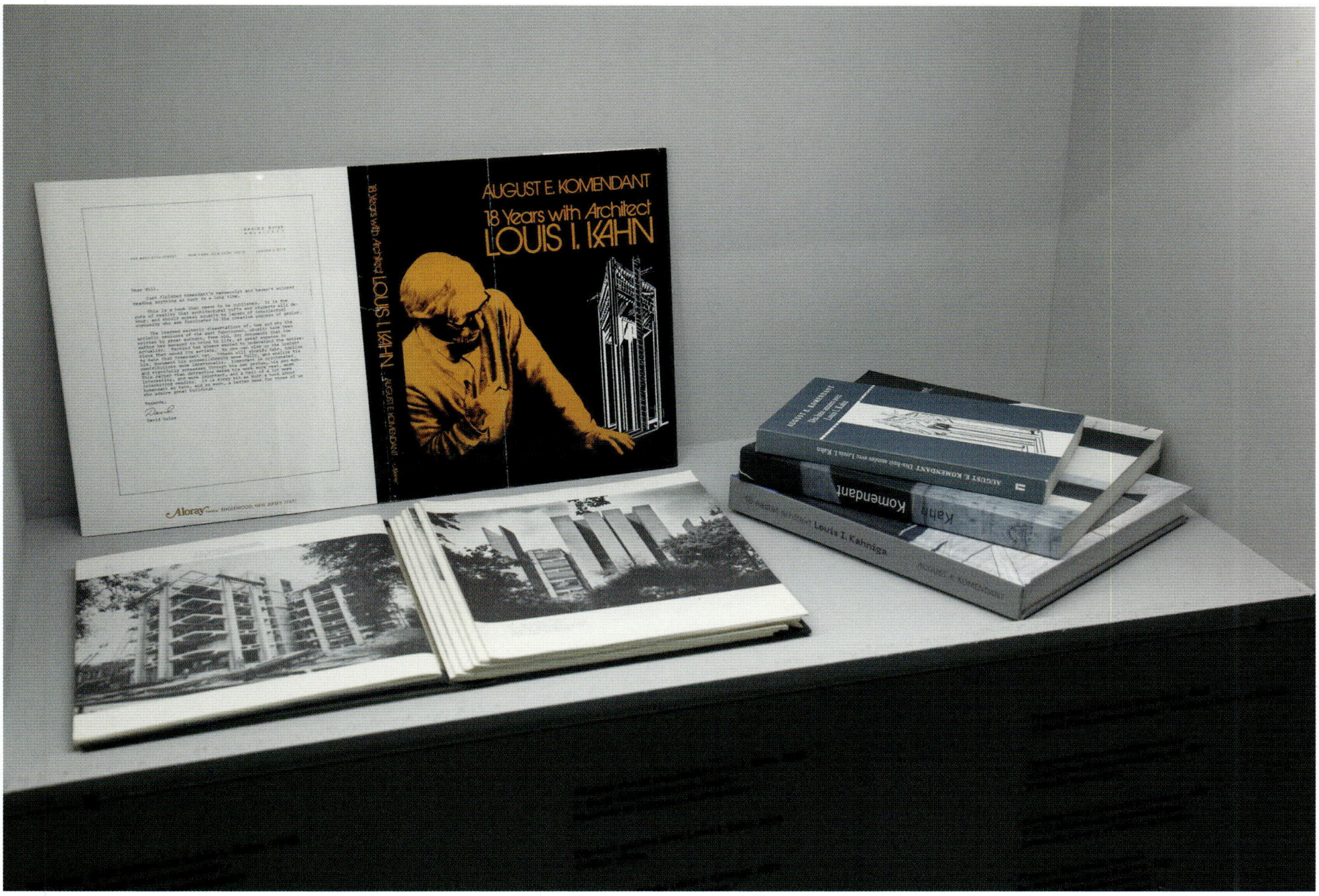
AUGUST E. KOMENDANT
18 Years with Architect
LOUIS I. KAHN
Komendant
Kahn
Louis I. Kahniga

Ühine hüve
The Common Good

Betoon
Concrete

List of Works

Estonia, 1934–1944

Symbols

+	built
+/–	built, but not after August Komendant's design
–	not built or missing information

Buildings or Structures Designed by or with the Participation of August Eduard Komendant

	Project	Location	Architect / Head Designer	Year	Built
	**Võhma Export Slaughterhouse, Sausage Factory floor slabs**	Võhma, Estonia	Hendrik Otloot	1934–1935	+
	**Seaplane Harbor of the Ülemiste Airport, landing bridge and dredging operations**	Tallinn, Estonia	August Komendant	1934–1935	+
	Ülemiste Airport, runways, taxiways, railway, hangars, customs building, drainage	Tallinn, Estonia	Konstantin Bölau, Johannes Pikkov, August Komendant et al.	1934–1936	+
	**Military Aircraft Hangar**	Tartu, Estonia	August Komendant	1935–1936	+
	Männiku Ammunition Depots and Laboratory, extensions	Tallinn, Estonia		1935–1937	+
	National Archives and Library	Tallinn, Estonia	August Tauk	1935–1937	+
	Tallinn City Government, minor projects	Tallinn, Estonia		1935–1938	+
	University of Helsinki, extension, floor slabs	Helsinki, Finland		1936	+
	Nõmme Hydrophore Basement	Tallinn, Estonia		1936–1937	–
	Underground gasoline tanks, 2 pcs, 1,600 tons, Eesti Kiviõli (Estonian Shale Oil)	Helsinki, Finland	August Komendant	1936–1937	–
	**Underground shale oil and gasoline tanks, 2 pcs, 1,600 tons, Eesti Kiviõli (Estonian Shale Oil)**	Tallinn, Estonia	August Komendant	1936–1937	–
	Warehouse, Eesti Kiviõli (Estonian Shale Oil), partial demolition	Tallinn, Estonia		1936–1937	–
	**Kadriorg Stadium Grandstand**	Tallinn, Estonia	Elmar Lohk	1936–1938	–

	Project	Location	Architect / Head Designer	Year	Built
	**Wound Clinic, Faculty of Veterinary Medicine, University of Tartu, concrete slab foundation**	Tartu, Estonia	Preliminary design Paul Mielberg, design Alar Kotli, Manivald Loite	1936–1938	+
	Aleksander Adamka Residence	Tallinn, Estonia		1937	+
	Johannes Komendant's Flour and Saw Mill	Nurmsi, Estonia	August Komendant	1937	+
	Keila-Joa Highway Bridge	Keila-Joa, Estonia	August Komendant, Ernst Kesa	1937	–
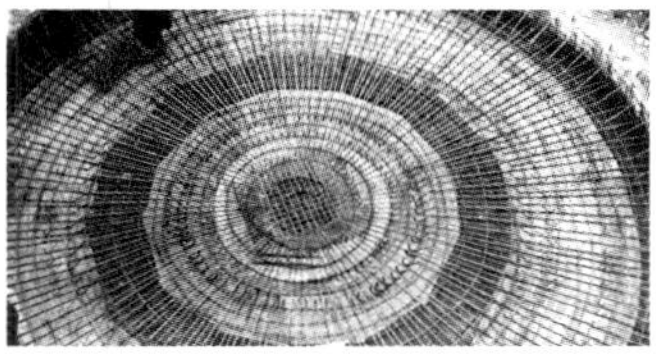	**Kehra Pulp and Paper Mill, glauber salt silo**	Kehra, Estonia	August Komendant	1937–1938	+
	Kehra Pulp and Paper Mill, pulp storage	Kehra, Estonia		1937–1939	–
	Aleksander Adamka Shoe Factory	Tallinn, Estonia	August Komendant	1937–1939	–
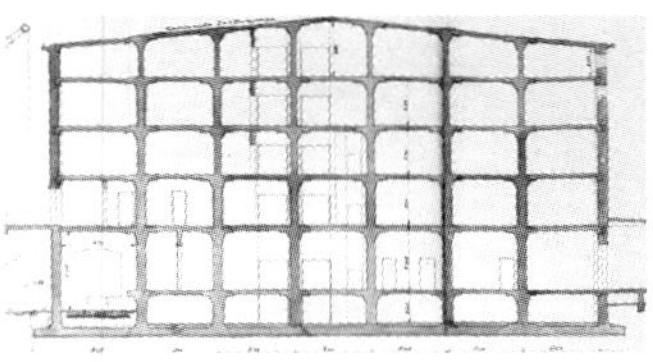	**National Cold Storage, Port of Tallinn**	Tallinn, Estonia	Preliminary design AS Franz Krull, design Roman Koolmar, August Komendant	1937–1941	+
	Narva Flax Mill, building No. 85, strengthening of floor slabs, reconstructions	Ivangorod, Russian Federation		1938–1939	+
	Fat Margaret Artillery Tower, strengthening of the gate vault	Tallinn, Estonia		1938–1939	–
	Vennad Kimberg Nail Factory, warehouse floor slab	Tallinn, Estonia		1938–1939	–
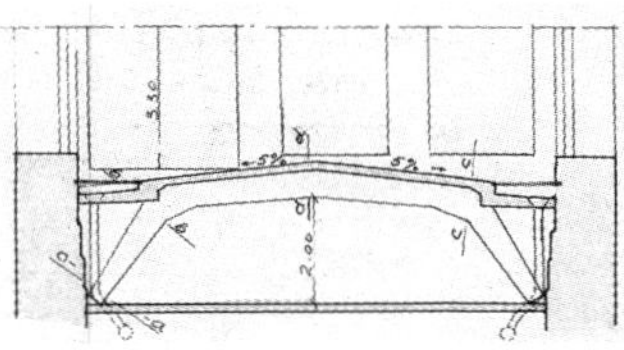	**Kawe Chocolate Factory, AS Volta Tehased, floor slabs**	Tallinn, Estonia	Eduard Kuusik, August Komendant	1938–1939	+
	Kawe Chocolate Factory, AS Volta Tehased, water tower	Tallinn, Estonia	August Komendant	1938–1939	–
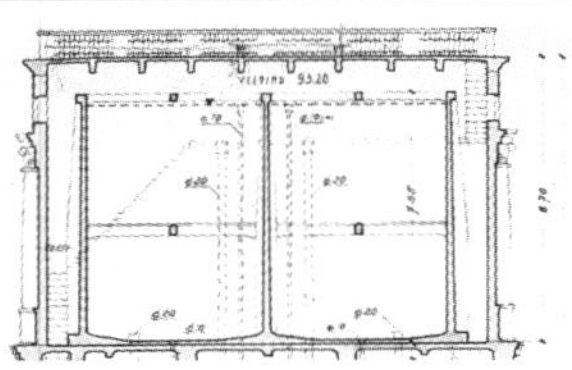	**Tartu Water Tower Apartment Building, water tanks**	Tartu, Estonia	Voldemar Tippel, Voldemar Onton, Hans Tari, August Komendant	1938–1940	+
	Apartment Building Heina 22, Tallinn	Tallinn, Estonia	August Tauk	1939	+
	Rauaniit Thread Factory, strengthening of floor slabs	Tallinn, Estonia	August Komendant	1939	–
	Apartment buildings	Tallinn, Estonia	Eugen Saarelinn (Sacharias)	1939–1940	–
	National Industries of the Port of Tallinn, workshop building	Tallinn, Estonia		1939–1940	+

	Project	Location	Architect / Head Designer	Year	Built
	**National Grain Silo**	Tartu, Estonia	August Komendant, Ernst Kesa	1939–1941	+
	Estonian Workers Insurance Association Building	Tallinn, Estonia	Artur Perna	1940	–
	Kehra Pulp and Paper Mill, conversion of a former grain dryer into a community center	Kehra, Estonia	August Komendant	1940	+
	Ulila Power Station, steam turbine foundations	Ulila, Estonia		1940	–
	**Estonian Phosphorite Ltd., enrichment plant, sifting plant, crushing plant**	Maardu, Estonia	Eugen Saarelinn (Sacharias)	1940–1941	–
	Estonian Phosphorite Ltd., bridges, sediment basin, dumper building	Maardu, Estonia	August Komendant	1940–1941	–
	Kehra Pulp and Paper Mill, lime reserve warehouse extension	Kehra, Estonia	August Komendant	1941	–
	Kohila Paper Mill, boiler house	Kohila, Estonia	August Komendant	1941	–
	AS Franz Krull, industrial building	Tallinn, Estonia	Elmar Lohk, August Komendant	1942	–
	Kehra Pulp and Paper Mill, boiler house ceiling and roof structure	Kehra, Estonia	August Komendant	1942	–
	Kehra Pulp and Paper Mill, dam	Kehra, Estonia	August Komendant	1942	–
	Tallinn Cellulose and Paper Factory, reconstructions	Tallinn, Estonia	August Komendant	1942	–
	Aseri Phosphorite, master plan and factory building	Aseri, Estonia	Anton Soans, August Komendant	1943	–
	Estonian Phosphorite Ltd., reconstruction	Maardu, Estonia	August Komendant	1944	–
	Kehra Pulp and Paper Mill, air raid shelters, pulp machinery building	Kehra, Estonia	August Komendant	1944	–

Germany, 1944–1950

	Project	Location	Architect / Head Designer	Year	Built
	**Reconstruction of war-damaged bridges**	Germany		1945–1950	+
	Buildings of prestressed concrete for the US Army	Turkey		1945–1950	+
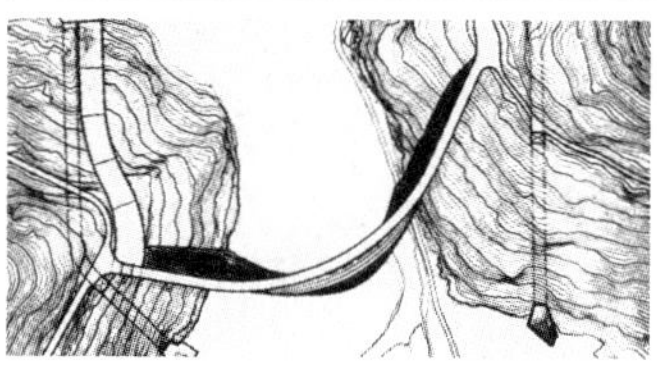	**Sylvenstein Dam of prestressed concrete on the river Isar**	Bad Tölz-Wolfratshausen, Germany	Franz Dischinger, August Komendant	1949–1950	–

United States of America, 1950–1992

	Project	Location	Architect / Head Designer	Year	Built
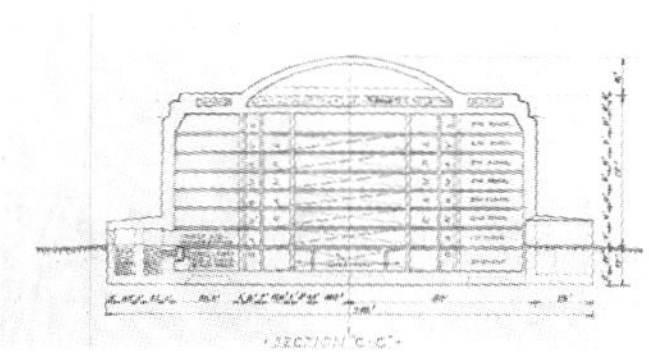	**Shelter network for Lower Manhattan**	New York, New York	August Komendant	1950	–

Devenco Inc., New York, New York, consulting engineer, 1951–1953

	Project	Location	Architect / Head Designer	Year	Built
	Beaumont Works, foundations, E.I.U. DuPont de Nemours & Co., Inc.	Beaumont, Texas		1951–1953	–
	Chemstrand Corporation nylon plant, E.I.U. DuPont de Nemours & Co., Inc.	Pensacola, Florida		1951–1953	–
	Edge Moor pigment plant, building #213-A, E.I.U. DuPont de Nemours & Co., Inc.	Wilmington, Delaware		1951–1953	–
	Memphis cyanide plant, building #501, E.I.U. DuPont de Nemours & Co., Inc.	Memphis, Tennessee		1951–1953	–
	Repauno Works D.M.T. plant, esterification building #1436, E.I.U. DuPont de Nemours & Co., Inc.	Old Hickory, Tennessee		1951–1953	–
	Sabine River Works chemical plant, buildings #539 and #547, E.I.U. DuPont de Nemours & Co., Inc.	Orange, Texas		1951–1953	–
	Various designs, insufficient data			1951–1953	–

Kelvin Engineering Co. Inc., New York, New York, consulting engineer, 1954

	Project	Location	Architect / Head Designer	Year	Built
	Precast Prestressed Houses/Kelvin Engineering Co. P.R. Inc., layout of prestressing plant and equipment	Puerto Rico	August Komendant, Helmi Aren	1954	–
	Bulk sugar storage silos and conveyors	Central Lafayette, Puerto Rico	August Komendant	1954	–
	Cotton yarn plant	South Korea	August Komendant	1954	–
	Elevated tank, prestressed concrete		August Komendant	1954	–
	Grain silo, capacity 10.000 tons	Pakistan	August Komendant	1954	–
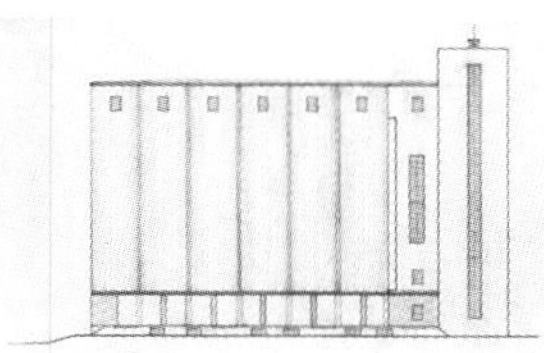	**Grain storage plant, capacity 10,000 tons, steel and concrete versions**	India	August Komendant, Helmi Aren	1954	–
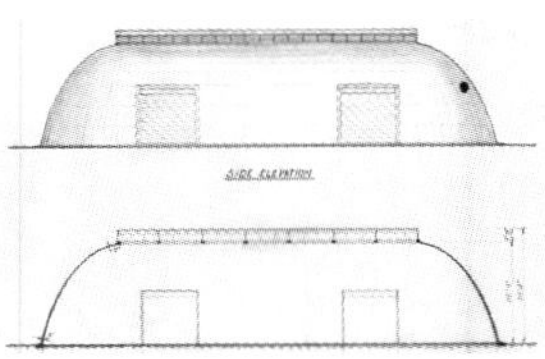	**Grain warehouse, concrete shell, type 1**		August Komendant	1954	–
	Grain warehouse, concrete shell, type 2		August Komendant	1954	–
	INA grain storage plant	El Banco, Magdalena, Colombia	August Komendant	1954	–

	Project	Location	Architect / Head Designer	Year	Built
	INA grain storage plant	Pasto, Nariño, Colombia	August Komendant, Helmi Aren	1954	–
	Low-Cost House no. 1, precast elements	Puerto Rico	V. Monsanto-Diaz	1954	–
	Raw sugar storage silos and conveyors, Kuksaing Industrial Co., Ltd.	South Korea	August Komendant	1954	–
	Straw and wood pulp plant, capacity 40 tons per day, Kuksaing Industrial Co., Ltd.	South Korea	August Komendant	1954	–
	Sugar refinery, capacity 100 tons per day, Kuksaing Industrial Co., Ltd.	South Korea	August Komendant, Helmi Aren	1954	–
	Textile plant	Puerto Rico	August Komendant, Helmi Aren	1954	–
	Water tanks, 20,000, 30,000, 50,000, 100,000, 2,000,000 gallons	Puerto Rico	August Komendant	1954	–
	Water tower, 50,000 gallons	Puerto Rico	August Komendant	1954	–
	Water tower, 50,000 gallons, Kuksaing Industrial Co., Ltd.	South Korea	August Komendant	1954	–
	Sumapaz river bridge on route Bogota-Girardot, prestressed concrete	Boquerón, Tolima, Colombia	August Komendant	1954	–

Precast Tilt Up Construction Co., Inc. P.R., Puerto Rico, consulting engineer, 1954

	Project	Location	Architect / Head Designer	Year	Built
	Prestressed concrete hangar, San Juan International Airport	San Juan, Puerto Rico	August Komendant	1954	–
	**Prestressed concrete nose hangar, San Juan International Airport**	San Juan, Puerto Rico	August Komendant, Osvald Mitt	1954	–
	Water tank, 50,000 gallons, Automatic Sprinkler Co.		August Komendant	1954	–

Precast & Prestressed Products Corporation, Norwalk, Connecticut, consulting engineer, 1955

	Project	Location	Architect / Head Designer	Year	Built
	Precast & Prestressed Products Corporation, layout of prestressing plant and equipment	Norwalk, Connecticut	August Komendant, Helmi Aren	1955	+
	Westcott & Mapes, pipe supports	Norwalk, Connecticut	August Komendant	1955	–
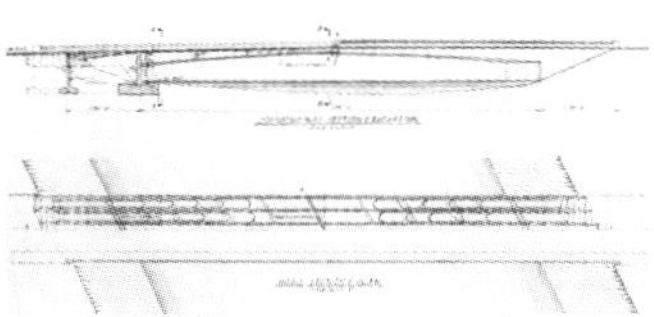	**Broad Street Bridge, prestressed concrete, versions A, B**	Norwalk, Connecticut	August Komendant	1955	–
	Cross Street Bridge, prestressed concrete	Norwalk, Connecticut	August Komendant	1955	–
	James Street Bridge, prestressed concrete	Norwalk, Connecticut	August Komendant	1955	–
	Perry Avenue Bridge, prestressed concrete	Norwalk, Connecticut	August Komendant	1955	–

	Project	Location	Architect / Head Designer	Year	Built
	**Dr. Mario Julia Office Building, concrete slab foundation**	Santurce, Puerto Rico	Henry Klumb	1955	+/–
	Pine Neck Concrete Building			1955	–
	Union Parts MFG Co. building, prestressed concrete shell			1955	–
	AMC Warehouse			1956	–
	Arenas Lavadas Pedregal, Ltda., layout of prestressing plant		August Komendant	1956	–
	**Enrico Fermi Memorial, architectural competition**	Chicago, Illinois	Louis I. Kahn	1956–1957	–
	K-System, lightweight concrete roof and floor system		August Komendant	1956–1958	–

Lakewood Prestressing Company, Inc., Howell, New Jersey, consulting engineer and partner, 1956–1958

	Project	Location	Architect / Head Designer	Year	Built
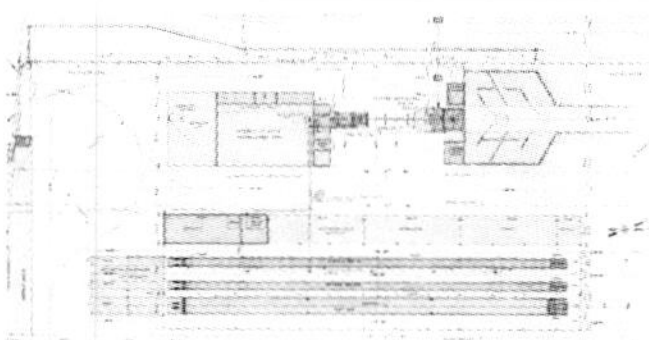	**Lakewood Prestressing Company, Inc., layout of prestressing plant and equipment**	Howell, New Jersey	August Komendant, Helmi Aren	1956–1958	+
	Frank Sarpolus Shop and Showroom, roof			1956	–
	Neptune Garage			1956	–
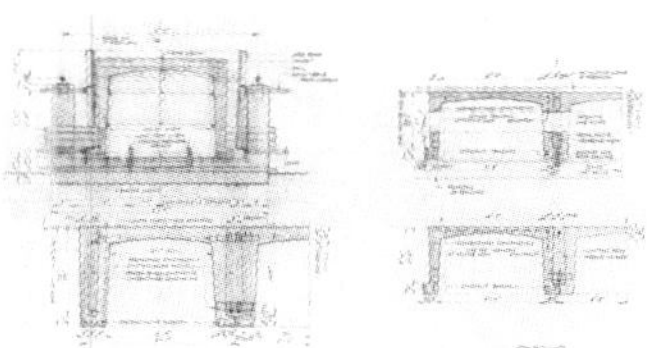	**Various prestressed concrete products: beams, roof and floor planks, girders etc.**		August Komendant	1956	–
	Industrial buildings #300, #305, #306, #307, Cincinnati Chemical Corporation, precast concrete canopies, purlins	Toms River, New Jersey	A. M. Kinney, Inc.	1956–1958	+
	Airplane hangars, two types		August Komendant	1957	–
	Albertini Motors, prestressed concrete girders		August Komendant	1957	–
	American Stores Co. Warehouse	Flemington, New Jersey	August Komendant	1957	–
	Bowling hall		Paul B. West	1957	–
	Brick Presbyterian Church, concrete frames		Paul B. West	1957	–
	Glerum Concrete, batching plant foundation, approach bridge, girders	Brick, New Jersey	August Komendant	1957	+
	Metal and Thermit Corp., laboratory building			1957	–

	Project	Location	Architect / Head Designer	Year	Built
	New Jersey Motor Vehicle Field Installation Buildings	New Jersey	Frank Grad & Sons. Architects & Engineers	1957	+
	Patuxent River Bridge, two types			1957	–
	Pine Street Bridge #D4.9, girders	Mt. Holly, New Jersey	Burlington County Engineer's Office	1957	+
	Precast prestressed concrete hangar			1957	–
	Railway loading platform			1957	–
	Skating hall, prestressed concrete shell roof		August Komendant	1957	–
	Sprout Brook Bridge			1957	+
	W. M. Birtwell Inc., storage and garage building			1957	–
	Y.M.C.A., swimming pool roof space girders	Stamford, Connecticut	August Komendant	1957	+
	**Trenton Jewish Community Center, community building**	Ewing Township, New Jersey	Louis I. Kahn	1957–1958	–
	Harlem River Bridge			1958	–
	St. Joseph's High School, columns and beams	Camden, New Jersey	Thomas J. Early	1958	+
	Zaperts Tavern and Liquor Store	Toms River, New Jersey	Paul B. West	1958	+
	**Richards Medical Research Building and Biology Building (Atlantic Prestressed Concrete Co.)**	Philadelphia, Pennsylvania	Louis I. Kahn	1957–1965	+

Structural Concrete Products Corporation, Carolina, Puerto Rico, consulting engineer, 1958–1960

	Project	Location	Architect / Head Designer	Year	Built
	Structural Concrete Products Corporation, layout of prestressing plant and equipment	Carolina, Puerto Rico	August Komendant, Helmi Aren	1958	–
	Transmission poles, prestressed concrete, P.R. Water Resources Authority	Puerto Rico		1958	–
	Rio Grande de Añasco Bridge	Puerto Rico		1958	–
	Lawnside Motel, concrete shell roof	Lawnside, New Jersey	Fruchtbaum & Maitin (Morris Fruchtbaum, Irving J. Maitin)	1958	–
	The Liberty Corp., layout of concrete plant	Philadelphia, Pennsylvania	August Komendant	1958	–
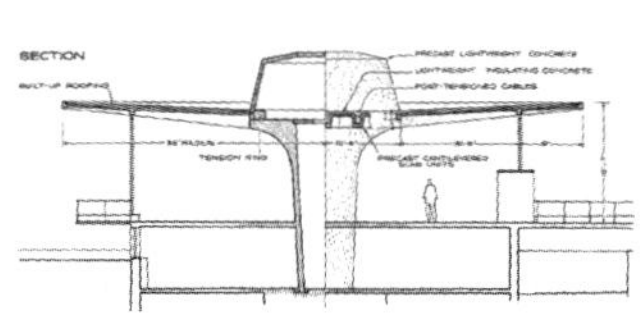	**Philadelphia Hospitality Center**	Philadelphia, Pennsylvania	Harbeson, Hough, Livingston & Larson (Roy Larson)	1958–1959	+/–

	Project	Location	Architect / Head Designer	Year	Built
	**Tribune Review Publishing Company Building**	Greensburg, Pennsylvania	Louis I. Kahn	1958–1962	+
	Concrete shell roof	Horsham, Pennsylvania		1959	–
	Muckinipates Creek Bridge			1959	–
	**Parroquia Nuestra Señora del Carmen—Parish Church of Our Lady of Mount Carmel**	Cataño, Puerto Rico	Henry Klumb	1959–1960	+/–
	U.S. Consulate and Residence	Luanda, Angola	Louis I. Kahn	1959–1962	–
	**Philadelphia Police Administration Building**	Philadelphia, Pennsylvania	Geddes Brecher Qualls Cunningham	1959–1963	+
	**Salk Institute for Biological Studies**	La Jolla, California	Louis I. Kahn	1959–1965	+
	**First Unitarian Church**	Rochester, New York	Louis I. Kahn	1959–1969	+

Atlantic Prestressed Concrete Co., Trenton, New Jersey, consulting engineer, 1960

	Project	Location	Architect / Head Designer	Year	Built
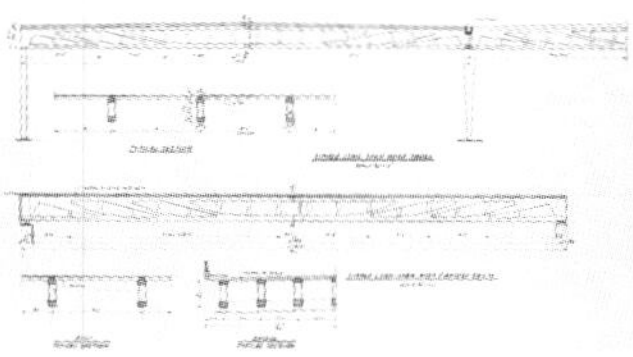	**Long-span roof and bridge trusses**		August Komendant	1960	–
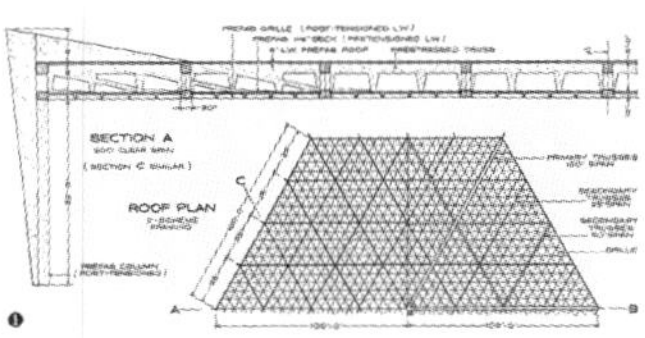	**Paterson State College Auditorium**	Wayne, New Jersey	LaPierre, Litchfield & Partners	1960	+
	Prefabricated auxiliary coaxial repeater station		August Komendant	1960	–
	Railway Express Warehouse			1960	–

	Project	Location	Architect / Head Designer	Year	Built
	**Colegio San Ignacio de Loyola Gymnasium Building**	San Juan, Puerto Rico	Henry Klumb	1960	–
	**August Eduard Komendant Residence**	Upper Montclair, New Jersey	Osvald Mitt, August Komendant	1960–1961	+
	Classroom and administration buildings, Scranton University, K-System framing	Scranton, Pennsylvania	Robert P. Morain	1960–1961	–
	**Cold Storage and Distribution Center, Merchants Refrigerating Co.**	Secaucus, New Jersey	Abbott Merkt & Co.	1960–1961	+
	**Ezra Stiles and Samuel Morse Colleges, Yale University, roof structure of the dining halls**	New Haven, Connecticut	Eero Saarinen	1960–1961	+
	Ponce Shopping Center and Bank, IBEC Realty Company Inc. (Structural Concrete Products Corporation)	Ponce, Puerto Rico	Luccarelli Associates (Anthony Luccarelli)	1960–1961	–/–
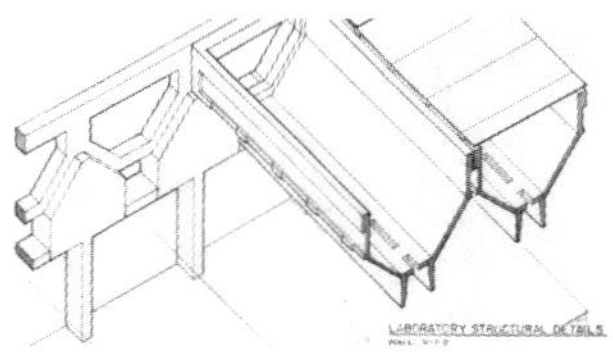	**Chemistry Building, University of Virginia**	Charlottesville, Virginia	Louis I. Kahn	1960–1963	–
	Erdman Hall, Bryn Mawr College	Bryn Mawr, Pennsylvania	Louis I. Kahn	1960–1965	–/–
	Various bridge and roof girders, prestressed concrete		August Komendant	1960–1968	–
	**Collingswood Sr. High School, cafetorium roof**	Collingswood, New Jersey	Howell Lewis Shay & Associates	1961	+
	Health & Agriculture Building for the State of New Jersey	Trenton, New Jersey	Alfred Clauss Architects	1961	–/–
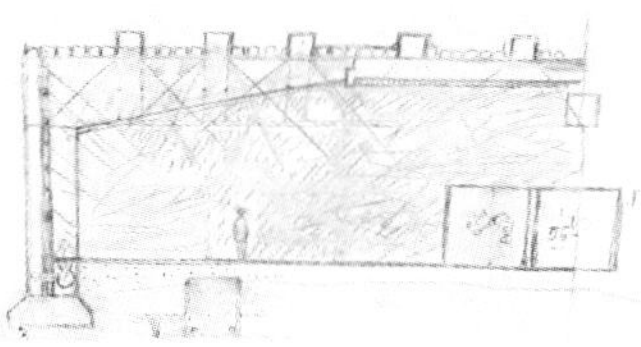	**Carbonorum Company Warehouse and Office Building**	Atlanta, Georgia	Louis I. Kahn	1961–1962	–

	Project	Location	Architect / Head Designer	Year	Built
	Physical Education Building, The Pennsylvania State University	Philadelphia, Pennsylvania	Kneedler, Mirick & Zantzinger	1963	–
	Grand Stand of the University of Delaware Stadium	Newark, Delaware	Howell Lewis Shay & Associates (Howell Lewis Shay Jr.)	1963–1964	+
	**Sher-e-Bangla Nagar, Dacca, Capital of East Pakistan (now Dhaka, Bangladesh)**	Dhaka, Bangladesh	Louis I. Kahn	1963–1982	+/ –
	Life Science & Chemistry Building, University of Illinois	Urbana-Champaign, Illinois	Earl L. Wall	1964	–
	The Moore School Graduate Research Center, University of Pennsylvania	Philadelphia, Pennsylvania	Geddes Brecher Qualls Cunningham	1964	+/ –
	**Habitat '67**	Montreal, Quebec, Canada	Moshe Safdie; associate architects David, Barott, Boulva	1964–1967	+
	**Temple Beth Hillel**	Wynnewood, Pennsylvania	Norman Rice	1964–1968	+
	**Parking Garage No. 2, University of Pennsylvania**	Philadelphia, Pennsylvania	Mitchell/Giurgola Architects (Romaldo Giurgola)	1966–1969	+
	**Olivetti-Underwood Factory**	Harrisburg, Pennsylvania	Louis I. Kahn	1966–1970	+
	**Kimbell Art Museum**	Fort Worth, Texas	Louis I. Kahn; associate architect Preston M. Geren	1966–1972	+
	National Headquarters Building, American Institute of Architects	New York, New York	Mitchell/Giurgola Architects (Romaldo Giurgola)	1967	–
	University City High School, structural system for auditorium			1967	–
	Broadway United Church of Christ and Office Building	New York, New York	Louis I. Kahn	1967–1968	–

	Project	Location	Architect / Head Designer	Year	Built
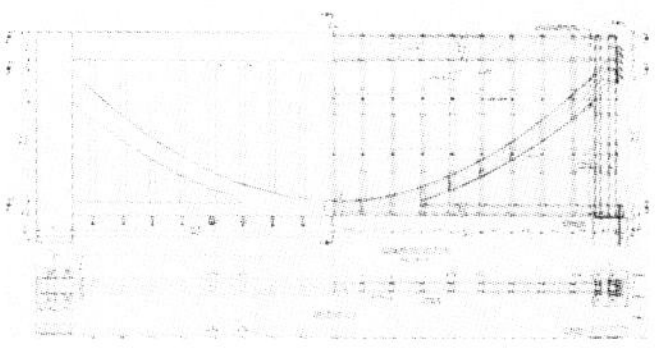	**Kansas City Office Building**	Kansas City, Missouri	Louis I. Kahn	1967–1974	–
	One-Family Home			1968	–
	**National Airlines Inc., Miami International Airport, Parking Structures No. 1 and No. 2, taxiway bridges, maintenance hangar (Kellermann & Dragnett Inc.)**	Miami, Florida	Greenleaf/Telesca. Planners. Engineers. Architects	1968–1970	+
	**Vivienda 70, apartment buildings (Shelley Enterprises)**	Sabana Llana, Puerto Rico	Louis Fernando Coll Arana	1968–1970	+
	**Vivienda 70, apartment buildings (Shelley Enterprises)**	Jersey City, New Jersey		1968–1974	+
	**Palazzo Dei Congressi**	Venice, Italy	Louis I. Kahn	1968–1974	–
	Jersey City Garage	Jersey City, New Jersey		1969	–
	Y.M.C.A. Building, natatorium addition and alterations	Reading, Pennsylvania	Frederick R. Schenk – Lee V. Seibert Architects	1969	+/–
	School of Engineering Building, University of Pittsburgh	Pittsburgh, Pennsylvania		1969	–
	Rapid Speed Elevated Bridge, study	Buffalo, New York		1971	–
	Prefabricated housing	Panama		1973	–
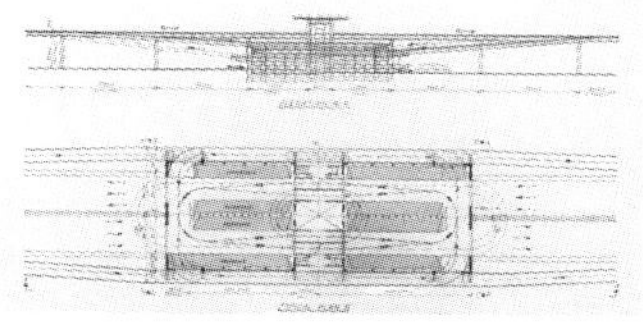	**Highway parking garage with helipad, conceptual project**		August Komendant	1973	–
	Pillsbury elevator, stabilization and repair after explosion	Memphis, Tennessee		1974	+
	Rock storage building, Lone Star Industries Inc., stabilization and strengthening of roof (Kellermann & Dragnett Inc.)	Nazareth, Pennsylvania		1974–1975	+

	Project	Location	Architect / Head Designer	Year	Built
	Crude oil or water tanks, 10.000 m^3 (Kellermann & Dragnett Inc.)		August Komendant	1975	–
	Fuel storage tanks, Consultores Asociados Ltda. COAS	La Paz, Bolivia		1975	
	LNG storage tank, 135.000 m^3, Pittsburgh-Des Moines Steel Company (Kellermann & Dragnett Inc.)		August Komendant	1975	–
	LNG tanks 9500 m^3 and 130.000 m^3 (Kellermann & Dragnett Inc.)		August Komendant	1975	–
	Container vessels, prestressed concrete, for LNG, crude oil, gasoline etc., Abe Kogyoshe Co., Ltd.	Japan	August Komendant	1975–1976	–
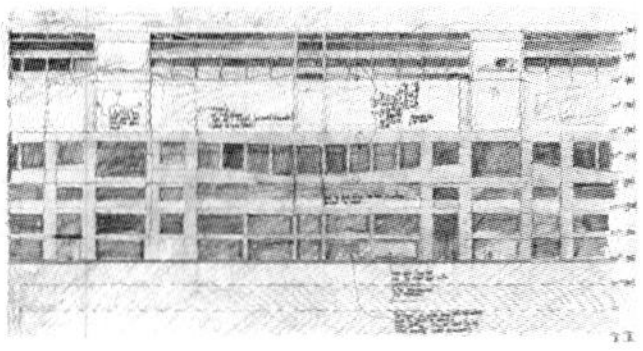	**Caracas Bus Terminal**	Caracas, Venezuela	Oscar Tenreiro	1976–1977	–
	**Pandock warehouse**	Venezuela	Oscar Tenreiro	1977	–
	Apartment buildings, hotel, club	Isla de Margarita, Venezuela	BMPT Arquitectos (M. Bemergui, J. M. Menendez)	1977–1978	–
	**K-System apartment building**	Juangriego, Isla de Margarita, Venezuela	Oscar Tenreiro	1977–1978	–
	**K-System Modular Building System**		August Komendant	1977–1980	–
	**Habitat Tehran**	Tehran, Iran	Moshe Safdie	1978	–
	Head Office of the Mercantile Bank of Iran & Holland	Tehran, Iran	Mandala International/ Mandala Collaborative (Nader Ardalan)	1978–1979	–
	Nuran, The City of Illumination, New Community for the Atomic Energy Organisation of Iran A.E.O.I.	Isfahan, Iran	Mandala International/ Mandala Collaborative (Nader Ardalan)	1978–1979	–

	Project	Location	Architect / Head Designer	Year	Built
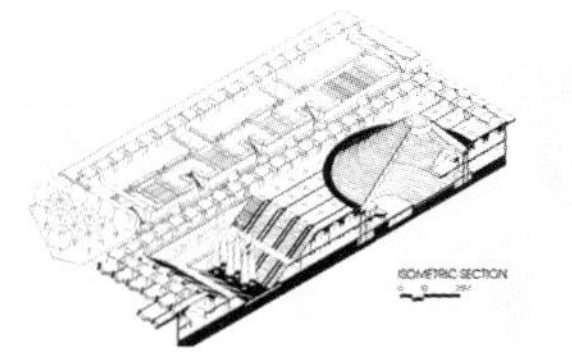	**Tehran Center for the Celebration of Music**	Teheran, Iran	Mandala International/ Mandala Collaborative (Nader Ardalan)	1978–1979	–
	Residence for Bill and Merike Phillips	Kenosha, Wisconsin	Bill Phillips	1979	–
	**Office and Computer Building, Selected Risk Insurance Company**	Branchville, New Jersey	Architecture Partnership (W. Richard Wilson Jr.)	1979–1982	+
	**Law School with Auditorium**	Caracas, Venezuela	Oscar Tenreiro	1980–1981	–
	**GAN—Galeria de Arte Nacional**	Caracas, Venezuela	Oscar Tenreiro, Francisco Sesto	1980–1986	–
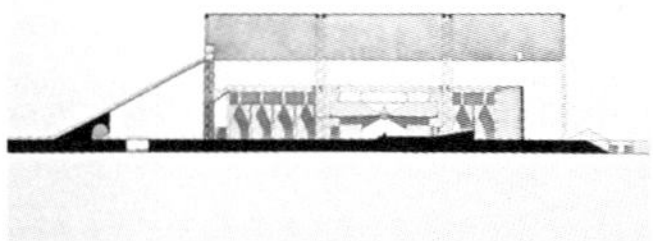	**Guayana Cathedral, architectural competition**	Guayana, Venezuela	Oscar Tenreiro	1981	–
	**Robina Casino Hotel**	Gold Coast, Queensland, Australia	Moshe Safdie	1981–1982	–
	**Ciba-Geigy Pharmaceutical Company, Medical Research Building, Scientific Information Center and Chemistry Building**	Summit, New Jersey	The Office of Henry Klumb, K.S.K. Associates (Henry Klumb, Salvador Soltero, Richard Klumb)	1981–1986	+
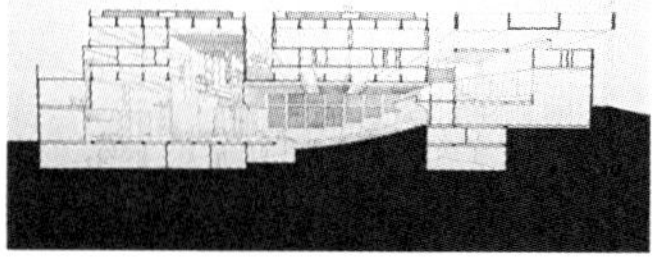	**Teatro del Oeste Dance Theater**	Caracas, Venezuela	Oscar Tenreiro	1982–1983	+

	Project	Location	Architect / Head Designer	Year	Built
	**Plaza Bicentenario and the Presidential Palace Extension**	Caracas, Venezuela	Oscar Tenreiro	1982–1987	+
	The National Gallery of Canada	Ottawa, Ontario, Canada	Moshe Safdie	1983–1984	+/ –
	**Lehigh Valley Laboratory**	Allentown, Pennsylvania	Geddes Brecher Qualls Cunningham	1984	–
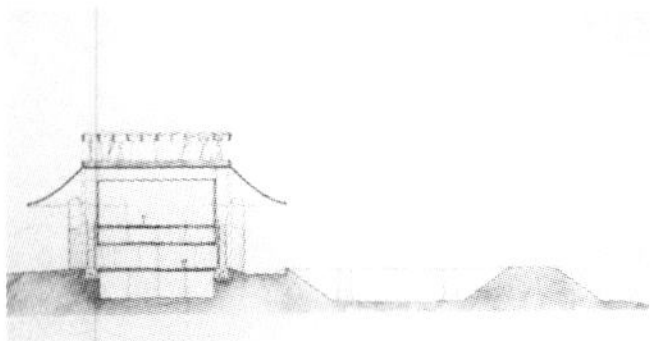	**Museo del Petróleo, Oil Museum**	Cabimas, Venezuela	Oscar Tenreiro	1984	–
	Newton Project, office building and parking garage	Newton, New Jersey	Architecture Partnership (W. Richard Wilson Jr.)	1985	–
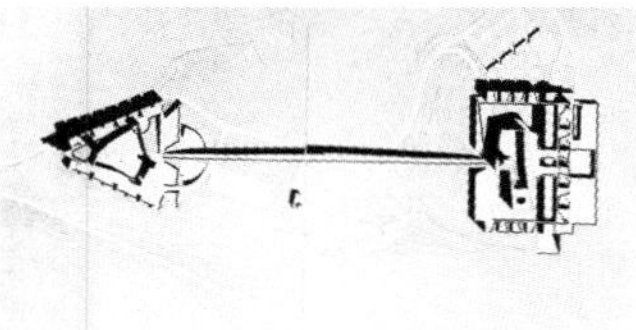	**The Castles of Romeo and Juliet, La Biennale di Venezia, conceptual project**	Vicenza, Italy	Oscar Tenreiro	1985	–
	Ciba-Geigy Pharmaceutical Company, parking garage	Summit, New Jersey	Soltero-Klumb and Associates	1985–1986	–
	Ciba-Geigy Pharmaceutical Company, Life Science Building	Summit, New Jersey	The Office of Henry Klumb (Richard Klumb, Gary P. Cirincione)	1986–1988	–
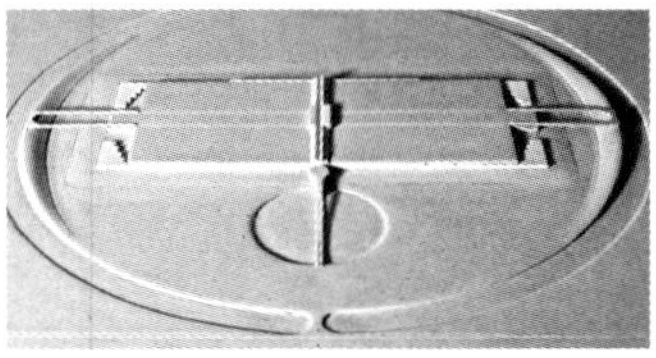	**General Motors 21st Century Manufacturing Facility, design research competition**		Oscar Tenreiro	1987	–
	Sparta Business Campus	Sparta, New Jersey	Architecture Partnership (W. Richard Wilson Jr.)	1987	–
	Sparta Office Building	Sparta, New Jersey	Architecture Partnership (W. Richard Wilson Jr.)	1987	+

Primary sources

August E. Komendant Collection, The Architectural Archives, University of Pennsylvania

August Komendant Collection, Estonian Museum of Architecture

Louis. I. Kahn Collection, The University of Pennsylvania and the Pennsylvania Historical and Museum Commission

Louis Kahn: The Power of Architecture. Weil am Rhein: Vitra Design Museum, 2013

Viisteist: Eesti Arhitektuurimuuseumi kogumik. Tallinn: Eesti Arhitektuurimuuseum, 2006

Bibliography

Publications by August Komendant

18 Years with Architect Louis I. Kahn. Englewood, NJ: Aloray, 1975. Translated into Japanese (1986), Spanish (2000), French (2006), Estonian (2019).

"Architect-Engineer Relationship." In Latour, *Louis I. Kahn: l'uomo, il maestro*, 315–19. Rome: Edizioni Kappa, 1986.

"August Komendant'i curriculum vitae" [August Komendant's Curriculum Vitae]. In "Arvustajate arvamused kandideerijate kohta puu-, massiiv- ja raudbetoonkonstruktsioonide professuurile," *Tallinna Tehnikaülikooli Toimetuste Lisad*, no. 4 (December 1939): 1–2.

Contemporary Concrete Structures. New York: McGraw-Hill, 1972; 2nd ed., Huntington, NY: Krieger, 1977.

"Cylindrical Shelled Arch Dams." In *Water Power & Dam Construction* (May 1977): 35–41.

"Earth-Covered Structures." In *Underground Space* 3, no. 6 (1979): 279–84.

"Economy and Safety of Different Types of Concrete Dams." In *Proceedings of the American Society of Civil Engineers* 81, separate no. 685 (May 1955).

"Entrevista con August Komendant" [August Komendant interviewed by Oscar Tenreiro]. In August Komendant, *18 anos años con el arquitecto Louis I. Kahn*, 58–77. Santiago de Compostela: Colexio Oficial de Arquitectos de Galicia, 2000.

"Kas on meil eeldusi betoonraua kui ka betooni lubatavate pingete kõrgendamiseks" [Are there prerequisites to increase the allowed stresses in reinforcing bars and in concrete]. In *Tehnika Ajakiri*, no. 1 (1938): 7–10.

"Komendant on Concrete." In *Progressive Architecture* (October 1966): 208–13.

"Konstantin Zeren ehitajana" [Konstantin Zeren as a builder]. In *Liivika võõrsil: Üliõpilasselts Liivika 75. aasta koguteos*, 96–99. Toronto: Üliõpilasselts Liivika, 1984.

"National Art Gallery, Caracas, Venezuela." In *GAN: Proyecto Nueva Sede Galeria de Arte Nacional Caracas / New National Gallery of Art Project Caracas: Arquitectos Oscar Tenreiro, Francisco Sesto*, 77–78. Caracas: Consejo Nacional de la Cultura, Galeria de Arte Nacional, 1986.

"Possibilities." In *Progressive Architecture* (October 1960): 178–85.

"Post-Mortem on Habitat." In *Progressive Architecture* (March 1968): 138–47.

Practical Structural Analysis for Architectural Engineering. Englewood Cliffs, NJ: Prentice Hall, 1987.

Precast Prestressed Products. Manual 1–55. Norwalk, CT: Precast & Prestressed Products Corporation, 1955.

Prestressed Concrete Products. Manual No. 1. Lakewood, NJ: Lakewood Prestressing Company, Inc., 1958.

Prestressed Concrete Structures. New York: McGraw-Hill, 1952. Translated into Russian (1959).

"Sandwich-type Construction Project is Cast-in-Place." In *Concrete International* (January 1988): 36–39.

"Tallinna Kadrioru staadioni raudbetoontribüün" [Reinforced concrete grandstand of the Tallinn Kadriorg Stadium]. In *Tehnika Ajakiri*, no. 12 (1937): 278–82.

"Tallinna külmhoone" [Tallinn Cold Storage]. In *Tehnika Ajakiri*, no. 3 (1938): 53–57.

Other Publications

"Application." In *Progressive Architecture* (October 1960): 186–91.

"Arvustajate arvamused kandideerijate kohta puu-, massiiv- ja raudbetoonkonstruktsioonide professuurile." *Tallinna Tehnikaülikooli Toimetuste Lisad*, no. 4 (December 1939).

Banham, Reyner. "Habitat." In *Architectural Design* (July 1967): 3–7.

Barizza, Elisabetta, and Gabriele Neri, eds. *Louis Kahn e Venezia. Il progetto per il Palazzo dei Congressi e il Padiglione della Biennale / Louis Kahn and Venice: The Project for the Palazzo dei Congressi and the Biennale Building*. Mendrisio: Universita della Svizzera italiana, Accademia di architettura, Fondazione Teatro dell'architettura, 2018.

Berger, Horst. "Book Reviews" [a review of August Komendant's *18 Years with Architect Louis I. Kahn*]. In *Architectural Record* (mid-August 1977): 106–7.

Beringer, Hubert. "Habitat 67: architectures d'images, images d'architectures." In *Journal of the Society for the Study of Architecture in Canada = Le Journal de la Société pour l'étude de l'architecture au Canada* 27, nos. 1–2 (2002): 3–20.

Boyd, Robin. "Habitat's Cluster." In *The Architectural Forum* (May 1967): 36–41.

Brownlee, David B., and David G. De Long, eds. *Louis I. Kahn: In the Realm of Architecture*. New York, NY: Rizzoli, 1991.

"Building a City with King Kong Blocks." In *Progressive Architecture* (October 1966): 226–37.

Burton, Joe. "The Limits of Reason." In *The Fifth Column* (Winter 1983): 17–19.

"Circling the Square." In *The Architectural Forum* (February 1963): 120–25.

Dagit, Charles E., Jr. *Louis I. Kahn – Architect: Remembering the Man and Those Who Surrounded Him*. London: Routledge, 2017; 1st ed., Transaction Publishers, 2013.

Donchin, Mark. "Kahn, Komendant, and The Kimbell Art Museum: Cooperation, Competition, and Conflict." In *The Collaborators: Interactions in the Architectural Design Process*, edited by Gilbert Herbert, Mark Donchin, 205–36. London: Routledge, 2016; 1st ed., Ashgate Publishing, 2013.

Eaton, Leonard K. "The Engineer Kahn" [a review of August Komendant's *18 Years with Architect Louis I. Kahn*]. In *Progressive Architecture* (April 1976): 97–98.

"Economical Post-Tensioning System, Done with an Expert Hand, Frees Insurance Offices of Columns." In *Architectural Record* (April 1982): 140–43.

"Eesti insener Korea ülesehitustöödel nõuandjaks." In *Vaba Eesti Sõna = Free Estonian Word*, July 29, 1954.

"Eesti insener projekteeris Kanada maailmanäitusel ehitusime." In *Vaba Eesti Sõna = Free Estonian Word*, April 20, 1967.

Eller, Mart-Ivo, ed. *Eesti kunsti ja arhitektuuri biograafiline leksikon*. Tallinn: Eesti Entsüklopeediakirjastus, 1996.

"Esimene uustulnukast tehase asutaja." In *Vaba Eesti Sõna = Free Estonian Word*, July 7, 1955.

Frampton, Kenneth. *Studies in Tectonic Culture: The Poetics of Construction in Nineteenth- and Twentieth-Century Architecture*. Cambridge, MA: MIT Press, 1995.

Gargiani, Roberto. *Louis. I. Kahn: Exposed Concrete and Hollow Stones*. Lausanne: EPFL Press, 2014.

Huxtable, Ada Louise. "Habitat: Flawed but Exciting Prefab Housing." In *New York Times*, April 30, 1967.

"Imaginative Engineering Ties Habitat's Many Elements into Unified Structure." In *Stressteel Corporation Technical Bulletin*, no. 27 (August 1967).

"Insener A. Komendant Koreasse." In *Vaba Eesti Sõna = Free Estonian Word*, June 24, 1954.

Jordy, William H. "Book Reviews" [a review of August Komendant's *18 Years with Architect Louis I. Kahn*]. In *Journal of the Society of Architectural Historians* 39, no. 1 (1980): 85–89.

Kaasik, Imbi ed. *Tallinna Tehnikumi ja Tallinna Tehnikaülikooli õppe- ja abijõud 1918–1944. Eluloolisi andmeid*. Tallinn: Tallinna Tehnikaülikooli Raamatukogu, 1993.

"Kahn's Kimbell: A Building in Praise of Nature and Light, the Vault-Room Art Museum in Fort Worth, by Louis Kahn." In *Interiors* (March 1973): 84–91.

Karimi, Pamela. *Domesticity and Consumer Culture in Iran: Interior Revolutions of the Modern Era*. New York: Routledge, 2013.

Kivi, Raul-Levroit. *Tartu planeerimisest ja arhitektuurist. Artikleid ja mälestusi*. Tallinn: Eesti Arhitektuurimuuseum, 2005.

Korrovits, Harri. "Maailmanimega ehitusteadlase juubel." In *Tehnika ja Tootmine*, nos. 9–10 (1991): 39–42.

Kries, Mateo, Jochen Eisenbrand, and Stanislaus von Moos, eds. *Louis Kahn: The Power of Architecture*. Weil am Rhein: Vitra Design Museum, 2013.

Kulbach, Valdek, Armas Luige, Enno Soonurm, eds. *Ehitusinsenerid TPI-ist*. Tallinn: Valgus, 1986.

"Lakewoodi eelpingestatud raudbetooni tehas käigus." In *Vaba Eesti Sõna = Free Estonian Word*, February 14, 1957.

Latour, Alessandra, ed. *Louis I. Kahn: l'uomo, il maestro*. Rome: Edizioni Kappa, 1986.

Legault, Réjean. "The Making of Habitat 67: A Tense *Pas de Deux* between Moshe Safdie and August Komendant." In *Journal of the Society for the Study of Architecture in Canada = Le Journal de la Société pour l'étude de l'architecture au Canada* 46, no. 1 (2021): 30–50.

Leslie, Thomas. *Louis. I. Kahn: Building Art, Building Science*. New York: George Braziller Inc., 2005.

Leslie, Thomas. "Vältimatud nuhtlused: August Komendant, Louis I. Kahn ja arhitektuuri ning insenerikunsti keerulised suhted." In *Maja: Eesti arhitektuuri ajakiri = Estonian Architectural Review*, no. 4 (2006): 72–75.

Lige, Carl-Dag. "Architect, Engineer and the Culture of Building." In "Louis I. Kahn," special issue, *kunst.ee*, no. 1 (2012): 83–89.

Lige, Carl-Dag. "Arhitektuur kui tervikprotsess: ümber hinnates ehitusinseneride panust 20. sajandi ehituskultuuri." In "Louis I. Kahn," special issue, *Maja: Eesti arhitektuuri ajakiri = Estonian Architectural Review*, no. 3 (2010): 58–60.

Lige, Carl-Dag. "Eesti mees maailma ehituskultuuri tipus – August Komendant." In *100 aastat TTÜ ehitusinsenere*, edited by Karl Õiger and Ivo Pilve, 417–20. Tallinn: SA Karl Õigeri Stipendiumifond, 2018.

Lige, Carl-Dag. "Julgus liigutada piire." In *Sirp*, May 10, 2019.

Lige, Carl-Dag. "Tippinsener August Komendant ja tema koostöö arhitekt Louis I. Kahniga." In August Komendant, *18 aastat arhitekt Louis I. Kahniga*, 188–205. Tallinn: Eesti Betooniühing, Eesti Arhitektuurimuuseum, In Nomine, 2019.

Lobell, John. "Books" [a review of August Komendant's *18 Years with Architect Louis I. Kahn*]. In *AIA Journal* (July 1976): 176–78.

"Logic and Art in Precast Concrete." In *Architectural Record* (September 1959): 232–38.

Loud, Patricia Cummings. *The Art Museums of Louis I. Kahn*. Durham: Duke University Press, 1989.

"Louis I. Kahn 1901/1974," special issue, *Rassegna* 7, no. 21 (1979).

"Louis I. Kahn, Architect: Richards Medical Research Building, Museum of Modern Art." *Museum of Modern Art Bulletin* 28, no. 1 (1961).

"Louis I. Kahn: Silence and Light," special issue, *a+u Architecture and Urbanism* 3, no. 1 (1973).

Mägi, Vahur. "August Komendant maailma ehitustandril." In *Eesti teadlased ja insenerid välismaal*, edited by Vahur Mägi and Anne Valmas, 190–200. Tallinn: Teaduste Akadeemia Kirjastus, 2011.

Mägi, Vahur. "Mees, kes ei mahtunud paati." In *Ajapulss*, no. 20 (1991): 6–10.

Mändel, Maris. "Betoonarhitektuur vabariigi ajal." In *Eesti Betoonehituse Ajalugu = The History of Estonian Concrete Construction*, edited by Toomas Kään, 114–27; English summary p. 329. Tallinn: In Nomine, 2014.

Masso, Tiit. *100 Ehitist*. Tallinn: Valgus, 1983.

McCarter, Robert. *Louis I Kahn*. London: Phaidon, 2005.

Merkel, Jayne. *Eero Saarinen*. London: Phaidon, 2005.

"More Than Just a Volume." In *The Architectural Forum* (April 1971): 20–25.

Murphy, Diana, ed. *Moshe Safdie I*. Mulgrave: The Images Publishing Group Pty, 2009; 1st ed., Academy Editions, 1996.

Newman, Oscar. "Habitat '67: A Critique." In *Canadian Architect* (October 1964): 38–46.

"Obituary: A. E. Komendant, 85, A Structural Engineer." In *New York Times*, September 18, 1992.

"Operation Breakthrough." In *Architectural Record* (April 1970): 137–52.

Osanov, Mikhail. "Evaluation of the Design of Komendant's Cycloidal, Thin Shell Roofs at the Kimbell Art Museum Using Finite Element Analysis." Honors thesis, Bucknell University, 2014. https://digitalcommons.bucknell.edu/honors_theses/250.

Pelkonen, Eeva-Liisa, and Donald Albrecht, eds. *Eero Saarinen: Shaping the Future*. New Haven: Yale University Press, 2011.

"Pioneering in Precast Concrete." In *Engineering News-Record* (October 13, 1960): 56–60.

Polivka, Jaro J. "Discussion of Economy and Safety of Concrete Dams." In *Transactions of the American Society of Civil Engineers* 121, no. 1 (1956): 922.

"Poured-in-place Concrete Stabilizes Parabolic Roof." In *Modern Concrete* (October 1976): 55–56.

"Prestressed Concrete Trusses Save Time and Money for Big Plant." In *Engineering News-Record* (February 2, 1961): 40–42.

Raam, Villem, ed. *Eesti Arhitektuur 1–4*. Tallinn: Valgus, 1993; 1996; 1997; 1999.

Raney, Don, and Suzanne Stephens. "Operation Breakthrough: Operation P/R." In *Progressive Architecture* (April 1970): 120–33.

Rosellini, Anna. *Louis. I. Kahn: Towards the Zero Degree of Concrete*. Lausanne: EPFL Press, 2014.

Rowan, Jan C. "Wanting to Be: The Philadelphia School." In *Progressive Architecture* (April 1961): 130–63.

Safdie, Moshe. *Beyond Habitat*. Montreal: Tundra Books; Toronto: Collins Publishers; Cambridge, MA: MIT Press, 1970.

Safdie, Moshe. *For Everyone a Garden*. Cambridge, MA: MIT Press, 1974.

Safdie, Moshe. "Habitat '67: Towards the Development of a Building System." In *PCI Journal* (February 1967): 60–66.

Saint, Andrew. *Architect and Engineer: A Study in Sibling Rivalry*. New Haven: Yale University Press, 2007.

Seymour, A. T., III. "The Immeasurable Made Measurable: Building the Kimbell Art Museum." In *Via*, no. 7 (1984): 76–85.

Siilivask, Karl, ed. *Eesti teaduse biograafiline leksikon 1. A-Ki.* Tallinn: Eesti Entsüklopeediakirjastus, 2000.

Simonson, Juhan. "Eestist pärit arhitekti ja inseneri pärandite tutvustamine laieneb." In *Vaba Eesti Sõna = Free Estonian Word*, April 25, 2002.

Solomon, Susan G. *Louis I. Kahn's Trenton Jewish Community Center*. New York: Princeton Architectural Press, 2000.

Suits [Mändel], Maris, and Carl-Dag Lige. "Insener Heinrich Laul ja Eesti XX sajandi ehituskultuur." In *Sirp*, September 17, 2010.

"Suri dr. ins. A. E. Komendant." In *Vaba Eesti Sõna = Free Estonian Word*, October 1, 1992.

"Systems: Myth or Reality?" In *Architecture Plus* (July–August 1974): 70–75.

Tammik, Toivo. "Geeniuste tagasitulek: Louis Kahni päevad Kuressaares." In *Sirp*, October 6, 2006.

Tammik, Toivo. "Kahn and Komendant." In *Life in Estonia* (Autumn 2006): 59–63.

Tammik, Toivo. "Kahn jõudis Eestisse tagasi, Komendant mitte veel." In *Sirp*, October 27, 2006.

Temko, Allan. "Evaluation: Louis Kahn's Salk Institute after a Dozen Years." In *AIA Journal* (March 1977): 42–49.

Tenreiro, Oscar, ed. *Todo Llega Al Mar: Pensamiento y obra del arquitecto Oscar Tenreiro*. Valencia: Ediciones ETSAV, 2019.

Tenreiro, Oscar. "La enseñanza de dieciocho años." In August Komendant, *18 anos años con el arquitecto Louis I. Kahn*, 23–54. Santiago de Compostela: Colexio Oficial de Arquitectos de Galicia, 2000.

"The Mind of Louis Kahn." In *The Architectural Forum* (July–August 1972): 42–89.

Tor, Abba. "Book Reviews" [a review of August Komendant's *18 Years with Architect Louis I. Kahn*]. In *Architectural Record* (mid-August 1977): 107.

Treier, Heie, ed. *Kahn: The Islander.* Tallinn: Louis Kahn Estonia Foundation, 2016.

Valk, Kristel. "Arhitektuurielu Saksa okupatsiooni aegses Eestis 1941–1944" [Architectural life in Estonia during the German occupation in 1941–1944]. In *Viisteist: Eesti Arhitektuurimuuseumi kogumik*, edited by Kristel Valk, 93–132; English summary pp. 199–202. Tallinn: Eesti Arhitektuurimuuseum, 2006.

Vallhonrat, Carles. "Tectonics Considered: Between the Presence and the Absence of Artifice." In *Perspecta* 24 (1988): 123–35.

Vivoni-Farage, Enrique, ed. *Klumb: Una arquitectura de impronta social / An Architecture of Social Concern*. San Juan: La Editorial, Universidad de Puerto Rico, 2006.

Vivoni-Farage, Enrique. "Modern Puerto Rico and Henry Klumb." In *Docomomo Journal*, no. 33 (September 2005): 28–37.

Wickersheimer, David J. "The Vierendeel." In *Journal of the Society of Architectural Historians* 35, no. 1 (1975): 54–60.

Williamson, James. *Kahn at Penn: Transformative Teacher of Architecture*. London: Routledge, 2015.

Wiseman, Carter. *Louis I. Kahn: Beyond Time and Style: A Life in Architecture*. New York: W. W. Norton & Company, 2007.

Wittgenstein, Ludwig. "A Lecture on Ethics" (1929). In *Philosophical Review* 74. no. 1 (1965): 3–12.

Wurman, Richard Saul, ed. *What Will Be Has Always Been: The Words of Louis I. Kahn*. New York: Access Press Ltd., 1986.

Žantovská Murray, Irena, ed. *Moshe Safdie: Buildings and Projects, 1967–1992*. Montreal: McGill-Queen's University Press, 1996.

Illustrations

20 aastat ehitamist Eestis: 1918–1938 (1939)
411 (first from the top)

Alexander Architectural Archives, University of Texas Libraries, the University of Texas at Austin
Preston M. Geren drawings
August Komendant 100, 274

The Architectural and Construction Archives, University of Puerto Rico
Henry Klumb Collection
47, 324–325
August Komendant 179 (bottom)
Henry Klumb 172, 178, 179 (top), 415 (first from the top), 417 (second from the top), 418 (first from the top)
J.L.Houser 326–327, 422 (seventh from the top)

The Architectural Archives, University of Pennsylvania
August E. Komendant Collection, by the gift of Merike Komendant Phillips and George Jüri Komendant
17, 22 (bottom), 26 (bottom), 55 (bottom), 77, 132 (top), 136, 146, 157 (top left, bottom left), 187 (bottom), 189, 221 (bottom), 224, 231 (top), 234–235, 238–243, 262–263, 265, 286 (bottom), 301, 360 (bottom), 366 (top), 374, 379 (bottom right), 412 (first, fourth from the top), 419 (second from the top), 420 (second from the top), 422 (second from the top)
August Komendant 26 (top), 63, 85, 147 (bottom), 149 (bottom), 152, 168 (top), 187 (top), 198 (bottom), 251 (top), 260–261, 294, 306 (bottom), 309, 319, 347 (left), 413 (second, third from the top), 414 (first from the top), 415 (third from the top), 417 (sixth from the top), 420 (sixth from the top), 423 (second from the top)
Louis Kahn 291 (bottom)
Merike Komendant Phillips, Bill Phillips 50, 54, 275, 296 (top)
Oscar Tenreiro 299, 300, 421 (first from the top)

John Dorio Nicolais Collection, by the gift of Robert Nicolais and Drexel University
John Dorio Nicolais 98, 166, 168 (bottom), 194, 197, 208, 218, 280 (bottom), 282, 417 (fifth from the top)

Marshall David Meyers Collection, by the gift of Anne P. Meyers and Pamela Meyers Schaefer
Marshall David Meyers 24 (bottom), 25, 42, 51, 55 (top), 56, 78, 80–81, 97 (bottom), 99, 101, 153–155, 158, 160–161, 163 (bottom), 169, 209–212, 216, 268, 276–279, 280 (top), 281, 283–285, 368, 419 (first, sixth from the top)

Mitchell/Giurgola Architects Collection, by the gift of Ehrman B. Mitchell, Romaldo Giurgola and MGA Partners
248–250, 251 (bottom), 252–257, 419 (fourth from the top)

Norman N. Rice Collection, by the gift of Norman Rice
August Komendant 246

Norman N. Rice Collection, by the gift of William Strauss
244–245, 419 (third from the top)

Richard Saul Wurman Collection, by the gift of Richard Saul Wurman
379 (top)

The Architectural Forum (February 1963)
186

Art & Architecture Library, University Libraries, Virginia Polytechnic Institute and State University
Architectural Drawings Collection
August Komendant 82, 228–229

Avery Architectural & Fine Arts Library, Columbia University
Abbott Merkt & Company Collection
53, 181 (top), 182–183, 418 (third from the top)

Estonian History Museum
106, 108–109, 410 (second from the top)
Hans Voolmann 118, 410 (fifth from the top)
Johannes Koitmets 123 (top)

Estonian Maritime Museum
Rudolf Linnuste 124

Estonian Museum of Architecture
49, 107 (bottom), 110, 113, 117 (top), 410 (third from the top)
August Komendant 20–21, 117 (bottom)

August Komendant Collection, by the gift of Martin Komendant
August Komendant 378

August Komendant Collection, by the gift of Merike Komendant Phillips and George Jüri Komendant
62, 70, 4, 76, 79, 105, 132 (bottom), 147 (top), 159, 345–346, 347 (right), 348–357, 359, 360 (top), 361–365, 366 (bottom left), 369–370, 376–377, 382–383, 412 (third from the top), 418 (second, sixth from the top), 420 (third from the top)
August Komendant 413 (first from the top), 414 (second from the top), 415 (fourth from the top)
George Jüri Komendant 206–207, 417 (fourth from the top)
Johannes Ehrenwert 358
John Ebstel 164, 217
Karl Akel & Ko. 18
Lawrence S. Williams Inc. 184, 188
Malcolm Smith 162
Merike Komendant Phillips 308
Office of Oscar Tenreiro 421 (second from the top)

August Komendant Collection, by the gift of Oscar Tenreiro
28, 87, 91 (bottom), 93, 298, 304, 312 (top), 322–323, 328–329, 332–334, 336–342, 372–373, 421 (third from the top), 422 (fourth), 423 (first, fourth, fifth from the top)
Office of Oscar Tenreiro 307
Oscar Tenreiro 40, 89 (bottom), 91 (top), 302–303, 305 (bottom), 306 (top), 312 (bottom), 313, 315, 317–318, 335

Carl-Dag Lige 420 (fourth from the top)
Elmar Lohk 119 (top)
Marje Eelma 385–387, 389, 391–395, 396 (top), 397–402, 403 (top), 404–407, 408 (bottom)
Martin Siplane 21, 125–127, 142, 144–145

Reio Avaste 388, 390, 396 (bottom), 403 (bottom), 408 (top)
Stanislav Stepashko 366 (bottom right), 367, 375, 379 (bottom left), 380, 381 (top left, top right)

Estonian National Archives
116, 128, 129 (bottom left, bottom right), 131 (bottom), 139, 143, 410 (first, fourth from the top), 411 (second from the top)
Aleksander Koitla 138
Artur Kalm 122 (top)
August Komendant 111, 129 (top)
Eugen Saarelinn (Sacharias) 141
Oskar Viikholm 122 (bottom)

Estonian Sports and Olympic Museum
123 (bottom)

Family of Harald Laupa
156, 157 (top right, bottom right), 180

Foundation of Haapsalu and Läänemaa Museums
140, 412 (second from the top)

George Jüri Komendant
Merike Komendant Phillips 310–311, 421 (fourth from the top)

Jari Jetsonen
219

Manuscripts & Archives, Yale University
Eero Saarinen Collection
174, 175 (top)
Joseph W. Molitor 176–177, 418 (fourth from the top)

McGill University Library
Moshe Safdie Archive
60, 64, 83, 230, 232 (top, bottom right), 233, 236, 237, 421 (fifth from the top)
August Komendant 223
Graetz Inc. 220
Moshe Safdie 221 (top, middle), 226 (top)
Office of Moshe Safdie 225, 226 (bottom)

Nader Ardalan
103, 422 (first from the top)

Oscar Tenreiro
88, 89 (top), 305 (top), 314, 316, 320–321, 330–331, 343, 422 (third, fifth, eighth from the top), 423 (third from the top)

Pilt ja Sõna (no. 10, 1941)
137

Progressive Architecture (October 1960)
173, 175 (bottom), 181 (bottom), 185, 416 (third from the top), 417 (seventh from the top)

Safdie Architects
45, 227 (top), 231 (bottom), 232 (bottom left), 422 (sixth from the top)
Jerry Spearman 43
Moshe Safdie 222

Special Collections Research Center, Temple University Libraries
George D. McDowell Philadelphia Evening Bulletin Collection
Charles Higgins 190–191, 417 (third from the top)
Joseph McGuinn 66
Joseph Wasko 68
Sonnee Gottlieb 192–193

Steven Lawrey
69

Stressteel Corporation Technical Bulletin (no. 27, August 1967)
227 (bottom)

Tallinn City Museum
107 (top)
Hans Soosaar 131 (bottom)

Tallinn City Planning Department
Eduard Kuusik 411 (fourth from the top)
Roman Koolmar 130, 411 (third from the top)

Tartu City Government
112, 114–115
August Komendant 22 (top), 133
Voldemar Onton, Voldemar Tippel 411 (fifth from the top)

Tartu Mill
134–135

Tehnika Ajakiri (no. 3, 1937)
119 (bottom), 121

Tuumik Stuudio
Marje Eelma 381 (bottom)

The University of Pennsylvania and the Pennsylvania Historical and Museum Commission
Louis I. Kahn Collection
16, 148 (bottom), 163 (top), 167 (bottom), 170–171, 199 (bottom), 213 (bottom), 215, 258, 259 (bottom), 264, 266–267, 290, 296–297 (bottom), 416 (first from the top), 417 (first from the top), 419 (fifth from the top), 420 (fifth from the top)
August Komendant 97 (top), 202, 214, 288, 420 (first from the top)
Cervin Robinson 150, 416 (second from the top)
Dick Whittington 204 (top)
Louis Kahn 148–149 (top), 151 (top), 167 (top), 195–196, 200 (top), 213 (top), 259 (top), 270–271, 273 (top), 286 (top), 287, 291 (top), 292–293, 415 (second from the top), 418 seventh (from the top)
Marvin Rand 203, 204 (bottom), 205
Matt Wargo 151 (bottom)
Office of Louis Kahn 24 (top), 198–199 (top), 200 (bottom), 201, 269, 272, 273 (bottom), 418 (fifth from the top)
Ronald C. Binks 15

Index